Acclaim for the Polish edition:

Reading 'The Auschwitz Photographer' left a lasting impression on me. It is neither an academic thesis nor a proper memoir, but it significantly expands general public's knowledge about not just the camps, but about the system that created them.

Władysław Bartoszewski
Former Auschwitz prisoner
(Inmate No. 4427)

Anna Dobrowolska chose images for this album which depict many aspects of the camp life, not only the ramp where transports of deportees were unloaded, but also the camp orchestra, the boxing and soccer matches and even a wedding.

Interia.pl

A large album—designed by Ryszard Kajzer, lecturer of the Academy of Fine Arts in Warsaw, renowned for his posters and illustrations—contains, in addition to Brasse's story, about 300 photographs, historical notes and sketches, many of which are published for the first time... A valuable publication.

Monika Żmijewska
Gazeta.pl

The Auschwitz Photographer was not a 'war correspondent', 'reporter' or 'observer', but another victim of those events. One should keep that in mind looking at these pictures which —quoting Susan Sontag—'terrify and so they should'. It makes our contemporary perspective more humble.

Agnieszka Sabor
Tygodnik Powszechny

Brasse paints a nuanced view of the camp reality, of the relationships between the inmates and the staff of KL Auschwitz-Birkenau. The recollections of a man who helped save 40 thousand pictures illustrating the tragedy of the inmates of this camp are remarkable. I've read this story with highest interest.

Grzegorz Berendt
Historian,
Remembrance National Institute

CONTENTS

CHILDHOOD	6
ŻYWIEC—MY TOWN	10
PHOTOGRAPHY—BEGINNINGS	16
WAR	20
AUSCHWITZ—BEGINNINGS	26
„ARBEIT MACHT FREI"	54
A GOOD KOMMANDO WAS ESSENTIAL	60
ERKENNUNGSDIENST	70
MUG SHOTS	78
PHOTOGRAPHIC PORTRAITS OF GERMANS	96
PENAL COMPANY	104
KOMMANDO ZEPPELIN	114
PHOTOGRAPHS OF PRIESTS	116
TYPHUS	120
PICTURES OF „EXIBITS" AND STRANGE CASES	124
PHOTOGRAPHS FOR MENGELE AND OTHER DOCTORS	130
PHOTOGRAPHS OF „GUINEA PIGS"	134
PHOTOGRAPHS OF EXPERIMENTS ON MEN	138
PHOTOGRAPHS OF WOMEN	144
PHOTOGRAPHS OF CHILDREN	150
SPECIAL PHOTOGRAPHS —THE RAMP, THE GAS CHAMBERS AND THE CREMATORIUM	158
ILLEGAL PHOTOGRAPHS	168
PHOTOGRAPHS USED IN FORGING BANK NOTES	172
PHOTOGRAPHS OF PRISONERS' ART	176
PHOTOGRAPHS OF THE ORCHESTRA	178
HELPING OTHER PRISONERS	182
CAMP LIFE	188
TRADE	196
CAMP VALUES	202
LOVE IN THE CAMP	210
TRUE LOVE	214
WEDDING IN AUSCHWITZ	220
POSTCARD PHOTOGRAPHS	224
SAVING THE PHOTOGRAPHS	226
EVACUATION	232
END OF PHOTOGRAPHY	242
AFTERWORD	248
AUSCHWITZ CHRONOLOGY	250
PRISONER BADGES	254
SS RANKS	255
PRISONERS	256
BIOGRAPHIES OF PRISONERS	258
BIOGRAPHIES OF THE SS STAFF	263
GLOSSARY	268
LIST OF ILLUSTRATIONS	270
BIBLIOGRAPHY	282

THE AUSCHWITZ PHOTOGRAPHER

Anna Dobrowolska

Translated by
Anna Samborska
and Clayton Young

Warsaw 2015

My name is Wilhelm Brasse. I am a photographer. In September 1940 I became prisoner of Auschwitz Concentration Camp, where I took over 50.000 pictures for the camp records and provided photographic documentation of experiments by Dr. Mengele.

6 BRASSE WITH YOUNGER BROTHERS

CHILDHOOD

I was born on December 3rd 1917. My parents gave me the ancient Germanic name of Wilhelm. At that time Wilhelm II was the German Emperor.

My grandfather Albert Karol came from Alsace[1] but he considered himself Austrian. During the Franco-Prussian war many people from there came to our land[2]. My grandpa worked as an ornamental gardener for the Habsburg Archduke and in those days he was doing very well. Among other things, he created the Żywiec[3] Castle Park; he planted trees and established flowerbeds. In his daily life he used three languages. He spoke French, German and very nice Polish. I was amazed and proud, when he was naming the trees and flowers in all those languages plus Latin. My grandpa would visit us often and I remember him well. He died in 1934.

My mother's name was Helena, née Kucharska. She was a very good person and a great mom—loving and caring. She took great care of us—quite a job given that I have five brothers and no sisters.

I WAS THE ELDEST AND HAD TO LOOK AFTER MY BROTHERS.

Mom mother loved us dearly and would watch over us, care for us, cook delicious food and bake fabulous cakes. I also soon learned how to cook and could manage quite well by myself. I would make sandwiches for my older brothers and for the younger ones I would prepare "zacierka"—you mix milk, flour, egg and salt with a fork to create tiny noodles. Then you pour it over boiling milk and finally serve it with melted butter. Later I learned to make more complicated dishes - bullions or even roasts.

---

[1] Alzace-Lorraine became incorporated into the German Empire after the Franco-Prussian war of 1871. (If no other source quoted, footnotes by Anna Dobrowolska)
[2] The Żywiec region
[3] Pronuciation: "ZHI-vyets" (Translator's note.)

To my eyes my mother was a very pretty woman. And a hard working one. She would sew from early in the morning, although she wasn't a professional seamstress. I remember her sitting at the sewing machine and humming religious songs. This is an image that keeps coming back to me...

My mom was Polish in the full meaning of the word. She told my brothers and me that we were Polish and that Poland was our country. From early childhood she imbued us with patriotic spirit, a strong work ethic, honesty and piety. "You have to love your country", she kept repeating. She was all steeped in it.

In 1920 my father took part in the Anti-Bolshevik campaign. Even before the war he was a member of "Friendship" ("Przyjaźń"), an organization that was active in Żywiec, and in spite of his German name he would only socialize with Poles. He did not hang out with Germans. He kept telling stories about "Friendship" and later joined a Polish choir "Lutnia". As soon as Poland regained independence in 1918 he joined the Polish Socialist Party (PPS) and was active in it up until the outbreak of WWII.

MY FATHER SPOKE OFTEN ON PATRIOTIC SUBJECTS.

My father was a mechanic whose specialty was precision metalwork. He was an expert worker and earned good wages.

But what fascinated me much more was his musical passion. I loved to listen to him play flute and violin, which he played often and well. Later he even played in an army band. He would practice a lot, daily by himself and twice or three times a week with his friends. There was one other violin, plus a clarinet and a cello. They would mostly play Strauss's waltzes and polkas. In those days I was quite well versed in music. I also tried to play some violin, but I wasn't very good at it.

Sometimes I looked out into the courtyard and could see a group of neighbors who sat by the house and listened to my dad's music through open windows. There was no radio yet; people only had just begun to get the first gramophones. It was around 1925-26.

Later my father played less and less. He kept saying he had no time. He worked in a screw factory outside Żywiec and would give himself to other pleasures, such as vodka.

My parents got married on February 17th 1917. My father had already chosen his nationality earlier on, not influenced by my mother: Polish. They all—by this I mean his whole extended family—considered themselves Polish. That included him and his four brothers—Alfred, Bruno, Oswald and Adolf—as well as his two sisters Luiza and Ilona. My father was a strong Polish patriot. The fact that he married my mom only helped to emphasize his Polishness.

In our house only Dad spoke German. He had been a soldier in the Austrian army, so he spoke it quite well. I started to learn German early, after a few years in school. At that time they taught German beginning in 5th grade of elementary school and later through middle school. Although my father knew German he would not teach me or help me with it; but it was not hard because I had German speaking pals, who among themselves spoke either German or both languages. The Kubicas and the Hibners, for example, which were well known and respectable families, spoke at home in both Polish and German, sometimes mixing up words in the same sentence.

In our house, however, we spoke only Polish because my mom did not know any German. However, I would often hear my dad and grandpa communicate in German outside the house.

I went to the local elementary school. I passed a placement exam and went straight into the second year of Żywiec Middle School, because I was doing very well. It wasn't so easy in those days. The youth of today complain, but I had to pass exams from fifth grade onward.

LEARNING GERMAN WAS EASY FOR ME.

I have a fond memory of one professor of German. The first day he came to school looking like a typical teacher: skinny, tall, dressed in the old fashioned way with a stiff collar. One of the Jewish guys immediately nicknamed him "Pipshtock", which in our dialect meant a thin stick. So the poor professor remained Pipshtock thereafter. No one called him anything else, neither the parents nor the other teachers. "Where is Pipshtock? Haven't you seen Pipshtock?" Sometimes a person would come to the school conference and ask:

"Professor Pipshtock?" and he would answer, "With your permission, my name is not Pipshtock but Łaszczynski, but do come in..."

It didn't bother him. I liked that professor a lot. He did a good job teaching me grammar, which was the basis from which I later quickly moved to fluency. Unfortunately, his life had a sad ending. In 1945, just after the war, nobody wanted to learn German any more. That professor threw himself under a train.

ŻYWIEC - MY TOWN

View of Żywiec and Zabłocie between the wars

Prewar view of Żywiec – town square on a market day

ŻYWIEC – MY TOWN

At the beginning of the 20th century Żywiec was a Polish town, with some nice international flavor, thanks to the Habsburgs, who owned a huge brewery and also thanks to whom the local community prospered. They were much respected and employed a few hundred people from Żywiec so nobody objected to their foreign background.

Renewing the royal charter granted by King Jan Kazimierz during the Polish-Swedish war, the Austrian Emperor Franz Joseph II athorized the town of Żywiec to ban Jews from settling within its limits.

By contrast the towns of Oświęcim (Auschwitz), Chrzanów and Sosnowiec had large Jewish populations. In the case of Oświecim, before WWII Jews constituted nearly 60% of its inhabitants.

My Jewish acquaintences lived in the suburbs of Żywiec, in Zabłocie. I was friends with those boys. And anyway, there were many nationalities intermingled in the area, including a big German community since there were many Germans working there, as well as many Austrians. And too, many Czech people settled there. It was a real international hodgepodge. Many worked in the local paper mill and in the screw factory.

IT WAS NOT IMPORTANT FOR US AT THAT TIME WHETHER SOMEONE WAS JEWISH, GERMAN OR CZECH.

We hung out together, played soccer together. Jews liked it just as much as we did. Bornstein... Weiss... Forner... Kornhouse... Ritter...

Later "Makkabi"[4] built a nice soccer field and we would often play there. They were good friends. They helped us at school, because they often had ability for languages and were particularly good in German. Of course, the Jews in those days often spoke German among themselves.

My colleagues and I used to talk about what we'd like to be someday. Some of us wanted to be great artists, others—mechanics, doctors or lawyers. I myself did not aim that high. There were boys who dreamt of military careers. Two others wanted to be professors of Polish. They were both very good at Polish. One had the name Ritter, the other, Kornhauser. Both of them died. So did Forner and Weiss. Only Bornstein survived and he went to Israel.

A few boys dreamt of becoming airplane pilots—as did I. Especially since the summer when Żywiec was visited by the pilots of the 2nd Air Regiment from Krakow. They took part in military maneuvers on the giant meadows nearby, normally used for grazing cattle belonging to Archduke Habsburg. I would go with the other boys to have a closer look at the planes. You could come up quite near to them; the pilots would not chase you away. My friend and I were dreaming up ways to build a plane powered by a battery. We would get in and just fly away...

[4] Makkabi - name of Jewish Sports Association.

PHOTOGRAPHY - BEGINNINGS

One day professor Nowak, the school principal, entered the classroom and uttered the words:
- The following students will leave the class...

The first one was Barcik, then Bornstein, and then I. That's how it went. We did not have the money for tuition and so were expelled from school. I was just in the sixth grade out of eight. At that time—it was spring 1930—there was massive unemployment; my father was out of work and the middle school cost money.

I hated principal Nowak at that moment. But later, when I met him in the camp, it turned out he had a heart of gold. First and foremost, he proved himself as an older and wiser friend. He gave me the spiritual support that I sorely needed. I liked him enormously. As to the matter of my expulsion... I regretted that it happened but there was no other way, since we hadn't the money. My mom and dad conferred and concluded it was time to find me some kind of trade.

My father's sister—my aunt in other words—had a big and busy photography shop in Katowice. I thought, and so did my mom, that it might be be my path.

I started my photographer's apprenticeship in the fall of 1933. At the beginning I was an assistant. I had a good mentor: his name was Edward Siudek. He taught me the trade and I pride myself on having studied with such a master. He taught me camera technique, portraiture, lab work and retouching.

In those days the movie theatres had already started showing advertisements, pre-show slides on 6x6 centimeter film. This is what we worked on. Someone would do the design and then we would make the photos and diapositives. They would advertise local stores—for example, for a smoked meat manufacturer or Forner's Soda.

It was in 1933 in the studio of Mr. Siudek that for the first time in my life I held a camera in my hands. There were already some simple Kodak box cameras available, but I couldn't afford those. Only later did my mom buy me a 9x12 "Voglender" which I began to use for some work "on the side", so to speak, to make some extra dough. Of course my boss knew nothing about it; if he had he wouldn't have liked it. But, after all, I was not paid during my apprenticeship. I worked for three years completely for free, that is to say in exchange for the job training. So I felt justified to work on the side.

I was aiming to become a master of photographic portrait. In those days it was a distinct, specialized profession and required passing a higher bar of proficiency because it involved sculpting a model's face using soft lighting.

In professional portrait photography, or, more precisely, in running a photography shop, one creates portraits for postcards and IDs.

A GOOD PHOTOGRAPHER IS ONE WHO CAN SET UP CORRECT LIGHTING IN RELATIONSHIP TO THE HUMAN FACE

and then retouch the picture well. A lot depends on the retouching. You can make the face slimmer, or shorten the nose, or remove the wrinkles... Of course it all must be done artfully. Sometimes you can see old photographs dreadfully over-retouched. The faces there are so smooth it's as if the wrinkles didn't exist.

First you have to take a quick, thorough look at a person, since each of us has irregular features and one half of the face is different from the other. Sometimes one eye is a little bit bigger or the nose is too long. In that case, you must position the face in a special way to make the nose shorter. If someone has a long nose, you can lift the face slightly and illuminate it from below. That way there's no long shadow from the nose. Or if someone has a short nose you can take the picture a little bit from below; if they have short legs—same thing. With women, a lot can be done with clothes and also highlighting of the eyes.

Most importantly, the photographed subject should act naturally. He must not strain the face or force a smile. This is what makes for a good portrait.

After working with Mr Siudek for some time I got to do practically all the lab tasks myself. I made prints, enlargements and touchups. My boss did not yet let me take photographs in the studio. Only after about six months did I take my first school ID picture. I was very excited. Later my boss looked that picture over. Of course he had some comments, but finally he said it was good.

Brasse in Katowice, 1937

One day, at the beginning of 1935, a lady came to the atelier with her daughter and asked me to take a few shots of the girl wearing a ballerina costume. She wasn't particularly happy that such a young lad as myself was going to take care of it. I said I would take several photos and that she'd be able to choose the ones she liked. I shot five or six full figure views as well as some portraits. And it was those portraits she ended up liking the most. She was the first client truly pleased with my work.

After that my boss allowed me to take the simplest pictures more often. I worked for him until the end of June 1935. Then I passed my apprenticeship exam and officially became a professional photographer.

Next I worked for "Foto-Korekt", a studio in Katowice at No. 36, 3 Maja Street, in a building which still exists, although under a different owner. In those days it was the best photo shop in town and specialized in portraits almost exclusively. The highest priority was to have prints ready for pick up on time. I spent a lot of hours in the lab. I copied, enlarged, and retouched... and I was given individual assignments. Sometimes I even got praised. I liked that job a lot. It was easy and I was allowed to work at my specialty.

In Katowice I met some German girls. They wore pendants similar to the sacred ones with saints, but you could open them. Inside the medallions, in a gold plated envelope, were portraits of Hitler. It was the first time that I met girls so deeply steeped in Nazism. I wondered about them, since they had such Polish sounding names. One of them was Miss Małgorzata Dziadek. She was my first love. I remember that maiden to this day... I will always remember her...

In Katowice, wherever you went you would encounter Nazi propaganda. It was everywhere. I took meals at the home of a lady named Wolny (Pol. "free"). Her son became a declared Nazi supporter later on when the Germans took over Silesia in 1940, and he divorced his wife because she spoke no German.

Financially, I was doing well in Katowice. I was a young guy making 120 zlotys a month and I had free lodging. I paid just 40 zlotys a month to the lady who did the cooking. She was very generous with her food! I'd be lying if I said I was not having a good life. I went to coffee shops and the movies. The first time that I went to the cinema my aunt sent me to see "The Lady of the Camelias". It was for me a wonderful experience

and thereafter I became a regular movie goer. I also signed up with a dance school so as to be able to go to the dance clubs. I was young and free. But I did not drink very much! Maybe occasionally I would have a shot or two but that was all.

AND I WAS IN LOVE...

Besides that girl and photography, both of which for me were great passions, I also took a strong interest in motor vehicles, especially motorcycles. In a townhouse next door there was a motorcycle mechanic. I went to see him and helped clean the bikes, sometimes getting all smeared up with grease in the process. He would take those things apart and I would wash all the pieces. From him I learned how to fix a motorcycle and to this day dealing with cars and motorcycles comes easy to me.

I even started saving up for a motorcycle, but it was still out of reach. Anyway, it turned out that the one I had my eye on had defects... Eventually I gave up on motor vehicles and began to focus more fully on photography. What a pleasure that was, shooting with my 9x12 camera!

I photographed my mom in her Żywiec folk costume. I took a portrait of my father at home lit by a kerosene lamp. I also shot photos of my brothers when they were little.

I photographed landscapes as well, such as the mountains and views around Żywiec. I took an interest in art photography and began using the so-called gum technique[5]. I had a how-to manual and did some experimenting with that material. You see, gum arabic in conjunction with gelatin and potassium dichromate is photosensitive. That means that the exposed gum is very reactive to light, so that in the areas where the pictures were covered with gum the color remained, while in the spots where the light sensitive material was not used it washed out. Sometimes I added also color tints—blue, brown or green. I would then make a print from the negative in different colors. After exposure I developed it and there would come the most beautiful moment when that artistic effect emerged, rendering the landscapes very beautiful and rather mysterious. I found it most intriguing. Today this technique is completely abandoned.

[5] Dichromate technique, "gum printing".

I also photographed kids. In the beginning, all kids' photos looked the same. I would put the baby on a white sheepskin or goatskin and photograph him naked. There were so very many of such photos! Older children were usually brought in by their mothers on Sundays. I strove to make their heads appear bigger and to get the light just right. I also needed to capture the child's attention so that he or she would look straight into the lens. I would show them a ball, a bird or a rattle. For a full body view, I would put them on a rocking horse or next to either a tall bicycle or a kids' tricycle that we had in our shop.

I worked in Katowice until 1938. It was a wonderful time.

WAR

In 1938 I reached the military draft age of 21 and appeared in front of the Selective Service Board[6]. I was given category A and assigned to the Air Force. I was told that in the Fall I would join the Army. That's why in September of the same year I gave up my job in Katowice, because I thought by the end of September or early October I would be in the Polish Army. At that time a conflict had broken out between Poland and Czechoslovakia and the Poles had annexed part of the Zaolzie region. So I was certain I would soon be called up; but it didn't happen then and so I remained in Żywiec.

In February 1939 I went to Zakopane to watch the FSI Ski Competition. There was no snow when I arrived, but it did fall right on the day of the ski jumping. Our man did not take first place. The winner was an Austrian jumper—by then a German national, since this was after the German annexation of Austria. I was devastated.

I was restless and wanted to change something in my life. So from Zakopane I went to my aunt's, who had a pension in Krynica and with whom I asked if I could stay. She agreed gladly, so from March 1939 I lived in Krynica and worked as a lab technician in a photography shop. There was a small photo service in the New Spa House. It did not shoot the pictures but rather made prints and enlargements of amateur photographers. I worked there only about 5-6 hours a day so I had lots of leisure time. I remained until August 26th 1939.

YOU COULD FEEL THE BUILDUP OF THE WAR PSYCHOSIS…

Now I was certain I would be taken into the Army. I decided to go back to Żywiec. This was a period of great uncertainty. I could feel something was up and was looking forward to my conscription. I was category A—in top physical condition—and I was ready. From the very beginning I didn't like the way the Germans were acting. I understood quickly that my valuues were completely opposed to theirs.

„Our primary goal is the destruction of Poland. […] I will provide the excuse for the attack, whether the world believes it or not. […] I have put my death-head formations' in place with the command relentlessly and without compassion to send into death many women and children of Polish origin and language. Only thus we can gain the living space that we need. […] Poland will become depopulated and settled with Germans."

Source: Adolf Hitler's Obersalzberg Speech[7]

At last I got my draft summons to the 6th Air Regiment in Lwów. I was to turn up on September 1st, so I tried to get there by all means possible. I did not make it to Lwów, but only as far as Rawa Ruska, where I was arrested by German troops. They transported me with others in a column on foot to Jarosław. I was still in my civilian clothing. I managed to escape from this transport and return to Żywiec.

My father had a train engineer's license and had been summoned to Krakow, to the Bonarka train station. Later he was assigned to an armored train - a giant engine protected by steel armor with at least two cars armed to the teeth.[8] He crossed the Hungarian border and was interned there. Thus it happened that in 1939 my father was gone and I became the oldest male in the family.

When the Nazis took over Silesia and incorporated it into the Reich they took a census and decreed the so-called "optioning"—everyone had to declare themselves as Polish or German.

At the end of 1939 there was a nationality registration in the occupied territories, the Fingerabdruck (the so-called "palcówka" in Polish). People living in those areas obtained an ID with a fingerprint instead of a photo. Every person had to declare the language used at home, their nationality, the beginning of their residence, information on military service in the Polish Army, their religion, marital status, occupation and property or business ownership.[9]

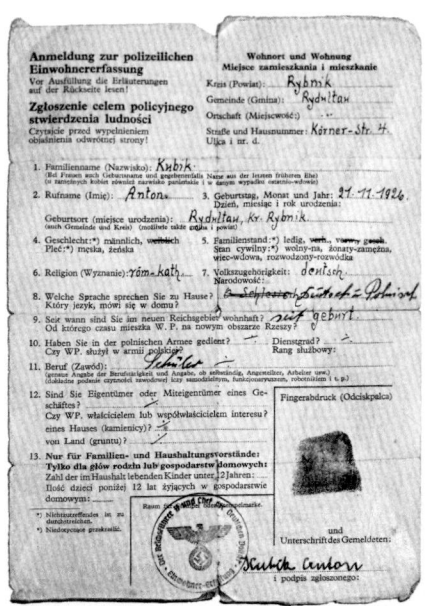

---

6 It was December 17th

7 Fragment of the November 7th Obersalzberg speech given by Hitler to the Wehrmacht commanders. Nurmberg Document No 798—PS

8 There were two armored trains in the "Kracow Army": No 51 "Pierwszy Marszałek" ("The First Marshall") and 54 "Groźny" ("The Fearsome"). They were part of the 2nd Armored Trains Division in Niepołomice. Wilhelm Brasse's father probably served at the PP54 "Groźny", as the PP 51 had been taken over by the Soviets.

9 The scholarly notes appearing in this font were prepared by the Author in cooperation with the historians of the Auschwitz Museum

I declared that I was Polish. The German clerk who was looking over my papers hesitated to accept them from me, explaining that since my grandfather had been Austrian and my father was Austrian and since I spoke a decent German I was not therefore Polish. He handed the papers back to me and declined to issue me a document with a fingerprint. I thought he would keep insisting, but instead he just waited silently. After a long while he let me go.

One of my brothers was severely wounded while escaping East, and so he came back at the end of November needing medical treatment. I decided then to take up smuggling from Slovakia. You would go there to get food: sugar, flour, margarine… That was the way I earned a living and supported my family including the therapy for my brother. He had a blind physical therapist come in to massage his wounded arm. It helped him.

I would take a train from Żywiec to Milówka, which was about 20 kilometers towards Zwardoń. That was the border checkpoint. I would get off at Milówka and walk through Koniaków, from whence I would descend South through Zapasieki village. That was at the border itself. I would cross over to the Slovak side and buy food. The Slovaks were glad to sell. Sometimes I would get the food in Zapasieki, because they had plenty there. Then there was the return trip: about 20 kilometers on foot, Koniaków, Milówka and the train to Żywiec.
It was drudgery. The Germans were guarding the border and sometimes there were inspections at the train station. If that happened we would lose all we'd carried and would have to go back and figure things out all over again. We could not come back empty handed…

The winter of 1939 was particularly severe—snowy and very cold. A group of us including Stanisław Kucharski[10], my mother's brother

who was nearly my age, traveled that route on skis. I was a decent skier, so it was not a problem to cross from Milówka and Koniaków to the border. The German border guard, called Grenzschuts, kept watch over that section, but the locals were friendly towards us and informed us when a patrol was passing and when there would be another. They had some idea of how it operated. So between the patrols we would quickly go down across the border to a village on the Slovak side. There we would get what we needed and would return the same way. We would sit in the forest and wait for the German patrol to pass. When they had passed and were far enough away we would continue. We had to walk up a steep mountain, but at least that way the forest hid us from view. From Koniaków we would ski some 18 kilometers down to Milówka.

IN MY FREE TIME I LISTENED TO THE RADIO.

Although people were required to turn in all their radios, I cheated. I turned in an old, primitive set, a crystal radio, and kept a very good Phillips, which I used regularly to listen to foreign stations. There was no Polish language BBC yet. Polish radio was broadcasting from Toulouse in France. They were calling on all able people to escape through Hungary to France and enlist with the Polish forces. Every now and then we would hear that so-and-so had fled, that someone else had made it and that another one hadn't. I felt that as a young, healthy man subject to military duty, I simply had to make it to Hungary.

Four of us started the preparations to go: me, my brother, my mother's brother and a friend. A week earlier two friends set out and later we saw them beaten up and being led by the Slovak Gestapo. We realized that things were not looking rosy and so decided to speed up our escape.

10 Stanisław Kucharski, b. April 26th 1918 in Żywiec.
More → BIOGRAPHIES

WE SET OUT FOR OUR MOBILIZATION POINT A WEEK BEFORE EASTER 1940.

We tried crossing the border near Zwardoń. We made it. In Zwardoń we were joined by another volunteer who had already been in the military but somehow got arrested. There was a mass movement of volunteers heading toward the Polish forces through Slovakia, so the Germans reinforced their border checks.

The Slovaks whom we got to know during our previous trips warned us not to try crossing just then because of increased inspections and searches on the trains.

So we went back to our side at the Gubernia[11] near Sucha Beskidzka and later, through Maków Podhalański, we made it to Sanok. We had to make one stop along the way.

In Tarnów we met Jews who had been expelled from Żywiec. They fed us and put us up for the night. The next day they directed us towards Sanok, to a Jewish woman who told us how to proceed. We crossed practically all of the Bieszczady Mountains on foot, from Komańcza through Bukowska Pass, and made it almost to the Hungarian border. At that time the Hungarians had taken over Carpathian Ruthenia[12], which shared about forty or fifty kilometers of border with Poland. We tried to cross there, with disastrous results because all around the Lemko[13] and Ukrainian villages had sided with the Germans. The Germans had fanned Ukrainian separatist passions by giving them hope for a Ukrainian state.

A day after Easter we were low on water. On March 28th we entered a village and were surrounded by ten or twelve local Lemkos. They intimidated us with stanchions and sticks, until their leader came with a gun and took as all the way to Baligród, through the mountains. In Baligród there was a Gestapo unit. The Lemkos had been told that the more they brought of us, the bigger their bounties. I saw that they were getting money for capturing us. It was an area of great poverty. That is how I explained it to myself.

In Baligród we went through a preliminary interrogation. It turned out there were plenty more guys just like us. We were searched. We had a few German marks. I had a gold watch and a signet, which my father had told me to sell in Hungary if need be. They took all of it. I was surprised to see there a young German whom I knew from dancing clubs in Katowice. He stood out since he was wearing a typical Nazi uniform: tall boots, short trousers and white stockings. He was already a Gestapo employee in Baligród, a translator. He wore a uniform without any rank marks, but he recognized me. He asked me why I was fleeing. I told him briefly how things were. Some of my friends then got beat up, but I wasn't. I might have been spared because of his support.

From there we were put on a wagon and escorted to Sanok prison. It was April 2nd 1940. For a moment we considered jumping off the wagon, but it was not so simple. The Germans positioned us in such a way that we could not reach any of them. We were lying down in the front and were not allowed to move. If anyone budged he would be shot with a short, fast rifle. It didn't make sense to try to run away. We didn't stand a chance.

Later they separated us and we each ended up in different cells. If my memory serves me right, mine was number 27. I spent four months in that prison. I was interrogated. The Germans wanted me to admit to being a ringleader of the whole escape. But we did not have a leader or a superior—that was the story we had planned to tell in such a situation, anyway. Half of the prisoners from my cell were court martialed. They were sentenced and executed by firing squad.

The word Gestapo was not much used at that time but I more or less knew what they were all about. In Żywiec, just before my escape, they had arrested many young men; among them a friend of mine named Stanisław Sanetra, a year my senior and a former cadet. He had been interrogated and subjected to extreme beating. They let him out for two or three days and then locked him up again. He got beaten yet again with fists and sticks. Later he became a prisoner at Sachsenhausen. He remained there for the next five years, but luckily survived the war.

---

11 "Gubernia" was a colloquial term for the General Government, the German occupied region of Poland roughly resembling an administrative area of the former Russian partition, or more precisely – the old General Government of Warsaw (1844–1917).

12 In March 1939, at the collapse and partition of Czechoslovakia, Hungary annexed Southern Slovakia and Carpathian Ruthenia, which led to a shared Hungarian-Polish border.

13 Lemkos: small ethnic group in the Carpathian Mountains.

I was now being taken to the Sanok Gestapo and I was terrified. Since the moment we were captured I could sense it would be hard. My father, who by that time had returned from his internment, warned me that if they caught me I would be a goner. He knew what to expect from them. I knew about the beatings and that they were very bad, but even so not to such an extent as the reality.

During our interrogations by the Sanok Gestapo the Germans asked who organized those trips to Hungary. They wanted to know precisely who was behind it. I got such a beating that when I went into the questioning I had to hold up my pants, but when I left they stayed up by themselves—I was that swollen. I was beaten by an assistant to the Gestapo, a big, strong man. He used his fist and a "vein"—a bull's tail dried up and made flexible.

I had heard earlier that those who inflicted such punishments wanted to be really good at their job and made sure that every strike of the "vein" cut the prisoner's skin. The typical penalty was 25 lashes on the whipping horse.

After each interrogation the prisoners were handcuffed and a uniformed man would take them to the train station. I feared they were about to execute me, so in my broken German I asked my guard: "Where To?" (*Wohin?*). "To Tarnów", he answered. That calmed me down a bit.

Also, one of my friends with whom I was fleeing to Hungary had earlier been detained and interrogated by the Gestapo in Żywiec. Someone informed on him, saying that he had been listening to the radio and spreading the news. He had in fact told some stories about the Gestapo. So that's how I already knew it was a secret Nazi police that was known not to handle people with kid gloves.

WILHELM BRASSE BEFORE LEAVING FOR HUNGARY

I was put on a train to Tarnów, where I was held in prison for another month.

> The majority of the arrested would not reveal to the investigators the real purpose of their hikes in the mountains and maintained they were "tourists". Those who confessed were executed on the spot.

In a short time they executed one hundred and five prisoners. Ten were from my cell. My family members and friends who tried to go with me to Hungary were not among the dead. Mostly they were youths, students, and some soldiers. Some others were educated people, often teachers or lawyers who tried to cross the border individually at a randomly chosen place. If they used a local guide then they probably had followed smugglers trails.

One of those beautiful young people was called Babiński who was the son of a pre-war Polish ambassador to Paris and Amsterdam. I got to know him a bit better, because in prison I had nothing to do and out of boredom began to study French. It was Babiński who became our teacher, since he had gone to French schools and was really fluent. He came to Poland in the summer of 1939 for his vacation in Warsaw where—his bad luck—the war found him. He attempted to escape via Hungary to join his father in Paris. But he got caught. He was executed on July 5th 1940.

There was also a math student, Bakinowski, Czesiu Malczewski from Piotrków, Attorney Bielnicki from Warsaw, Dr. Łazarczy—a judge—and a pre-war Communist Warzyszyn. Eighty percent of the people in my cell were fugitives who counted on making it into the Polish army. They were arrested in various spots around Sanok, near the border. Practically all the people in that prison were captured on their way to Hungary.

At the end of my stay in Tarnów two prisoners were called: a guy named Adler and me. I was put in front of an elegantly dressed officer. He told me, that if I agreed to join the German military I would be released and I would not be put "in transport". This is what they called it. They did not say where we were going, only "in transport". I refused. If I did this, how could I look my friends in the eye? The other guy also refused—but he died after a month in Auschwitz.

Then the Germans offered me an opportunity to sign the Reichslist[14]. They thought it would be only natural since both my name and surname were German. They even told me during my interrogation that I was a German and that I was bringing disgrace upon the German nation. "My father is Polish and so am I," I retorted.

"If your father is stupid, you don't have to be." (*Wenn dein Vater ist dumm, mussen Sie nicht.*), was their answer.

IT NEVER OCCURRED TO ME THAT I SHOULD HAVE SIGNED THAT DEVIL'S BARGAIN AND BE LEFT ALONE.

---

[14] As a son and grandson of a German. Brasse was probably offered to apply for German citizenship (*Staatsangehörigkeit*).

On the morning of August 29th 1940, heavily guarded, we were taken into the showers. Then four hundred and sixty of us prisoners formed a column and were escorted to the train station. We were heading into the unknown...

"The parade wound itself among the streets like a long snake, and you couldn't help thinking of a herd being taken to the slaughterhouse. The guards' shouting quieted things down some, but the noise did not cease. We were serious and downcast as we walked. Among us there were local people, the Tarnovians. It was they who had the hardest time."[15]
SOURCE: The Memoires of Jerzy Bielecki[16]

"Although the street where we were marching was still empty, in some of the windows you could see faces hiding behind the curtains. Startled, they would disappear quickly, to come back in the next moment.
This town, stunned with terror, was doubly struck by the sight of such a huge transport (...). Suddenly, thrown by an unknown hand, a bunch of red flowers fell down and got immediately trampled under the boot of a passing guard. This is how the good folk in Tarnów were saying goodbye to its prisoners: quietly... in secret... warmly."
SOURCE: Jerzy Bielecki's account[17]

---

[15] Bielecki was taken to Auschwitz in the first Tarnów transport on June 14th; Brasse came in the second one – August 30th 1940.

[16] Bielecki J., *Kto ratuje jedno życie, ratuje cały świat*, Oświęcim 1999, p. 59

[17] Archives of Auschwitz-Birkenau State Museum; later: Auschwitz Museum [APMA-B, Zespół Oświadczenia t. 132, k. 43]

AUSCHWITZ - BEGINNINGS

2ND TARNÓW TRANSPORT THAT TOOK BRASSE TO AUSCHWITZ

AUSCHWITZ-BEGINNINGS

AUSCHWITZ - BEGINNINGS

We reached Oświęcim on August 30th 1940 around 3 or 4 PM.

THE NAME OŚWIĘCIM DID NOT MEAN MUCH TO ME AT THE TIME.

I had some vague notion of what a concentration camp was. None of the people I was with had known that such a thing existed on Polish territory. We were told we were going to a labor camp. The SS men who escorted us were saying exactly that: "You are traveling to work" (*Ihr fährt zu arbeiten*). There were even some lawyers among us who claimed that for what we had done, meaning illegaly attempting to cross the border, we could get, according to the Criminal Code, one or two years at most.

The buildings, which in May of 1940 were used for the location of the concentration camp, were built in 1916–1919. They were supposed to serve as a quarantine station for seasonal workers emigrating from Galicia to North and South America. After Czechoslovakia annexed Zaolzie in January 1919 they were used as refugee camps for people from Zaolzie and Silesia. In 1925 the site was given to the Polish Army. They served as barracks for the 2nd Batallion of the 73rd Regiment of Infantry and for the 3rd Division of the 21st Regiment of Light Artillery; from the spring of 1939 for the 5th Division of Horse Artillery.

After the Nazis decided to establish Auschwitz, the first transport of prisoners was housed in the Monopol building. They fenced in the courtyard in front of the building and put up watch towers in the corners.

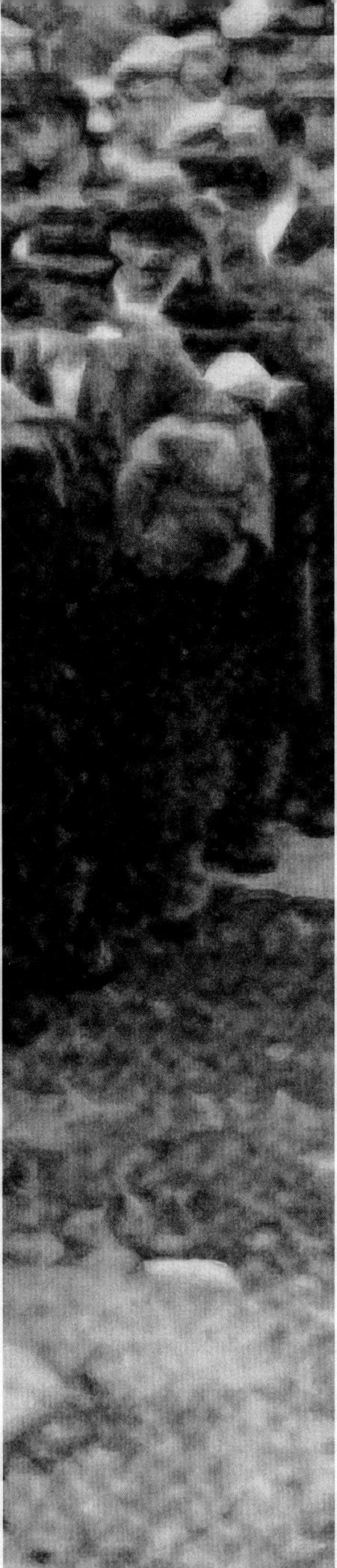

We were leaving the train amidst incredible sounds of screaming and beatings. It was the first time that I saw prisoners in striped uniforms. Someone said that they were surely Navy mutineers, but they all were German prisoners who a few days earlier had been brought from Sachsenhausen.

"Thirty common German criminals, wearing striped clothes, were the first inmates of Auschwitz. They were convicts, mostly hardened murderers with life sentences. Under Nazi laws they were facing long years of punishment, which could be lessened if they volunteered to build a camp for the so-called Polish bandits in Oświęcim. They were informed by the SS men that if they could match them in the task of finishing off the Poles, the authorities would pardon them and let them out, and maybe even allow them to join the ranks of the Nazi military."

SOURCE: Deposition no 1.. In: *Oświęcim w systemie RSHA*[18]

After five months of prison I had become somewhat accustomed to the screaming but I had never heard anything like this. I was terrified.

---

[18] Rajewski L., *Oświęcim w systemie RSHA*, Warszawa 1946, p. 89-90

„The tumult and clamor of voices gradually increased. At last the door of our carriage was violently opened. We were blinded by strong lights aimed inside.

"*Alle raus! Rrraus! Rrrraus!*" ("All out!") yelled the SS-men, while their rifle butts were hitting the shoulders, backs and heads of my colleagues.

We had to hurry outside. (...) A gang of SS-men were hitting, kicking and making incredible noise: „*Zu Fünfe!*" ("In fives!") The soldiers incited their dogs to attack those on the wings of the five-man ranks.

Blinded by the lights, pushed, beaten, kicked, attacked by dogs, we suddenly found ourselves in conditions that none of us had ever experienced. The weaker among us were so stunned that they degenerated into a thoughtless mass."
SOURCE: Witold Pilecki's Report[19]

We crossed the gate and stood in the roll call yard

WE WERE ORDERED TO LAY DOWN ALL OUR POSSESSIONS.

Most of us had nothing, but some people had provisions from their relatives in Tarnów. An SS-man standing by said to us in Polish, "Eat what you have; they will take it from you anyway."

I remember him. His name was Malisch[20] and he was from Bielsko. He was right. They were taking everything. Sometimes someone smuggled something in, but to be honest I don't know how they did it...

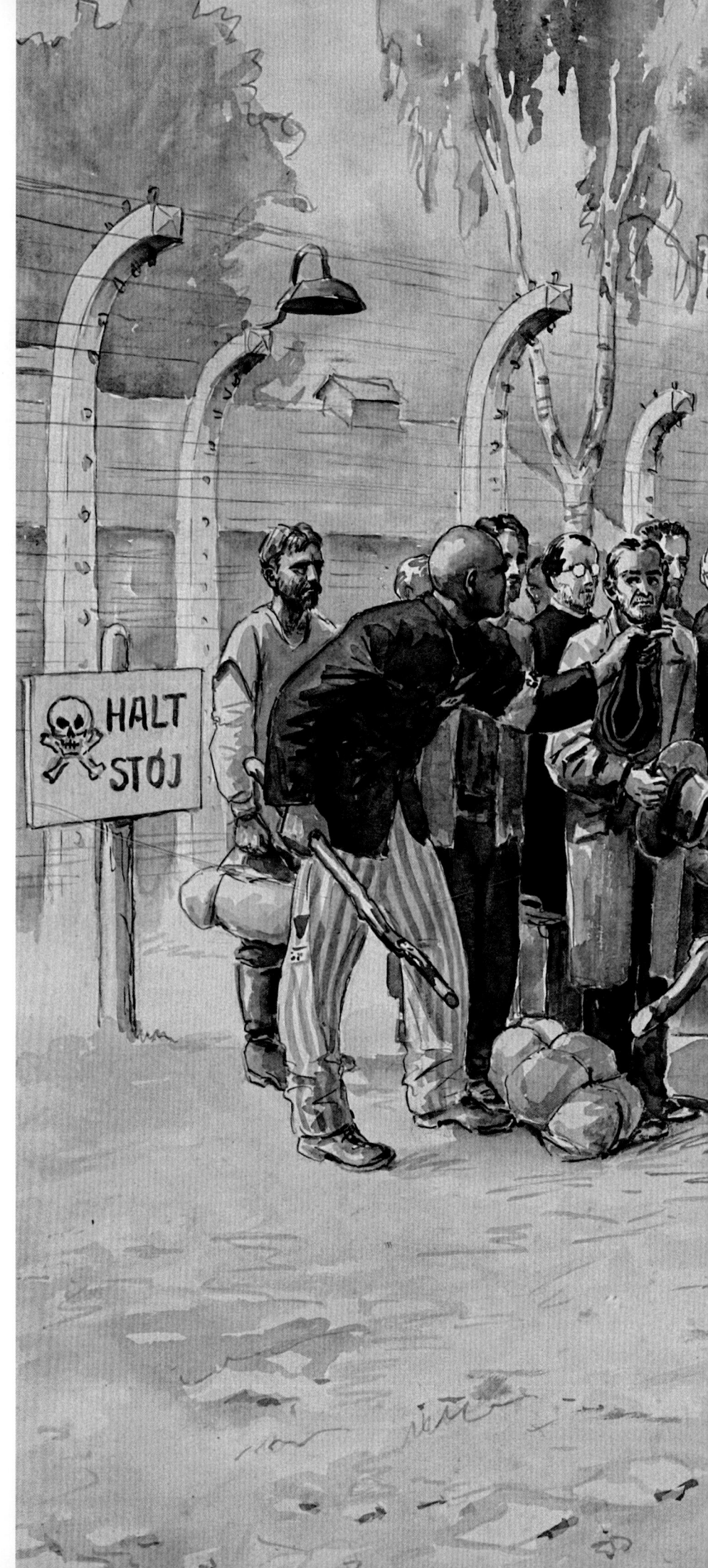

---

[19] Cyra A., *Ochotnik do Auschwitz. Witold Pilecki 1901-1948*, Oświęcim 2000, p. 266-267

[20] Erich Malisch (SS-Unterscharführer) b. Aug. 23rd 1910 in Świętochłowice, worked as a driver at the main camp and at the sub-camp in Jaworzno. More → BIOGRAPHIES

Welcome to the Newcomers, Władysław Siwek

KL Auschwitz II-Birkenau. Jews during camp registration, after selection

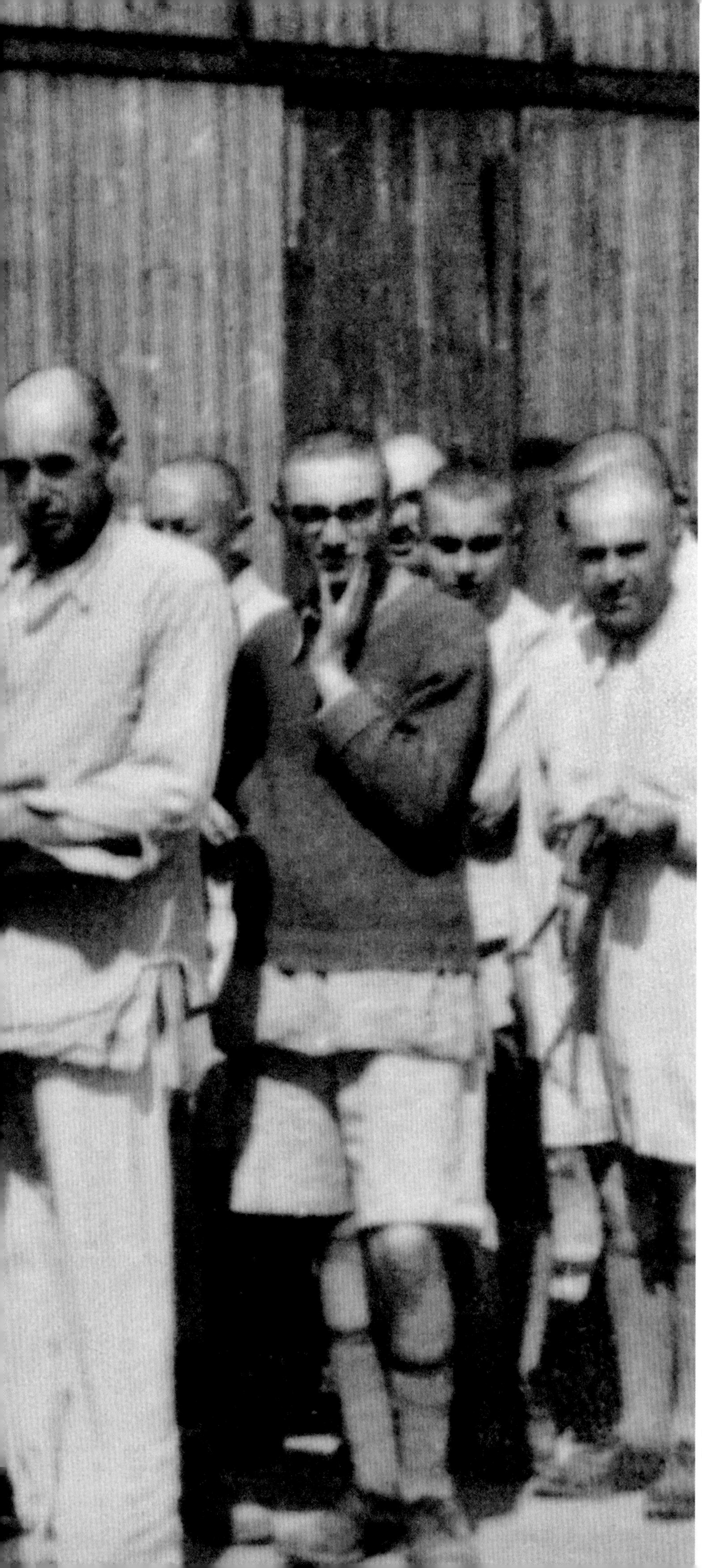

"I was brought out of my stupor by a strong and persuasive voice:

"Listen, colleagues, we know that some of you have dollars, soft and hard, and also diamonds, gold, silver, marks, currencies. You have it hiding in your mouths, noses, ears, asses.

I advise you to give it up immediately, as we have the means to make you do it, even if it's hidden in your stomachs or guts. "[...] We kept looking at each other suspiciously. I was so impressed by those words that I really began to suspect people of hiding valuables inside themselves. A moment passed, then another moment and everybody just stood there and no one gave anything away. They looked at one another with pleading eyes and the eyes said: "Give it to them... Give it... Give it...!

I regretted deeply not having anything to give. I went through my pockets, creases in my clothes, but unfortunately I had nothing. Neither did the others, although they all did the same feverish search."

SOURCE: Abraham Kajzer's account[21]

"They let us keep only a handkerchief. For men, also a belt. All the other objects were put into large paper bags and taken to a deposit room (Effektenkammer), where they were supposed to be kept during prison time. Of course there was no invoice, even if a prisoner had gold valuables, or a watch or large sums of money. Next he was given a carton with the camp number on it and was rushed to another room for other procedures."

SOURCE: Tadeusz Iwaszko's account[22]

---

21 Kajzer A., *Za drutami śmierci*, Wałbrzych 2008, p. 29
22 Iwaszko T., Więźniowie.. In: *Oświęcim: hitlerowski obóz masowej zagłady*, W. Michalak ed., Warszawa 1984, p. 46

My name was read from the transport list. When they called a name, we would step out, hand over our clothes and receive underwear and prison uniforms. Those who had hair on their heads had it immediately shaved off.

Then we went straight to the showers. We got sprinkled with some water.

"We were rushed in single line along a hallway and put in front of prisoners who, painfully yanking, cut our hair (which was to be used for the manufacture of hats). On other stools there were prisoners shaving off the rest of what was left on our heads. Women were going through the same procedure."
SOURCE: Jan Szembek's account [23]

"It was an unpleasant operation because of both the hurry and the dull tools that were used. The roughly shaven spots were disinfected by rubbing them with a rag dipped in some sort of antiseptic liquid."
SOURCE: Tadeusz Iwaszko's account [24]

"... Shaven, in groups of about 30, we were taken to the showers, which sprinkled the entire area of a small room. The water, from which you could not hide, was so cold, that compared to it the snow seemed warm. Whereas the people in the next group got severely scalded. All wet, we proceeded in line towards an open door at the top of the corridor. There, items were thrown at us from the rooms we passed: shirts, pants, striped fatigues, clogs, caps, towels."
SOURCE: Jan Szembek's account [25]

---

[23] Szembek J., *Obozowe wspomnienia Auschwitz--Birkenau. Zugang - Block,* , July 27th 2012
www.auschwitz88369.republika.pl

[24] Iwaszko T., *Więźniowie..* In: *Oświęcim...*, op. cit., p. 46

[25] Szembek J., *Obozowe...*, op. cit.

Beginnings of the agon— the bath, Władysław Siwek

AUSCHWITZ - BEGINNINGS

KL Auschwitz II-Birkenau. A group of Jews directed to the camp after selection

After the shaving and showering we got prison clothes. Some people looked funny because their uniforms were too small, like one giant chap with pants just down to his knees. They did not have caps at that time; we walked bare headed up till January 1941. When the frost came, we received earmuffs, which had flaps. They covered the ears, attached by a springy headband. There were no coats or socks. In the beginning we had our own shoes. Mine were all burnt, in shreds, from the time I tried to dry them and had put them too close to the fire. It was only the following week that we got our camp footwear, wooden shoes with leather in the front. Later it would be all-wood Dutch-style clogs, which turned out to be quite good for the winter.

IT WAS THEN THAT I HAD MY FIRST ENCOUNTER WITH HUMAN CORPSES.

It was especially bad to be confronted with the sight of dead bodies close up. The Germans told us they needed a few young strong bodies and so I volunteered, not knowing for what. It turned out we were to carry the corpses of the Jews from our transport to the basement where the dead were stored. When we arrived, the camp had already been in operation for two and a half months and the Nazis had already managed to set up storage houses for the dead. That sight was one of the first of many nightmare images...

Later they divided us into separate *blocks*[26]. I was assigned to what was then Block 9[27]. I spent a few first nights there. In the beginning we were not allowed to sleep. They tormented everybody with sleep deprivation.

---

26 Block: housing building for the inmates.
27 Initial numbering of blocks lasted till August 1941. Block 9 is today's Block 24, which houses the Archives of the Auschwitz-Birkenau State Museum in Oświęcim.

"The first night. We were sleeping probably on the second floor. The room was large with the floor covered in sawdust, wood chips and other trash. We were lying close to each other. At night when the SS men came, they would hit us and shoot at the ceiling. And there were the drills: Down! Up! Hinlegen! Auf! Hinlegen! Auf! Clouds of dust everywhere. It took a while before the SS men got tired and left, though not for long. They repeatedly tormented us with those visits until morning."
SOURCE: Józef Paczyński's account[28]

"At the camp, same as in prisons, there was no chance for normal sleep.[...] What is your chance to get any sleep, which brings rest and relaxation, if:
- you are hungry and thirsty
- you sleep in your clothes, which during the day had been soaked with snow, rain or fog
- you sleep with 8 other people on the lower, middle or top level of a bunk bed in a brick dorm or later in a wooden dorm at Birkenau
- the cold on the block wakes you up and you have to walk to a distant sanitary quarters (the name "sanitary" is an overstatement)
- you sleep breathing air from the crematorium chimneys
- you sleep so close to the ramp that you hear every train full of people pull up and get unloaded.[29]
SOURCE: Zofia Podhorecka's account[30]

---

28 Auschwitz Museum [APMA-B. Zespół Oświadczenia, t. 100, k. 95]
29 Zofia Pohorecka was in the women's camp. The situation she describes was similar in both men's and women's camps, especially in the first weeks of imprisonment.
30 Jagoda Z., Kłodziński S., Masłowski J., *Więźniowie Oświęcimia*, Kraków-Wrocław 1984, p. 215

Then prisoner-clerks (block writers) took down our personal data based on the lists provided by the Germans.

These files contained the personal data cards of prisoners and sometimes other documents, such as, for instance, an order for preventive imprisonment, or confirmation of transfer from a prison facility to the camp (Überführungsvordruck). The files had updated information about punishments, transferals to other blocks and hospitalizations. There were also copies of any correspondence concerning the prisoner. The files – which also contained classified information, for instance, about the status of ongoing investigation and remarks such as „Rückkehr unerwünscht" ("return undesirable") – could be accessed only by SS and a very few inmates working as block writing clerks.[31]

I WAS ASSIGNED CAMP NUMBER 3444.

At that time there were as yet no tattoos. They just wrote the number on a card and that was it. I wore mine in a small breast pocket. They first started tattooing prisoners in early spring of 1943.

"KL Auschwitz was the only concentration camp where they branded prisoners with tattoos. In other camps, for example in KL Mauthausen, they wore small metal tags with engraved numbers, which were fastened to the wrist with wire, chain or a string.
In Auschwitz, in addition to the tattoo, the number had to be sewn in next to the triangle indicating prisoner category, which was placed on the left breast part of the shirt and on the right trouser leg, above the thigh, under the pocket.
Introducing tattoos in Auschwits was due to the high mortality rate of prisoners, sometimes several hundred a day."

"[...] Tatooing began in the hospital when they started to pencil the numbers on prisoners' chests. The same method was used for prisoners shot in executions. [...] Initially they made the tattoos with a special metal stamp with changeable digits. The digits were made up of 1 centimeter long needles. That instrument, by means of striking the prisoner in the upper part of the left breast, made it possible to tattoo the whole number at once. Ink was then rubbed into the bleeding wounds. [...] But because this method turned out to be impractical they started tattooing with individual needles. [...]. They also switched the location to the left forearm."[32]

---

31 Paczuła T., *Izby Pisarskie w KL Auschwitz.*. In: *Księgi zgonów w Auschwitz. Relacje 1.*, , Munich 1995, p.30

32 Iwaszko T., *Przyczyny osadzania w obozie i kategorie więźniów.*. In: *Auschwitz 1940-1950: węzłowe zagadnienia z dziejów obozu – więźniowie – życie i praca*. T. 2, W. Długoborski, F. Piper (edit), Oświęcim 1995, p. 18-19

We were told that we no longer had names; we were numbers. We were not persons, but prisoners. Then Liutenant Lagerführer Fritzsch[33] gave a short speech:
"You, Polish legionaires..." – he knew that the transport was made up mostly of guys fleeing to become soldiers –

"YOU ARE NOW IN AUSCHWITZ CONCENTRATION CAMP AND THE ONLY WAY OUT OF HERE IS THROUGH THE CREMATORY CHIMNEY."

He added, that the longest life span there was three months and that all needed to obey the orders of the SS men and the kapos[34] and every case of disobedience would be immediately punishable by death. The translator was Count Baworowski.[35]

I listened to that speech and wondered if Fritzsch was lying, just trying to scare us...

"If somebody doesn't like it they can go and throw themselves on the wires. If there are any Jews in the transport they will be allowed to live no more than two weeks; priests – one month, the rest – three months."
Source: Wiesław Kielar's account[36]

"I listened to those words with more than incredulity. Who could have thought that in the 20th century, in the heart of Europe, such a venerable nation as Germany would build a death factory? I didn't do anything wrong enough, I thought, to lose my life."
Source: Józef Paczyński's account[37]

KL Auschwitz II-Birkenau.
The camp latrine

I think that maybe as much as fifty percent of my survival I owe to the fact that I could communicate in German and that from the very beginning I tried to speak German even to the kapos, although at that time it was still a broken German. With the SS men we had to speak German. That was the order, plain and simple. Naturally, those who had trouble with, for instance, singing in German, were getting additional beatings. That was the procedure.

"In those conditions language isolation could be a death sentence. That was why all the Italians died. In the first days it turned out they did not understand the commands, and that was unacceptable. It was not tolerated. They did not understand the orders; they could not be understood. All they were getting where some shrieks, as the German soldiers were always yelling."

SOURCE: Primo Levi's account[48]

---

[48] Camon F., *Rozmowa z Primo Levim*, E. Kabatc (tłum.), Oświęcim 1997, p. 26

THE PRISONERS HAD A TERRIBLE TIME WITH THE COUNT OFF.

There were, let's say, four hundred people at a roll call. They formed ten rows, but no one wanted to be in the front because often the prisoners did not know how to count to forty. The short ones would push themselves into the middle, not wanting to be in the front, but if a tall guy was in the first row an SS man would beat him up because he should have stood in the back. So setting this up was very chaotic. By the way, no one wanted to stand in the back either, because there it was easy to get kicked by an SS man. Later the prisoners became smart and the one who, for instance, who knew how to say "eighteen" would stand in a particular spot and report: "achtzehn", and the one further up could say "nineteen" and would position himself in such a way to be able to say this number.

The Germans always kept counting us and if something didn't add up they kept us standing in roll call. Then they would hit, poke, kick and drill us as usual.

"Can there be anything easier than to stand up in fives, zu fünfen? It seems a child's play, but the reality was different. The blows, which are so generously bestowed upon us, make it even more difficult. I don't know why, but suddenly there are only four people in the preceding row, the "hole" has to be immediately patched up by someone from the row behind. But by whom? Two guys jump in at once. So now we have six in front and behind again four. The game lasts a good hour. The skies begin to slowly lighten. No one knows what time it is, three, four? It begins to drizzle.
SOURCE: Szymon Laks's account[49]

authorities would get themselves under some roof, apparently to do some simple math – while we were tormented by staying out in the cold rain and snow, required to stand in one spot completely still. You had to struggle with your whole organism, flex and release the muscles and in this way generate some body heat, to remain alive."
SOURCE: Witold Pilecki's report[50]

For every escape the rest were punished with roll calls lasting several hours. I had it better than other prisoners, as I did not always have to stand outdoors like them in the cold and rain.

"Since our jobs at the *kommando*[51] often required working there until evening hours, we were excused from participating in the evening roll call. It took place directly at our kommando, where an SS man would receive the report of the status of the kommando given by kapo Tadek. It was only for the morning roll calls that we joined other residents of the block, but those did not last long. The missing prisoners were always found out at the evening roll call, as the majority of escape attempts took place during work in the area enclosed by a large chain of posts.
SOURCE: Janusz Karwacki's account 📷 [52]

49 Laks S., *Gry...*, op. cit., p. 26

50 Cyra Adam, *Ochotnik do Auschwitz* [A Volunteer to Auschwitz]. Witold Pilecki 1901-1948, Oświęcim 2000, p. 291
51 Kommando — work detail
52 Auschwitz Museum [APMA-B, Zespół Wspomnienia, t. 175, s. 60]

📷 This symbol indicates members of Erkennungsdienst

Both at the roll calls and in the block we were bullied and punished for every trifle.

Whippings were sometimes performed on the naked butt. The skin was broken, and if the prisoner survived his buttocks were often badly slashed. One of my colleagues' butt looked like a cauliflower, because of all the cuts and scar tissue. That was, by the way, how he got his nickname.

A very unpleasant punishment was called "the post" where the prisoner's arms were tied behind the back and then he was hoisted up.

> "That was an extremely painful punishment, which made prisoners pass out from pain. It was also very dangerous due to the consequences that often followed. After a long suspension from the post the tendons in the shoulders would rupture; the prisoner would lose the use of his arms and if he couldn't work he would become subject to "selection"."[53]

Sometimes the punishment was "*Stehbunker*", or the standing cell. The prisoner had then to remain standing all night; he was not allowed to lie down or even to sit.

> "Standing cells, which were also called dark cells, were created in cell 22, dividing it with partitions into four spaces, each measuring less than 1 sq meter. Four prisoners would spend several nights there, sometimes more than 10 nights. They entered the space through a small opening above the floor, which was secured with bars and a wooden flap.

THE ONLY AIR VENT FOR EACH OF THOSE CELLS WAS A HOLE OF FIVE BY FIVE CENTIMETERS LARGE,

which was covered from the outside with a metal shield punched like a sieve. Prisoners incarcerated in those cells were deprived of adequate oxygen and faced asphyxiation."[54]

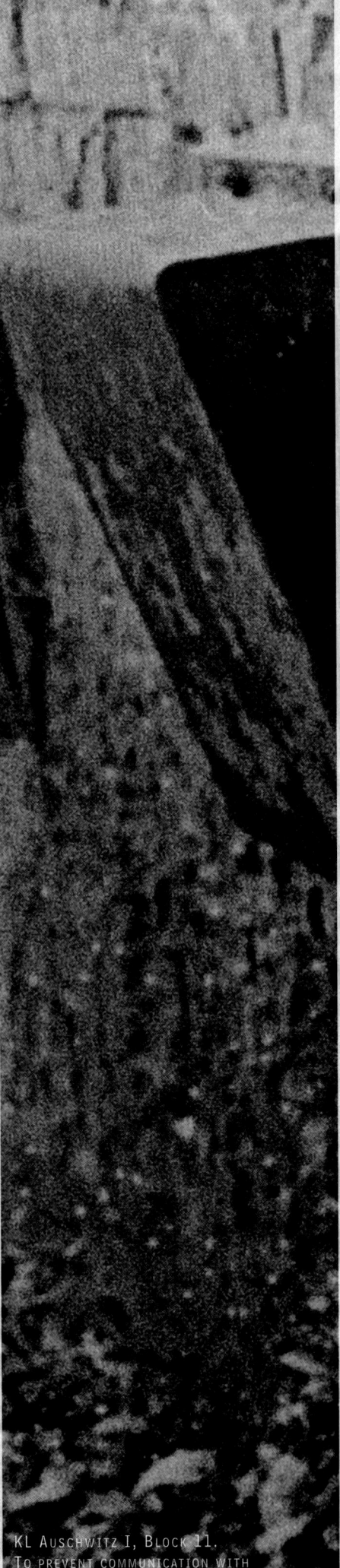

KL Auschwitz I, Block 11.
To prevent communication with prisoners in the standing cell metal shields were installed over the air vents

In the morning the prisoner had to go to his usual work. A good friend of mine, Wiesław Kielar[55], talks about that. He was a smarty pants and a dodger, but a good sport and I have fond memories of him. Kielar got this punishment several times and... he survived.

> "[...] I put on warm underwear from '*Kanada*'[56], protected my back with a cement paper sack, on top of that put on two shirts and bandaged my legs with paper. My feet, in woolen socks, I wrapped additionally in rags and only then did I put on the stripy uniform, not forgetting two sweaters and a scarf. Instead of leather shoes I put on clogs several sizes too big. Dressed like this I looked enormous. To match the look I moved like a hulk, so my friends watching my preparation couldn't stop laughing. I also checked the contents of my pockets: cigarettes, matches, a piece of bread with margarine, a candle. [...]
>
> On all fours—otherwise I wouldn't fit—I pushed myself through the black hole of the stehzel. The cell was narrow and stank of feces and while I was clumsily struggling to get inside, the *Blockführer*[57] would help me out with a forceful kick in the butt. [...] The SS man slammed the door closed and I heard him turn the key in the padlock. Through the vent above I could see the light in the corridor go out. Then there was complete darkness and silence, the only sound being the slam of the *bunker's*[58] main door. [...] I felt damp coldness creeping up from the concrete floor. I had increasing piercing pain under my shoulder blades. With each passing minute the pain in the legs got worse."[59]

SOURCE: Wiesław Kielar's memoirs[60]

WNIOSEK O UKARANIE WIĘŹNIA CHŁOSTĄ

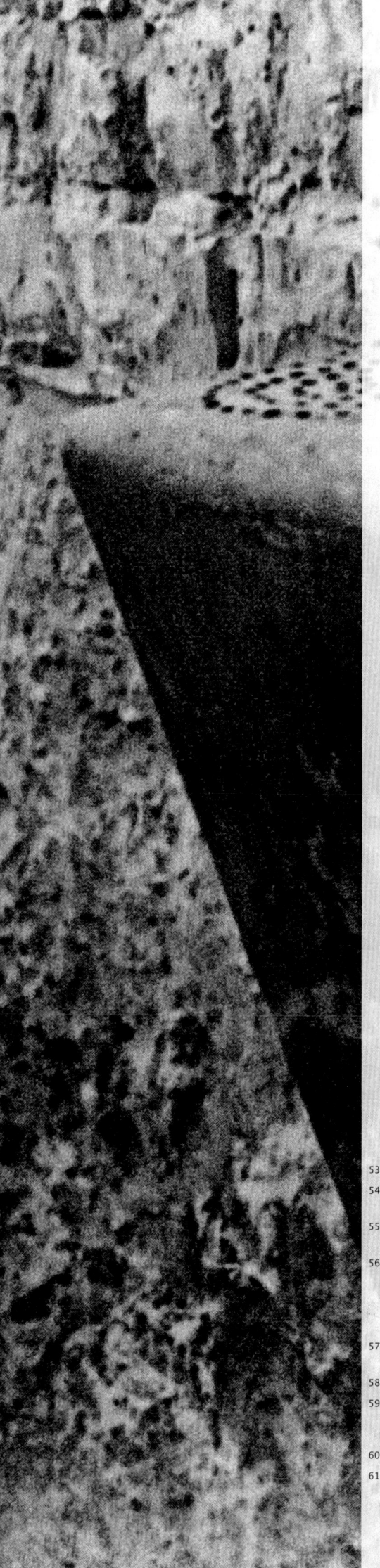

In the late summer of 1940 I was working throwing dirt around a freestanding building. We were putting dirt next to the side walls making a berm that is there to this day. There were about 150 of us, mostly from the transport in which I came. I was sure we were securing the walls of a bakery. It turned out it was the first crematorium[61]

Next few weeks in the camp I spent at the carpenter workshop, in block 9. I volunteered, as I hoped there would be a chance to get something out of it. First we had again to carry the bodies of six or eight murdered people. They lay there naked. They had been dreadfully kicked. One of them had been so badly kicked around his penis that was just horrific. They had swollen heads and faces destroyed by the blows. It was a horrible sight.

Some people broke down at the very start. But many of us, especially the young guys, were saying that we would hang in there just to spite them. Some prisoners had been at Auschwitz for almost three months so we comforted ourselves thinking we might also make it. The most important thing was to get some sort of job.

---

[53] Piper F., *Eksterminacja*.. In: *Oświęcim...*, p. 88–89
[54] Strzelecka I., *Kary i tortury*. In: *Auschwitz 1940--1950...*, op. cit., p. 285
[55] Wiesław Kielar (Inmate No. 290), b. Aug. 12th 1919 in Przeworsk, student. More → Biographies
[56] Storehouses for goods looted from gas chambers'-victims, located near the main camp (Kanada I) and in Birkenau in the B II section (Kanada II). Name origin: Canada—the country—was a popular term for a land of plenty.
[57] Blockführer - an SS man overssing one or several blocks.
[58] Bunker - basement prison cell
[59] Wiesław Kielar describes standing cells in one of the brick buildings in the men's section of Birkenau, which operated there till July 1943.
[60] Kielar W., *Dzieła...*, op. cit., p. 203–208
[61] The photograph of this building is the background on p. 44–45

When I first arrived at the camp there was an awful racket. They walked us among screams and beatings and I actually never noticed the sign "Arbeit macht frei". I noticed it the next day and thought it was ludicrous.
"How is such hypocrisy possible?", I thought. We were obviously not working, but getting tortured and murdered. In the first days there was not even a question of work. There were just the exercises, non-stop running and the yelling kapos.

"Arbeit macht frei" (Germ. Labor makes free) – the German slogan based on "Wahrheit macht frei"—"The Truth shall make you free"—a popular Bible quote from the Gospel of John (J 8, 32); commonly used in the Protestant tradition. In 1872 German right wing writer Lorenz Diefenbach used a paraphrased quote "Arbeit macht frei" as the title of his novel published in Vienna. The slogan became very popular among nationalist groups. In the 1930s it was used in Nazi propaganda in programs fighting unemployment.
By order of SS General Theodore Eicke it was used at the gates of several Nazi concentration camps (Auschwitz, Dachau, Gross-Rosen, Sachsenhausen, Theresinstadt, Flossenbürg), which were also camps of exhausting slave labor.
In some camps other slogans were used. In KL Buchenwald, for example, the sign on the gate read: "Jedem das seine" which can be translated as: "To each his own."

"They wrote 'labor makes you free', although we were experiencing first hand that labor in Auschwitz was just one of the ways of murdering prisoners. So we quickly made up a saying: 'Arbeit Macht Frei durch den Schornstein', which meant: 'Labor makes you free (to leave) through the chimney.' "
SOURCE: Kazimierz Albin's account [62]

"I was entering the camp through the gate. Yes, now I understood the words: 'Arbeit macht frei'! Oh, yes, indeed... Labor makes you free... frees you from the camp... from the consciousness that I had a moment ago. Frees the spirit from the body, making the body go to crematorium..."
SOURCE: Witold Pilecki's report [63]

62 Albin K., *W Oświęcimiu i konspiracji. Rzeczpospolita*, Sept. 25th 1984.
63 Cyra A., *Ochotnik...*, op. cit., p. 286

THE SIGN "ARBEIT MACHT FREI" WAS MADE BY MY COLLEAGUE JAN LIWACZ[64]

I would see him quite often, especially in the later part of my camp time. I would mostly go there to visit Józef Szajna[65],

with whom I was a close friend. Liwacz worked in a very good kommando, where all of the prisoners were artists: painters, sculptors...

"One of the first jobs we had was making the sign "Arbeit macht frei". Kapo Schlosserei Kurt Müller drew on the ground the shape he wanted. After we bent the pipes and cut the letters the parts were welded together. The whole ironworks shop worked at that project."

SOURCE: Artur Krzetuski's account[66]

Liwacz was very talented and he did special jobs as a blacksmith-artist for the commander and the top officers. He had incredible skills. I read a beautiful story about him...

"[...] There was a woman in that group. Somebody told her that I could light a cigarette with a hot iron. She wanted me to demonstrate it. I told her I did not have a cigarette. When she gave me a cigarette in a case I apologized and said I could not accept anything without the consent of my superiors. When the Lagerführer gave me permission, I apologized, because my hands were dirty and I would have soiled the other cigarettes. The woman took out one cigarette and put it in my mouth.

---

64 Jan Liwacz (Inmate No. 1010) b. Oct. 4th 1898 in Dukla, blacksmith. More → BIOGRAPHIES
65 Józef Szajna (Inmate No. 18729) b. March 13th 1923 in Rzeszów, artist, came to KL Auschwitz on July 7th 1941 in a transport from Krakow. More → BIOGRAPHIES
66 Auschwitz Museum [APMA-B, Zespół Oświadczenia t. 12 s. 113]

I heated up a metal bar by hitting it with a hammer. I lit the cigarette with the bar. Then the woman said: "After all, those Poles are not a stupid nation"."
SOURCE: Jan Liwacz's account[67]

Liwacz made lanterns, decorative lamps and sconces.

"The first chandelier that I made was a big, 6-sided one. Part of it was made of intertwining deer antlers, and the lights were fixed to those antlers.
The second chandelier was the one with 6 Nazi eagles tied together. Each eagle had a decorative lamp in its beak. It was a substantial and pretty piece.
[...]
For Commandant Höss I made a set which included a bridge table, ashtrays, a cigar cutter, a standing lamp etc.
From sheet metal I cut signs or individual letters used in signs. I also made symbols or decorations, like the figures sitting on beer barrels (Fassreiter), which still remain on the building of the former SS Revier, (inside there was a small canteen)."
SOURCE: Relacja Jana Liwacza[68]

Janek Liwacz is said to have made a toy airplane for Höss's son[69]. I heard that it was a real masterpiece.[70]

"From Lederfabrik Kommando I remember also prisoner Liwacz, who designed and made a metal airplane for Höss's children. The airplane would slide down a rod and its size permitted the child to sit inside the plane. The toy stood in the Commander's garden."
SOURCE: Wiktor Pasikowski's account[71]

„[...] With my friend Weszek, carpenter by trade, we made for Höss's kids a plane with wings about four meters wide, which went round like a carousel and was powered with an electric engine. With the wheelwrights we made two autos, which look exactly like real cars, to be pulled by a single horse, very nice work. One of them was used by Höss; the other one was sent to Berlin, to Himmler."
SOURCE: Jan Liwacz's account[72]

Even if Liwacz was making such things as the little airplane for Höss's son and so pleasing the Germans, he remained honorable. Of that I am sure.

"[...] Höss came into the Schlösserei[73] and asked what I would do if I were released. I explained that I would immediately go home. Then he asked me if after the release I would stay there, bring my family and work. I answered something to the effect that I was there already. Of course I never got released."
SOURCE: Jan Litwacz's account[74]

---

67 Auschwitz Museum [APMA-B, Zespół Oświadczenia, t. 65, k. 78]
68 Auschwitz Museum [APMA-B, Zespół Oświadczenia, t. 65, k. 76–77]
69 Rudolf Höss (SS-Obersturmbannführer) b. Nov. 25th 1900 in Baden-Baden, Commandant of KL Auschwitz-Birkenau 1940–1943. More → BIOGRAPHIES

70 The airplane was fitted with an electric engine and had a power supply cord 15 meter long. The propeller turned as in a real airplane. There was a swastika on the rudder. It was named "Brummer" and the name was painted on the wings. Source: IFZ Munich
71 Auschwitz Museum [APMA-B, Zespół Oświadczenia, t. 105, k. 156]
72 Jagoda Z., Kłodziński S., Masłowski J., Oświęcim..., op. cit., p. 124
73 Trans.: metal workshop
74 Auschwitz Museum [APMA-B, Zespół Oświadczenia, t. 65, k. 78]

A GOOD KOMMANDO WAS ESSENTIAL

Those, who continued to live, did so because they figured out, or learned from others, that

YOU SURVIVED IF YOU GOT INTO A GOOD KOMMANDO.

"In order to obtain some function on the block or work "under a roof" you had to buy into it with food, cigarettes or influential friends, who themselves had gotten better jobs through favoritism"
SOURCE: Jan Dziopek's account[75]

"Under those conditions there was a chance for those working in the construction workshops established soon after the camp started operating. These were the workshops: ironworks, carpentry, installation, painting, glass, electric, flooring, waterworks and concrete. The work in these shops was considered a privilege, as it usually took place indoors. [...]"[76]

"The labor—a common reality at the camp, was mostly experienced as torment and threat, which was also reflected in the language. Usually it was schwerarbeit—hard labor, sometimes punitive, as distinguished from light labor (*leichtarbeit*), secure indoor employment, which was a dream for the prisoners who wanted to survive. Tasks in the aussens, in the aussenkommandos, meaning in the groups going outside the "small *Postenkette*"[77], enabled occasional secret contacts with people outside the camp. Aussenarbeiters had more chances of getting something to eat, so it was hard to get a job in one of those kommandos. The prisoners became expert in working with their eyes and ears (augenarbeit), i.e. watching out and faking labor, so that the post guards, kapos, vorarbeiters and other overseers would not notice they were pretending to work."[78]

I went through a few kommandos. In the very beginning I was assigned to road building work in Strassenbaum Kommando. I would not wish that upon my worst enemy...
The work was accompanied by incessant shouting and beating. My first kapo wore a green triangle, which meant he was a professional criminal. His name was Teresiak[79] and he was from Drezno.

At work he would beat people to death. On his first day he killed six prisoners with a shovel handle. The next day our supervisor just noted that the six were dead and was not curious what had happened. The SS man did not ask any questions and just accepted the fact that there were casualties. That was it.
I was shocked by this attitude. I could not understand that nobody cared about what was done to those people.
Later I was put to work at the Planierungskommando, making foundations for future horse stables, cattle barns and garages. There were about one hundred and twenty of us and the buildings, which were built on foundations we had prepared, still stand.
After that I spent two or three days demolishing a house, unloading coal, carrying beams, tearing down a roof and floor, and pulling down walls with a pick. It was very hard labor. It was awkward to fill a shovel; we had to use hands and all the skin on our palms was chafed raw. I was always pushed around to do the hardest task, since the better positions were already taken. I ran away from that hard kommando. Then one kapo, a vulgar redhead and degenerate, found me, smacked all over my face and kicked me. I had to go back to that job but again I escaped. I found out that another kommando was looking for people - one block clerk said it would be for light and easy work with extra food.

---

75 Dziopek J., *Walka o życie*. In: *Pamiętniki nauczycieli z obozów i więzień hitlerowskich 1939-1945*, K. Bidakowski, T. Wójcik (ed.), Warszawa 1962, p. 327
76 Piper F., *Eksploatacja pracy więźniów*. In: *Auschwitz 1940-1950...*, op. cit., p. 68-69
77 Kleine Postenkette - inner security perimeter of the camp.
78 Jagoda Z., Kłodziński S., Masłowski J., *Oświęcim...*, op. cit., p. 39
79 Franz Teresiak (Inmate No. 3231) b. January 23rd 1914. A German brought to the Camp on Aug. 27th 1940 from KL Sachsenhausen. More → BIOGRAPHIES

A few other colleagues and I volunteered immediately. As it turned out, it was again transporting the corpses. We would put eight or ten bodies on a cart and haul them from block 28, that is, the hospital.

All day, corpses and more corpses. We were taking them to the crematorium. After a week I became numb to the horror. Once, we were roasting slices of potato on a grill as if the deceased were not right there beside us. They were giving us extra bowls of soup, but I didn't care for that soup. I suffered dreadfully...

Some kommandos were simply murderous. The worst one – Neubaum, or the construction kommando – had concrete mixers and transportation columns for unloading bricks, pouring concrete, woodworking, digging sand and gravel. There was a horrible kapo there, Siegruth[80]—a German.

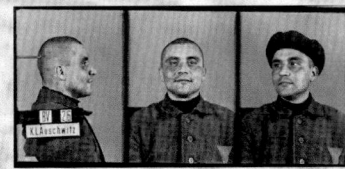

He hated the Poles because he had once served in the "Freikorps", which were militias made up of WWI vererans that were active in Greater Poland from 1918 till 1922. Initially they were fighting the Communist revolution in Germany. Later they fought on the outskirts of Germany to maintain the pre-war borders, mostly in Silesia and Greater Poland. Siegruth was particularly violent, a murderer. He treated prisoners horrifically. In his kommando – and it was a giant one of about 1000 people – he had subordinates, German kapos, who supervised different sections of the work. He told them they had to meet the quotas no matter the cost.

[80] Johann Siegruth Inmate No. 26) b. March 24th 1903 in Katowice; came to Auschwitz on May 20th 1940 from KL Sachsenhausen. More → BIOGRAPHIES

KL AUSCHWITZ II-BIRKENAU. INMATES DIGGING A DRAINAGE DITCH

One day I saw that a certain kapo, a German more or less friendly towards me, was in the potato room. I wanted to ask him to take me into this work group, but I couldn't get through to him. Finally I took the risk and just entered the block. I was immediately caught by the prisoners and taken to the kapo – such were the rules. The kapo's name was Markus[81] and he was from Hanover. He wore a black triangle, which meant he was an "asocial" prisoner. Those were mostly pimps and panders. He said he got the black triangle because in 1926 he had joined the French Foreign Legion and after his training in Toulouse had been sent to Morocco in order to fight against the Arabs. He had spent 10 years there. He told awful stories about the encounters between the native people and Legion troops. He described the battles and the cruel treatment of the Arabs. After 10 years of service he returned home to Hanover, where he got immediately arrested and was taken to Sachsenhausen, later to be transferred to Auschwitz.

Ninety percent of German kapos were common murderers. Compared to them, Marcus was human. At first I was surprised. He was the first kapo I had experienced who did not hit or yell.

When I turned up at his block he noted that I had snuck in illegally, but then he recognized me, because a while earlier we had had some contact in the building kommando. He said, "You are a good worker. And I know you are a photographer. So you will stay here in the potato room." (*Du bist ein gutter Arbeiter, ich weiss dass du bist ein Photograph. Du bleibst hier in der Kartoffellagerhalle.*)

---

81 No data

POTATO KITCHEN AT THE MAIN KITCHEN BUILDING

So I stayed, but I did not peel potatoes. Instead I carried them to the other end of the long and narrow kitchen, some fifty meters, to the vegetable unit. It was light work without beatings or screaming, and it was quiet.

THERE I LAY LOW, LIKE A HARE IN THE FIELD, HOPING TO STAY IN THIS BETTER PLACE.

There were about one hundred and thirty people working in the potato unit, mostly from the intelligentsia. There were informal groups of educated professionals such as teachers, university professors, MPs, counts, judges, senators. If they were really senators, I cannot say for sure. But there was for certain a pre-war Peasant Party parliamentarian, Putek[82], who was an MP from Wadowice.

In the beginning I invited myself into the teachers' group—but they kicked me out. They went to the kapo and complained that a stranger had turned up among them.

In the end I did not join with any professional group. Instead, I become something like a personal translator to Markus. The most important was to be working in a warm space where there was heating, because the weather outside was getting colder. My new kapo did not allow the others to take away his workers, so I was protected.

---

[82] Józef Putek (Inmate No. 829) b. July 4th 1892 in Wadowice, PhD, attorney, Member of Parliament from the ZPL, Polish People's Union; came to KL Auschwitz on June 20th 1940 in the Krakow–Tarnow transport. More → Biographies

Oświęcim. Inmates employed at tearing down buildings

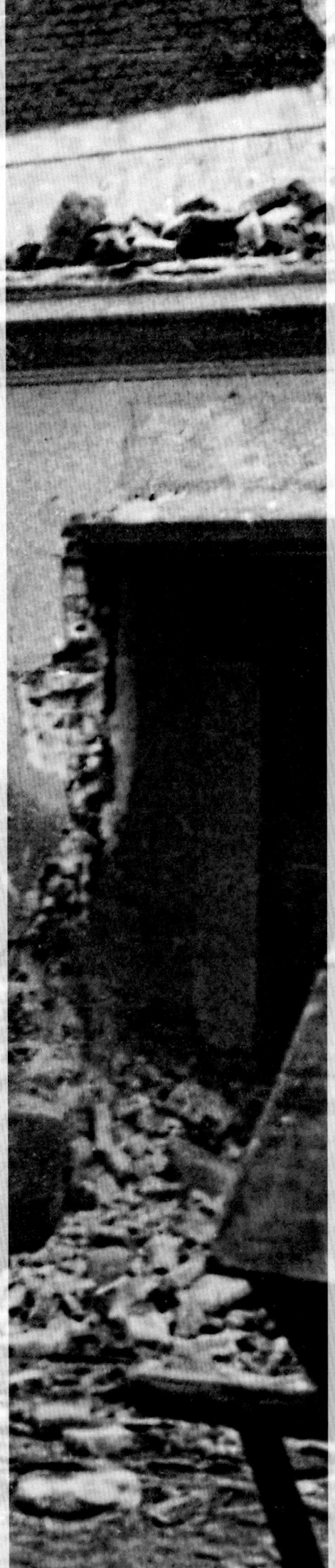

Once, after the roll call, the Lagerführer turned up and accused us of talking politics while working in the potato unit. Indeed; that was true. While peeling the potatoes we would discuss current affairs or even developments on the front. We were also making political plans for after the war. An older friend of mine, editor of pre-war daily Kurier Ilustrowany, was particularly energetic on that subject. His name was Artur Popiel[83]. He would often tell me his political predictions and sure enough, many turned out to be accurate.

"Those working in the potato unit acted as if they were chatting members of a gentlemen's club that just happened to be peeling potatoes. They used the pre-war titles, told stories of various people in the camp, and reminisced about their pre-war positions. They talked Big Politics, even "creating" post-war governments."
SOURCE: Władysław Fejkiel's account[84]

"Supposedly there had been an investigation in the potato unit over a secret organization 'Politische Ecke' – 'political corner'. Indeed, there was a corner where a group of officers, MPs, professors, in the early going also priests, attorneys etc. peeled potatoes and talked on political subjects, but they didn't form any secret organization. [...] Apparently some prisoners interrogated at the 'Politische Ableitung' thoughtlessly claimed, that there had been such an organization, but its members were already dead (Barlicki, Dubois, Czapiński, Rybarski, Jaracz[85], Stawarz, Zajączek) or left in a transport (Putek, Wrona, Rev. Węgrzyn); so the organization had already dissolved."
SOURCE: Józef Putek's account[86]

Although my kapo covered for me,

MY STAY IN THE POTATO UNIT WAS SHORT

and I still twice got pulled out of there to lug bricks. Evidently some informers had told Lagerführer about our discussions. As a penalty the whole potato unit had to go to the building site. The weather was dreadful, and many inmates did not make it back to the camp. I pulled through, somehow. I worked for a few hours and later swung the lead in some barn. I dove under the straw but I was not the only or first one. Other dodgers like me started hissing:
"Why did you come here?"
I said just the same thing to the next guy. There were already quite a few of us there and there was no more room under the straw. Luckily, only that particular day was so hard, and then I went back to the potato unit. I had it good there. I figured out ways to get extra food. I would go to the vegetable unit, so sometimes I would steal something, or sometimes the cook would pour me a bit more soup. Besides, the kitchen unit chief, a low level SS man named Egersdörfer[87] –  a little corporal we nicknamed "Uncle" – was going through regulation channels to get an extra cauldron for the potato unit. With a piece of salt pork inside! He would also give us an extra pot of food if the potatoes were very neatly, cleanly peeled—about twice a week.

---

83 Artur Popiel (Inmate No.951) b. May 24th 1885 in Warsaw, came to KL Auschwits on June 20th 1940 in the Krakow-Tarnów transport. More → BIOGRAPHIES

84 Fejkiel W., Więźniarski szpital w KL Auschwitz, Oświęcim 1994, p. 152

85 Renowned actor Stefan Jaracz was released from the camp on May 15th 1941. He died soon after the war and this is probably why Putek mistakenly listed him among the deceased.

86 Auschwitz Museum [APMA-B, Zespół Wspomnienia, t. 255, k. 37]

87 Karl Egersdörfer (SS-Unterscharführer,), b. June 20th 1920 in Rosenbach, Bavaria. In KL Auschwitz from 1940 to 1944, manager of camp's kitchen. More → BIOGRAPHIES

I worked in the potato unit until November 18th 1940, about 2 months. In spite of Marcus's protection, I could not stick around there because all the young and strong guys were being rounded up to do other work.

And then Markus suddenly disappeared. After Markus was gone we had it hard in the kitchen. The new kapo had a green triangle, which meant that he was a common criminal. He made me and my friend carry a kettle that was much too heavy, weighing at least fifty kilograms. We had to carry it thirty times a day. It was tough.

The thing was, though, that in the kitchen you could always get yourself something to eat. Sometimes I managed to pinch a few potatoes, for my roommates. Later there was a guy who informed the kapo that I was stealing potatoes. The kapo called me, but did not even smack my face, as was the norm. He just asked what I was doing with those potatoes and when I told him I was giving them to my friends he just nodded his head.

Later I was again assigned to much harder labor at the Strassenbau kommando, this time building a road leading from the camp to the train station. That was back-breaking. You had to break up the ground with picks, shovel the dirt into wheelbarrows, wheel it away, dump it and come back with the empty.

"We were unloading the freight trains which were backed onto the sidings. They carried iron, glass, bricks, pipes, drains; all the materials needed for the construction of the camp. The cars needed to be unloaded fast. So under the threat of a stick we would hurry, carrying, stumbling, and falling. Sometimes a two-ton beam or a rail would crush some of us.

[...]

Yes, there even arose a kind of contempt for those who were shown to be human by their bodily weakness. But there was at the same time an increasing appreciation for human nature, whose spirit was so strong that it made you believe in immortality."

Source: Witold Pilecki's report[88]

---
88 Cyra A., *Ochotnik...*, op. cit., p. 285

Later I got into ground leveling and then into the laying of eclectic cables. The conditions were dreadful and

MY COMMANDO WORKED ONLY OUTDOORS.

We were beaten for everything. Either we were pushing the wheelbarrow too slow or too fast. One day there was a visit by a Corporal – the infamous Plagge[89]. My colleagues said he was one of the sportführers, a robber and a sadist. The first blow I had received in the camp came from him. I remember him.

Plagge had the nickname "Fajeczka" (Little Pipe), because he did have a pipe. A strange, short one, and he enjoyed puffing on it. While my kommando was working he would stand there and look on. Apparently, he concluded that they were throwing me too little dirt or that I was not taking enough. So he took up a shovel leaning next to him and whacked the handle of it across my back, or more precisely, across my kidneys. I fell to my knees. When I got to my feet I got another blow. My back got wrenched. When the Kommandoführer left I asked the kapo to let me rest a bit. He said okay. I pretended to be taking back the tools. I threw some of them into the wheelbarrow and took them to the shed. I sat there a couple of hours until I got better.

---

89 Plagge Ludwig (SS-Oberscharführer) b. January 13th 1910 in Landesbergen; farmer. Trained in KL Sachsenhausen to serve in concentration camps. From July 1940 in KL Auschwitz in dept. III: manager of blocks 2, 24 and 111. More → Biographies

Auschwitz II-Birkenau. Building drainage ditches by Crematorium II

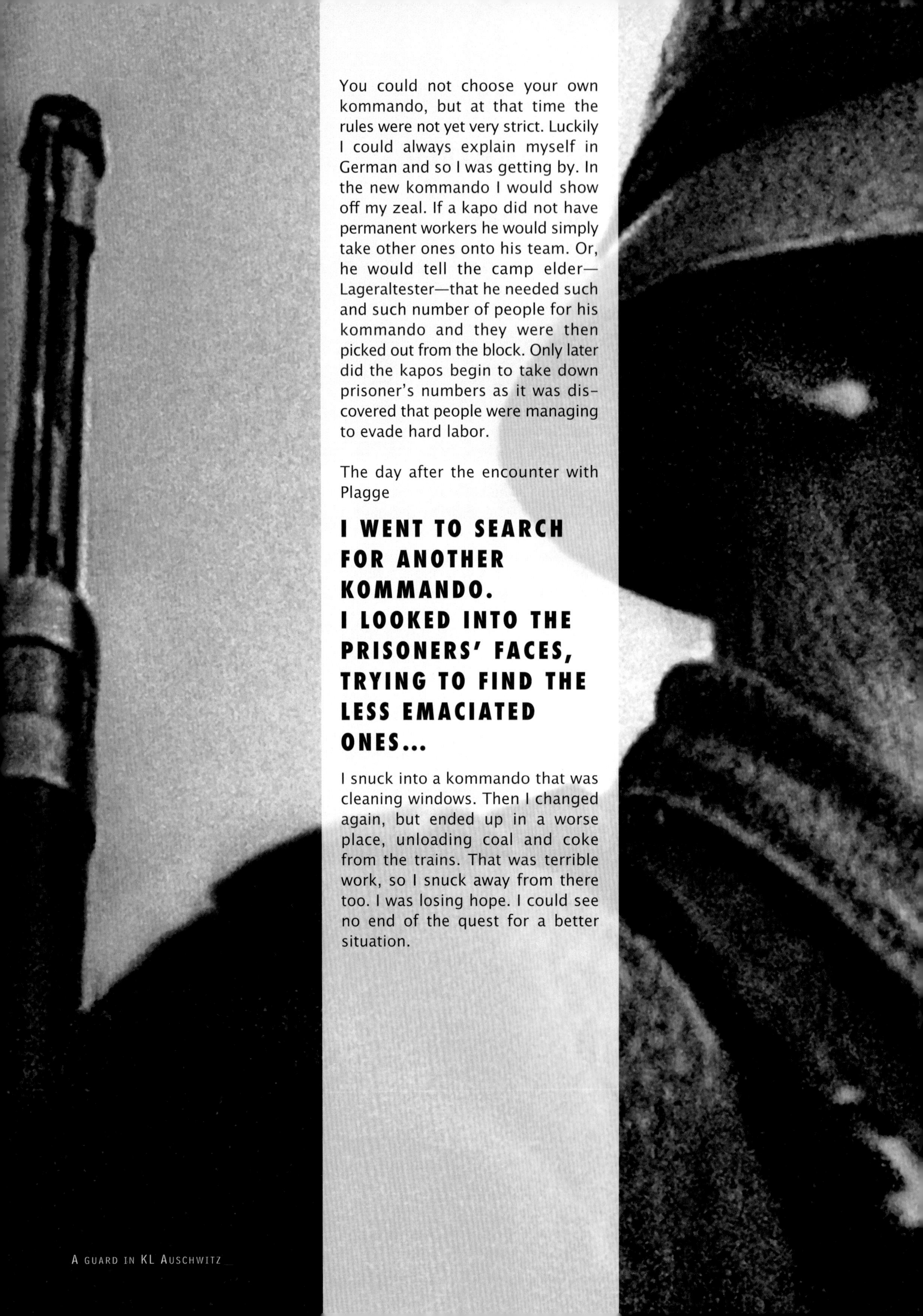

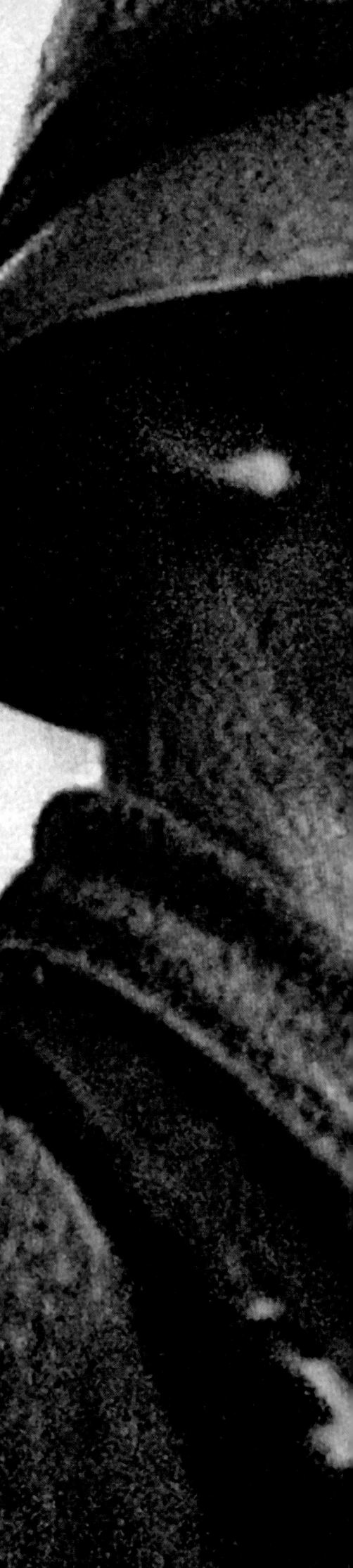

You could not choose your own kommando, but at that time the rules were not yet very strict. Luckily I could always explain myself in German and so I was getting by. In the new kommando I would show off my zeal. If a kapo did not have permanent workers he would simply take other ones onto his team. Or, he would tell the camp elder—Lageraltester—that he needed such and such number of people for his kommando and they were then picked out from the block. Only later did the kapos begin to take down prisoner's numbers as it was discovered that people were managing to evade hard labor.

The day after the encounter with Plagge

I WENT TO SEARCH FOR ANOTHER KOMMANDO. I LOOKED INTO THE PRISONERS' FACES, TRYING TO FIND THE LESS EMACIATED ONES...

I snuck into a kommando that was cleaning windows. Then I changed again, but ended up in a worse place, unloading coal and coke from the trains. That was terrible work, so I snuck away from there too. I was losing hope. I could see no end of the quest for a better situation.

As penalty for leaving work without permission or changing kommando on your own you could be thrashed on the face or ass with a truncheon. After a blow you had better fall down or you'd be whacked again. We learned to collapse immediately. It made the German proud to have dealt such a mighty blow.

If a prisoner-functionary was not authorized to beat you, then he would insult you verbally. There were numerous insults: mostly very short, vulgar names. The whole camp language was saturated with curse words that I'd never even heard of before when I was free.

> "Among the most popular volleys of abuse were the words such as: Arsch (ass), Dreck and Scheiss (shit), Mist (dung), Schweine (swine), Kuh (cow), Hure (whore). [...]
>
> German language lent itself to "impressive" combinations: du Arsschloch! (you asshole!), du Scheissdreck (lit. you shitty dung!), du Drecksack (you bag of shit!), du Scheisswagen! (you cart of shit!), du Misthaufen! (you pile of dung!) ihr verfluchte schweinerei (damn pigs!), du blöder Hund! (you stupid dog!) du Sauhund! (you dirty dog!), du Schweinedreck! (you pig shit!), du Schweinehund (you swine dog!), du alte Hure (you old whore!), du alte blöde Kuh! (you old stupid cow!), du inteligenter Kühtreiber! (you intelligentsia sodomite!), du Hurentreiber (you whore fucker!), du Läusenfresser! (you louse eater!), du Rattenfresser! (you rat eater!) and so on and so forth. The primitive criminals could sometimes become more creative with insults like, for example, du Hosenscheisser! (you shitty pants!), du pariser Puffleiter! (you Parisian whoremaster!)"[90]

Finally, when the SS crew, or even the simple prisoners-functionaries could not get at a guy by beating him or insulting him, they would simply unleash the dogs.

> "They trained dogs, which were part of the camp crew. The Dog kennel and school was located in Brzezinka in the former farmhouse of Jan Krzemień, near Birkenau camp. Training was conducted by SS men who were already established members of the camp's garrison. At one point the school had about 200 dogs of various breeds, mostly German Shepherds. The dogs had their own book of rules and their lives reflected the lives of the SS men. To make the dogs hate prisoners, various kinds of torture were applied. During training the SS men would put on striped uniforms with thick protective padding underneath. The dogs were beaten and tormented in various ways. Although some of them were not aggressive by nature, the beating made them explode with rage. The dog would attack the man in striped clothes. After making sure the dog was well prepared for the guard service it was assigned to a particular kommando."[91]

> "At the order of Oct. 16th 1942[92] from the headquarters in Berlin they built luxury kennels that could house 250 service dogs. It cost 81 thousand Reich Marks. The analysis of the blueprints for this building shows that it was designed in consultation with the camp's veterinary expert and no effort was spared to ensure proper sanitary conditions. The dogs had access to proper green spaces; they built and equipped a dog hospital and a special kitchen."[93]

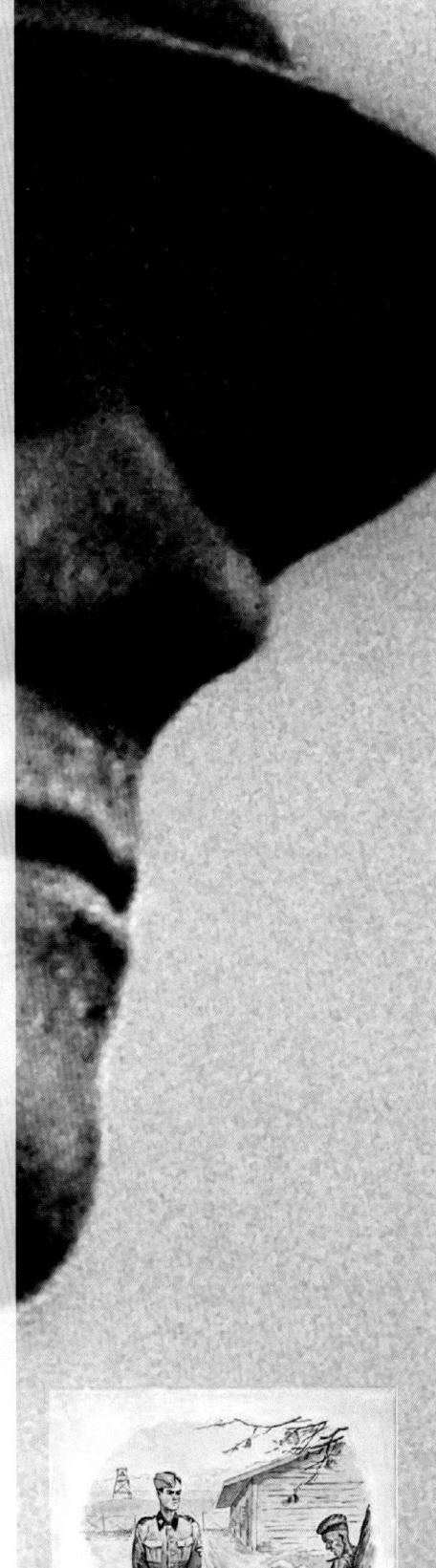

90 Jagoda Z., Kłodziński S., Masłowski J., *Oświęcim...*, op. cit., p. 31-32

91 Jagoda Z., Kłodziński S., Masłowski J., *Więźniowie...*, op. cit., p. 22

92 The dogs were used by Germans from the beginning of the camp. The dog company was created in the summer of 1942.

93 Sehn J., *Obóz koncentracyjny Oświęcim-Brzezinka/Auschwitz-Birkenau*, Warszawa 1964, p. 49-50

ERKENNUNGSDIENST

ON FEBRUARY 5TH 1941 I WAS SUDDENLY CALLED IN BY THE POLITICAL DEPARTMENT.

I got scared; such a summons could not be expected to mean anything good. You could likely end up in Block 11.

There were five other prisoners who turned up besides me, all of us photographers. SS officer Berhard Walter[94] questioned us each in turn about our skills, including our knowledge of lab work and retouching. In fact, he was looking for someone who could do both portrait photography and lab work. He asked what cameras I had used, what equipment was necessary, and if I knew how to make film developer. We spoke in German without a translator. In those days my German was still basic, but it was good enough to satisfy him. Besides, I really knew photography. So I got selected.

From what I know, only one of the other photographers who were there that day survived the camp and after the war had a photographic shop in Krakow. The rest of them perished.

The next day I was called into the office and went from there to the ID Service—*Erkennungsdienst*.
There I reported to my boss, Bernhard Walter, then an Oberscharführer, who in civilian life had been a plasterer from Fürth in Bavaria. Even before the war he joined the SS and had been trained as a projectionist. He arrived in the camp sometime in the first months of 1941. He was transferred from the Sachsenhausen camp in order to organize the Erkennungsdienst in KL Auschwitz.

"The structure of Auschwitz Concentration camp was based on camps established earlier on the territory of the 3rd Reich. There were 6 departments, one of which—Department II—was the Political Department (Politische Ableitung), also known as the camp Gestapo. Within its scope of operation were the keeping of the camp prisoner records; interrogations and investigations of both the prisoners and the SS garrison; fighting corruption and illegal trade; prosecuting criminal cases; and supervision of the mass extermination."[95]

"Erkennungsdienst, the Identification Service, was formally under the Political Department headed by the infamous Grabner. This distinction put the commando, and the prisoners working therein, in a privileged position. The Political Department was a state within a state of the camp's structure and only formally answered to the camp commander. It had its own political goals connected to the interests represented by the Gestapo, independent and regardless of the opinion of the camp's command. That situation made it possible for the department bosses to create privileged positions for the prisoners who worked for them."
Source: Janusz Karwacki's account[96]

"When Adolf Hitler rose to power, Walter was unemployed. He was offered a job in the SS formations. He got trained in photographic technique and in the other aspects of the Ergennungsdienst. Then he got assigned to one of the concentration camps, Dachau or Sachsenhausen[97]. From there he went to Oświęcim to be a kommando chief. His passions were motorbikes and card games. [...]
The work at the Erkennungsdienst was physically one of the lightest in camp. But it involved other dangers: as a division of Politische Ableitung the kommando and its workers were subject to the "*streng geheim*" (top secret) rule. As a result even the smallest

---

94 Bernhard Walter (SS-Hauptscharführer) b. April 27th 1911 in Fürth, Frankonia; plasterer. In KL Auschwitz from Jan. 1941 to Jan. 1945. Member of Dept. II; manager of the photography and Identification Service. More → Biographies

95 Smoleń K., "Erkennungsdienst". In: *Fotografie więźniów z Obozu Auschwitz-Birkenau*, T. 1, J. Parcer (ed.), Oświęcim 1993, p. 14
96 Auschwitz Museum [APMA-B, Zespół Wspomnienia, t. 175, k. 50]
97 to Sachsenhausen

imprudence could result in instant extermination. It was easy to fall under suspicion, since all political prisoners were a priori suspects and also because of B. Walter's frequent drunkenness."

SOURCE: Alfred Woycicicki's account 📷 98

In the beginning, Walter had to establish a proper photo lab. The most important part of Erkennungsdienst equipment came from the Sachsenhausen photo lab including a swivel chair, a 6x12.5 centimeter frame camera with sliding adapter, and a wind-up movie camera, the Agfa Mofik 16mm.

"Offices and labs were situated in Block 26, on the ground floor, to the right of the end entrance (opposite Block 20). However, Erkennungsdienst did not have the full use of the ground floor.
There was some remodeling done in Block 26 to ensure better operation of the unit.
The first room was the office of SS men Walter and Hoffman. Walter had a cabinet where he kept all classified or secret letters, materials and photographs. The second room was the secretariat. There was no direct entry to this room from the hallway. It was staffed by the kapo and the clerk Woycicki. The third room had direct hallway access and this is where the retouchers Dembek and Josefsberg worked and also Myszkowski, who as an artist was in charge of putting together albums (he did not know German, so the captions were provided to him by the SS men.) Myszkowski would often draw portraits, sketches and sculptures. In the photo work he was occasionally used as an assistant.
The fourth room had the copying and enlargement equipment. It had no corridor access. The rest of the spaces were darkrooms."

SOURCE: Bronisław Jureczek's account 📷 99

Next to the atelier where we took pictures were three darkrooms. One was set up for developing negatives, the two others for making copies and enlargements.

Our atelier was a relatively large room, about four by four meters in dimension. It had a platform with a mounted camera and a swivel chair that could be moved by a lever next to an old, wooden camera. The camera was mounted to a strong and stable Zeiss frame, which you could set up vertically or horizontally. The camera had a Zeiss lens with 1.5 speed and focal lengths of 15 and 18 centimeters, set up for mug shots. We had also two large round reflectors. They used two 500W bulbs covered with special matte screens. Two main lights were used for mug shots. It was very harsh light.

For portraits we used an additional smaller light to enhance the face. The background was a curtain stretched on a frame and set up in one spot. The portrait pictures used a gray backdrop, the mug shots a lighter colored one.

"The exact date of the beginning of Erkennungsdienst in KL Auschwitz is not known. Prisoners mention December 1940 or January 1941 but since Hauptscharführer Walter arrived on January 1st 1941 one can assume that it was then that the organization of the department first began. [...] Because various spaces (i.e. the darkrooms) still needed to be built one may estimate that the beginning of the photographing of prisoners falls sometime in the first quarter of 1941."[100]

---

98 Auschwitz Museum [APMA-B, Zespół Oświadczenia, t.9, k. 1313–1314]
99 Auschwitz Museum [APMA-B, Zespół Oświadczenia, t. 19, k. 30]

100 Smoleń K., "Erkennungsdienst". In: *Fotografie...*, op. cit., p. 14

In the beginning Walter filled out my card and sent me to the Badenraum, or baths. Later I was given fresh underwear and a new uniform because all prisoners who were in contact with SS men had to be clean. The rules of hygiene were strictly observed. I was immediately moved from Block 3a to Block 26. My colleagues who lived there worked either in the kitchen or in the kommandos, which worked directly with SS men such as Kommando Effektenkammern, prisoner deposit storage, or Bekledungskammern, the prison uniform warehouse.

"It was populated by prisoners from choice kommandos [...] and was not representative of the rest of the camp. It was the block of the privileged ones, whom I joined while working in Erkennungsdienst."
SOURCE: Janusz Karwacki's account 📷 101

I moved into the new kommando with new comrades. This is where I met Tadek Myszkowski[102], who became my great friend.

"That young Highlander from Zakopane or Zakopane area had various artistic talents. He drew, painted and sculpted. His nickname at the camp was "Nosal" or "Nase" ("Nose"). [...] In his camp art there was a theme of nostalgia for the mountains. The mountains and anything connected to them were his favorite subjects.""
SOURCE: Mieczysław Kościelniak's account[103]

„Myszkowski Tadeusz was considered a Highlander which – as far as I know – he was not. He had only lived for some time near Zakopane. [...] For Lagermuseum he painted a big oil picture of harvesters. He was also a good graphic artist—his caricatures were very popular. He was also an official lettering specialist and made sketches and descriptions for Erkennungsdienst."
SOURCE: Relacja Franciszka Targosza[104]

PHOTOGRAPHIC CAMERA SUCH AS THIS ONE WAS USED BY BRASSE TO TAKE PICTURES AT THE CAMP

From Walter I went to Bródka¹⁰⁵, who was from Poznań and who came to Auschwitz with the first Polish transport. He greeted me warmly. Then he introduced me to the guys who already worked there.

The group was made up of maybe three students and Tadek, who knew a little bit about photography. Before the war he had worked for a big company trading in photographic equipment.

Later the eight of us were joined by Bronisław Jureczek¹⁰⁶, who spoke fluent German, and Józek Pysz¹⁰⁷.

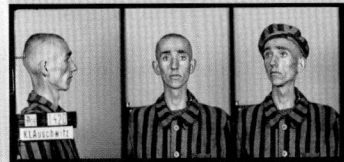

Another colleague from Warsaw named Janusz Karwacki¹⁰⁸ came into the camp at the age of 17. Then there was Josefsberg¹⁰⁹ and a kapo – Frantz Malz¹¹⁰, who passed for a photographer, although he didn't know much. None of my colleagues was a professional.

Neither our boss nor the other kommando prisoners had a high opinion of Malz's professional qualifications. They called him a "village" photographer (Dorfphotograph). He was from Szczecin (Stettin) and was brought to the camp with Walter from Sachsenhausen, in the second transport of German criminals. Maybe he knew how to develop and print a picture but retouching, for instance, he could not do.

SO AT THAT TIME I WAS THE ONLY PROFESSIONAL PHOTOGRAPHER IN ERKENNUNGSDIENST.

Tadek Bródka informed me that I would be taking regular portrait pictures for the Gestapo files. Up until then they had been made by Tadek and kapo Malz.

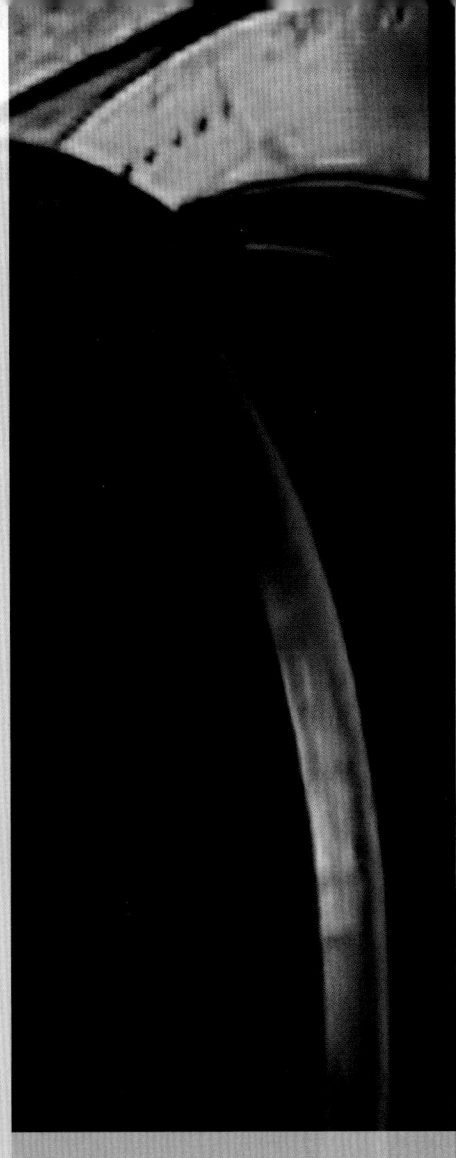

101 Auschwitz Museum [APMA-B, Zespół Wspomnienia, t. 175, k. 60]
102 Franciszek Tadeusz Myszkowski (Inmate No. 593), b. Sept 25ᵗʰ 1912 in Zakopane, graphic artist Graduated from State School of Decorative Arts in Krakow. He was brought to Auschwitz on June 14ᵗʰ 1940. More → BIOGRAPHIES
103 Auschwitz Museum [APMA-B, Zespół Oświadczenia, t. 73, k. 202]
104 Auschwitz Museum [APMA-B, Zespół Oświadczenia, t. 64, k.56]
105 Tadeusz Bródka (Inmate No. 245) b. Jan. 1ˢᵗ 1920, came to KL Auschwitz on June 14ᵗʰ 1940 in the Krakow-Tarnów transport. More → BIOGRAPHIES
106 Bronisław Jureczek (Inmate No. 26672) b. July 7ᵗʰ 1920 in Brzozowice Kamień. Brought to KL Auschwitz on March 3rd 1942 in the Katowice transport. More → BIOGRAPHIES
107 Józef Pysz (Inmate No. 1420), b. March 9ᵗʰ 1915 in Dresseldorf; photographer. Came to KL Auschwitz in the July 29ᵗʰ 1940 Katowice transport. More → BIOGRAPHIES
108 Janusz Mieczysław Karwacki (Inmate No 93186) b. July 22ⁿᵈ 1925 in Ostrowiec. More → BIOGRAPHIES
109 No data
110 Franz Malz (number unknown) b. Sept 25ᵗʰ 1896 in Brandenburg, photographer. More → BIOGRAPHIES
111 Eugeniusz Dembek Inmate No. 63764) b. 1900. Came to Kl Auschwitz on Sept 15ᵗʰ 1942 in the Warsaw transport. More → BIOGRAPHIES
112 Tadeusz Krzysica (Inmate No. 120557) b. Oct. 22ⁿᵈ 1914 in Krakow. Brought to Kl Auschwitz in a combined transport on May 8ᵗʰ 1943. More → BIOGRAPHIES
113 Auschwitz Museum [APMA-B, Zespół Oświadczenia, t. 19, k. 29]
114 Smoleń K., „Erkennungsdienst". In: Fotografie..., op. cit., p. 18

In September 1942 we did get another professional photographer. He was from Ostrów Mazowiecka and his name was Eugeniusz Dembek¹¹¹, camp nickname "Genuś". He was to help me with the retouching. He was an expert.

Later they employed a zinc engraver from Krakow – Tadek Krzysica¹¹². But he had not worked in a photographic shop before, only at IKC – "The Illustreated Daily Courrier" as a photographer dealing with zinc plates. From him I learned some zinc engraving technique.

I knew that my boss wanted me to learn how to do screen printing and Tadek introduced me to the principles of zincography. From him I also found out about the process of etching.

Walter also needed someone to take individual pictures of the SS men.

"The prisoners took pictures of the newcomers /the so-called Zugang/ and often of SS men or even civilians who had clearance to enter the camp or were brought in by an SS man. Those persons had ID photos /Passbilder/ taken for their passes. It was the prisoners who developed and fixed the film, then prepared contact sheets and enlargements."
SOURCE: Bronisław Jureczek's account 📷 ¹¹³

„[...] it cannot be ruled out that those civilian pictures might have been made in connection with some legal disputes (such as a divorce, alimony etc.). An order to take such a picture was given by the Political Department or by the legal division (legal-intervention division), matters which were dealt with by SS-man Uscha Draser. It is also possible that a similar procedure was initiated at the request of the families of prisoners who were citizens of German allies (ex. Italy) or of a neutral country.

It also may be that Erkennungsdienst made ID photos for workers from companies employed at the construction and development of the camp. Civilian workers (Zivilarbeiter) had to use such IDs, although inside the camp they had to be accompanied by SS men."¹¹⁴

I VALUED WHAT I HAD

regardless that had I had a lot of work to do every day. In the morning I worked in the darkroom, mostly copying. I did that till about 10. Later the prisoners would come for their mug shots so I was at the camera for some 5 or 6 hours, with short breaks. When I was done photographing prisoners in the atelier I went back to the darkroom to do copying, printing or enlarging. After a batch of negatives was developed, one of my colleagues made contact sheets. At first it was Tadek Bródka, later Jureczek or Józek Pysz.
The enlargements were done by Pysz, Josefsberg or Jureczek, depending who had time.
I was the main one making copies and when I was swamped another colleague would do it, for instance Edward Josefsberg.

I felt that my kommando was extraordinary and working in the atelier was, given the camp conditions, a dream job. I worked in peace, without anyone lurking behind my back. At the camp it was very important to have a safe haven where no one would beat you. And here, thanks to our skills, we were protected. We could not be mistreated, beaten or killed for no reason.
In the potato unit I had not gone hungry, but it could happen that an SS man or another German who wanted to show off would beat prisoners. And here, firstly, I was working in my profession, and secondly I was in a heated, safe space. Nobody raised their voices. The boss did not interfere and did not yell at us without cause. So there was a big difference, even compared to the potato unit.
Work there was giving us a greater chance of survival. Besides, my comrades and the good companionship that we shared helped me forget what I was seeing each day.

THE EXCHANGE WALDEMAR NOWAKOWSKI

"We here at the studio make something of a small family, although each of us comes from a different part of Poland. We stay here almost the whole day – this is where we work, eat, chat, sometimes secretly playing at cooking, competing with each other in our culinary talents. We only sleep in our own block, where each one has his own bed with a hay mattress and 3 blankets. We still get up at 5 (on Sundays 1.5 hour later), to retire in the evening after all day at work to lie down again and even while asleep to revel in the dream of future freedom and seeing you all soon".
SOURCE: Józef Światłocha's account[115]

We had underwear, clothes, shoes, coats...

We also had much better sanitary conditions. We got to bathe twice a week, not once a month. There was a lavatory with running water whereas in the previous block there was no lavatory and you had to wash outside. There was also a flush toilet. This is where I first saw three tiered bunks, whereas in the previous block we had slept on the floor.

Food rations did not change. In Erkennungsdienst we got regular food, like everybody else. The same soup as other prisoners, normal portions of bread and a chunk of margarine. For breakfast we had coffee or herbal coffee, then ate at 12 or had a combined dinner-supper after the evening roll call. For dinner we had one third of a loaf of bread and 2 dekagrams of margarine. Twice a week, marmalade or a slice of horse sausage.

---
115 Auschwitz Museum. Excerpt from illegal letter smuggled from the camp, dated November 23rd 1942. [APMA-B, t. 60, k. 65]

I will remember that menu till the end of my life. Every week looked the same: on Monday and Thursday the "awo" soup[116]; on Tuesday, water with slices of barreled kohlrabi; Wednesday and Saturday, vegetable soup, or more precisely, water with cabbage; on Fiday "wodzionka" (water and bread soup) on ox tail. And twice a week, jacket potatoes.

We would get a liter of wish-wash – coffee or tea – and after the roll call, generally without breakfast, we went to work. I say generally, since we at the Erkennungsdienst were sometimes able to procure ourselves something resembling breakfast.
Sometimes Walter would send a note to his boss asking for some extra soup for us. Then one of my colleagues would take a bucket and walk to the kitchen. That happened maybe twice a week... Still, I appreciated the fact that I could eat a bit more and be of help to others.

Sometimes on Sunday a noodle or a piece of potato would fall into my bowl, depending on how the server stirred. And you had to eat it immediately because food could be stolen right from under your mouth. Everybody kept saying: "When I get home, my mom will make me such thick soup that a spoon will stand in it."

FOOD WAS GOD,

although I know that it is a blasphemy to say so.

116 Awo soup – a very thin pulp from ground bones

"Near our job, behind the wires at the end of the 'larger chain of watch posts' there were two grazing goats and a cow, all of which were enjoying some cabbage leaves growing on the other side of the wires.
There were no more cabbage leaves on our side—they all had been eaten. Not by the cows, but by human-like creatures—the prisoners—us. We ate raw cabbage and fodder beets, which didn't agree with us. We envied the cows because the beets didn't bother them. A great percentage of us had stomach trouble. [...]"
SOURCE: Witold Pilecki's report[117]

"Food storage rooms and kitchens were supervised by SS personnel. (...) Even at the stage of food preparation the amount distributed was smaller than stipulated by the rules.
Based on the archives of Institute of Hygiene in Rajsk, which after 1943 analyzed samples of food and food products given to prisoners, it was determined that the soup, for example, was lacking 60-90 percent of margarine called for by the official recipe. (...)"[118]

The table below shows differences in the food amounts at the three stages of preparation, always to the prisoners' disadvantage.

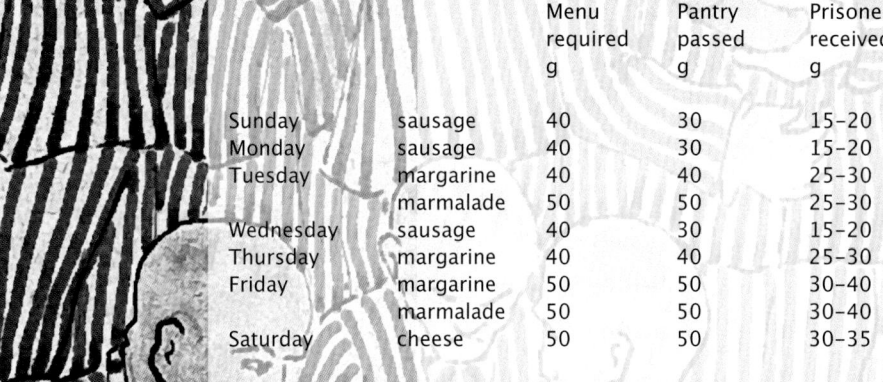

		Menu required g	Pantry passed g	Prisoner received g
Sunday	sausage	40	30	15-20
Monday	sausage	40	30	15-20
Tuesday	margarine	40	40	25-30
	marmalade	50	50	25-30
Wednesday	sausage	40	30	15-20
Thursday	margarine	40	40	25-30
Friday	margarine	50	50	30-40
	marmalade	50	50	30-40
Saturday	cheese	50	50	30-35

SOURCE: tab. in: Biuletyn...[119]

117 Cyra A., Ochotnik..., op. cit., p. 284
118 Iwaszko T., Zakwaterowanie, odzież i wyżywienie więźniów. In: Auschwitz 1940-1950..., op. cit., p. 44
119 Biuletyn... op. cit., Vol. 1, Poznań 1946, p. 103

My sense of smell at the camp was so acute that I could detect a piece of bread that a passer-by had secreted somewhere on his person. He who had bread was a big shot; it meant he hadn't had to finish eating it.

I STILL OFTEN CARRY IN MY POCKET A DRIED PIECE OF BREAD.

As a matter of fact apart from the bread, I do not recall other camp smells. Maybe because of the perfumes that the Jews, especially from France, were bringing. They had also colognes and mouth wash. The colognes were very much in demand by the German kapos. They drank them and then reeked of a characteristic odor.

"A hungry person's smell sharpens. The wind brings to the camp the cooking odors from nearby villages, or maybe we are only imagining it. We talk more and more about food. At night hungry people make up dream menus for when they are free. Sometimes in the coats of the deceased you find those recipes, written down on a piece of cement sack. A dream: a huge pot or pan, and in it, mixed together, anything that is fit for eating."
SOURCE: Roman Trojanowski's account[120]

"Apart from dreams some more imaginative guys would make various notes and memos. They would put together recipes for various extremely greasy and, from the culinary point of view, nonsensical treats."
SOURCE: Władysław Fejkiel's account[121]

"People sick from hunger had dreams of parties at opulent houses or in good restaurants and joints; the "Polonias", the "Bakchuses", the "Pollers" or nice and friendly provincial Jewish inns. Unfortunately, it always so happened that when everything on the table was ready you still had to wait for someone, or at the last moment something was missing and the feast had to be postponed. When everything was ready to go and all you had to do was to grab a fork and knife, you heard the camp's gong calling you to get up and get back to work."
SOURCE: Władysław Fejkiel's account[122]

120 Kołodziejczyk M., " Pierwszy transport do Auschwitz". July 18th 2010 Polityka
121 Fejkiel W.,*Pamiętniki lekarzy*, Warszawa 1964, p. 434
122 Fejkiel W., *Więźniarski szpital ..., op. cit.*, p. 70

MUG SHOTS

78

Mug shots were the bulk of the photos taken at Auschwitz. Those pictures also survived in the greatest numbers.

"Since 1947 the pictures of prisoners of the former concentration camp Auschwitz-Birkenau have been preserved in the archives of the Auschwitz Museum. [...] The collection is made up of 38, 916 photographs; 31, 969 of men and 6947 of women, usually in 3 views."[123]

The prisoners would come into the atelier in large groups, usually 20-25 people at a time. It sometimes happened that we had a hundred or two hundred prisoners at once. I worked then like a robot. There were either the new ones, the Zugang, or those who for some reason did not yet have a picture. One of our duties required that we check whether a prisoner had been photographed. If not, the block writing clerk would send his number to the camp's office and the prisoner would be brought to us under a block supervisor's escort.

"The word "Zugang" is best translated as "newcomer". But this is not exactly the same. In the camp slang it also means that the newcomer is "green", that he is new to the secrets of life in the camp. He is treated like a new recruit in the army. Of course the camp is not the army. It is a particular community with its own ethical norms and customs."
SOURCE: Janusz Karwacki's account 📷 [124]

---

[123] Parcer J., *Zdjęcia więźniów KL Auschwitz ze zbiorów PM w Oświęcimiu*. In: *Fotografie...*, op. cit., p. 3
[124] Auschwitz Museum [APMA-B, Zespół Wspomnienia, t. 175, k. 20]

Prisoners would come in one by one and sit on the chair. Actually, it was not a chair but a special cuboid with a crescent shaped support fixed to the back. The prisoners would lean their heads on that support to remain still. The crescent was mounted at about occiput level. It maintained a fixed distance between the face and the camera and thus made work more efficient. There was a special stand mounted to the chair which displayed information with inmate numbers, nationalities and their categories—for instance, a political prisoner or one under preventive arrest. That information had to have a set format according to the so-called Zugangliste, or the newcomer list.

We filed the pictures by their numbers, in increasing order, separately for men and women. There were three takes: the first one – prisoner wearing a cap and in three quarter view; the second one – with bare head and full face. For the third one the whole setup with the prisoner on the chair was turned ninety degrees and we shot his profile.

THE WORK PROCEEDED EFFICIENTLY,

mainly thanks to the fact that the seat was securely mounted on a round rotating platform about 10 centimeters thick. Inside the platform there was a hole housing a metal bolt which stuck out from the floor. Thus, the whole platform with the seat on top could turn around the vertical axis of this bolt. Inside the seat and the platform there was a transmission mechanism leading to the photographer, who could use a lever to position the prisoner in a precise way.

"The sitter would be automatically photographed "en face" and later, with two moves of a lever, from his left and right profile. It happened so quickly that the line of prisoners moved through smoothly."
SOURCE: Jan Szembek's account[125]

"It all happened quickly and easily, like clockwork. The three pictures did not take longer than a minute including the time to insert the information panel on the side of the chair [...]"
SOURCE: Janusz Karwacki's account [126]

We used factory cut glass plates. We had only to insert them into the frame in the cassette and move it along. The system kept the photographer tied to the camera. At the command "Leave" the prisoner would get down, or jump down, as the Germans insisted that it be done quickly.

"Each day they would shoot forty or fifty negatives. In the early days of the camp the film was easily available and ordered by Walter either from Agfa or Opta in Bromberg (Bydgoszcz). The prints made from those negatives were attached to index cards measuring 8x8 centimeters, with prisoner's name, number, date of birth and the place he was transferred from. The records were divided into 3 categories: the living, the dead, and those moved to another camp."[127]

---

[125] Szembek J., *Obozowe wspomnienia Auschwitz-Birkenau. Zugang – Block*, July 27th 2012
http://www.auschwitz88369.republika.pl/
[126] Auschwitz Museum [APMA-B, Zespół Wspomnienia, t. 175, k. 58]
[127] Struk J., *Holocaust w fotografiach*, Warszawa 2004, p. 145-146

Our kapo Malz was a Communist, so theoretically his treatment of prison mates should have been humane. In reality it was quite different. When a prisoner was descending he could pull the lever and make him stumble. Malz became an expert at this little trick and acted wildly happy when he managed to make someone fall to the ground. There were situations when they would bring us the sick from the hospital. Those were usually very frail people, who could barely stand on their legs, let alone descend from that chair. So when the kapo pulled the lever the miserable person would collapse and get seriously bruised. The kapo was especially fond of doing that to women.

"They sometimes played those pranks on us, where the SS man pressed some button and we got catapulted out of that chair."
SOURCE: Anna Stefańska-Tytnoniak's account[128]

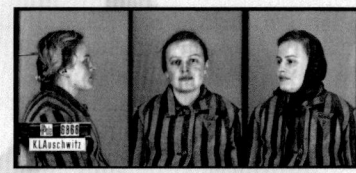

„Under the seat there was a spring which – if you did not get up quick enough – ejected you to the ground. You would clumsily fall, which made the attending SS man burst out with laughter."
SOURCE: Franciszek Hillman's account[129]

Because of Malz we had a bad name among the other inmates. For a long time we could not do anything to stop him. But later on we did find a way: we would give him a mark or two and after that he would no longer interfere with the picture taking. From then on it was quieter and our reputation improved.

---

[128] Auschwitz Museum [APMA-B, Zespół Oświadczenia, t. 137, k. 88]
[129] Auschwitz Museum [APMA-B, Zespół Oświadczenia, t. 95, k.118]

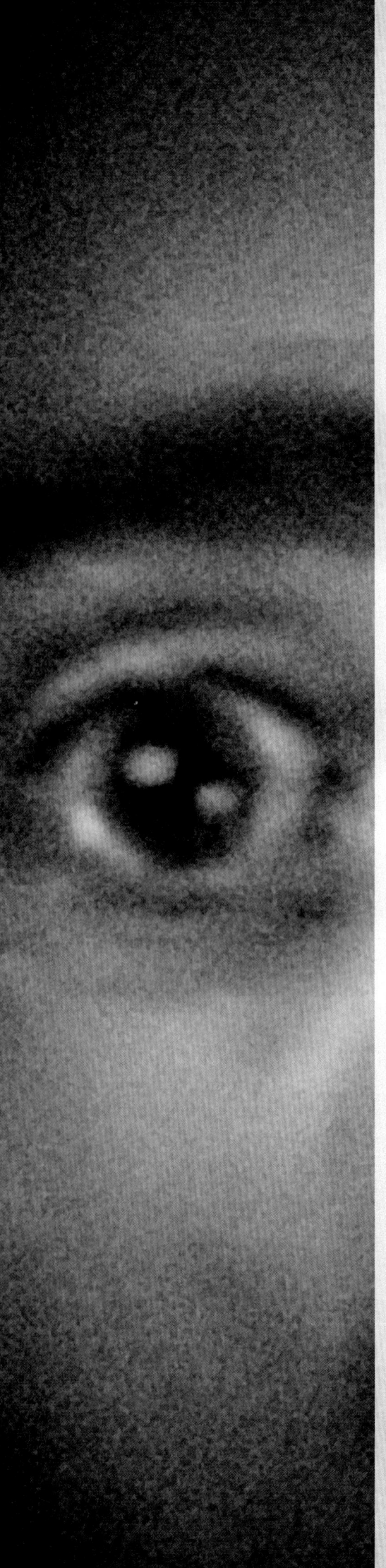
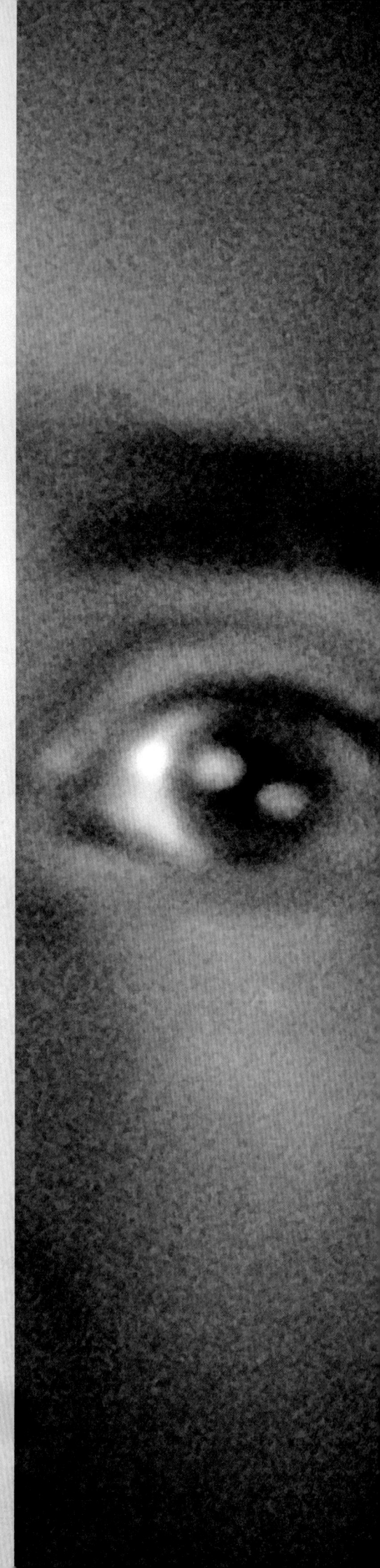

People knew they would have to get their picture taken. Anyway, I did not have time for individual chatting so I could not explain everything to them, unless I was having a break or taking down the prisoner's data. Then I could ask a question or two. Usually I asked where they were from, how long they'd been in the camp, even though this would be obvious. If the prisoners were from Żywiec or nearby areas I asked them what was going on at home. They practically never asked me anything. If at all, my appearance was suspicious. I wore a decent, clean uniform and my number showed I had been in the camp for a long time.

While taking photos I asked the prisoners not to look directly into the lens, but just to the side of the camera.
"No smiling, no crying…" – I said.
And so they went by, one by one… If a prisoner moved during shooting we would retake the picture. The lights were set up, as was the camera, and the distance from the lens was fixed. All you had to do was change the plate case which was handed to me by one of my colleagues, Bródka or anybody else who was available. Those were routine photographs, so I didn't much care about them.

ALL I COULD SEE WERE THE PRISONERS' EYES,

hour by hour, one after the other…

At first the prisoners' eyes were wide with horror, but with time they became indifferent. The look on the face of a starving human, especially a "Muselmann", is hopeless, staring into infinity. Nothing interests him, his whole mind is focused on food. It's his only dream, goal, fantasy…

"The conversations between "Muselmann" prisoners were very typical. They promised themselves that on return home they would live wiser. They would eat several bowls of thick barley with cracklings at a time, a few loaves of bread with butter and bacon at a time…. they would always be at home and always help their wives with the cooking."[130]
Source: Władysław Fejkiel's account

„The prisoners, who as the result of starvation and hopelessness looked like the living dead, are called „Muselmänner". Their organism has used up all the fat reserves and now is making up the calorie deficit by feeding on its own proteins. When a prisoner loses about one third of his body weight he begins to die.
The will to live disappears. "Muselmann" prisoners urinate and defecate lying down or standing, soil the hallways, the pallets, everything. They get beaten up but they no longer care, as if they have separated themselves from the beatings with an invisible wall."[131]

"Their willingness to die did not resemble (…) an act of will; it was more an expression of a complete lack of it. […]. They don't fear death because they are too tired to understand it."[132]

During picture taking I had to make sure the prisoner did not smile or make a pained face. Sometimes the prisoners were so terrified that they were unfit to be photographed. You couldn't do anything. They did not look good in the photos and such photos were not to be made. But since the routine mug shots were not repeated sometimes you can see it – the look on the face is all wrong.

---

[130] Fejkiel W., *Pamiętniki…*, op. cit., p. 434
[131] Klee E., *Auschwitz. Medycyna III Rzeszy i jej ofiary*, Kraków 2001, p. 13
[132] Levi P., *Czy to jest człowiek*, H. Wiśniewska Trans., Warszawa 1996, p. 99–100

Occasionally my boss Walter would send the prisoners to get better shaved, since in the pictures they had to be clean shaven with a clean uniform.
Sometimes I over-exposed the negatives in the x-ray machine because – though rarely – that would buy the victims a little more time, some more life. In that case you called such a prisoner back again. Often he would be completely terrified, as if he did not know what was going on and expected the worst.

We usually communicated with the prisoners in German. I would say, „Cap off and look ahead" (*Mütze ab und gerade schauen*), "Cap on" (*Mütze auf*) and at the end "Go away (*Weg*); those were the set formulas required by the regulations. But the prisoners knew what to do and often I did not need to say a thing. Besides, I mostly photographed Poles. I would tell them: "Hat off. Look here" or "Look straight", at the third picture: "Look ahead", and finally "Hat on" and "Descend". Sometimes one had to add: "Sit still. Look to the right. Behave calm."

If someone did not understand what was going on I tried again in French, because I knew that language well enough to communicate in it. Later, slowly, I learned basic phrases in several languages that I used in my work.

When I had to ask a Serbian woman to take off her scarf I spoke to her in Serbian: "rubetz dolu", to the Czech women I would say: "Chepitzu dolu", which meant "scarf down", and they understood that.

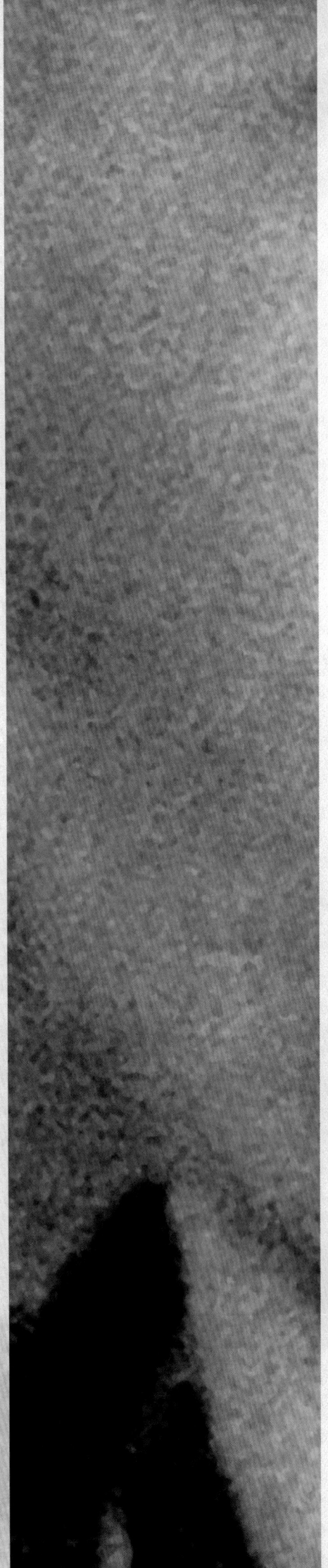

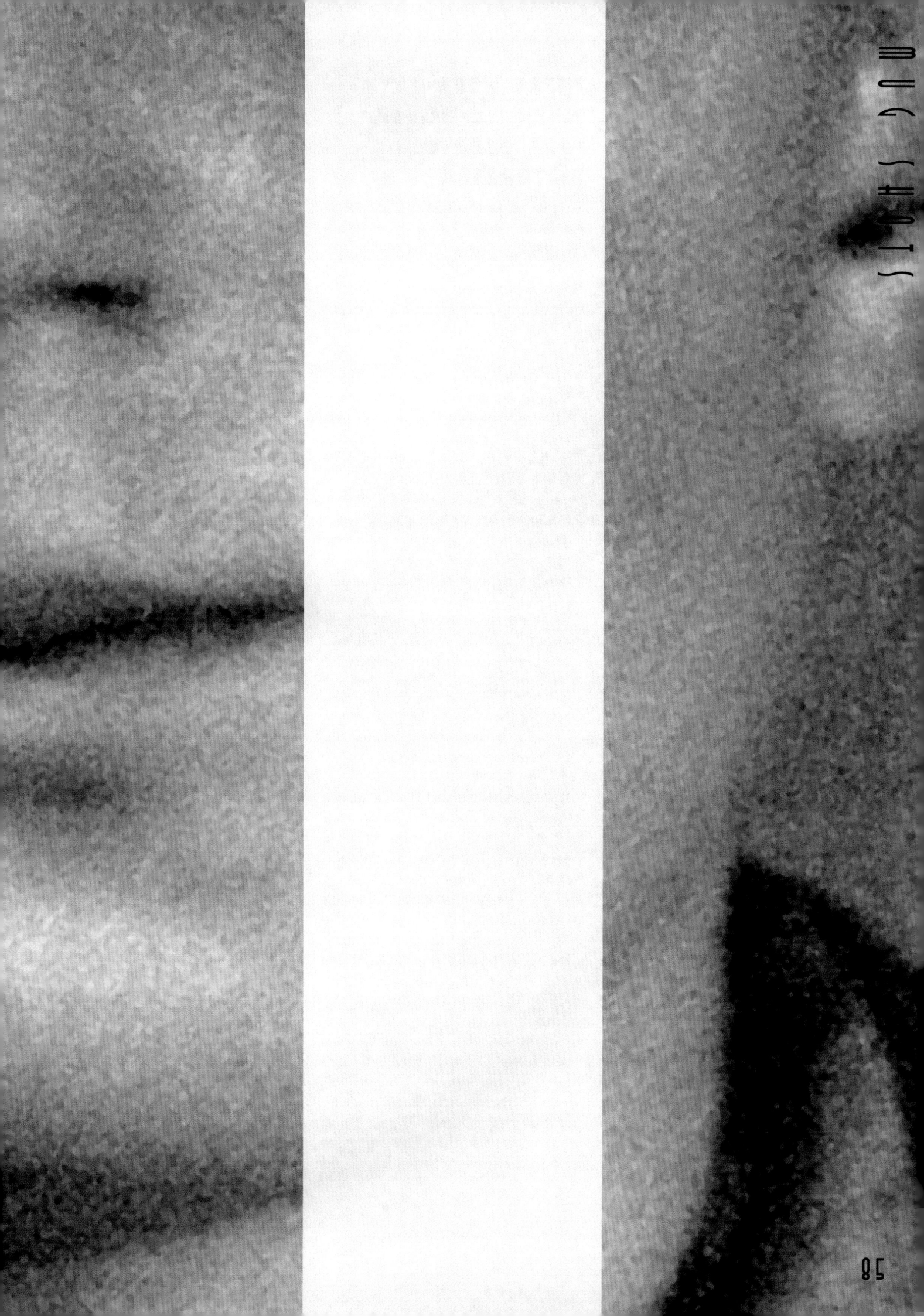

THERE WERE DAYS WHEN WE WOULD TAKE OVER 1000 PICTURES.

Sometime in the summer of 1942 our boss Walter came in and said there was going to be overnight work. There was a transport of prisoners who needed to be photographed by morning, according to his orders. In that transport were a thousand people from Paris.

> "[...] On August 8th 1942 KL Auschwitz received a transport of 1170 prisoners, non-Jews, from Paris. They had numbers from 45,157 to 46,326. [...] Stark ordered to mark their records with words 'Nacht und Nebel' (night and fog).
> In this transport came members of left-wing (Communist) and anti-Nazi organizations, so they were political prisoners. [...] Although their nationality was put down as 'F'(French) there are reasons to believe that there were citizens of many countries (for ex. brothers Hans and Robert Bachmann, nos 45,215 and 45,219 respectively, were Dutch, and their father was a professional Dutch officer)."[133]

> "In the camp they were given green triangles, designated for criminal offenders. It was supposed to hinder their contacts with other political prisoners."[134]

After roll call we went back to the atelier. Just as Walter said, we worked all night. I took seventy percent of all the pictures. When I needed to rest, my colleague Bródka, who was just as good at that job as I, took over. By the morning the whole transport had been photographed. We did it fast, as there were six of us. One would exchange the film case, another the numbers, while an assistant brought on the prisoners. Two others were on standby, as after hours of rushing one got exhausted. I became hoarse from constant talking, but overall everything went very smoothly. Our boss sat in his office. Sometimes he would

---

[133] Smoleń K., "Erkennungsdienst". In: *Fotografie...*, op. cit., p. 19
[134] Czech D., *Kalendarz wydarzeń w KL Auschwitz*, Oświęcim 1992, p. 197

ask something, but generally he did not interfere. Malz didn't interfere either and we did our job.

I suppose that that whole transport was destined for extermination. The French were assigned extreme hard labor carrying bricks and pouring concrete. They dropped like flies. Almost all of them died. Maybe a few survived.

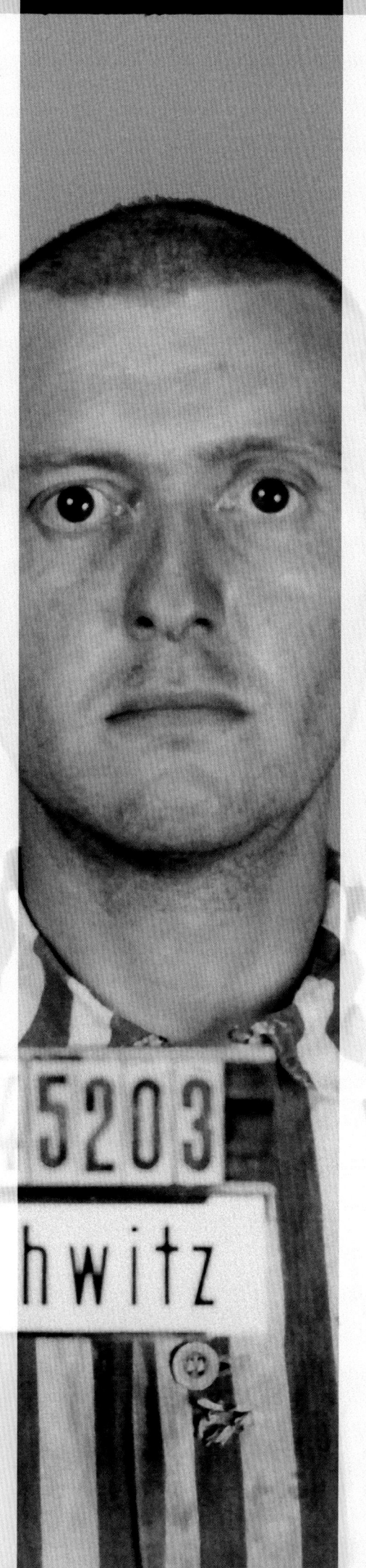

Initially we took mug shots of all nationalities, even the Jews, but that was only until the numbers got up to about 50 thousand, that is until 1942.[135]

Then is when the mass extermination began. The Jews were murdered and cremated two or three weeks after arrival at the camp. Taking pictures of Jews was, according to the Nazis, wasteful. This is how we found out

THE ENDLÖSUNG OPERATION HAD STARTED.

"In the summer of 1941[136] – I cannot provide a specific date-- I was suddenly called to Berlin to see the leader of SS. The call was put through directly from his adjutant office. Unusually for him, Himmler was without his adjutant and declared, 'The Führer has ordered the final solution to the Jewish question. We at the SS have to carry it through. The places of extermination located in the East will not accommodate such a wide scale operation. Therefore I designate Auschwitz to fulfill this purpose, both for its convenient location and because that area can be easily isolated and covered up.

You have to keep this order a top secret even from your superiors. After talking with Eichmann you will immediately send me the design plans for the facility. Jews have forever been the enemies of the German nation and must be exterminated. The Jews that fall into our hands during this war will all be, without exception, eradicated. If we don't manage to destroy the biological forces of Judaism, one day the Jews will destroy the German nation.'"
SOURCE: Rudolf Höss's deposition[137]

„The purpose of it was to coordinate all the operations involved in the implementation of the so-called Final Solution to the Jewish Question (a plan of total extermination of Jews). At the conference plans were made regarding the number of Jews destined for extermination in various countries. After the conference mass deportation of Jews to the extermination centers began."[138]

"The question is often asked whether the Jews sent to Auschwitz in the death transports knew what awaited them there. Jews from Poland and Lithuania, and those, who had spent years in ghettos and knew of the atrocities of extermination, realized what fate was in store for them. There were some who had heard rumors of the death camps and of mass murders. Mostly, though, the scant and incomplete quantity of information failed to give any idea of the scope and progress of the "Endlösung" operation."[139]

„The Jews brought to Auschwitz (except the Polish ones, and those much later) did not have any idea what would happen to them. It was (we found this out from the French and Dutch Jews) because of the information that the Germans had given them. They were told that they had to leave their country and that they were going to Poland, where everybody would work in their profession or would get a business equivalent to the one they were giving up. So they had to take with them all their possessions and provisions for six weeks. As a result, people brought with them to Auschwitz enormous treasures (such as the Dutch bankers or diamond cutters), which later were mostly stolen by SS men and criminal prisoners."
SOURCE: Jerzy Tabeau's account[140]

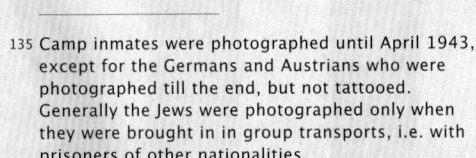

---

135 Camp inmates were photographed until April 1943, except for the Germans and Austrians who were photographed till the end, but not tattooed. Generally the Jews were photographed only when they were brought in in group transports, i.e. with prisoners of other nationalities.

136 Rudolf Höss was mistaken in this doposition. It could be in the summer of 1942.

137 Testimony on the Extermination of Jews at Auschwitz camp, recorded during his investigation at the Krakow prison, 1946. In: *Biuletyn...*, op. cit., vol. VII, 1951, p. 223

138 *Raporty uciekinierów z KL Auschwitz*, H. Świebocki (ed.), Oświęcim 1991, s.95

139 Gutman Y., Krakowski S., *Żydzi w Kl Auschwitz*. In: *Księgi zgonów w Auschwitz. Relacje*, Munich 1995, p. 168

140 *Raporty...*, op. cit., p. 112

"It is communicated to the newcomers (all of them Jews, since during the time of the testifier's work at Sonderkommando only the Jewish transports were going to gas chambers) that the group of able bodied workers would go on foot to a job camp; the rest will be taken by cars to a camp where you don't have to work. So there were cases when the men from the able workers' group asked Kathke if they could join their wives and children in the other group. As a general rule, Kathke would agree, eagerly saying "bitte". The prisoners from the Sonderkommando, on the other hand, ushered into the cars those released from work. Three or four prisoners would get into the back of the car, the cars would take off and on the way the guards would reassure the women (such were their orders) by saying they would be fine at the camp and that upon arrival they would take a bath, get some hot coffee and milk for the kids, etc. The cars took them to the crematorium which on the outside, with its tall rectangular smokestack, resembled a factory. They gently helped them out of the cars and said "Here's the bath house."

SOURCE: Deposition 14. In: *Oświęcim w systemie RSHA*[141]

"One of the mothers, who was despairing while walking with a little girl became hopeful when she saw a car with the Red Cross logo on it. One of the prisoners working on the ramp heard her say: 'Thanks God, we are saved!' The prisoner whispered to her that the Red Cross car was carrying toxic gas for the crematorium and that she would get burned there. The frightened woman saw Broad and asked him if that was true. Broad reportedly said: 'Dear madam, how can you believe a prisoner? They are criminals, just look at their shaven heads.' Then he asked her to point to the prisoner who warned her and wrote a report. The prisoner got 150 blows with a truncheon and the other men from his kommando received 10 each."[142]

SOURCE: Erich Kulka's deposition[143]

---

[141] Rajewski L., *Oświęcim...*, op. cit., p. 120-121

[142] From the later part of the account we learn that the inmate who gave information about the Red Cross car died. As a cover up, Zyclon B was brought into the camp in ambulances marked with the Red Cross symbol.

[143] Langbein H., *Auschwitz przed sądem. Proces we Frankfurcie nad Menem 1963-1965. Dokumentacja*, Wiktor Grotowicz (Trans.) Wrocław-Warszawa, Oświęcim 2011, p. 391

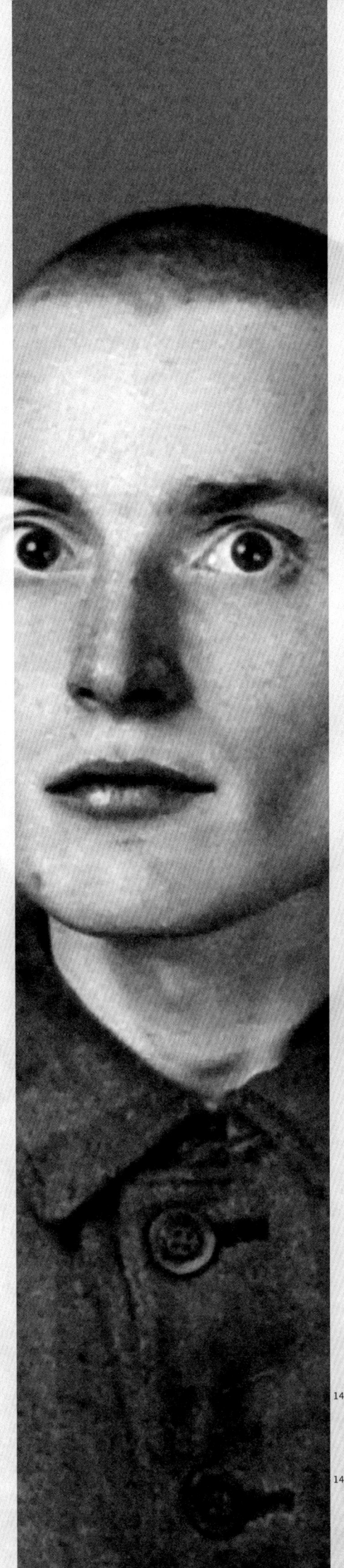

SOME TIME AT THE END OF 1943 OR THE BEGINNING OF 1944 HOFMANN[144] **SAID THAT WE WOULD NO LONGER BE PHOTOGRAPHING THE POLES.**
He said "It's a waste of materials for that shit." (Es ist schade des Materials fur so einem Mist).

Thus, Polish prisoners with numbers higher than 125 thousand were no longer photographed.

"[...] As a general rule you might note that the gaps (omissions) in the pictorial records of prisoners with numbers over about 70,000 are quite frequent, even more so for numbers approoaching 100,000 and ubiquitous (there exist only a few) above 100,000 [...]
Apparently shortages of photographic supplies forced the halt of universal prisoner photo documentation, especially of the Jews, who came to Auschwitz in mass transports and the majority of whom (without camp registration) were killed in the gas chambers."[145]

144 Ernst Hofmann (SS-Unterscharführer) b. Nov. 11th 1901 in Witkendorf. In Auschwitz from May 16th 1941 to Sept. 14th 1944, deputy chief of the Identification Service at the camp's Political Department. More → BIOGRAPHIES

145 Smoleń K., "Erkennungsdienst". In: *Fotografie...*, op. cit., p. 20–21

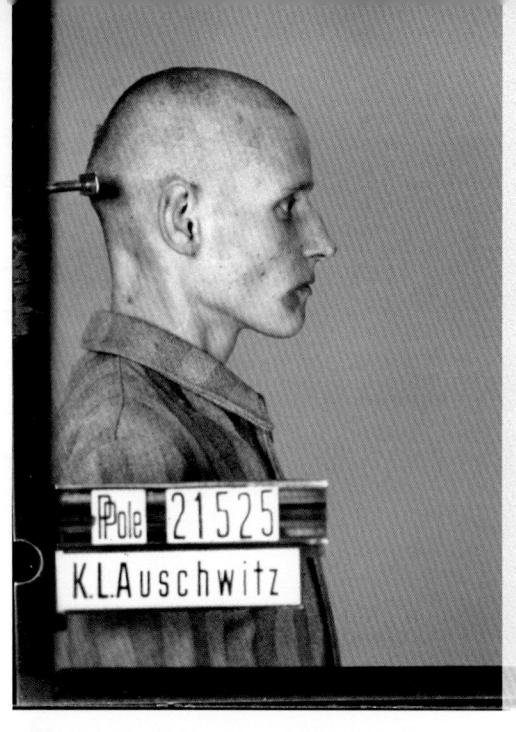
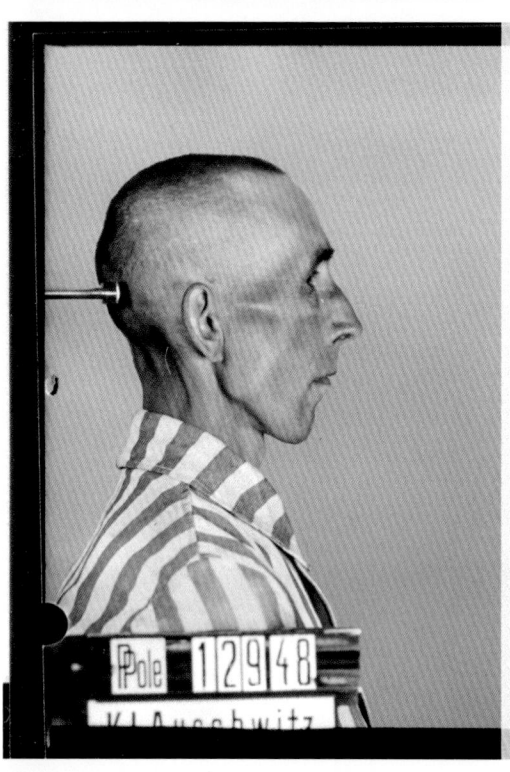
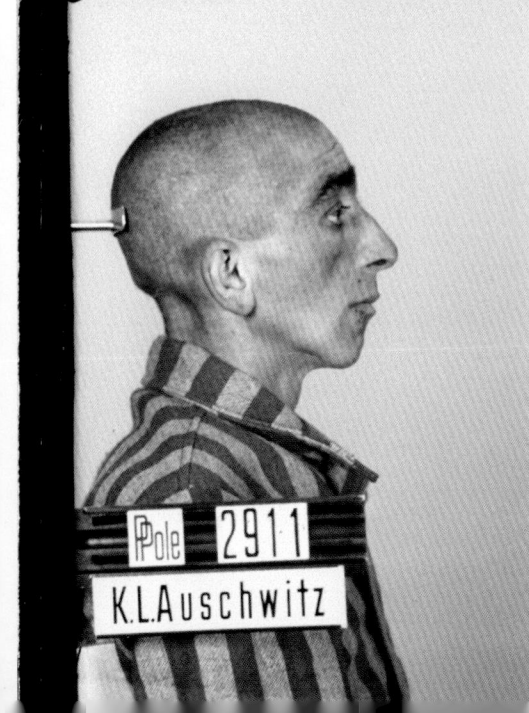

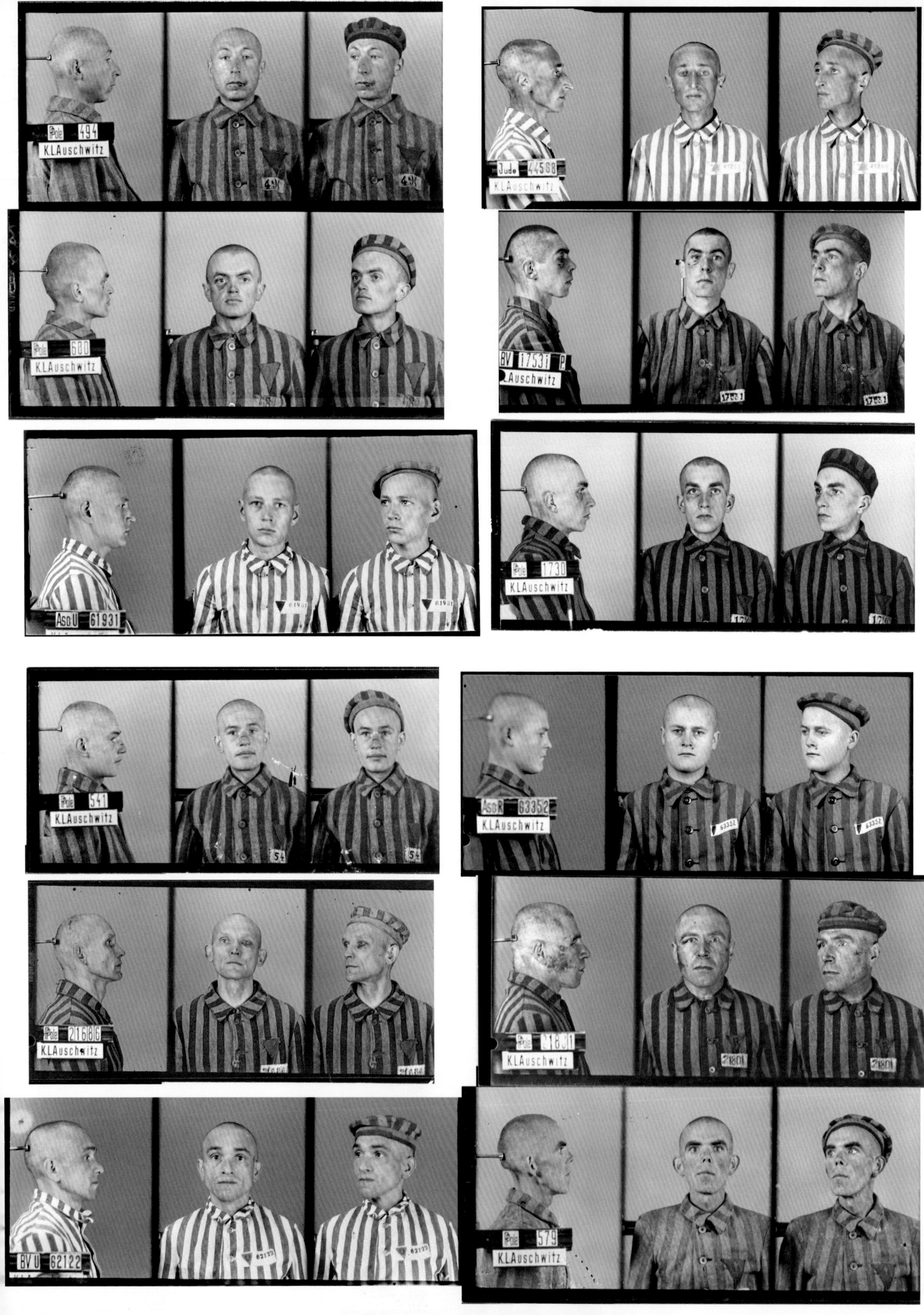

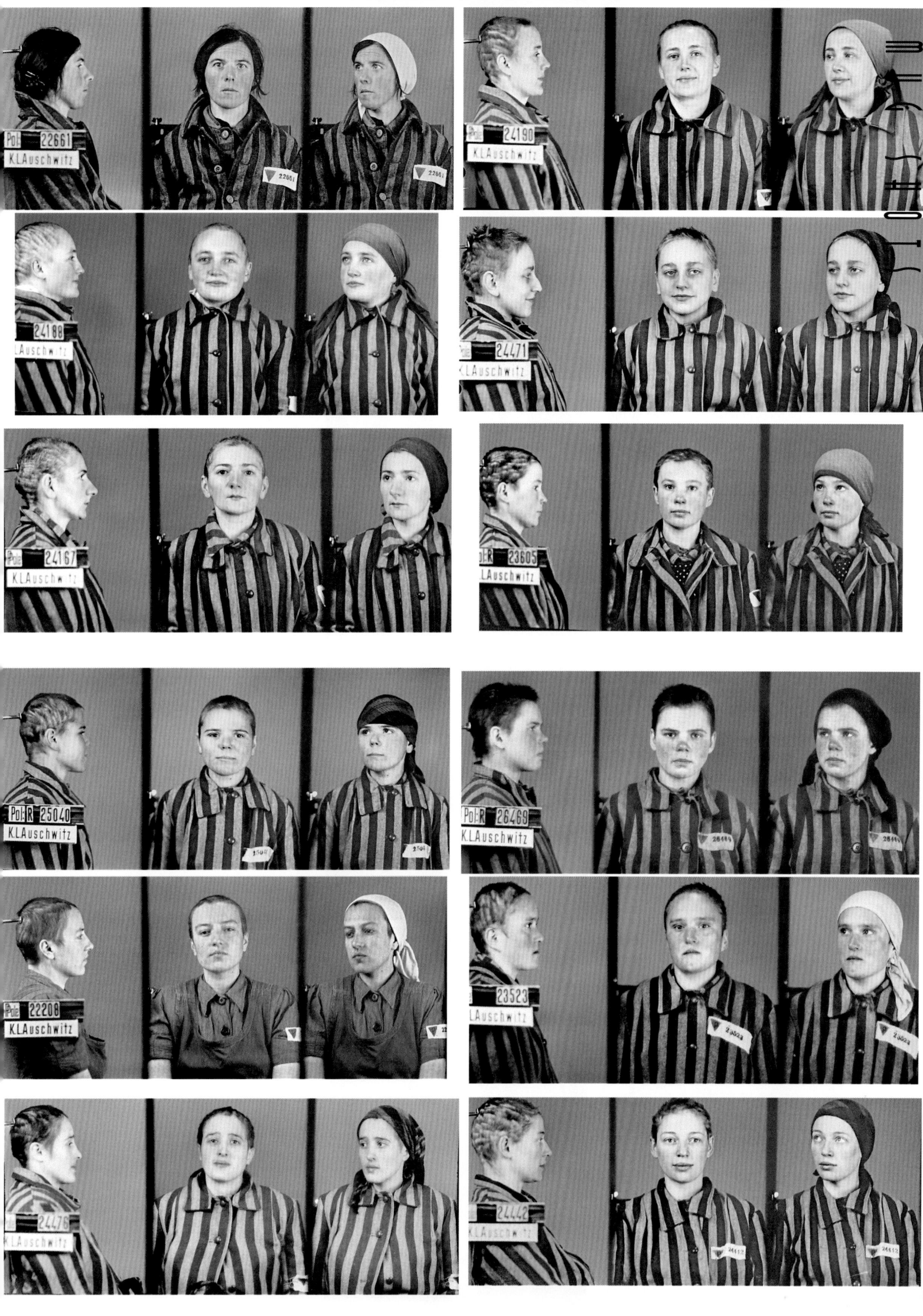

PHOTOGRAPHIC PORTRAITS OF GERMANS

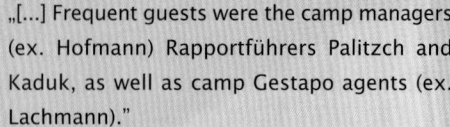

Mug shots did not require much artistry. The lighting setup was always the same and the camera sat in a fixed position. In portraits, however, you had to arrange the lights more carefully and move closer to the subject. At that time and for those pictures we no longer used glass plates but instead various sizes of film. Portrait photography was a completely different kind of work...

> "Pictures for photo IDs were made also for civilian employees of the camp, SS men and high ranking officials. SS men often used the facilities at the Erkennungsdienst to take their own pictures or have them taken by the prisoners."[146]

At the beginning of 1942 Walter called me to his office at the atelier and wanted to know what we needed in order to do portrait photography. I said we mostly needed retouching materials and I named them. My boss then went to Katowice and in a short while I had three retouching boards, 3H and 4H pencils, and delicate spotting brushes and paints.

I took the portraits with a monocle, which is a very primitive lens, just one long focal length – about 25 cm. The monocle that I attached to the camera softened the focus of the lens; that, coupled with some delicate retouching made my photographs a great success with the Germans.

> "The kommando [...] made also portraits of SS men and prints from their small-frame amateur cameras. The best photographer was Willi, and all our clients ordering portraits of themselves or their family members wanted them to be of top quality."
> SOURCE: Janusz Karwacki's account [147]

„[...] Frequent guests were the camp managers (ex. Hofmann) Rapportführers Palitzch and Kaduk, as well as camp Gestapo agents (ex. Lachmann)."
SOURCE: Tadeusz Krzysica's account [148]

I made portraits for the best known and most important figures at the camp.

OUR ATELIER HAD MANY HIGH AND LOW RANK SS VISITORS.

They would come to us and I would take postcard or desktop size shots, slightly larger than the ones for official IDs. Usually you had to photograph them in helmets (worn by regular SS soldiers) or in a hat (worn by officers). Private pictures were taken without hats.

Among others I took a postcard picture for the later lagerführer Schwartz[149]. He was a handsome man. Probably the only person I never photographed was Commandant Rudolf Höss. Höss simply didn't stop by our atelier and I never visited his house. The pictures of him, his wife and children were taken by Walter.

> „I don't remember Commandant Höss ever coming to Erkennugsdienst. At some point his son Klaus came though. He was interested in photographic lab technique.
> He would usually bring his own film and, instructed by the prisoners, develop it, dry it, make contact sheets and enlargements, etc. He was merely learning."
> SOURCE: Bronisław Jureczek' account [150]

---

146 Struk J., *Holocaust...*, op. cit., p. 146
147 Auschwitz Museum [APMA-B, Zespół Wspomnienia, t. 175, k. 63]
148 Auschwitz Museum [APMA-B, Zespół Oświadczenia, t. 67, k. 118-119]
149 Heinrich Schwarz (SS-Hauptsturmführer), b. June 14th 1906 in Munich, chemical engraver. Since end of September 1941 in Kl Auschwitz; member of the IIIrd Department - manager of the Labor Deployment Service. Since April 1942, after the establishment of Dept IIIa, he became its chief. From August till November 1943 chief of the main camp. Later Commandant of Kl Auschwitz III-Monowitz. More → BIOGRAPHIES
150 Auschwitz Museum [APMA-B, Zespół Oświadczenia, t. 19, k. 29]

I heard from my colleagues, especially from Janek Liwacz[151], that Höss was doing very well for himself and that he treated the camp as his own private estate and factory. Stanisław Dubiel[152] – the gardener to the Höss family, confirmed that:

"During the day Höss would often stop at home. He would ride horses or drive various vehicles all around the camp, watching things and taking interest in all camp matters. The least amount of time would be spent in his office. Files requiring his signature were brought to his house and he dealt with them there. At his home he would often receive various SS officials, including two visits by Himmler. During the first stay Himmler had a friendly chat with Höss and his wife. He took Höss's children on his lap, and they called him "Onkel Heini" (…). During those visits the Hösses would throw glamorous parties for his guests. (…). The Hösses accumulated so much stuff which were kept in the co-called Haus Höss, that after his transfer[153] they filled four train carriages."
SOURCE: Stanisław Dubiel's account[154]

„It was true that my family did well in Auschwitz. Every wish of my wife and children was fulfilled. The kids could run wild. My wife had so many of her favorite flowers around that she felt she was in paradise."
SOURCE: Rudolf Höss's memoirs[155]

"Höss's children, except for the eldest, Klaus, did not harm the prisoners who worked there. They would run around the garden and watch the work. One day they came to me asking to sew for them armbands similar to those worn by the prisoners. I did not realize the consequences of doing that. Klaus put on a kapo arm band, and the rest had colored triangles which I had sewn onto their clothes. While the happy kids were running around the garden, they came across their father who tore off those insignias and took them into the house. I was not punished, but was forbidden to do such a thing ever again."
SOURCE: Janina Szczurek's account[156]

"The older boy, 14 or 15, went to school and was very ambitious. He played with a pistol and a rifle, shooting right into the garden. Often it was unsafe for us. The kid would stupidly point at people and boast, 'I will shoot a Polish swine'."
SOURCE: Stanisław Dubiel's deposition[157]

The Commandant's House
The house of the camp commandant, where he lived with his family, was built in the years 1935–1937. It had belonged to Sergeant Józef Soja of the Polish Army, who after the September 1939 campaign escaped to Romania, where he was interned. His family was forced to leave the house on May 8th 1940. The Germans rebuilt the roof of the house in mansard style. After the war the Sojas returned to the house, but after a time they sold it. The windows of the house overlook the buildings of the camp commandant's office at a short distance and on the other side, some 150 meters away, the crematoriums and the gas chambers, in front of which stand the gallows where on April 16th 1947 camp Commandant Rudolf Höss was hanged.

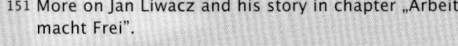

---

151 More on Jan Liwacz and his story in chapter „Arbeit macht Frei".
152 Stanisław Dubiel (Inmate No. 6059) b. Nov. 13th 1910 in Chorzów. Came to KL Auschwitz in the Nov. 6th 1940 transport from Katowice. More → BIOGRAPHIES
153 On Nov. 11th 1943 Höss was transferred to Berlin and became chairman of the Inspectorate of Concentration Camps at the SS-WVHA (SS Main Economic and Administrative Department).
154 Auschwitz Museum [APMA-B, Zespół Oświadczenia, t. 4, k 45-46, 51]
155 Oświęcim w oczach SS. Höss, Broad, Kremer, I. Polska, ed., Katowice 1972, p.101
156 Ibidem, p. 282
157 Auschwitz Museum [APMA-B, Höss's trial, t. 5a, k. 92]

One day I was taking a picture of Walter with his wife and child. Our studio was not set up for group pictures, so the Walter family photograph didn't turn out too well. On one side of the faces the light was too sharp and the other side had too much shade. We did not have the right light to soften that shade. But Walter liked it anyway.

I think he was fond of me since I discussed professional subjects with him in German. He spoke bad German himself, using some kind of dialect, and was unable to put together any sort of official document. Roman Karwat[158], and later another block writing clerk, from Krakow, Alfred Woycicki[159], did it for him. Alfred was an art historian who spoke French, German and Italian. Before he had been the artistic director of one of the Krakow theatres. In the Erkennungsdienst he was in charge of the photographic card index and the archive. I often consulted with him about my German.

Walter was genuinely interested in photography and sometimes I would mentor him, showing him how to do certain things. He did not understand why I had declined German nationality and kept saying I was a disgrace. He put it even stronger:
"You are our shame." (*Du bist unsere Schande.*)

---

[158] Roman Karwat (Inmate No. 5959), b. Nov. 15th 1904. Brought to Auschwitz in the Oct. 10th 1940 transport from Katowice. More → BIOGRAPHIES

[159] Alfred Woycicki Inmate No. 39247), b. June 21st 1906 in Lwów. Brought to Kl Auschwitz in the June 11th 1942 transport from Krakow. More → BIOGRAPHIES

One day Walter had a visit from his boss, the head of the whole Political Department, Untersturmführer Grabner[160]. He requested a post-card-size portrait. Walter informed me that the picture must be especially good and meticulously done. He invited Grabner into his office and told him in my presence that I was a professional photographer. I was extremely nervous. To take a picture of the top camp Gestapo officer was unheard of. Even Walter himself was terrified of him.

Grabner started a polite conversation with me. He said he would like a nice picture to send home to his family. He even addressed me as "Mr" (*Bitte Sie*). He spoke in Austrian dialect, so he was no intellectual. I heard that before the war he had been a shepherd in the Austrian meadows. Other prisoners told me he was a simpleton.

He led me into the atelier. I asked him to sit on the chair, look ahead and relax. I set up the lights: two regular shadeless reflectors and an additional one for enhancing facial features.

"Please take your seat and don't be tense. (...) Don't think about the camp, think about the Alps."

I also asked Walter to look under the black cape to check how it looked.

Walter approved. After a few minor adjustments and a request for a smile, I shot two takes. Then I did a nice retouching job and my boss took the finished prints to him. He returned and said Grabner was most satisfied. The negative stayed in our files and by some miracle survived.

That picture indeed did turn out well. He had highlighted eyes and a slight smile.

IN THIS PHOTOGRAPH HE LOOKED LIKE A MAN OF GENTLE DISPOSITION,

while in reality he was an embodiment of all the evil and crime in the camp. He was our master of life and death. We feared him like the devil.

The things Grabner did were told to me by my colleague Jan Pilecki[161], who at that time worked as a writing clerk at Block 11.

---

[160] Maximilian Grabner (SS-Untersturmführer), b. Oct. 2nd 1905 in Vienna, criminal police employee. From June 1940 till Dec. 1st 1943 in KL Auschwitz as Chief of the Political Department. More → Biographies

[161] Jan Pilecki (Inmate No. 808) b. April 27th 1913 in Warsaw. Came to KL Auschwitz on June 20th 1940 in the Krakow-Tarnów transport. More → Biographies

Once a week Grabner would enter the bunker in block 11 and start some kind of kangaroo trial. He and Fritzsch called it a purge. It took place in a small room in block 11. The SS men would sit at a table and the inmates serving at the prison cells (kalifaktors) would bring in prisoners, one a time. Grabner and Fritzsch asked a prisoner through an interpreter what his sentence was and decided whether he would be executed or be given 6 months in the Penal Company. Each prisoner would give an account of his transgression; for instance, that he had stolen some bread or margarine, or that they had found on him a bottle of vodka. If someone had been caught sending illegal messages, he was doomed to be put against the wall. Those sentenced to death were immediately taken to the bathroom where they were made to undress and then were shot. More than once I saw Grabner and Fritzsch exit Block 11 happy and smiling.[162]

"The 'trials' usually take place on Saturday mornings. Grabner used to—as he ironically put it—use every weekend to 'dust off the bunker'. After the briefing the whole unit had to go to Block 11. Actually, he only needs three or four clerks but Grabner brings in everybody, as he likes to have his whole staff gathered around. In the staff room of Block 11 they wait for SS-Lagerführer Aumeier. After some delay, which enhances his status, a short Bavarian strides into the room. His high, screechy voice tells us he is drunk. The air of cruelty in his eyes and features shows his true nature. He boasts that he is a personal friend of Himmler's, decorated with a Party's Gold Medal. Later, in comes the SS doctor. The block supervisor and some Blockführers complete the committee which now descends to the basement to start the 'dusting'. [...] A muffled murmur comes from behind the cell doors and bright lights bring out stark contrasts between the black floor, the white walls and the shining skulls on the hats of SS men, creating an eerie atmosphere."
SOURCE: Pery Broad's account[163]

"The Lagerführer, chief of the Political Department, Grabner and his whole entourage would always run into the bunker from some party, almost always drunk, and go from cell to cell. [...] So the prisoner's life depended not on a sentence but on the Commandant's mood and the impression that the prisoner made on the drunken gang. If it was favorable, he lived (sometimes just until the next, mock trial; if unfavorable he went straight to his death. In such cases they never failed to humiliate and torment the convict. Most often, 85%-90% of the bunker went against the wall[164] to make room for new inmates."
SOURCE: Jerzy Tabeau's account[165]

STANDGERICHT IN BLOCK 11/SUMMARY COURT IN BLOCK 11, WŁADYSŁAW SIWEK

---

162 Wilhelm Brassse while not bein an eyewitness to those events, confuses the field sessions of the Katowice Gestapo Summary Court with the „dusting" of the prison bunker, when the selection took place directly in the prison cells located in the basement of Block 11.

RUDOLF HÖSS

They did these things to increase their job approval; indeed, they received bonus pay by taking part in these executions.

"A precondition of job security was an exemplary record of tormenting and wearing down the prisoners, enemies of the 3rd Reich. Unsatisfactory service records exposed them to negative assessment by their superiors; carrying with it the danger of getting transferred from the camp to the front—especially the terrifying Eastern Front."
SOURCE: Arnold Andrunik's account[166]

"Young SS men hungered for promotion. The more positive reports, the faster and bigger the reward. We were not wrong in this observation. We noticed that when an SS man was alone without any witness, he was a quite different person, even a kinder one. But if there was another SS around, they would show off.
[...]
The truly evil and inhumane would act in this manner whenever they could. There are many dormant instincts inside a man."
SOURCE: Professor Mieczysław Brożek's account[167]

Eventually Grabner was arrested by his superiors, ostensibly for unauthorized killing of prisoners, but in truth because information of his criminal activities had been leaked to the BBC. There were also financial irregularities.

163 *Oświęcim w oczach...*, op. cit., p. 138-139
164 It could have happened that such a large percent of inmates was executed, but it was not a rule.
165 *Raporty...*, op. cit., p. 124
166 Jagoda Z., Kłodziński S., Masłowski J., *Więźniowie...*, op. cit., p. 19
167 Brożek was the inmate in Sachsenhausen and Dachau. *Ibidem*, p. 19

After 1943, in spite of the new restrictions, I still photographed the Germans. For instance the last commandant of the camp, Lieutenant Colonel Baer[168], although I did not know at the time that he would be the commandant. I took a postcard and an ID picture of him. I also photographed Commandant Liebehenschel[169], who followed Höss.

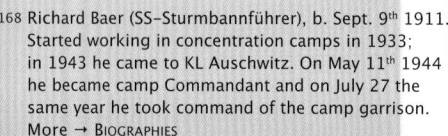

I had visits from: Lieutenant Sell[170] who was the chief of human resources, dr Wirths[171], and various sub-officers including the infamous Palitzsch[172], Plagge, and Stiewitz[173].

"Rapportführer Palitzsch called on us many times. He would come sometimes directly from the executions at Block 11. He would inevitably sit at the corner of the table, quietly pull out a cigarette, light it without speaking a word and then, after a bit, he would leave."

SOURCE: Bronisław Jureczek's account 📷[174]

---

168 Richard Baer (SS-Sturmbannführer), b. Sept. 9th 1911. Started working in concentration camps in 1933; in 1943 he came to KL Auschwitz. On May 11th 1944 he became camp Commandant and on July 27 the same year he took command of the camp garrison. More → BIOGRAPHIES

169 Arthur Liebehenschel (SS-Obersturmbannführer), b. Nov. 25th 1901 in Poznań, tax authority employee. In November 1943 he became the Commandant of KL Auschwitz. In May 1944 he was named Commandant of KI Lublin. More → BIOGRAPHIES

170 Max Sell (SS-Obersturmführer), b. Jan. 8th 1893 in Kiel, tradesman. In Sept 1939 in FKL Ravensbrück; later in KL Auschwitz as deputy chief and since 1943 chief of Department IIIa. More → BIOGRAPHIES

171 Eduard Wirths (SS-Sturmbannführer), b. Sept. 4th 1909 in Würzburg, MD. Since Sept.1942 till Jan. 1945 chief physician of the SS garrison in Auschwitz; he carried out medial experiments on prisoners. More → BIOGRAPHIES

172 Gerhard Max Arno Palitzsch (SS-Hauptscharführer), b. June 17th 1913 in Grossopitz-Therandt near Dresden; farmer. In KL Auschwitz since May 1940 till November 1943. In Department III initially as a reporting officer in KL Auschwitz I and KL Auschwitz-Birkenau II. More → BIOGRAPHIES

173 Friedrich Stiewitz (SS-Unterscharführer), b. May 15th 1910 in Sobernheim, Pfalz; locksmith and turner. In 1941 in Auschwitz as a sentry and since July as a block chief; later deputy of the KI Auschwitz reporting NCO; later in Department IIIa. More → BIOGRAPHIES

174 Auschwitz Museum [APMA-B, Zespół Oświadczenia, t. 19, k. 29]

THE GERMANS LIKED MY PICTURES.

I don't know what would have happened to me if they hadn't liked them. Maybe I would have been thrown out of the kommando. I don't think I would have been immediately put against the wall; there would definitely have been unpleasant surprises.

However, I was not too worried, since by that time I was a seasoned expert. I could properly position the photographed subject and apply suitable lighting. Later, with some retouching, the photo was bound to turn out well.

For taking those private photographs of the SS men I would occasionally be rewarded with food and cigarettes. Often they would offer them on their own and I would not have to ask. Only after some time did I dare to ask for something outright if they didn't volunteer it. First I tried to get a feel of an SS man when he came to see me. I asked him what kind of picture he would like and how he envisioned it. If I noticed that he was polite towards me, that I could talk to him, I would make him understand that yes, I could do something extra for him, but perhaps it would turn out better for a few cigarettes, some bread or a piece of sausage. It occasionally happened that they had additional requests with which they preferred not to go through my boss. For instance, they might request extra copies of their family photos.

There were other situations too. For instance, there were visits from the so-called Flak[175] artillery soldiers – the antiaircraft artillery unit which was stationed near the camp. I photographed them for cigarettes. Theoretically they were entitled to one picture, but if they talked nicely to me I would make them more. Their platoon leader even brought me some rum a few times.

---

[175] Abbreviation of Flegerabwehrkannonen, German antiaircraft artillery. The Flak batteries were placed around Auschwitz as a protection for the "Buna Werke" synthetic rubber factory constructed by the inmates and for other industrial plants in the area.

PENAL COMPANY

I took pictures of prisoners from the Penal Company.

"Compared to the Penal Colony the rest of the camp was a resort. Any contact with prisoners from outside the Penal Company was out of the question. Under the threat of heavy penalties you were not allowed to even approach Block 11. Everything had to be done running. Krankemann said:
"There is only 'Laufschritt' (running) at the Penal Company, you must stand neither at the block nor at work, whether you are carrying a load or not. [...]"
SOURCE: Paweł Żur's account[176]

Ever since the beginning of my time at the camp I was aware that the Penal Company meant certain death. In December of 1940 the Penal Company was lined up behind the kitchen. They stood out there completely naked, in heavy frost. Every now and then one of them would collapse to the ground. I walked past the undressed prisoners but of course I dared not stop. I was not even allowed to look in their direction. However, from the corner of my eye I saw a friend of mine from middle school. Naked. Awaiting death. I could not help him.

---
[176] APMA-B, Zespół Oświadczenia, t. 55, k. 168–171

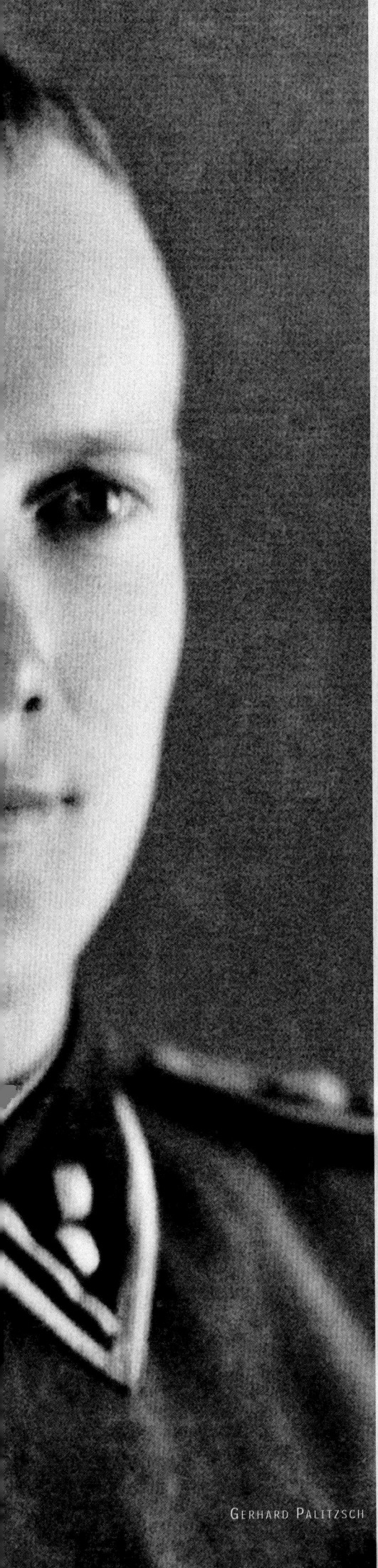

GERHARD PALITZSCH

Since November 1941 very bad news had been coming out of Block 11, where at the Wall of Death there were mass executions of both Poles and others.

"A black wall was erected in front of a stone[177] wall in the yard of Block 11. The Wall, constructed of black insulation sheets, became the final way station in the lives of thousands of innocent people: patriots, who did not want to give up their country in exchange for their lives; prisoners, who had managed to escape the Auschwitz hell, but by a bitter twist of fate had got recaptured; nationalistic folk from all the countries occupied by the Nazis."
SOURCE: Pery Broad's account[178]

"That is where, in that closed courtyard, the butcher Palitzsch –

A HANDSOME GUY, WHO NEVER LAID A HAND ON ANYBODY AT THE CAMP, BECAUSE THAT WAS NOT HIS STYLE

– staged his macabre scenes. The convicted stood in a row, naked by the "wall of tears," and he would approach them one by one, put a small caliber rifle at the base of their skulls, and terminate their lives. Sometimes he would use a plain bolt of the kind used for slaughtering cattle. This automated bolt pierced the brain under the skull and erased life. [...] Palitzsch liked to order the girls to undress and run around the yard. Standing in the middle he would take his time to pick a target then aim, shoot, and kill – one by one, all of them. None of them knew if she would be next or live another few moments, or whether they would take her back for "examination"... He was using them for target practice.
SOURCE: Witold Pilecki's report[179]

"I would often watch him, but I could never see any trace of emotion. Always indifferent and calm, in no hurry and with a stone face, he carried out his gruesome deed. During my service at the gas chambers I did not detect in him any trace of sadism. His demeanor was always still and expressionless. He was so hardened psychologically that he could kill non-stop without a thought."
SOURCE: Rudolf Höss's memoirs[180]

---

[177] It was a brick wall.
[178] *Oświęcim w oczach...*, op. cit., p. 140
[179] Cyra A., *Ochotnik...*, op. cit., p. 295
[180] *Biuletyn...*, op. cit., Vol..7, Poznań 1951, p. 257

Prisoners from the Penal Company were usually brought in to the atelier by Wacek Ruski – one of the butchers of the camp, renowned for his brutality. He was a kalifaktor from Block 11. His actual name was Wacław Szymborski (Szemborski)[181], but we called him "Wacek Ruski" because before the war he had served in the Eastern Borderlands of Poland as part of the Border Protection Corps. He was strongly built, short, and well fed, a working class Pole who spoke in dialect. Szymborski felt a particular hatred for the Russian POWs, who since the inception of the camp had been treated with particularly extreme cruelty. Skinny, tattered, haggard...

"Another contingent was made up of the Soviet prisoners-of-war, who were supposed to build a POW camp at Birkenau. They were brought from the Łambinwice camp in Upper Silesia in a state of total exhaustion. They got into Łambinowice after weeks of marching. On the way, they received almost no food. During the short rest stops they were allowed to go out into the neighboring fields and eat whatever they could find. 200,000 Soviet POWs were reported to be kept at Łambinowice. They lived mostly in dugouts, which they made themselves. Their nutrition was completely insufficient and irregular. They cooked for themselves in dirt holes. The majority "devoured" – you could no longer call it eating – their rations raw, on the spot."
SOURCE: Rudolf Höss's memoirs[182]

"In their drenched uniforms they marched back and forth from Birkenau to Auschwitz in the dead of winter, in -15 degrees and less."
SOURCE: Adam Stręk's account[183]

"People went insane with hunger. They would throw themselves wildly at any frog or beet. Each day, cartloads of corpses were carried into the Auschwitz crematorium. Half-dead, unable to take any more of that indescribable torture, the Russians would climb onto the cart by themselves to be slaughtered like cattle."
SOURCE: Pery Broad's account[184]

Wacek Ruski's speciality was murder by strangulation. He pushed a Russian POW into the wall with his hands and strangled him. He would also place a man in front of him at attention and swing at his jaw with his elbow. The poor fellow would fall as if cut down and Szymborski would finish him off with a thick stick or kick him to death.

I can also tell you that Wacek Ruski killed prisoners at his block in order to get at their food rations. A certain number of prisoners meant a certain quota of bread.

"[...] Those block leaders murdered the prisoners not merely out of joy for killing, sadism or (moral) degeneracy, but for profit."
SOURCE: Wiesław Kielar's memoirs[185]

"[...] The block chief at the time was the madman Wacek Ruski, a common sadist and criminal, who would boast that to get a portion of bread he killed two Jews a day. He said and did those things consistently and with impunity."
SOURCE: Stanisław Głowa's memoirs[186]

---

[181] Wacław Szymborski (Szemborski) (Inmate No. 1976), b. 1913. Arrived in Auschwitz on August 15th 1940 in the Warsaw transport. He was not a "kalifactor" (prison orderly) but a deputy block leader.
More → BIOGRAPHIES
[182] Oświęcim w oczach..., op. cit., p. 56
[183] Stręk A., Bóg ocalił nielicznych. In: artykuł E. Tylus, www.fakty.interia.pl/wiadomosci/podkarpackie/news/bog-ocalil-nielicznych,1251240,3328, 30.01.2009 r [Jan 20th 2013]

[184] Oświęcim w oczach..., op. cit., p. 161
[185] Kielar W., Dzieła zebrane 2. Anus mundi, Wrocław 2004, p. 66
[186] Auschwitz Museum [APMA-B, Zespół Wspomnienia, t. 181, k. 57-58]

WHEN WACEK WAS HUNGRY, HE MURDERED FIVE, EIGHT OR TEN JEWS

and took their bread. He would share it with the block supervisor, the block writer and certain others. They would calculate how many Jews or other weaklings they would need to kill that day and then divide up the food. They killed with a truncheon or they strangled the victim and then dragged the body off to the showers. Then they made up a so-called "death report." The next day they would murder somebody else in the same way. The SS men did not interfere at all. Somebody died, then he died. Nobody cared how.

The leftover food from prisoners who died at night never remained unclaimed.

"The block chiefs were supposed to report to the main Schreibstube the updated number of prisoners in their barracks. The number the supervisor reported determined the quota of food the block would receive during the day. There was not one block where there weren't at least a few overnight deaths. [...] For obvious reasons the supervisors preferred the corpses to be taken away after the roll call so that they could report them as living and appropriate their day's rations."
SOURCE: Wiesław Kielar's memoirs[187]

---

[187] Kielar W., *Dzieła...*, op. cit., p. 66

Before Szymborski brought the prisoners to us he beat them at any opportunity and for any reason: because they did not line up straight, because they moved too much... When the prisoners stood in the hallway waiting in line for their turn they tried to figure out what was going on and became somewhat unruly—perhaps because they wanted cigarettes. That's when their supervisors, especially Szymborski who was infamous for it, brutally established order. Szymborski would find any excuse.

In some instances I told him not to, because the prisoners were not supposed to have bloody or bruised faces. I reminded him that they shouldn't have any signs of hitting, no oozing wounds or bruises. Sometimes that reminder worked.

The SS men also intervened when prisoners were brought in with a black eye or bruises, especially if they were Jews. Under these circumstances the SS man would forbid the picture to be taken. They would order the block supervisor to bring the prisoner back another time, when he appeared unmarked. Ninety percent of prisoners pulled out from the queue that way never came back. They were more likely to be murdered than healed.

Sometime around the beginning of 1942 Szymborski brought in a group of prisoners from the Penal Company and to my horror I found out two of them were the very same Jews from Tarnów, who had given me shelter during my attempted escape to Hungary. One was named Wachsberger[188], who had owned a restaurant opposite the Żywiec train station. The other was Enoch[189] who had been a store owner in Zabłocie, even closer to my home. He was about 35. They recognized me. I gave them some bread and cigarettes. It was all I could do. Wachsberger, already an older man, had part of his ear torn off. I knew they were going to be murdered.

I would take their picture and then they would be taken to Block 11 and in a day or two Wacek or some other butcher would murder them by beating them to death during work.

I asked Szymborski not to take away their food and cigarettes and I did something else, which to this day I find hard to believe. I begged that torturer not to make them suffer. I asked him not to torment them. I pled with him to treat them humanely and not to murder them in some wretched drawn-out manner. If he must kill them, let him not be cruel. A single lethal blow would be a preferable death.

Szymborski answered crisply: "Done". And that was it. Today it still seems unbelievable that

I WAS PLEADING FOR A MERCIFUL DEATH FOR SOMEBODY...

That story has been dragging me down all my life since. It keeps coming back to me. I see that fellow Wachsberg, a decent man, haggard with his torn ear. I keep seeing his battered head. His face wasn't in too bad shape, but his head was horribly bruised. That image keeps haunting me...

Wacek Ruski always called Jewish people "kasztany" (chestnuts). A Jew for him was not a human being, but a being lower than a worm. I saw more than one case of his perverse, murderous cruelty. He would shove the prisoner to the ground face up, jam a shovel handle on his neck, then stand on the handle and, lurching from one side to the other, strangle his victim. This is one thing he did to the Jews.
Finally, Wacek Ruski himself got killed off. By his own people—with God's help, you might say.

"During the raging typhus epidemic, in the spring of 1942, he fell sick and was taken to the isolation hospital at Block 20, where the author of these words was working as a nurse and a block writer. After a few days of intensive treatment Wacuś moved on to the Hereafter through a crematory smokestack. No one shed a tear for him. On the contrary, the prisoners who had any close contact with him regretted that it had taken so long to happen."
SOURCE: Stanisław Głowa's memoirs[190]

---

188 Felix Wachsberger (Inmate No. 31504), b. Sept. 29th 1889 in Tvrdosin. More → BIOGRAPHIES
189 Armin Enoch (Inmate No. 27148) b. April 27th 1900 in Petroutz, Romania, chemist. More → BIOGRAPHIES

190 Auschwitz Museum [APMA-B, Zespół Wspomnienia, t. 181, k. 57-58]

Another sadist similar to Wacek Ruski was a Ukrainian named Bogdan Komarnicki[191], who came to

the camp in the same transport as me. He immediately surrendered and began cooperating with the camp authorities. He beat his fellow prisoners and did everything the kapos or the SS men told him to do. He became a sub-kapo, or an Unterkapo, in the Penal Company. He was strongly built and over six feet tall. He wore a black triangle, which identified him as an "antisocial element." He was famous for his killer instinct and I was relieved that he did not come to our studio. His specialty was breaking the spine of weak and suffering prisoners. He would grab one of them by the collar of his jacket with one hand and with the other seize his pants by the belt. He would then drop them over his knee and break their spine. Such a prisoner died on the spot. One day I saw the Penal Company pass in front of my kommando. The prisoners were returning from work, exhausted, barely able to stand on their feet. One prisoner was so weak that he couldn't keep going and so Bogdan lunged at him, seized him and shouted:
"I will do you in, you son of a bitch!"
I heard the blow of the knee and the crack and watched the limp prisoner fall to the ground. His friends picked up his body and carried it to their block.

"He would take pride in the number of prisoners he murdered. I remember, one time he killed 6 or 7 Jews with his own hands and then reported it to the Blockführer SS man."
SOURCE: Michał Mysiński's account[192]

„The bestiality of the German bandits—criminals, who had been through years of German KLs and now were our overlords in Auschwitz—played perversely on the instincts of the youngsters. The sickness took many forms. At SK[193] the torturers made a game of bludgeoning the testicles—mostly of the Jewish men—with a wooden hammer on a stump handle. At "Industriehof II" an SS man, nicknamed 'Perełka' ("Pearly"), trained his wolf-dog to attack by using it on real people, which bothered no one."
SOURCE: Witold Pilecki's report[194]

"SS men and kapos sometimes employed the so-called 'pilot's death.' This consisted of shoving the selected victim over a steep earthen slope after kicking him unconscious. A kapo or Vararbeiter would be waiting below with a shovel. As soon as the unlucky fellow landed the kapo would bury him alive and after compacting the soil over the body would jam a stick on top to mark where 'the pilot' was buried."
SOURCE: Edward Ciesielski's account[195]

FOR THOSE BUTCHERS KILLING WAS ENTERTAINMENT.

They watched and laughed.

---

191 Bogdan Komarnicki (Inmate No. 3637), b. July 28th 1913 in Synowodzko. More → BIOGRAPHIES
192 Auschwitz Museum [APMA-B, Zespół Oświadczenia, t. 63, k. 109]
193 Strafkompanie - Penal Company
194 Cyra A., Ochotnik..., op. cit., p. 289
195 Auschwitz Museum [APMA-B, Zespół Wspomnienia, t. 55, k. 37]

My worst moments happened when I had to photograph people who had escaped and been recaptured. They had to hold a sign on a stick, which said: "Hurray, I'm back!"[196], sometimes they also had to play a drum. Later they typically were hanged.

"A person caught after an unsuccessful escape attempt had to wear a cap with donkey ears and other odd bits of clothing. He had to wear a sign saying: 'This is an ass... tried to escape...' etc.."
Source: Witold Pilecki's report[197]

The whole camp inside a radius of 2000 meters is surrounded with watch towers standing 150 meters apart[198].
[...]
To escape through that matrix of guards - and there are many such attempts - is nearly impossible."
Source: Alfred Welzler's account[199]

"The first prisoner who fled from Auschwitz through the still single-stranded and not yet electrified fence, was called, as if to mock the camp authorities, Tadeusz Wiejowski[200] (Pol. "someone who flees"). The authorities were infuriated. At the roll call, whenever they discovered a prisoner missing, the whole camp would be ordered to keep standing at attention for as much as 15 hours. Obviously, no one managed to stand that long. By the end of that punishment the state of people who spent all that time without food or opportunity to relieve themselves was deplorable. [...] The fugitive, if caught, invariably paid with his life, executed immediately after capture, either put into the bunker or publicly hanged. [...] The barracks, facing the roll call square, witnessed that macabre comedy in deadly silence."
Source: Witold Pilecki's report[201]

[196] Orig. German: Hurra! Hurra! Ich bin wieder da!
[197] Cyra A., *Ochotnik...*, op. cit., p. 290
[198] They were primitive sentry towers free standing about 200 meters apart.
[199] *Raporty...*, op. cit., p. 136-137
[200] Tadeusz Wiejowski's escape took place on July 6th 1940, 25 days before Wilhelm Brasse's arrival at the camp. The prisoners had to remain standing for 19 hours. Source: D.Czech, *Kalendarz...*, op. cit., p. 19
[201] Cyra A., *Ochotnik...*, op. cit., p. 290

BOGDAN KOMARNICKI

"[...] Made him wear a colored cap and an embroidered robe, gave him a drum with a stick and made him march around very slowly while playing the drum as laud as he could with his depleted strength. He walked, drummed and shouted: 'After escape there is a penance' and 'All the loved ones at home are dead!' "
SOURCE: Józef Jędrych's account[202]

"Later they displayed the bodies of prisoners shot during escape in front of Block 24. Passing inmates were made to turn their heads and look at those corpses."
SOURCE: Jan Dziopek's account[203]

„[...] Lagerführer Fritzsch announced at the camp that prisoners must spy on each other and that anyone who alerted the SS about a planned escape would be released."
SOURCE: Alojzy Drzazga's acoount[204]

From the establishment of KL Auschwitz until its liquidation and evacuation (January 18–19 1945) 757 men and 45 women attempted to escape, or a total of 802. Among those the largest group were:
- Poles – 396 (386 men and 10 women)
Citizens of USSR – 179 (164 men, including 50 POW, and 15 women)
- Jews – 115 (112 men and 3 women
- Gypsies – 38 (36 men and 2 women)
- Germans – (22 men and 9 women)
- Czechs – 23 (19 men and 4 women)
- Austrians – 2 men
- Citizens of Yugoslavia – 2 (1 man and 1 woman)
- and another 16, nationality unknown.

144 ATTEMPTS WERE SUCCESSFUL

and the majority of those people survived the war. 327 were captured during the attempt or sometime afterwards --months, a year, or even a few years later -- and returned to the camp. That number includes those shot down during the manhunts. There are no outcome records of 331 of the escapees, who may or may not have succeeded. It could be that some of them got lucky."[205]

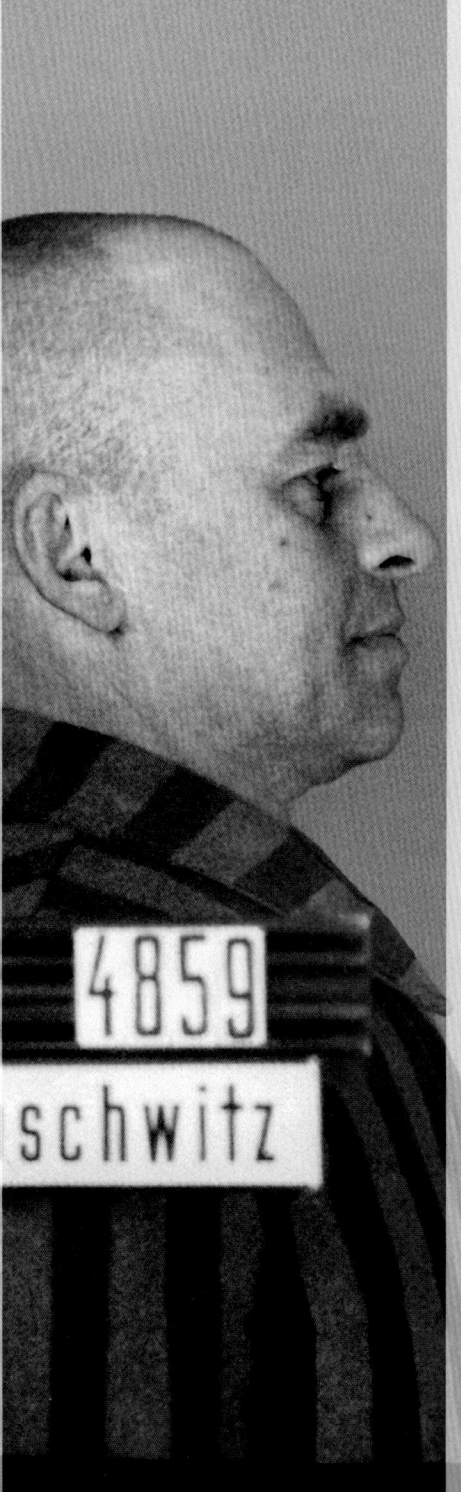

The most famous escapee was Tomasz Serafiński, otherwise known as Witold Pilecki[206], who originally got himself arrested intentionally and was brought to the camp on purpose. Once there, he organized the inside resistance movement, and then somehow escaped.

British historian Michael Foot in called Witold Pilecki one of the six most significant figures of the European resistance during World War II.

He was born on May 13th 1901 in Olonets, Karelia region, Russia, where his father worked as a forester. To strengthen national spirit, his mother decided to educate her children in Wilno (Vilnius).
Young Witold faught to secure the eastern borders of newly resurrected Polish Republic. He was a scout, a soldier in the defense of Wilno and a volunteer in the Polish-Soviet War of 1920.
Between the wars Pilecki settled in his family estate in Sukurcze near Lida.
He was a soldier during the 1939 campaign and soon became an active member of the underground resistance movement.
In the summer of 1940 he volunteered to get into Auschwitz in order to build a resistance network inside the camp, establish communication channels between the Underground and the Polish inmates, gather reliable intelligence about SS war crimes, and make contingency plans for future action.
He got himself arrested during a street roundup and was taken to Auschwitz on 22nd of September 1940.
At the camp he created a secret organization which sent reports to the Home Army headquarters in Warsaw. From there the intelligence passed via London to the Allied Forces, so that the world would know the Nazi crimes against Poles, Jews, Roma and other nationalities.
Pilecki contemplated the possibility of freeing the prisoners and planned to present his proposal to the Home Army Command.
On the night of April 26 1943, with two other inmates, he escaped. His superiors did not think his plans for liberating the camp were feasible.
He faught in the Warsaw Uprising of 1944, was captured at Lamsdorf (Łambinowice) and sent to Murnau, where he was liberated by American troops on April 29th 1945.

For a time he became an officer of the 2nd Polish Corps stationed in Italy. Then, in the last months of 1945 he undertook one more mission: he returned to Communist-ruled Poland to set up an intelligence network reporting to the Polish Government in Exile. In the spring of 1947 he was arrested in Warsaw and a year later, after a long investigation and trial, was sentenced to death.[207], The sentence was carried out on May 25th 1948 in the Mokotow Prison in Warsaw."[208]

One of the most spectacular escapes from KL Auschwitz was the one of Kazimierz Piechowski.

Piechowski came in the second transport and was registered as Inmate No. 918. His companions in the escape were Józef Lempat (No. 3419), Stanisław Jaster (No. 6438) and Eugeniusz Bender (No. 6805). Taking advantage of teir employment at the workshops and storage depots of the camp they stole SS uniforms and weapons and on June 20th 1942 left the camp perimeter in the commandant's office car. Although they lacked the exit pass they were not stopped at the checkpoints thanks to the assertive behavior of Piechowski who spoke fluent German. While in the vicinity of Żywiec they destroyed the car and sent an ironic thank you note to the Commandant for facilitating their escape. Of the four escapees only S.Jaster did not survive the war; most probably he was tried in error by the underground Polish court and executed. After his escape Piechowski joined the partisan unit of the AK (Home Army) and actively fought the German invaders. After the war he was arrested by the Polish security police and sentenced to 10 years of prison, of which he served 7.[209]

202 Auschwitz Museum [APMA-B, Zespół Wspomnienia, t. 101, k. 19]

203 Auschwitz Museum [APMA-B, Zespół Oświadczenia, t. 10, k 28]

204 Auschwitz Museum [APMA-B, Zespół Oświadczenia, t. 85, k. 71]

205 Świebocki H., Ucieczki z obozu. In: Auschwitz 1940-1950: węzłowe zagadnienia z dziejów obozu. Ruch oporu. Tom IV. W. Długoborski, F. Piper (edit.), Oświęcim 1995, p. 110-111

206 Witold Pilecki (Inmate No. 4859) b. May 13th 1901 in Ołoniec (Olonetz), officer of the Polish Army. More → Biographies

207 Witold Pilecki was posthumously pardoned in 1990 and the sentence of his Stalinist trial annulled. He is honored as one of the bravest man of WWII .

208 Adam Cyra, PhD

209 Kazimierz Piechowski (Inmate No. 918), b. Oct. 3rd 1919 in Rajkowy, ironworker. More → Biographies

KOMMANDO ZEPPELIN

In the summer of 1942 a group of Russian officers was brought to Auschwitz. They came in a civilian bus and were put into Blocks 3 and 4. Judging from their appearance they were not native Russians but rather people from the Southern Soviet republics such as Uzbeks, Georgians and others.

Suitable candidates could have been selected from among the POW in various stalags and oflags mainly according to nationality:
- People from the Caucasian Republics, especially Osmenians, Azeri, Georigians, Carbadinians, Circassians, Armenians, Iranians, Kurds, Daghestanis and Ossetians
- People from Turkmenistan, especially Kazakhs, Kyrgyz, Uzbeks, Tajiks, Mongolians (Kalmyk and Buryats) and Volga Tatars
- Russians from the not yet invaded Soviet territories

[...] The POWs initially qualified as the Unternehmen Zeppelin candidates had to be sent to three training camps, in the approved locations: Auschwitz n. Katowice–for prisoners of nationalities in the "A" group; Zielonka n. Warsaw for group "B" and Sachsenhausen n. Oranienburg for group "C"."[210]

"Kommando Zeppelin was a company which was stationed in Birkenau wearing Russian uniforms."
Source: Stefan Beretzki's testimony[211]

"The purpose of their training was known. Kommando Zeppelin trained in Auschwitz. I can still see those Russians in their czakos."
Source: Pery Broad's testimony[212]

Those prisoners were completely isolated within the camp. I remember their registration in great detail. One of the inmates in our kommando, Gieniu Dembek, who knew Russian, was assigned to fill out their special, white *Fragebogens* (questionnaires). Later those prisoners had their ID photos taken.

"Once a week, most often on Friday or Saturday, two Gestapo agents would come to Auschwitz accompanying a few Soviet citizens who sometimes wore SS uniforms. After speaking to the SS men at the admissions office the SD agents informed the "Russians" that they were going to the canteen to have their breakfast. When they left the office SS-Unterscharführer Stark or one of his deputies ordered the writing clerks to take down the particulars of the Soviets. Their data were written on special forms; the new arrivals did not receive inmate numbers. As for the institutions assigning them to the camp they put "Staatspolizei Oppeln"[213] with a note: "Sonderkommando Zeppelin"; as for the reason of incarceration they always wrote: "Geheimnistrager" (bearer of secrets)"[214]

Those POW were of particular interest to a group of SS officers who came from Berlin. They received some kind of training. All of it was very mysterious, especially since, when we were handing over those pictures, one of those SS officers took away with him not only all the film and the prints but also anything in the waste baskets in the lab, pulling out some rejected shots. Afterwards, there was literally no trace left of their existence.

The training of these Soviet POWs was assigned to an officer with the high rank of SS-Hauptsturmführer. By a curious coincidence I remember his name. When he came to us in Erkennungsdienst to pick up the pictures and the films I asked him to sign the receipt. That's when that he gave his name: Kudriavtzev.[215]

---

210 Setkiewicz P., *Sonderkommando Zeppelin - Volager Auschwitz*. In: Łambinowicki Rocznik Muzealny, Opole 2006, t. 29, p. 51
211 Langbein H., *Auschwitz przed sądem...*, op. cit., p. 115
212 *Ibidem*, p. 397

213 The Opole Police Headquarters
214 *Death records in Auschwitz... op. cit.*, p. 138
215 Pol. spelling: Kudriawcew, no data

Several months after those events we had an unexpected visit by one of the officers who had trained the mystery inmates. He came to Erkennungsdienst and spoke directly with our boss. From their conversation I inferred that he wanted us to do develop a small frame film that he had brought along. The matter must have been really urgent, for my boss decided to develop the film himself. However, he asked me to assist him in the dark room. The film was processed, and while checking the quality I had the opportuynity to see what was in it. In several frames you could see some white balloons and some human figures. When that SS officer spoke to Walter I overheard geographical names such as Crimea and Kerch (a town.)

I am convinced that these Soviet POWs trained in KL Auschwitz were members of the infamous Zeppelin Kommando, renegades whom the Nazis trained and sent in balloons as saboteurs behind the Soviet front lines.

"It was planned for them to train as paratroopers and be used for sabotage operations and fighting partisans over the vast territories of the Soviet Union. These POWs trained as secret agents were formed into military units divided into particular teams. Those taking part in the "Operation Zeppelin" were known as "the activists". [216]

That group stayed in Auschwitz for two or three months. Later they were transferred to some unknown location.

"As with many facts pertaining to the story of Sonderkommando Zeppelin in Auschwitz the exact date of its disappearance cannot be established. After March 1943, in any case, the name no longer appears in the log of the camp Commandant's orders [...] one may assume that around this time the 'special unit' (Vorlager-Sondereinheit) Auschwitz ceased to exist. [217]

---

216 *Death records in Auschwitz...*, op. cit., p. 137
217 Setkiewicz P., *Sonderkommando...*, op. cit., p. 51

PHOTOGRAPHS OF PRIESTS

I did not make special pictures of priests. Sometimes in the photos of transports you could see priests among the new prisoners. They were treated wretchedly. The same with anybody openly manifesting his religious faith.

Immediately on arrival, the first German guards from Sachsenhausen started singling out religious people for extra beatings-those who wore lockets or scapulars (sewn-in pictures of Virgin Mary) for example. The Germans liked to show off in front of their superiors so they beat the priests without mercy. One, an old man white haired like a dove, got killed on the spot. First one of the kapos struck him on the head and then others joined in. They tortured him to death. He entered the camp in a wheelbarrow, already dead.

"An SS man, a young cub, summoned all the priests over, showed them a picture of the Virgin Mary that he had found and asked if they knew it. [...] Then Father Kolbe, whom we didn't know at the time and who spoke German, said that it was the Mother of Lord Jesus. The SS man hit him on the face saying this was not true, because she was the greatest whore in the world, using other even more vulgar words. The priests crossed themselves. Then kapo Krott and the SS men began to abuse them, beating and kicking them with their military boots. (...) After a while the SS man ordered them to get up and commanded Father Kolbe to spit on that image. [...] He refused to do it. [...] Then the SS man spat on it himself and stomped on it with his boot screaming: 'So then let me be punished by this almighty God of yours!'"
SOURCE: Edward Wieczorek's account[218]

I did not photograph this. But I watched as a group of priests who had come from a prison in Krakow, were forced by a group of rowdy and cackling Germans to "practice sports", or "air their lungs". The priests had to do frog jumps, pushups and roll on the floor while being subjected to verbal abuse. When I first came to the camp, while they read the transport list, a group of priests and rabbis were separated from the rest of us. There were twenty of them altogether, or rather nineteen, since one had already been murdered. They were assembled to the side and formed into two groups, priests and Jews, each of which was commanded to sing religious songs. First the priests had to sing in Latin and then the Jews began their songs in their language. They were bullied into it with screaming and beating. When the Jews sang louder the Germans berated the priests, telling them they were lazy and did not sing loud enough. When the priests got loud enough to drown out the rabbis, the rabbis were beaten. So then they all began just to scream. It made a horrible racket, which the Germans found most amusing. But for us it was a cruel show. It lasted maybe half an hour until both the priests and the rabbis ceased submitting to the evil commands and abuse.

"Particularly humiliating exercises were imposed on priests and rabbis. Most of them were older people, less physically fit. They were ordered to climb a tree; those who refused or could not were beaten and bullied, kicked in the head and stomach with steel toed boots. Once they climbed the tree the SS man commanded them to sing Jerusalem psalms."
SOURCE: Kazimierz Tokarz's account[219]

To me it was like a blow in my solar plexus; I had this terrible awareness of absolute evil. I realized that these were people who would stop at nothing, not even at beating a priest.

---

218 Auschwitz Museum [APMA-B, Zespół Oświadczenia, t. 104 k. 24-25]

219 Ryn Z., Kłodziński S., *Patologia sportu...*, op. cit., p. 102

Plagge, whom I knew well enough since since he was the one who in my early days at the camp had damaged my vertebrae, also abused the priests.

"During one of those exercises the aforementioned SS man Plagge ordered: 'Juden und Pfarrer raus!' (Jews and priests step out!) Several Jews stepped out and one priest, a vicar from Nisko. [...] Plagge took out a piece of paper, gave it to one of the Jews telling him to familiarize himself with the text (the other Jews had to do it too) and he hummed a melody and told them to sing it. [...] So they marched and sang, of course in German. The meaning of the song was a plea to Moses to look on the tormented Jews, to come back to Earth, take them to the Red Sea and make a miracle with his rod: make the waters part and close over the Jewish nation, so that finally there could be peace on Earth."
SOURCE: Adam Jurkiewicz's account[220]

A particular beast with regard to the priests was a certain Krankemann[221].

Once I saw a group of over twenty priests harnessed to a paving roller. It was a very heavy machine that was used before the war for road repair, pulled by four pairs of horses.

AT THE CAMP THEY HARNESSED EIGHT PRIESTS TO IT.

All day long they had to compact one spot, going back and forth over it. During roll call in the yard I saw them at this more than once. If one of them fell from exhaustion, the roller went right over him. Krankemann, who was their work gang boss, stood on top of the roller and drove them with a whip.

"[Krankemann]. Reportedly, he had been a hair dresser. He was a repulsive, horrible toad. A giant chunk of meat and fat, endowed with unusual strength. He was the supervisor of Block 13[222], if I'm not mistaken, and a terror to the people there. He liked to show how he could kill a man with a single blow. He struck the jaw with the edge of his hand, swinging upwards in a slanted motion. It dislocated the atlas, or the topmost vertebra, and thus broke the spinal cord. Death was instantaneous."
SOURCE: Artur Krzetuski's account[223]

"There were two rollers 'working' right next to us, in the square. Supposedly, it was about leveling the terrain. However, their true purpose was to kill off the people who pulled them. Priests and some other Polish prisoners were harnessed to the smaller one, about 20-25 of them. The other, bigger one was pulled by some 50 Jews. Krankenmann and another kapo stood on the towing bars, adding to the load with the weight of their bodies, making the harnesses press deep into the necks and shoulders of the prisoners. From time to time the kapo or block chief Krankenmann would coldly drop a blow of his club onto somebody's head, as if he was beating a draft animal, and he did it with such force that he would sometimes kill the person outright or make him pass out to be crushed under the roller. Krankenmann would keep beating the rest of the prisoners to make them keep going. Daily, there were victims who would get pulled out from that corpse factory by their legs and arranged in a row on the ground, to be counted at roll call.
In the evening Krankenmann, walking around the square with his hands behind his back would look with a satisfied smile at those murdered prisoners, now resting in peace."
SOURCE: Witold Pilecki's report[224]

---

220 Auschwitz Museum [APMA-B, Zespół Oświadczenia, t. 76, k. 45]
221 Ernst Krankemann (Inmate No. 3210), b. Dec. 19th 1895. Brought to KL Auschwitz on August 29th 1940 in the KL Sachsenhausen transport; kapo of the Penal Company. More → BIOGRAPHIES

222 Block 13, later renumbered Block 11.
223 Jagoda Z., Kłodziński S., Masłowski J., *Więźniowie...*, op. cit., p. 34-35
224 Cyra A., *Ochotnik...*, op. cit., p. 278

AT THE ROLLER WŁADYSŁAW SIWEK

"In the room where the Blockführer[225] [Krankemann] later had his office, we had to undress, give away all our things and then be thoroughly searched. [...]
On me the Blockführer discovered a little locket sewn into my prisoner triangle. He said to me:
"This goddamn Black Madonna is not going to help you." He threw it on the ground and stomped it."
SOURCE: Paweł Żur's account[226]

Even to admit that you were religious was dangerous. Once I saw an SS man grab a chain with a cross that one of my comrades was wearing and start to strangle him in front of my eyes, screaming:
"Where is your Jesus?" (*Wo ist dein Jesus?*)
I watched in shock. I had been taught in religion classes that God was omnipotent.
"Where is He now?" I asked myself. Neither a Catholic priest, called "Wujek" (uncle) nor a protestant pastor from Germany—both my brothers in misery—could give me an answer to that question. They too were asking themselves where God was.

The Germans thought that murder might be fun for us, too, and so one day they told us to abuse the priests. They divided us into groups of twenty prisoners and each got a supervisor—a kapo, some German criminal who had come to Auschwitz earlier.
Our kapo had a long stick and he began to beat two priests. He knew they were priests, even though they wore striped uniforms. Then he gave that stick to Count Sobieszczański[227], who was in my group—an unassuming man, nice in conversation—and said:
"Take this stick and beat him. He's a churchman."
And Count Sobieszczański replied, "Nein." (I won't.)
He gave the stick to me and I also refused.

Almost always we would follow orders without hesitation, because we were terrorized. But this time we refused. And nothing bad happened.
In 1942 the situation of priests improved somewhat. In any case, the Germans began sending them to Dachau.

"It was the beginning of 1942. [...] The treatment of priests had improved for some time, but for reasons other than mercy. Based on some agreement between Italy and the 3rd Reich authorities, influenced by the Vatican, the priests were moved to Dachau, first in 1941, and then via a second transport in July 1942. Apparently in comparison to Auschwitz, the priests in Dachau were provided with relatively decent living conditions."[228]
SOURCE: Witold Pilecki's report[229]

---

[225] Mistake in the account. Krankenmann was Blockältester, (block chief, position held by an inmate) not a Blockführer (SS block supervisor)

[226] Auschwitz Museum [APMA-B, Zespół Oświadczenia, t. 55, k. 168-171]

[227] No data

[228] It is hard to speak about a radical change in the priests' situation in Auschwitz. It improved somewhat in the end of 1940, beginning of 1941 as a result of efforts of Nuncio Cesare Orsenigo in Berlin, when most Auschwitz priests got transferred to Dachau, which became a kind of comprehensive camp for the Polish clergy. Thus ended the practice from the first months of the camp existence, which consisted of putting newly arriving Catholic priests as well as the Jews in the Penal Company, where they quickly perished. The first transport of priests left for Dachau in December 1940, the next ones in May and June 1941. The sick and the terminally exhausted were left behind, as well as those who kept their profession secret. There were 1746 Polish Catholic priests imprisoned in Dachau ;799 of them died. SOURCE: Jacewicz W., Woś J., *Martyrologium Polskiego Duchowieństwa Rzymskokatolickiego pod okupacją hitlerowską 1939-1945*. Vol. 1, Warszawa 1977, p. 28-29

[229] Cyra A., *Ochotnik...*, op. cit., p. 329-330

PHOTO SHADES of PRIESTS

THE FIRST TARNÓW TRANSPORT

TYPHUS

In 1942 a typhus epidemic broke out in the camp. Typhus is a disease transmitted by lice.

"The barracks were nests of all kinds of vermin. Dark and damp prison spaces were infested with hordes of fleas, black cockroaches, lice and bedbugs. Of those the lice were the most dangerous because they carried a dangerous disease—typhus—which spread throughout the camp with lightening speed. [...] Lice would crawl into ears, nose, and body crevices. Bitten by the vermin, the inmates scratched themselves until bloody and would sometimes die of infection."
SOURCE: Jan Otrębski's account [230]

Typhus usually lasts thirteen days. Toward the end typically there is a crisis: either you make it or not. It is characterized by very high fever and often on the ninth or tenth day the sick will die of heart failure or from other complications. For seventy percent of the infected, typhus was terminal.

Because our kommando worked with the SS men, we had special protection. We were not allowed to drink well water from taps, only the bottled mineral water— "Mattoni", imported from Czechoslovakia. The Germans brought whole container loads of it, for the water at Auschwitz was tainted.

"On March 26th [1941] Professor Zuncker, the engineer, who on March 7th tested the water at the camp wrote a report in which he said camp water could not be used even as a mouthwash." [231]

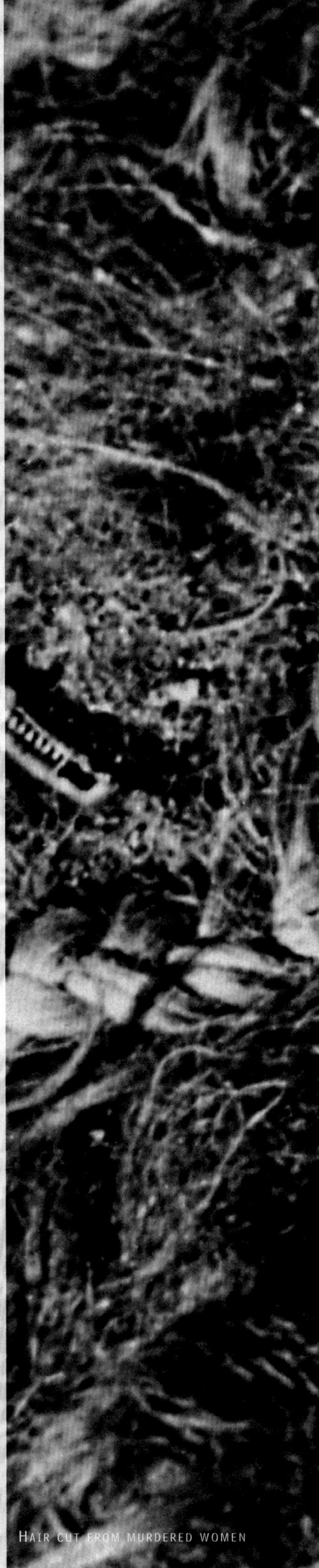

HAIR CUT FROM MURDERED WOMEN

Apart from that, we took a bath almost daily, changed our underwear weekly and for all practical purposes lived in a separate block with similarly privileged kommandos.

I REMEMBER WELL WHEN I GOT MY FIRST LOUSE.

I went to get 5 dekagrams of extra sausage. It had to be picked up behind the kitchen so I went there and stood in line with other prisoners who were getting it for their comrades—it was a bonus given to the privileged kommandos. Unfortunately, that is where I got the louse. And then it started. After a few days I came down with fever. Although I had the first signs of typhus, I still could walk.

My mother's brother, who worked in Birkenau, had already gone through typhus and was in so-called post typhoid quarantine. We started getting disquieting rumors that something was up at the camp. I told my uncle to get himself out of that quarantine. He said, "If something starts to happen, they will release me themselves."

And then I got very sick. I had an extreme fever. I reported it to my boss, who took me to the doctor. I was examined by Doctor Diem[232], a fellow prisoner. He immediately diagnosed it as *typhus—Fleckfieber* (*typhus fever*) in German—since I had all the characteristic symptoms: sudden fever, headache and redshot eyes. I was taken to Block 20, where the ground floor was used for typhus sufferers. I had a very bad case. Apparently my fever went up to 41 degrees Celsius, or so I was told. I was unconscious. I have one vague memory of a nurse putting cold water on me. I thought I was speeding down Grojec Mountain, where I'd skied a few years back, and that it was ice cold. Or I hallu-

---

[230] Auschwitz Museum [APMA-B, Zespół Wspomnienia, t. 236, k. 12]

[231] Czech D., *Kalendarz...*, op. cit., p. 55-56

[232] Rudolf Diem (Inmate No. 10022) b. August 23rd 1896 in Hermanów, physician, major of the Polish Army. Came to Kl Auschwitz in a transport from Warsaw. More → BIOGRAPHIES

cinated that I was somewhere in the tropics where it was terribly hot. I was looked after by Dr Fejkiel[233],

who later became a professor and an infectious diseases specialist at that. He was not always present, but luckily for me he was there on that particular day. My friends told me later that it was already the 8th day of my being unconscious.

Then things got worse. They ordered the transfer of all typhus patients to the gas chambers and crematoriums at Birkenau. We were dragged out of our beds and the unconscious were laid on the ground in the yard. Then they called our numbers, one by one. A truck pulled up and those who could walk were ordered to get inside. Among them was my uncle Staś Kucharski, who at that point was nearly recovered.

It just so happened that my kommando was opposite Block 20 and my comrades there saw me, unconscious, being dragged into the truck. Without thinking Tadek Bródka went running to SS man Walter, who lived in a house near the posts. Bródka asked him to intervene for me. I'm told he immediately jumped on his bike and went to the camp doctor. Since he was of lower rank, he saluted and asked for permission to speak. Dr. Entress[234] reluctantly asked him what he wanted and Walter explained that I was a valuable expert, that I was sorely needed, and to please make them let me stay. He didn't mention anything about me being taken to the gas chamber, he just asked that I be left behind and treated. Entress approved without protest. So I was pulled aside and moved to a temporary barracks. In the meantime the nurses loaded the rest of the unconscious patients onto the trucks and left.

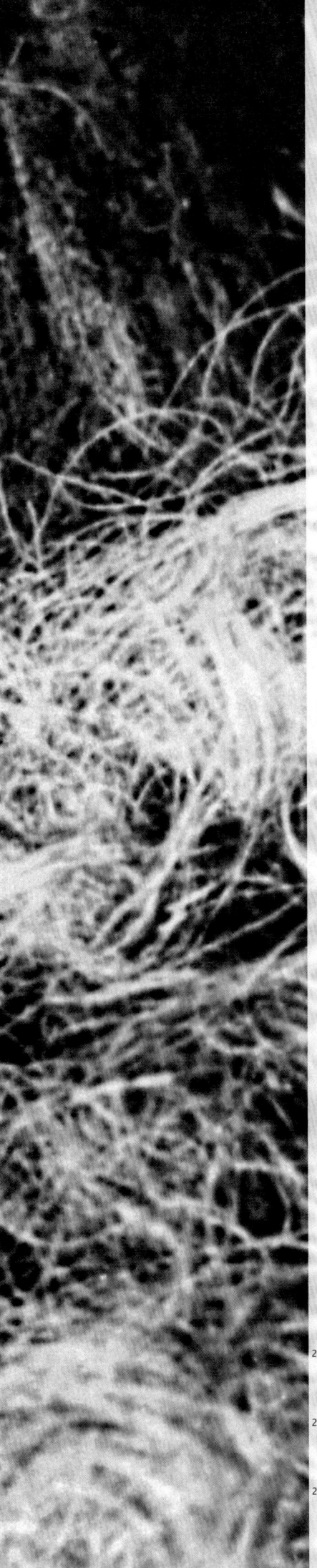

The next day I returned to the typhus block. As we later learned, all who were taken away, supposedly to be treated in Birkenau, were gassed and cremated the very same day— probably six hundred people.[235]

---

[233] Władysław Fejkiel (Inmate No. 5647) b. Jan. 1st 1911 in Krościenko, physician. Came to KL Auschwitz in Oct. 8th 1940 in the Krakow transport.
More → BIOGRAPHIES

[234] Friedrich Karl Hermann Entress (SS-Hauptsturmführer) b. Dec. 8th 1914 in Posen/Poznań, physician. Since Oct. 1943 camp SS doctor.
More → BIOGRAPHIES

[235] This happened possibly in the spring or summer of 1942

There were more of those mass transports of the sick. Apart from my own case I particularly remember the transport to Dresden. At the roll call we were told that all the disabled who limped or had some disability with their hands could leave for an additional treatment and later would be released. Many volunteered for that transport to Sonnenstein near Dresden[236], because they believed what they were told. It did happen that even some seasoned inmates bought into the lie. Such was the case with Maks (Maksymilian) Wylężał[237] whom I remembered from my days in the potato room when he bullied Julian Lachendro[238] in the judges group. He would tuck potato peels into his collar, I recall. Maks arrived at KL Auschwitz in a transport from Silesia. He spoke in Silesin dialect and his number was something between 1100 and 1200. He had a limp and walked with a stick since he had been wounded in the Silesian Uprising.

"The preparations for the Dresden transport of the selected sick were carefully camouflaged and the operation went so peacefully that in spite of our doubts about the purpose of moving the infirm, the old and the crippled we were generally convinced that they would end up in better living conditions. For instance there were cases when the SS doctors noticed some rough handling of the patients by the nurses, and would, in their typical German fashion, create a fuss and threaten consequences for the 'guilty ones', even when the nurses were German. That kind of camouflage reassured the sick that the life they were moving to would be better."
SOURCE: Adam Stapf's account[239]

The inmates were encouraged to go with the promise of release into general labor after their successful treatment. About 500-600 inmates were deported this way. We suspected something was not right and we were all surprised that Maks volunteered, as he was such a "sly fox".

THE SICK GETTING LOADED INTO A CAR
JERZY POTRZEBOWSKI

"The final destination was neither a sanatorium nor Dresden. The train with the KL Auschwitz prisoners went to Pirna, a town 20 kilometers east of the capital of Saxony. After the inmates left the train they were put into the buildings of the psychiatric hospital (closed since the fall of 1939) in Pirna-Sonnenstein. [...]"[240]

"Within the next few days our worst suspicions were confirmed. [...] The fact that the possessions of all of those unfortunates returned to the camp Bekleidungskammer[241] and that the Schreibstube[242] crossed them systematically from the records of the living indicated that they died."
SOURCE: Wiesław Kielar's memoirs[243]

I had a very nasty case of typhus.

I LOST ALMOST ALL MY HEARING AND MY HAIR TURNED GRAY.

After thirteen days I began to recover. I had to learn anew how to walk, as after typhus you walk like a baby. My hearing gradually returned. After three weeks I came back to my kommando. My friends there gave me extra food, because I had an enormous appetite.

I had excellent friends. Thanks to Tadek Bródka I am alive today; oherwise I would have been gassed like my uncle. They notified my family that he died of pneumonia. This is what the Germans would write: pneumonia, kidney disease, heart complications…

236 July 28th 1941
237 No data
238 Julian Lachendro (Inmate No. 265), b. Sept. 14th 1896 in Wieprz, PhD in law, judge of the town court. Brought to KL Auschwitz on June 14th 1940 in the Krakow-Tarnów transport. More → BIOGRAPHIES
239 Auschwitz Museum [APMA-B, Zespół Oświadczenia, t. 148, k. 101]
240 Johen A., "Transport 575 więźniów KL Auschwitz do Sonnenstein...". In: Zeszyty Oświęcimskie 24, Oświęcim 2009, p. 113
241 Bekleidungskammer – clothing storeroom
242 Schreibstube – office
243 Kielar W., Dzieła..., op. cit., p. 89

PICTURES OF "EXHIBITS" AND STRANGE

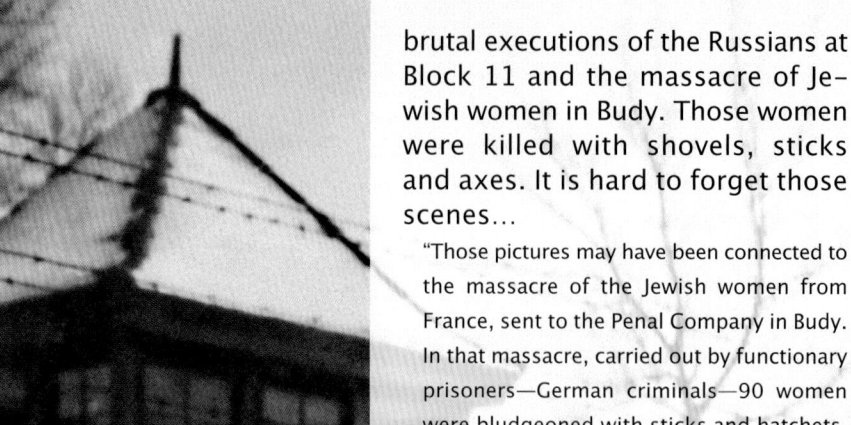

Soon after arriving at Auschwitz

I UNDERSTOOD THAT THE GERMANS WERE OBSESSED WITH RECORD KEEPING.

Everything they did at the camp they photographed and filmed.

"In one particular case there were pictures taken at the women's camp in Birkenau by a special Hauptsturmführer R.H.A, whose name I do not know. It was at the end of 1943 or in the beginning of 1944. The camp was notified of his visit by phone and he was to get all possible assistance. He came and took several pictures at the women's camp and on the same day he took the film to Erkennungsdienst to be developed and checked for quality. That's how I saw all of those pictures. I cannot understand why they were taken, for they were highly compromising to the camp authorities. One of them showed a pile of dead female bodies, on top of which stood two laughing SS women, while an SS officer held one leg of a female corpse and apeared very amused. Another picture showed the women's hospital, where the sick were lying around in disorder, several to a cot, some completely naked and in states of extreme emaciation.
SOURCE: Alfred Woycicki's deposition [244]

I remember my horror and the sadistic enthusiasm of my boss Walter, when he showed me and my friends a movie documenting the brutal executions of the Russians at Block 11 and the massacre of Jewish women in Budy. Those women were killed with shovels, sticks and axes. It is hard to forget those scenes...

"Those pictures may have been connected to the massacre of the Jewish women from France, sent to the Penal Company in Budy. In that massacre, carried out by functionary prisoners—German criminals—90 women were bludgeoned with sticks and hatchets. Some of them had their heads cut off. The massacre probably took place in the evening of October 5th 1942."[245]

Chief of Erkennungsdienst Walter also participated in photographing the fugitives and suicides. Together with his assistant Ernst Hofman they took pictures of prisoners who hanged themselves or threw themselves on the electrified wires.

"The Identification Service took pictures of the scene from all angles. Later, under strict supervision, the photo lab made a single print of each frame. The negatives were then destroyed in the presence of the Commandant and the prints were handed over to him."
SOURCE: Pery Broad's memoirs [246]

Tadek Bródka took pictures of prisoners shot "during escape". Location sketches connected to those photos were made by Tadeusz Myszkowski.

"There was an official ban on preventing fellow prisoners from taking their own lives. If someone was caught 'interfering', as punishment he got sent to 'the bunker'."
SOURCE: Witold Pilecki's report [247]

---

244 Auschwitz Museum [APMA-B, Höss's trial, t. 7, k. 4]
245 Smoleń K., "Erkennungsdienst". In: *Fotografie...*, op. cit., p. 24
246 *Oświęcim w oczach...*, op. cit., p. 158
247 Cyra A., *Ochotnik...*, op. cit., p. 272
248 *Oświęcim w oczach...*, op. cit., p. 135
249 Langbein H., *Auschwitz przed sądem...*, op. cit., s.87
250 Ryn Z., Kłodziński S., "Z problematyki samobójstw w hitlerowskich obozach koncentracyjnych". In: *Okupacja i medycyna. Trzeci wybór artykułów z: „Przeglądu Lekarskiego - Oświęcim" z lat 1963--1976*, Warszawa 1977, p. 114-115

CASES

When a prisoner did not manage to make it to the wires, he was a goner anyway. There was a neutral zone before the electric fence. If someone crossed into that zone a watchman would shoot before the fellow got electrocuted.

"If you heard shooting at night everyone knew that someone had given in to despair and threw himself toward the fence and was in the neutral zone. [...] In such cases the block supervisor briefly reported the suicide to the camp manager. Identification Service then went to the site of the event and photographed the body from all sides. [...]"
SOURCE: Pery Broad's memoirs[248]

"The rate of suicides varied. With the Dutch transports it was very high. I remember that one day it went up to thirty. With the Slovak transport there were less, from five to ten. The average might have been from eight to twelve a day."
SOURCE: Joserf Neumann's deposition[249]

"There were more suicides in the fall and winter, especially on rainy days. Bad weather significantly increased suffering and torment. On those days, after starting work, many prisoners crossed the safety lines in order to end their lives. Some crossed with a brisk stride, while others went slowly, stumbling from exhaustion, in a state of 'forgetting'."[250]

BIRKENAU. HOSPITAL OPERATION ROOM

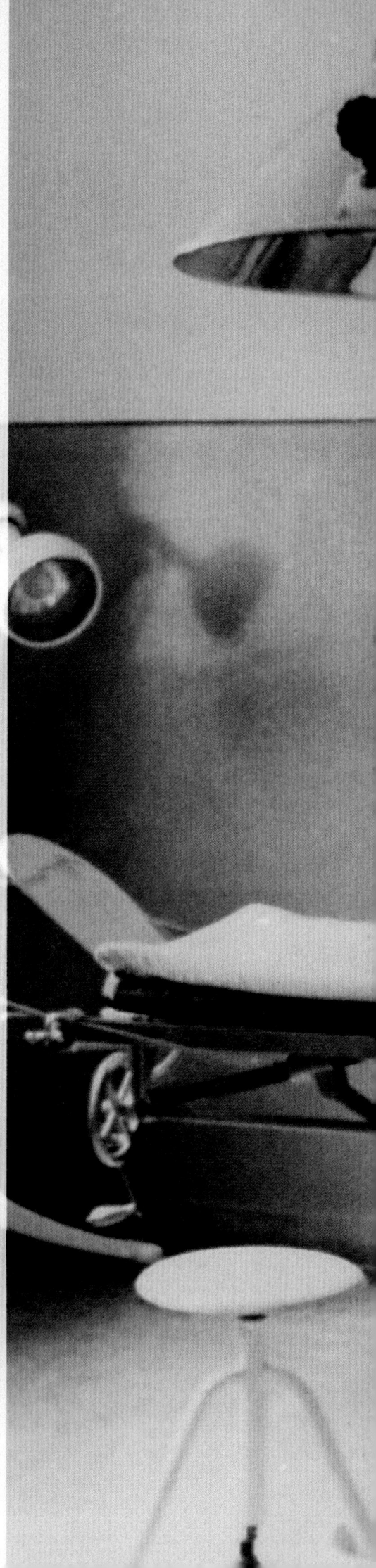

I was delegated to document the work of the camp doctors. I almost immediately went to see them.

MY FIRST THOUGHT ABOUT THE DOCTORS WAS A HOPEFUL ONE,

since from the beginning the prisoners were plagued by disease and there was merely an office, not a hospital. So it seemed there was a chance that they might take better care of us...

"Initially there was no health care at all at Auschwitz. There was just one office for SS doctors and one small operating room at Block 21. The severely ill would die without medical care."
SOURCE: Władysław Frejkiel's deposition [251]

"It was only at the end of 1941 (...) that a young SS doctor, Dr Entress, desiring to practice surgery, organized an operating room at the prison hospital. The equipment was primitive and only later did the prisoners manage to provide it with proper tools, stolen from the warehouses where goods from the exterminated transports were kept."
SOURCE: expert opinion of Prof. Jan Olbrycht [252]

"You went to the hospital. One prisoner held the head while another pulled out the tooth with an old pair of pliers. Many people died from diarrhea, which in our prison dialect was called durchfall. A dirty potato and that was the end of the game." [...]
As soon as you got durchfall, you helped yourself in whatever way you could, used any advice you got. [...]
The Russian prisoners invented a "knife" – it was an aluminum spoon sharpened on a stone. You used this to slice a potato into thin pieces and put it on some bread. You would sprinkle the sandwich with salt, just a tiny bit to make it last as long a spossible, for salt was one of the priciest items at the camp. If you had some salt, you would wrap it up in a piece of cloth and always carry it with you. Bread with potato and salt was supposed to stop diarrhea. The most expensive product of all was "cebion" [vitamin C] – a miracle cure-all. In Auschwitz it cost as much as a diamond. The prisoners would get vitamin C from folks living near the camp."
SOURCE: Józef Skrzypek's account [253]

[251] Deposition from June 7th 1960. The Auschwitz Trial, [APMA-B, Proces ZO k. 5791 and later.]
[252] Auschwitz Museum [APMA-B, Höss's trial, t. 31, k. 12]
[253] Skrzypek J., "Jak przeżyć?". In: *Dziecko szczęścia*, A. Morawska, http://www.fpnp.pl/swiadkowie/materialy/dziecko-szczescia.pdf, p. 10

One of the first doctors I met was Dr Friedrich Entress, who started sending me the so-called "exhibits". Those were either the owners of exceptional tattoos or prisoners who were extremely fat. I took pictures of some extremely obese Jewish men. They could have weighed over 200 kilograms.

Dr. Entress once sent me a Ukrainian with a particularly long penis. Then another time I took a photo of a very handsome Pole who was over six feet tall and well built, but whose penis was unusually small. He told me he had an inferiority complex, and whenever he went to visit a lady he would get dumped after one night and told not to return. They also sent me hermaphrodites—young Jews with beautiful female breasts and male lower parts. They were extremely popular with the kapos. There were maybe ten or twelve of them.

I photographed a man who had, for unknown reason, a giant, six to eight inch long nail stuck in the lower part of his abdomen. It pierced the whole diaphragm, but somehow he lived with it.

I would often see amazing tattoos and strange ornaments or mutilation of the body, but one prisoner I remember particularly well. Dr. Entress sent him to me in May 1941. He was a German from Gdańsk but had the Polish name Zieliński[254]. He was a sailor, a ship's stoker. He had been arrested when he declared Gdańsk rather than German citizenship[255]. I was asked to take a photo of the tattoo on his back. It was very beautifully made: red and blue, with great composition. It represented the Tree of Paradise with Eve handing Adam the apple.

The motif of Adam and Eve was common in tattoo art, but usually poorly executed, except for this case. Zieliński's tattoo must have been done by a great artist; it was rendered perfectly.

After a few weeks I learned that Zieliński was dead, either by shooting or by lethal injection. Mietek Morawa[256], a friend from Krakow who

came in the same transport as I told me to come and see something. He worked in the crematorium and at the doctors' request he cut out various specimens from the corpses. It took me two days to get to the crematorium—I went with the cadaver transportation commando—and there, stretched on the table, I saw the skin from Zieliński's back. Morawa had been ordered to flay it from the deceased prisoner and preserve it. Apparently some German wanted his Bible to be bound in it.

Mietek worked at the crematorium almost the entire time of the camp's operation. He started as a cleaner for Grabner's bicycle.

"One of our group's tasks at block 24 was to clean the bicycles. It was done by Lizak and Mietek Morawa. The latter would usually do it for SS man Grabner. After some time Grabner told Mietek that he could be delegated to do some 'light work'. That light work was burning corpses in the crematorium. In the beginning things went well enough. He was working under a roof, it was warm, and he had more food. But when I met him in Birkenau a few years later he was in deep despair. He wept, saying that he wanted to get out of that kommando but it was impossible. In any case, in 1940 he seemd genial enough, interested in boxing. Later, in Birkenau, however, he seemed to have changed for the worse."
Source: Kazimierz Smoleń's account[257]

---

254 No data
255 Gdańsk (Danzig) befor the war was a semi-autonomous city-state.
256 Mieczysław Morawa (Inmate No. 5730), b. March 19th 1920 in Krakow. Arrived in KL Auschwitz on Oct. 8th 1940 in the Krakow-Tarnów transport. More → Biographies
257 Auschwitz Museum [APMA-B, Zespół Oświadczenia,, t. 76, k. 173-174]

The doctors examined the freshly arrived prisoners,

SINGLED OUT THOSE WITH TATTOOS, AND SENT THEM TO ME.

The doctors examined the freshly arrived prisoners, singled out those with tattoos, and sent them to me. They were especially thorough in examining German citizens. Once a doctor asked me to photograph a German who had a scale tattooed on his penis in units of centimeters. On the side was a pointing hand with the caption "*NUR FUR DAMMEN*"[258]. Another time a prisoner had a tattoo of a similar hand pointing at his penis with the caption was "*NUR FUR MÄDCHEN*"[259]. I also saw an example of a tattoo over the anus: with a mouse at the sphincter and above it a cat, reaching his paw toward the mouse, all the way to the anus. It was artfully made.

There were a great many political tattoos. Some inmates had their left wrists tattooed with the image of a handshake. During Hitler's time those people were especially persecuted.

Jureczek informed me that Walter kept an album of the tattoo pictures in his office. The same album contained stills from a movie provided by camp Commandant Rudolf Höss himself. The originals were sent to Berlin and the copies returned.

"It was known that the tattoo pictures were kept in a special album. For unknown reasons they also photographed people who were crippled or of defective build or had hernias, scars etc."
SOURCE: Bronisław Jureczek's account [260]

In any case, they thought it interesting to photograph people who were considered strange, sick, deformed or on the verge of death. An example of the latter was photos of SS men sick with malaria, requested by Wirths and taken by Tadek Bródka. There were pictures of fever attacks of the patients in the wooden barracks next to the crematorium. I don't know why the *SS-Lagerarzt* (camp doctor) asked to film those scenes. But I saw the terribly twisted faces of the sick whose bodies were wracked with fever.

---

[258] Trans. "Only for women"
[259] Trans. „Only for girls"
[260] Auschwitz Museum [APMA-B, Zespół Oświadczenia, t. 19, k. 29]

PHOTOGRAPHS FOR MENGELE

In May 1943 Josef Mengele[261] arrived at the camp. I even took his camp ID picture but at that time I didn't know what he did. I found out later. He was said to be a high ranking SS officer decorated for his bravery at the front. Apparently, he'd been a sickly child. Now he was going to shamelessly exploit his victims and later, when he no longer needed them, send them to the gas chamber. He would pass time in their company. He would examine them, weigh and measure them, and then point to those who were to be liquidated.

"He visited us at the clinic like a benign uncle, bringing chocolate. Before he approached you with a scalpel or a syringe he would say, 'Don't be scared, you will be fine.' He made incisions in our testicles, injected us with chemicals, and once operated on Tibi's spine. After these experiments he would offer us gifts. I still see him walking through the door and I get rigid with fear. During later experiments he put pins into our heads. You can still see the scars from those. One day he killed Tibi, my brother. He was away for just a few days and when they brought him back his head was covered with a huge dressing. He died in my arms."
SOURCE: Moshe Ofer's evidence[262]

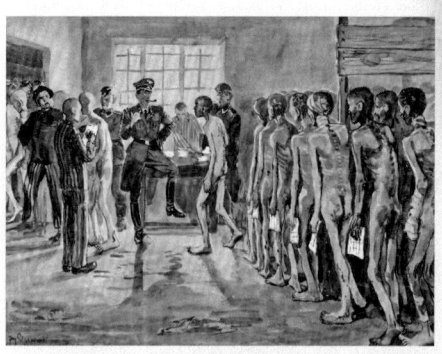

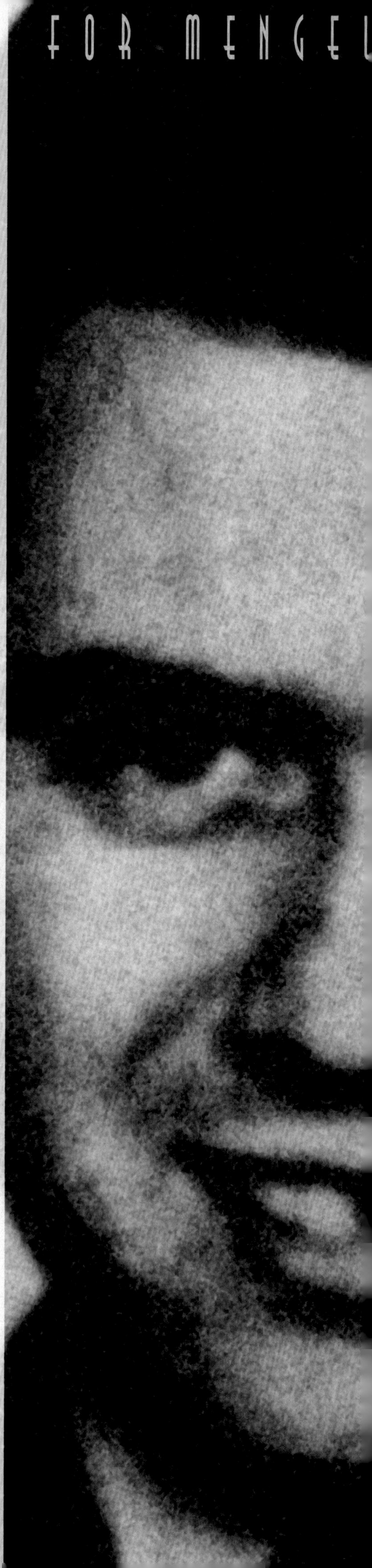

---

[261] Josef Mengele SS-Hauptsturmführer), b. March 16th 1911 in Grünzburg; PhD in humanities and a medical doctor. Physician in the Gypsy camp at KL Auschwitz II-Birkenau and in the women's camp. From August till November 1944 head SS doctor at the camp. After the merging of KL Auschwitz II-Birkenau and KL Auschwitz I into one administrative unit he was a doctor at the hospital for the SS. In KL he conducted experiments on multiple pregnancy, "water cancer" (noma) and heredity of traits in twins and dwarfs. More → BIOGRAPHIES

[262] Kubica Helena, *Dr Mengele i jego zbrodnie*. In: *Zeszyty Oświęcimskie 20*, Oświęcim 1993, p. 352

AND OTHER DOCTORS

Mengele did not look like a monster. His was an ordinary, wide face with an avuncular smile. He had a dark complexion, his height was just above average, and he was rather slim. Sometimes he would just come in, take his prints and leave. I would enter in the notebook what he took. In conversation, he treated me as an expert and behaved politely. He would say, "Can you do this? Do you understand what it is?"
Or, "Is it clear to you, or do I have to repeat myself?"
 So, he could be civil. And yet a few hours later he could send a whole ward of children he'd examined off to the gas chamber.
Photographing of Mengele's experiments started in the spring of 1943.

"The initiative came from the doctors, often university professors, who were looking for solutions to some medical problem and sought experimental subjects in the concentration camps. For this, they turned to Gravitz, who through Himmler got them permission to conduct the experiments. The experiments at Auschwitz were carried out by Dr. Clauberg, professor of Königsberg University, aged about 45, Air Force Oberleutnant Dr. Schumann, from Hitler's Chancellary and the camp garrison physician, Dr. Edward Wirths."
SOURCE: Rudolf Höss's deposition[263]

Mengele came to my boss Walter and talked things over with him for quite a long time. To me he said only that he would send in a group of women. They were to be photographed naked—front, side and back. As always, he addressed me politely. He said I would also be taking pictures of special medical exhibits, mostly twins, sometimes triplets. He told me that he himself was doing so-called racial research, but from time to time he would expand his interests to dwarves and retarded people. From then on he sent me groups of prisoners; twelve to fourteen twin Jewish girls in each group. Sometimes there would be boy twins too, brought in by a prisoner-nurse, an SS man or an aufseherin.[264]

> "Twins and crippled people were photographed and casts taken of their jaws and teeth. They fingerprinted their fingers and toes. Mengele ordered prisoner Dina Gottliebova, from Thersienstadt ghetto, to make comparison drawings of the heads, ears, noses, mouths, hands and legs of twins. The research papers of Mengele on the subject of twins were prepared by highly educated, mostly Jewish prisoners such as a world famous professor of pediatrics named Berthold Epstein, from Prague University and Dr. Rudolf Vitek (in Weiskopf camp)."[265]

> "According to Y.Ternon and S. Helman [...] Josef Mengele wanted to use his identical twin experiments to support the superiority theory of the Nordic race by proving the primacy of genetic over environmental determinism."[266]

> ""The great purpose" of that research is to increase the birthrate of the "superior race" that was predestined to rule. Practically speaking, it was intended to enable every future German mother to give birth to twins."[267]

DR. JOSEPH MENGELE

263 Auschwitz Museum [APMA-B, Höss's trial, t. 21a, k. 132]

264 Aufseherin - female supervisor of women-inmates at concentration camp
265 Strzelecka I., "Kary i tortury". In: *Auschwitz 1940--1950...*, op. cit., p. 269
266 *Ibidem*, p. 268
267 Nyiszli M., *Pracownia doktora Mengele. Wspomnienia lekarza z Oświęcimia*, Tadeusz Olszański (Trans.), Warszawa 1966, p. 44

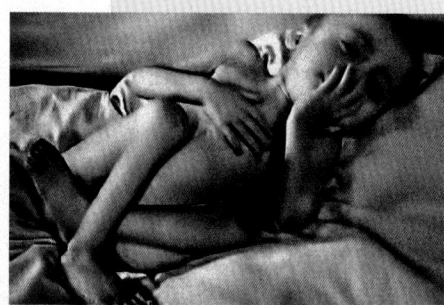

The next group sent in by Mengele was the disabled. Most of them came in the Hungarian and Greek transports. Some were so incapacitated that they couldn't stand, and I had to put them in a chair. Mengele ordered that the dwarves he sent should be photographed in the standard manner – naked, in three views. Once he sent me a whole family, two sisters and a brother. They all had normal torsos but abnormally short arms and legs. The women's breasts were of normal size, full and shapely. I managed to talk to that family and found out they were from Budapest. They told me they made a living as musicians. One sister played the guitar, the other the violin. The brother sang. They had taken part in many shows and cabarets; it was how they supported themselves. Sadly, I never met them again.

Mengele picked up the prints of their pictures himself and let my boss know he was happy with them.

Mengele would also send me cases, which, although I had seen plenty at the camp, were still shocking to me. A few times he told me to photograph Gypsy kids, and once a young Gypsy woman with a strange and frightening disease. The girl had a lovely face, but when she open her mouth I saw rot on her lower jaw, the flesh eaten to the bone. I asked Mengele what disease it was. He said it was noma, or water cancer, and that it occurred only in dark skinned races. He showed me what and how I should photograph.

IN ALL, I MADE PERHAPS 400 TO 500 PICTURES FOR MENGELE.

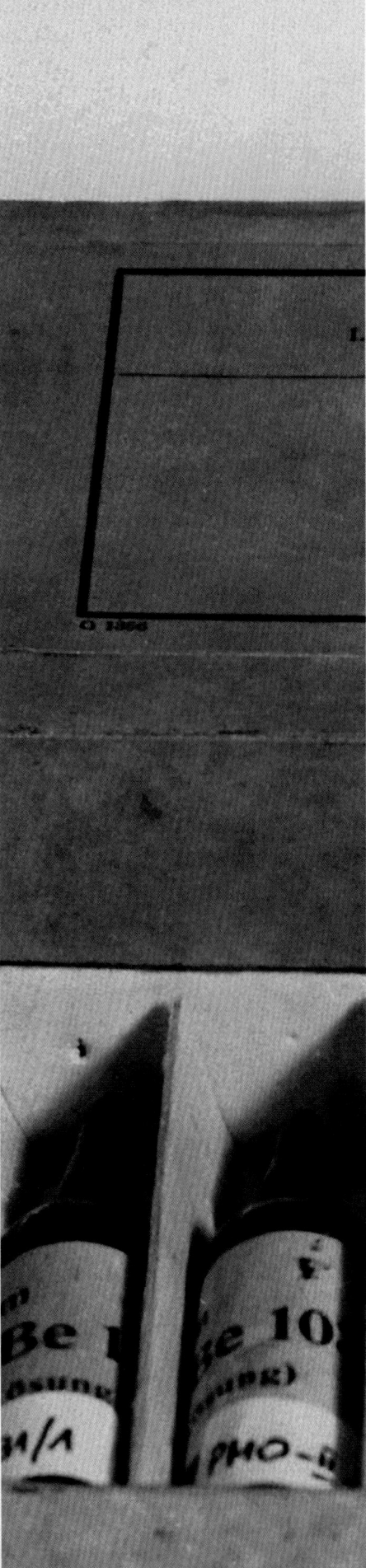

"The overall number of twins who were used by doctor Mengele is unknown. Elżbieta Warszawska, a former prisoner who worked at Block 1 as a caregiver for the twins says in her account that there were about 350 pairs of twins of both sexes aged from two to about sixteen, from various countries. The majority, however, were Jewish children from the Hungarian, Czech, (Terezin/Theresienstadt), and the German, Italian, Belgian and French transports. As for the number of twins in the men's hospital in barracks number 15, we know from the account of one of the twins who stayed there, that there were over 100 of them up to sixty years of age. Among them there were also triplets and dwarves from Hungary."[268]

Separate research was conducted by Dr. Wirths in Birkenau. He was SS Strurmbanführer. Initially I worked for him taking pictures of women's eyes. He would seek individual women who had eyes of different colors, for instance blue and green or brown and green. He found eight such women. A few times he sent me and Tadek Bródka to Birkenau to photograph just the eyes, in extreme close-up, with an excellent Leica camera. He wasn't very happy, since the black and white photographs did not show the effects he had expected and which would only have been possible with color images.

Later we had to retake the pictures of variegated eyes on color film. I did not see them because we did not develop them. We lacked the proper equipment.

I also worked on pictures of Dr. Emil Kaschub[269], who experimented on the limbs of healthy men in Block 28. First he injected them with various substances and later photographed various stages of decomposition—the ulcerations, swellings and oozings of the wounds. He would come to us with exposed rolls of film for developing.

---

[268] Kubica Helena, "Dzieci i młodzież w KL Auschwitz". In: *Auschwitz 1940–1950...*, op. cit., p. 205
[269] Emil Kaschub – physician in the rank of ensign. He came to Auschwitz in the summer of 1944.
More → BIOGRAPHIES

"Hofmann stressed very firmly that those pictures were top secret and extremely important; that he would count every print, and that all, even the bad ones, must be returned to him. He personally supervised those experiments in the lab."
Source: Alfred Woycicki's account  270

"In the years 1941–1944 camp doctors for the SS—Friedrich Entress, Helmuth Vetter, Eduard Wirths—tested on prisoners of Auschwitz the tolerances and effectiveness of new preparations and medications, with code names such as B-1012, B-1034, B-1036, 3582[271], P-111, and also of ruthenol and perystol, drugs which had not yet been introduced to the market. They were working for IG Farbenindustrie, including for Bayer, which was part of it. Those preparations were given to prisoners suffering from infectious diseases who had in many cases been intentionally infected."[272]

270 Auschwitz Museum [APMA-B, Zespół Oświadczenia, t. 9, k. 1319]
271 These chemicals were mostly sulfonamide preparations used for some cases of tuberculosis, typhoid, scarlet fever or unknown anti-typhus vaccines. They were given to prisoners as pills, granules, liquids, injections and enemas of various strengths. In case of positive outcomes they were to be marketed to the public.
272 Strzelecka I., "Eksperymenty". In: *Auschwitz 1940--1950...*, op. cit., p. 270

PHOTOGRAPHS OF "GUINEA PIGS"

The doctors experimented extensively on women.[273] At the end of 1943 they organized a special block for women (Block 10[274]), containing mostly Jewish women from Slovakia, Greece and Holland.[275]

I AVOIDED GOING TO THE WOMEN'S BLOCK.

Although some of those women were fond of male company, being mostly very young, I did not enjoy going there. Sometimes I had contact with the Jewish nurses who looked after the victims of those experiments. But I did not want to go to the victims themselves. I knew that after the experiments they would be killed. And anyway, some of them were already very ill. A regular, healthy woman is one thing and a human Guinea pig quite another.

The nurses told me they had seen horrible things there. So horrible that one French woman refused to assist the doctor.[276] She quoted the Hippocratic Oath.

"Dr. Samuel, at the order of Schumann, the Luftwaffe doctor – personally removed x-ray destroyed ovaries of the "Guinea pigs". Once he told her [Dr Hautvall] in very harsh manner (which she stressed in court) to give anesthesia to a victim designated for the operation. She was a 17-year-old Greek girl. After complying with the order Hautval declared that in future she would not participate in operations of this kind. Samuel informed the SS on her."
SOURCE: Hermann Langbein's memoirs[277]

---

[273] German doctors conducted a range of various medical experiments and tested pharmacological agents on both women and man (as described in the next chapter).

[274] The experimental station headed by Dr. Carl Clauberg existed in the Block 10 of the main camp from April 1943 till May 1944.

[275] At least 1,100,000 Jews from Germany, its allies and the occupied countries were deported into Auschwitz. It included 430,00 from Hungary, 300,000 from Poland, 69,000 – France, 60,000–Holland, 55,000 – Greece, Czech Republic – 46,000, Slovakia – 27,000, Belgium – 25,000, Germany – 23,000, Yugoslavia – 10,000, Italy – 7,500 and 37,000 from other places.

[276] „It was Dr. Adelaide Hautval from France, an imate-physician at the camp hospital, who according to the principle that there are higher values than life refused to cooperate in the experiments conducted at the camp by doctors Clauberg, Schumann and Mengele [...]."
SOURCE: Strzelecka I., Kobiety w KL Auschwitz. In: Auschwitz 1940-1950..., op. cit., p. 160

[277] Langbein H., Ludzie w Auschwitz, Oświęcim 1994, p. 253

Auschwitz I, gynecological chair inside Block 10

I spoke a few times with the women who were experimented on, but only in our atelier. Occasionally the SS man who brought them disappeared somewhere for half an hour and we could chat in peace, if they knew German. Once, for example, Mengele sent a young Jewish woman who was perhaps 30. I don't know how she ended up with us, since she wasn't a twin. I started taking pictures of her but she was terribly ashamed. I asked the nurse who came with her to calm her down. I tried not to look in her direction, put light on her only for the taking of the picture, and didn't even come over to position her. One of the prisoner physicians recognized her as a friend. So he asked through block writing clerk Woycicki to bring her back. He wanted to talk to her. He also thought that maybe he would be able to extend her life, that he'd be able to get her away from Mengele and into a regular women's camp. He was aware that after the experiments Mengele either killed the prisoners who were still in decent physical shape or sent them to hard labor. So I destroyed the negative, reporting to my boss that the work was faulty, and he tried to have the Hungarian woman brought in again. But it was too late. She had been sent to the gas chamber right away. I was very dismayed. She had been a woman in her prime, with a beautiful body...

The gynecological photographs I took in Block 10. A few times a gynecological chair was brought to our studio, a 17-18 year old girl was put in it and, in my presence, Dr. Samuel[278] – a prisoner, who conducted experiments for Dr Wirths, supposedly a former professor of gynecology in Munich— gave her a sleeping injection of evipan.

The prisoner would immediately lose conscioussness. The Jews suffered the worst because for them there was no anesthesia. The nurses would put a girl in the chair, pull up her skirt and open her legs. I put light on the genitals and the doctor stretched the vagina with forceps and with a special spoon pulled out the uterus. I did a close-up of that. The uterus was red on one side and on the other you could see white infiltrations. They possibly had put some poisonous liquids into the womb to create cancer. Dr Samuel explained to me that they were looking for methods to artificially fertilize women, detect uterine cancer, and—especially—find a quick method of sterilization.

"The story of Dr. Samuel, once a respectable professor of gynecology from Köln, is tied to the medical experiments which destroyed the name of Dering[279]. As a Jew Samuel had to immigrate to Belgium, later to France, from where at the end of 1942 he, with his wife and daughter, was deported to Auschwitz. (...) Dr. Lora Lorska-Kleinova, who was among the personnel of the experiment block, criticized his over-zealousness. Sara Spanjaard von Esso, who was a 'Guinea pig' in that block, characterized him as a 'disgusting man', who was also 'very eager'."
SOURCE: Hermann Langbein's memoirs[280]

278 Samuel Max (Inmate No. 62907), b. Sept. 15th 1880 in Frachen near Cologne, physician. Brought to KL Auschwitz in the Sept 2nd 1942 transport from Dranca. Worked at Block 10 at sterilization experiments conducted by Dr. Clauberg. More → BIOGRAPHIES
279 Władysław Dering was a well known Warsaw gynecologist and obstetrician.
280 Langbein H., *Ludzie...*, *op. cit.*, p. 250

"From conversations with Clauberg and the functionaries of the Reich Security Head Office Thomson and Eichmann I know that Himmler wanted to use the Clauberg method for the physical extermination of the Polish and Czech nationalities."
SOURCE: Höss's deposition[281]

"There is no doubt that the new method of sterilization was going to be used on women from nations bothersome to the Nazis. As early as July 7th 1943 Clauberg writes to Himmler that soon he will report that one able physician with ten assistants will be able to sterilize several hundred or as much as thousand women a day."
SOURCE: Władysław Fejkiel's memoirs[282]

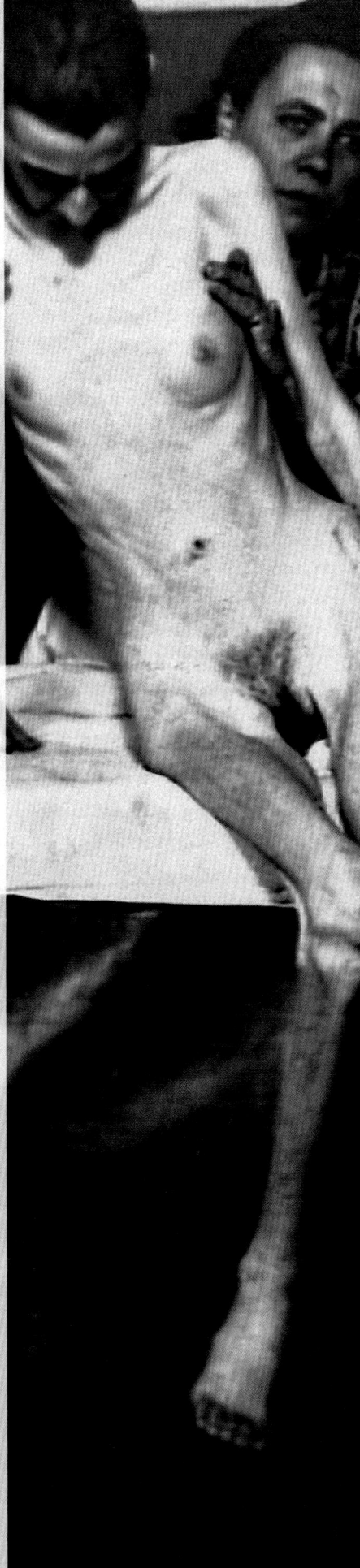

I took pictures of female experiments for Dr. Samuel for another few months. I took both black-and-white and color photographs but I would never see the color ones. Apparently my boss sent them to Katowice or Krakow or Berlin. I do know that Dr. Samuel was very pleased with those pictures.

It is worth noting that a few women from Block 10 survived. I read somewhere about three or four Greek Jewish women, who made it and went back to live in Salonika[283]. Indeed, there were a lot of Jews from there, since those areas were occupied by the Germans. No Jews from the countries occupied by Italy were brought to me.[284]

Taking pictures for the doctors made possible frequent visits to Birkenau. We could leave the main camp even during curfew, since we could easily obtain from Wirths an authorization.

We used this as an opportunity to sneak some medications into the women's camp. We smuggled them in the large tripod case. Instead of the tripod Dr. Fejkiel and Kłodziński[285] would fill the case with medicines, and we would tuck only the tripod head on top. In this way the medicines could be secreted into Birkenau.

---

281 Auschwitz Museum [APMA-B, Höss's trial vol. 21a k. 136-137]

282 Fejkiek Władysław, *Więźniarski szpital...*, op. cit., s.134

283 A popular story told in Israel is the one of Aliza Tzarfati, born in Salonika in 1927 and deported to Auschwitz in 1943, where as one of Mengele's "Guinea pigs" she was subject to sterilization experiments. In spite of having one of her ovaries removed in Auschwitz, after the war she married Ovadia Baruch, whom she had met at the camp, and soon they had two children.

284 Greece was divided into German and Italian zones of occupation.

285 Stanisław Kłodziński (Inmate No. 20019), b. May 4th in Krakow. Brought to Kl Auschwitz on August 12th 1941 in the Krakow transport. More → BIOGRAPHIES

PHOTOGRAPHS OF EXPERIMENTS ON MEN

I took specialty pictures for another of the doctors, Johann Kremer[286], an assistant professor at Münster University.

One day Kremer brought me five desperately starved Jewish men. They were mere skeletons, just skin and bones. Kremer was studying atrophy of the liver in prisoners suffering starvation. As soon as I photographed the prisoners, the professor terminated two of them with injections and then called the Polish doctors to perform autopsies. Normally an autopsy is done a few hours after death, but these doctors had to do it on still warm bodies.

Kremer took notes. As it turned out after the war, he described that episode plus one other where we took pictures for him.

"[entry from November 13th 1942]
I took fresh samples from previously photographed, severely atrophied Jewish prisoners (liver, spleen, pancreas). I preserved, as was usual, the liver and spleen in Carnoy and the pancreas in Zenker fluids. (prisoner's number 68030)."
Source: Johann Paul Kremer's diary[287]

And, of course, I recall the dialog between Dr. Kremer and his assistant:
„Where are those corpses?", asked the assistant.
"Probably still running around somewhere."– answered Kremer, chuckling.

---

[286] Johann Paul Kremer (SS–Obersturmführer), b. Dec. 26th 1883 in Stelberg; PhD in philosophy and medicine, professor at Münster University. At the end of August 1942 transferred to KL Auschwitz as SS physician. He conducted experiments on the atrophy of liver and on starvation.
More → Biographies

[287] Oświęcim w oczach..., op. cit., p. 221

I was all too familiar with nurse Klehr[288]. He was about 35, a platoon leader—an Unterscharführer—who would daily inject up to 50 people with phenol. Klehr would also deliver cans of Zyklon B. And then, as if nothing were going on, he would come to visit my boss for a chat. If Walter was not around, he would chatter to those of us who spoke German. He would go on about mundane matters such as the situation on the front; then inquire about our families.

HE SPOKE AS IF HE HAD JUST BATHED OR CHANGED SOMEONE RATHER THAN HAVING MURDERED THEM.

To inject lethal poison into a bunch of people was for him no more significant than reading the morning paper.

"In August 1941 there were larger scale attempts to kill off the sickest patients at the camp hospital. This was performed by intravenous injections of hydrogen peroxide, gasoline, evipan and phenol."
SOURCE: Stanisław Kłodziński's account[289]

"It was known that an intravenous dose of 10 milliliters of phenol caused death. [...] But that amount was still too large. After refining the methodology of phenol injection it turned out that a 3 milliliter dose given directly into the heart was equally effective, and a great economy! They would no longer need to apply phenol intravenously. The intracardiac method developed by SS medicine was so simple that even unskilled people could perform it, even guys like SS Oberscharführer Joseph Klehr who was so dumb that he had trouble signing his own name."
SOURCE: Tadeusz Paczuła's account[290]

"Klehr, dressed in a white doctor's coat, received each one individually in his 'surgery', carefully closing the door after each patient."
SOURCE: Wiesław Kielar's account[291]

"A prisoner was seated on a stool. He was approached by two nurses, Schwartz and Gelbhard[292]. Standing behind the sitting guy, they would grab his head with one hand, covering the eyes, and tilt it back. By jamming a knee into his spine they would make his chest stick out. Pańszczyk then stabbed the heart with a syringe. (...) Prisoners who had been waiting in another room would come in and haul away the body, bringing it to the *Baderaum*[293] and shutting the door."
SOURCE: Stanisław Głowa's account[294]

„After each peculiarly brief procedure, [Klehr] would look out into the hallway; beckoning the next one in. [...] The unsuspecting patients would enter the surgery one by one until the last one in the ambulatory was gone."
SOURCE: Wiesław Kielar's account[295]

"I had to carry the bodies of the murdered from the room in Block 20 where they had been 'pinned' through the corridor to the *Waschraum*. I sometimes stood just half a meter or so away from Klehr while he 'pinned'. On September 29th 1942, before my very eyes, Klehr murdered my father. [...] At that time Father had been lying in Block 21 with an infection on his left hand. I had visited him frequently. On that day he was among those taken to Block 20. Two were brought into the room at once, one of whom was my father. Klehr said to them: 'Please sit down, gentlemen, you are now going to get antityphus injections.' I began to cry. Klehr injected my father and I carried him to the washroom. [...] I did not then tell Klehr it was my father because I was afraid he would make me be the next to sit beside him on that chair."
SOURCE: Jan Weiss's account[296]

---

288 Josef Klehr (SS-Oberscharführer), b. Oct. 17th 1904 in Langenau; carpenter, nurse. Since September 1941 SS nurse at Department V - medical orderly of the SS garrison in KL Auschwitz and the head of the desinfection kommando. More → BIOGRAPHIES

289 Kłodziński S., *Fenol w KL. Auschwitz-Birkenau*, In: *Przegląd Lekarski*, Nr 1a, Oświęcim 1963, p. 62

290 Paczuła T., *Obóz i szpital obozowy w Oświęcimiu we wczesnych okresach istnienia*. In: *Przegląd Lekarski*, Nr 1a, op. cit., p. 53

291 Kielar W., *Dzieła...*, op. cit., p. 118.

292 Other people who performed the „pinning" executions were most often SS men Josef Klehr and Herbert Scherpe and inmates-nurses from the prisoner infirmary: Blockältester Otto Block and Poles: Alfred Stössel, Mieczysław Szymkowiak, Feliks Walentynowicz, Leon Landau and especially zealous Mirosław Pańszczyk.

293 Baderaum - communal washing facility

294 Auschwitz Museum [APMA-B, Zespół Oświadczenia, t. 36, k.5]

295 Kielar W., *Dzieła...*, op. cit., p. 118

296 Langbein H., *Ludzie...*, op. cit., p. 254

"Even while the camp was still operating, the prisoners, doctors and nurses who recorded the people exterminated with phenol in Auschwitz put the number at about 20,000."
Source: Stanisław Kłodziński's account [297]

We watched through our window every day as dozens of bodies from Block 20 were dragged by the legs down the stairs. One day I saw several boys aged 13–17 from the Zamość region. They stood at the wall, awaiting their executioner.

"On January 21st, February 23rd and March 1st 1943, by special order, 121 prisoners from Block 20 were killed by phenol. They were Polish and Jewish boys who had been deported from Zamość and other regions of Poland." [298]

"[February 23rd 1943] The boys were brought to the main camp on the pretense of taking part in nurse training. In the evening of that day they were murdered by intracardiac injections of phenol." [299]

"None of the prisoners resisted. They might have said, 'Oberscharführer, let me live.' But they didn't utter a sound. That was the most depressing thing."
Source: Joseph Klehr's, SS nurse's account [300]

BY THE AFTERNOON, ALL THAT WAS LEFT OF THOSE YOUNG BOYS WAS A PILE OF CORPSES.

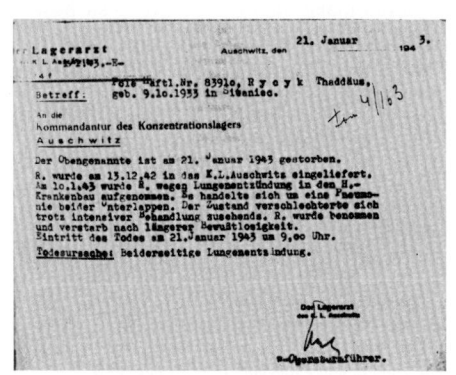

The death record of a 9 year old Tadeusz Rycyk from the Zamość region, who was killed with an intracardiac phenol injection on January 21st 1943. The cause of death was recorded as pneumonia.

[297] Kłodziński S., *Fenol w KL. Auschwitz – Birkenau.* In: *Przegląd Lekarski*, Nr 1a, op. cit., p. 63

[298] Strzelecka I., *Szpitale obozowe w KL Auschwitz* In: *Auschwitz 1940–1950...*, op. cit., p. 254

[299] Czech D., *Kalendarz...*, op. cit., p. 352

[300] Auschwitz Museum [APMA-B, Zespół Oświadczenia, t. 92, k. 85]

ABOVE: THE KOCH SIBLINGS: ROMAN, 13, DANUTA AND JÓZEF, 16. THEIR MOTHER MARIANNA BROUGHT THEM FROM WARSAW TO SKIERBIESZÓW VILLAGE IN THE ZAMOŚĆ REGION TO WAIT OUT THE TERROR OF NAZI OCCUPATION. IN THE FALL OF 1942 DURING THE PACIFICATION OF THE ZAMOŚĆ REGION THE KOCH WERE TAKEN TO KL AUSCHWITZ ON DEC. 13TH 1942 AND REGISTERED UNDER ASSUMED NAME SASIN.

LEFT: ROMAN AND JÓZEF KOCH SHORTLY BEFORE THEIR ARREST AND DEPORTATION TO KL AUSCHWITZ. ON MARCH 1ST 1943 ROMAN WAS MURDERED WITH A PHENOL INJECTION ("PINNING") IN A GRUP OF 80 BOYS UNDER 17, WHO WERE DECLARED UNFIT FOR LABOR. SS MEN LURED THEM BY PROMISING ENROLLMENT IN A COURSE FOR NURSES.

I also heard that the doctors would take sperm from the young Jews. We joked that those boys were forced to have intercourse. But it was not true of course; they masturbated.

"Apart from castration procedures and taking samples for histopathological analysis of irradiated organs, Schumann attempted also to take sperm samples from some prisoners. That procedure was reported by 'flegers' [nurses] from block 28 'Krankenbau'. Some prisoners brought from Birkenau waited in the hallway in front of the surgery opposite the ambulatory. The prisoners were taken in individually and the door was closed. They were forced to take off their pants; half naked, and then they were held by SS-Oberscharführer Büning. At that time Schumannn would put into the prisoner's anus a small object resembling a hand held ventilator fan. Probably, by stimulating the rectum, he was trying to induce sexual arousal. What was the actual effect of that macabre procedure, we don't know. The men wailed from pain."
SOURCE: Władysław Fejkiel's account[301]

Apparently, the men whose sperm was taken survived, while those who had been irradiated died in the gas chamber.

"April 29th 1944. Blankenburg, deputy chief of the 2nd Department of the Führer's Chancellary, in his letter to Reichsführer SS, reported on Dr. Schumann's Auschwitz experiments: 'At the order of Reichsleiter Bouhler I enclose the paper by Dr. Horst Schumann on the effects of X-ray irradiation of human reproductive glands. A while ago you instructed Oberführer Brack to commission this work and you even offered assistance by giving him access to the suitable material in KL Auschwitz. I refer especially to the second part of this work which demonstrates that castration of men carried out with this method is out of question, because of its significant cost. Surgical castration, as I have observed myself, takes 6 to 7 minutes and provides much greater certainty and speed compared to X-ray castration. Soon I hope to be able to provide you with further parts of this research...'"[302]

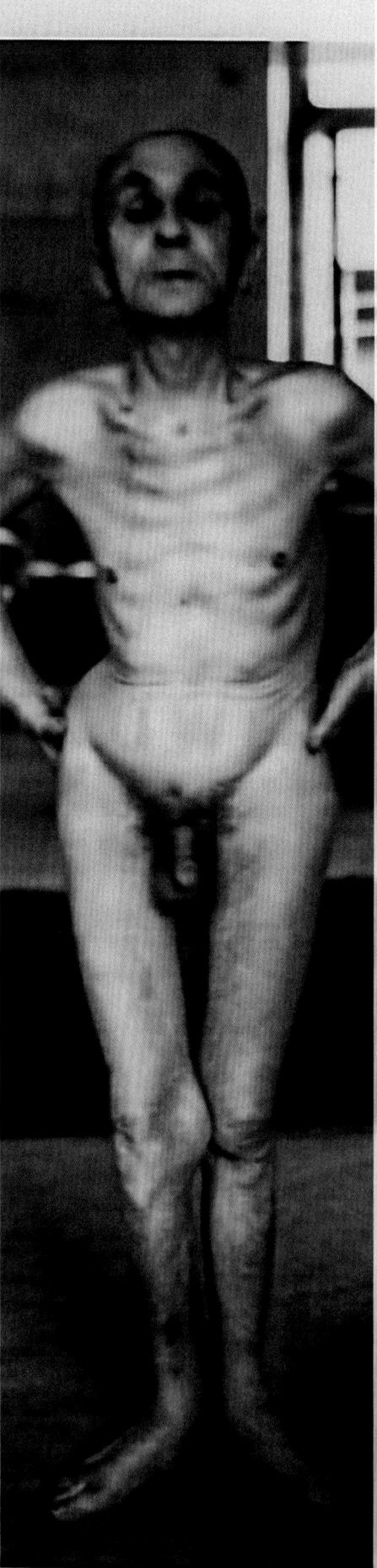

Because of the work I was doing for the doctors I saw much more than the other prisoners. There were also histopathological tests done at Auschwitz and specimens taken of various organs. They even preserved whole heads in formalin.

At the end of 1943 Dr. Mengele left Auschwitz and his experiments were suspended.[303] Dr. Samuel was himself given a lethal injection and the whole block was closed.[304] Other experiments ended sometime in October 1944.

"Why did the camp authorities have Samuel killed before the experiments were completed? Tadeusz Paczuła thinks that SS 'were unhappy with his garrulity and sloppiness.' Also because Samuel suffered from wet eczema, had an oozing face and caused disgust with his appearance. Dering wrote that Samuel was terminated because he was old, useless and all covered with eczema." However, at the trial in London, Dering offered other reasons: 'Samuel was arrogant. He knew too much and would start arguments with the other doctors.'"[305]

"Once he wrote a letter to Himmler. I read that letter, since all the prisoners who wanted to correspond had to leave their letters at the writing office. Doctor Samuel was asking Himmler to save his daughter, who was in Birkenau, emphasizing his meritorious service during World War I. He had been at the front and was wounded. Later he had been active in Bologna in the anti-occupation movement and for this had been decorated. Listing these merits he begged for the release of his daughter. It could be in the fall of 1943. A few days later Dr. Samuel disappeared from the camp. Word of his death followed. I heard he got shot either in Birkenau or in the old crematorium. He was a Geheimnisträger[306] [...]".
SOURCE: Tadeusz Hołuj's testimony[307]

---

301 Fejkiel W., Więźniarski szpital..., op. cit., p. 135-136
302 Czech D., Kalendarz..., op. cit., p. 648, 649
303 In fact Mengele left Auschwitz on January 17th 1945. Wilhelm Brasse did not know that Mengele got sick with typhus which excluded him for a time from activity at the camp. Moreover, he worked mostly in Birkenau, especially at the Gypsy camp.
304 Dr. Samuel indeed died at the camp in 1944 - no exact date is known; the last mention in the files: May 1944
305 Langbein H., Ludzie..., op. cit., p. 251
306 Geheimnistrager — "bearer of secrets"
307 Langbein H., Auschwitz przed sądem..., op. cit., p. 248-249

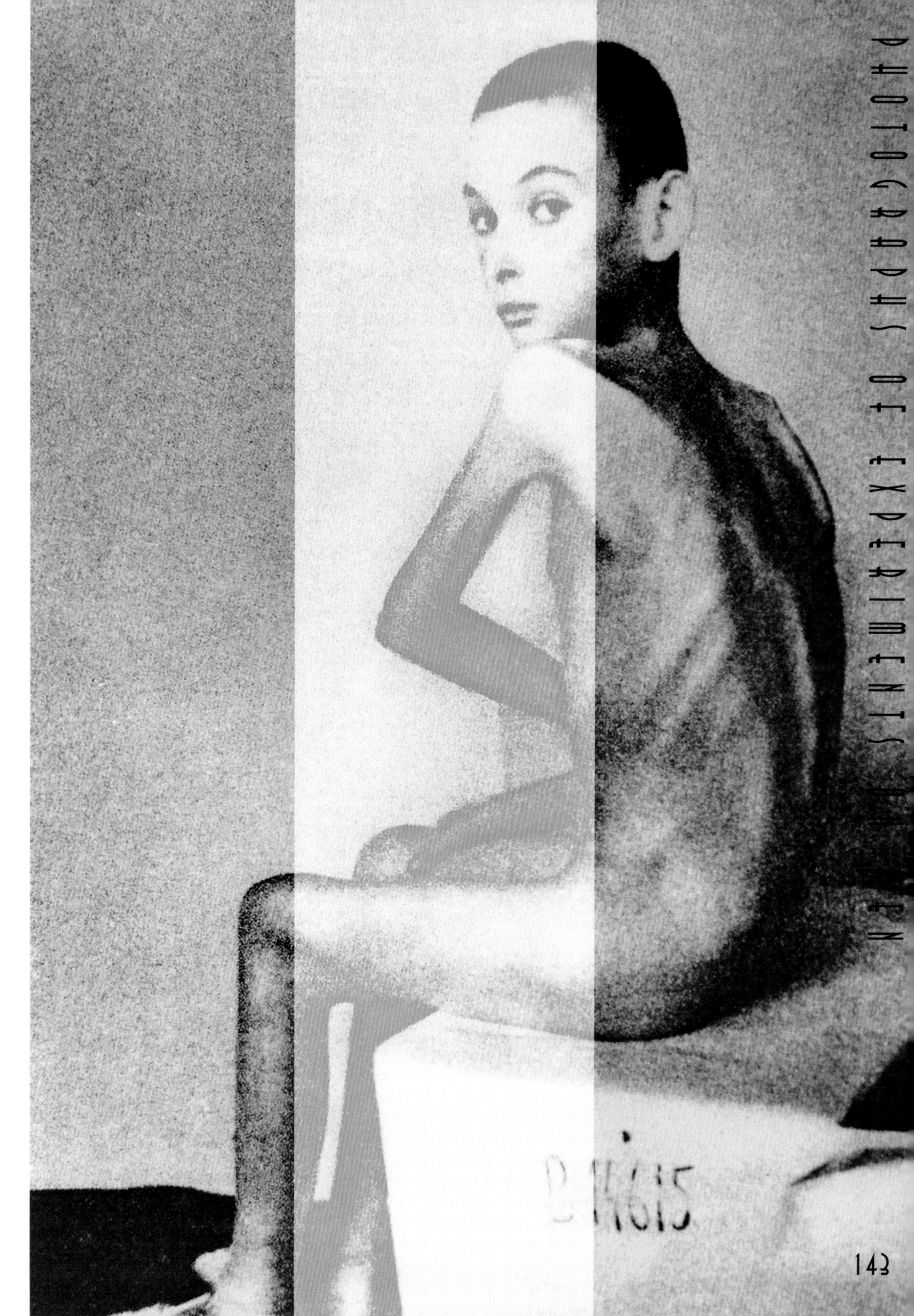

PHOTOGRAPHS OF EXPERIMENTS

PHOTOGRAPHS OF WOMEN

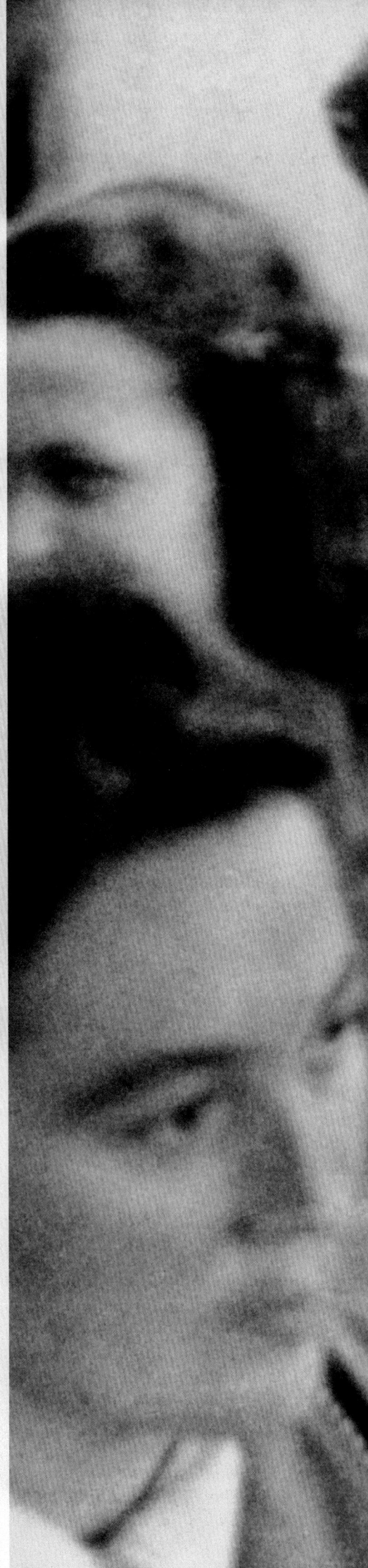

The women came to the camp in 1942. Later they were moved to Birkenau.[308] I saw them when they started coming into the atelier and also when we did jobs inside the women's camp.

A different numbering system was used for the women, and there were fewer of them than men.

> There were 131,560 women registered at KL Auschwitz, the majority of whom did not survive the camp. Most of the female prisoners were Jewish (about 82,000), Polish (31,000) and Roma (11,000). There were also Russians, Germans, Belarusians, Serbians, Ukrainians, Yugoslavians, French, Czechs and Dutch.
>
> "As part of the European Jew extermination plan, women probably made up half of the victims of the Auschwitz gas chambers and about 1/3 of all registered Auschwitz prisoners."[309]

Usually only German, Czech and Yugoslavian women—mostly Serbian—would come in for mug shots. Among the women used for medical experiments many were from Greece.

I had colleagues who thought of it in different terms and said, "Boy, we're going to have interesting stuff to look at!"

But I was not interested that way. Meaning, sure I appreciated beauty but the majority of women who came to us—and you can see it in the pictures—were already emaciated and haggard. It was a tragic sight.

The circumstance where a woman was still in healthy physical shape with feminine curves was extremely rare. Then my colleagues would of course show great interest. If they came across a picture of a young, shapely Jewish lady in full bloom they would try to stash it away somewhere.

---

[308] The first female inmates were registered at the camp on March 26th 1942. They came in two transports,; the first one came from Dresden with 999 German women from KL Ravensbrück (one inmate escaped from the transport). Among them there were political prisoners, Jehovah's Witnesses and also common criminals and prostitutes. The second transport was from Poprad in Slovakia and was made up of 999 young Jewish women (one died during the journey).

MEMBERS OF FEMALE SS AUXILIARY TEAM TRAVELING BY BUS TO AN SS RESORT NEAR AUSCHWITZ

There were some German girls from *Funkstelle* (the radio switchboard), who would come by during the photo sessions for the SS. They worked at the telephone exchange and at the "spark service"—the telegraph—in the local command office. They were not much older than twenty, wore uniforms, and their hair was always nicely done. I liked them plenty.

I remember a particular phone operator, a lovely blonde of twenty-three, in a jacket and skirt made from the same fabric as the SS uniforms. She came to have her photo taken accompanied by an SS man who watched over her (the women always came with a guard.) She had authorization for portraits and informed me she wanted a shot with deep décolletage. She even brought a piece of tulle to partly cover her breasts. At a certain moment she asked the SS man to leave the atelier. To my surprise, he obeyed.

WE WERE ALONE. SHE TOOK OFF HER BLOUSE AND BRA.

She said she wanted a photo where almost all of her breasts would be visible. I was stunned at that sight, for she was really pretty, well nourished and shapely. Her breasts were lovely. I stood there excited and a bit nervous. I took five pictures from different angles. In two of them her breasts were barely covered with the tulle. One was a close-up, one was from further back and another was just of her face and the top of her bust. I told her they'd be ready in three days. I did half-sharp copying and the breasts were not exactly visible, I nicely retouched everything. The pictures were handed over to her by my boss, Walter.

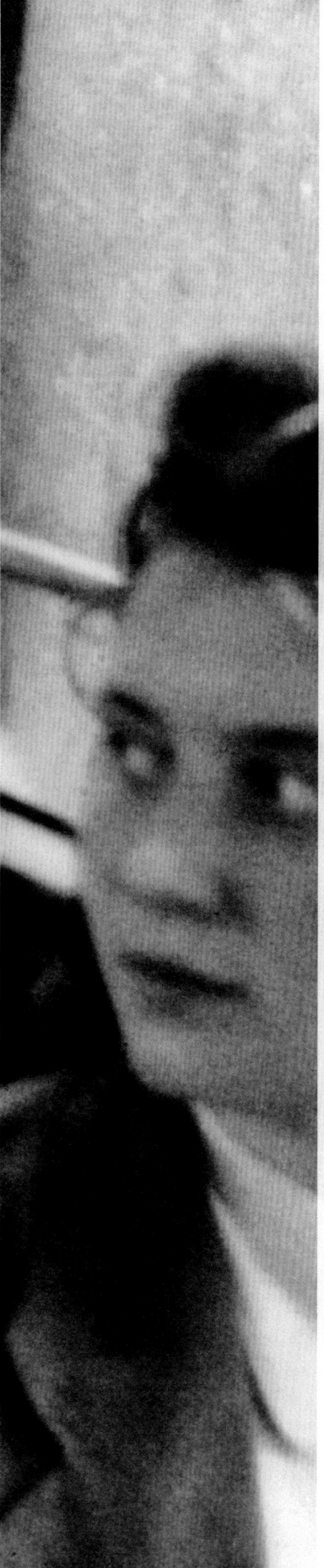

A week later during the evening roll call I was suddenly called to Lagerführer Schwartz. I went, saluting with the prescribed formula: "Inmate number so and so reports in order and at location"—hat on the side as required; hands hanging next to hips. He then asked me if I took pictures of that girl. I admitted that I had.

"Get the negatives and relinquish them to me", he ordered.

This was outrageous, since such negatives were generally a private thing, especially when the woman in them was half naked. But he was Lagerführer, so I could not refuse. I brought them. He looked at them against the light and asked a brief question:

"Did she at least have decent tits?"

I answered:

"Ja wohl, Lagerführer!"

From another SS woman I learned that this girl later poisoned herself. She probably couldn't stand what was going on in the camp. The radio station and the telegraph where she worked were located in the two story building next to the crematorium. The telephone operators saw everything through the windows—the whole death machine and the piles of bodies on the carts

---

309 Strzelecka I., *Kobiety w KL Auschwitz*. In: *Auschwitz 1940-1950...*, op. cit., p. 139

Apart from that beautiful girl who took her own life, there were other pretty young German girls. I spoke with them in their language. One also spoke Polish. Her name was Edyta Pinczer[310] and she was from Bielsko. A lovely girl, only her legs were not so great.

I remember also a young prisoner girl, 16-17 years old, who came with a larger group of women from the transition camp in Zamość. The others were already very gaunt, but she was still in reasonably good shape and extremely pretty. Czesia Kwoka[311], who attracted my attention, had blood on her lips. I was a young man, sensitive to the look of girls, so she immediately caught my eye. I politely welcomed her to the photo session. I reassured her by saying there was nothing to fear. Those girls were usually terrified. The SS women had terrorized them with yelling and beating at the formation of the columns. If one of them stuck out a few centimeters from the straight line she would get whipped. Those women did not know German so they did not understand what was going on when their numbers were called. The SS women would often slash them on the face with their whips. I heard of three SS women who stood out as particularly brutal: Hasse[312], Drehsler[313], Mandel[314]. The latter used to go around the camp on a bike.

310 No data
311 Czesława Kwoka (Inmate No. 26947), b. August 15th 1928 in Wólka Złojecka. Come to KL Auschwitz on December 13th 1942 in the Zamość transport.
More → BIOGRAPHIES
312 Hasse Elisabeth (SS-Aufseherin), b. Dec. 14th 1917. Came to Kl Auschwitz on October 7th 1942 from KL Ravensbrück, in 1944 promoted to Rapportführerin.
More → BIOGRAPHIES
313 Margot Elisabeth Drechsler SS-Aufseherin, B. May 11th 1908 in Neuersdorf, Saxony. Transferred to KL Auschwitz in early October 1942 from FKL Ravensbrück. Till end of June 1944 supervisor at the FKL in KL AuschwitzII-Birkenau. More → BIOGRAPHIES
314 Marie Mandel (SS-Oberaufseherin), b. Jan. 10th 1912, office clerk. Oct. 1942 - Nov. 1944 head supervisor SS at the women's camp in KL Auschwitz.
More → BIOGRAPHIES

"Mandel the beautiful [...] She was a thoroughbred, a flexible, springy and lovely wild animal; always enraged—a golden panther with eyes shining with murder lust; a lynx who could creep in from behind unnoticed, when least expected, and knock someone to the ground with a single blow of her small, iron-hard hand. [...]. To hit someone in a paroxysm of rage gave her pleasure and was for her perhaps a way to enhance her looks, because after every such execution she looked even more beautiful. You could see the muscle action under her perfectly fitted, very tight uniform. Her muscles moved like living snakes. Her greenish eyes shone star bright, her rosy face became vivid, and even her hair seemed to be more shiny."
SOURCE: Helena Tyrankiewicz's deposition[315]

"She speaks only German, a Vienna dialect. A boxer by profession, she was from Vienna, born January 10th 1912 and was popularly known as "Mańcia Migdał" [Almond Mary]. A cruel human being. She would abuse and torture the prisoners in person. The power of her blow was terrible. She dislocated a jaw with one swing of her fist. Her specialty was a kick to the groin."
SOURCE: Letter from the District Commission for the Investigation of Nazi Crimes in Poland[316]

"There was no mercy in her. Others would sometimes release certain people, but she was ruthless. She would send people to the gas if they had a scraped heel or a frostbitten finger. The pleas of the prisoners who kissed her shoes achieved nothing."
SOURCE: Anna Szyller's deposition[317]

Among the women that I met at camp, there was sometimes a face so beautiful, that I remembered her all my life. For me, one was a beautiful blonde from Krakow. I asked her offence. She said she had been a Home Army courier. Later, by a curious coincidence, I came across her photo. It had been taken by my boss's deputy Hofmann, when he was shooting women who worked cleaning the fishponds near Auschwitz. I remember that picture. Her

315 Auschwitz Museum . The Auschwitz Trial [APMA-B, Proces ZO, t. 57, k. 40]
316 Letter from April 13th 1946. Auschwitz Museum The Auschwitz Trial [APMA-B, Proces ZO, t. 65, k. 4]
317 Auschwitz Museum .The Auschwitz Trial [APMA-B, Proces ZO, t. 56, k. 84]

face was scrawny, but still pretty. The women in that kommando lived under extremely harsh conditions so I knew that the girl would soon die.

I also remember that sometime in September or October 1944 *Politishe Ableitung* (the Political Department, Gestapo) requested photographs of a Jewish woman from Estonia, who was said to be Palitzsch's lover. I do not remember the name of that prisoner.[318]

---

[318] Palitzsch, whose wife died of typhus in November 1942, fell in love in a beautiful inmate, a Slovakian Jew–Katja Singer. The camp Gestapo cell found out about the affair and Palitzsch got arrested. Katja Singer had a high position as a Lagerschreiberin— writing clerk. After her relationship with Palitzsch was discovered she was moved to the Stutthoff camp. She survived the war and later married a Czech officer.

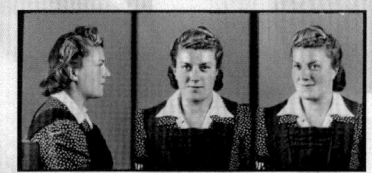

The women lived in barracks without beds, on three tiered boxes made from planks of wood. In each box four prisoners were crammed, one on top of the other. They had neither water nor toilets since the latrines were located only between the barracks.

"That women's camp was built on the worst swamps and bogs so that the mud ponds, two meter deep, never dried out from spring to winter."
SOURCE: Testimony No. 2[319]

„There were three level bunk beds placed tightly on both sides of a long barracks and on them sat hundreds of miserable figures, mere skeletons. Some women squatted on their cots, picking lice, while some others energetically squashed lice in the blankets which looked like rags. Still others lingered naked between the beds, trying to get as close as possible to a strange stove which ran the whole middle length of the barracks, deluding themselves that there they'd get a bit of warmth. Their naked feet were in mud that looked like manure."
SOURCE: Wiesław Kielar's account[320]

I felt terrible for those women. There were no opportunities for personal hygiene. Later I found out that

LIFE IN FEAR AND TERROR HALTED THEIR MENSTRUATION.

They simply stopped menstruating. In this, nature showed them some mercy.

"For eight months after we got moved to Birkenau I didn't wash. When we arrived there was a shower in one of the barracks which worked for three days, and that was it. There was no water. I washed only in the rain, if the SS men weren't looking."
SOURCE: Anna Stefańska-Tytoniak's account[321]

"We were all undernourished. None of us menstruated, which given the lack of underwear was a plus. But I keep asking myself if it was just the undernourishment, or would comparison with animals be appropriate? Even well nourished mammals in the zoo rarely give birth. Captivity is harmful, from the lowest to the highest level of evolution."[322]
SOURCE: Ruth Klüger's account[323]

---

319 Rajewski L., *Oświęcim w systemie...*, op. cit., p. 98-99
320 Kielar W., *Dzieła...*, op. cit., p. 184
321 Auschwitz Museum [APMA-B, Zespół Oświadczenia, t. 137, k. 100]
322 "Many women (according to research about 85%) stopped menstruation in the camp as result of disruption of hormone production due to malnutrition and extreme psychological stress. The disruption produced symptoms such as complete loss of menstruation (oligomenorrhea) or temporary or cyclical irregularities (amenorrhea)."
SOURCE: Giza Jerzy, Morasiewicz Wiesław, *Poobozowe zaburzenia seksualne u kobiet jako element tzw. Kz-syndromu*. In: *Przegląd Lekarski*, Nr 1, Kraków 1974, p. 68-71
323 Klüger R., *Żyć dalej...*, Wrocław 2009, p. 163

Women baracks—
KL Auschwitz II-Birkenau

PHOTOGRAPHS OF CHILDREN

Children came into the camp mostly because of their parents. For instance if a father ran away or was in hiding they took his child and kept it in the camp until he turned up. Children were also arrested when their parents committed some offense: listening to the radio, reading illegal newspapers, or spreading false (in the Nazi's opinion) news.

Generally I dealt with Jewish kids who were brought in by Polish nurses. They were not very small children; usually they were from 8–12. They came in so frightened that they wouldn't even talk to each other, especially in the presence of an SS woman. I reassured them, told them that nothing bad would happen to them here and then took the pictures. Sometimes one could not communicate with those children. Some understood German, some didn't. They were mostly children of Slovak, Hungarian and Greek Jews...[324] The Greek Jews spoke no German at all.

> "The Nazis deported to KL Auschwitz about 232,000 children and adolescents, including about 216,000 Jewish children of which only a few were admitted to the camp and the majority of whom were killed in the gas chambers without being registered in the prisoners' records. In the camp there were about 11,000 Roma children and about 5,000 Slavic, mostly Polish children"[325]

However, if a pregnant woman came to the camp and gave birth, the child would most often be drowned in a barrel of water. There was a specialist for this at the camp, a German midwife whom they called „Schwester Klara"[326]. She worked only at the hospital in Birkenau and practically all her work consisted of eliminating the newborn. She kept a bucket of water ready and just after birth she drowned the baby.

---

[324] With some exceptions, Jewish children subjected to selection would be taken to the gas chambers with their mothers. The exceptions were the children who caught the attention of Dr. Josef Mengele, who conducted criminal experiments on children from multiple pregnancies (twins, triplets), dwarfs and those with other physical disabilities.
[325] Kubica H., *Dzieci i młodzież w KL Auschwitz*. In: *Auschwitz 1940–1950...*, op. cit., p. 165–166
[326] Schwester Klara – German criminal inmate, block chief..

"Initially births took place in Barracks 24 in the 'hospital zone' of the women's camp (numbering from 1943). In Birkenau, it was section Bla. They were received by the supervisor of the block, the criminal prisoner 'Schwester Klara', and her assistant, Pfani, also a German criminal. The prisoners gave birth in extremely primitive conditions on the chimney pipe running along the barracks, in plain view of all the sick. Immediately after the birth the Germans killed the newborn, most often by drowning it in a bucket of water. There were instances of birth in the dorm barracks, in the cots. Immediately after labor, mothers had to appear at the roll call and report to their kommando for work."[327]

The parents tried to protect their children as best they could. Mostly it would end badly. Some SS men showed off their cruelty in the mother's presence by smashing the baby's head against the wall...

"[...] the surviving camp records from 1943--45 and the documentation of assistance for the liberated inmates, lists 680 child-prisoners, born in the women's camp in Birkenau and in the Gypsy family camp. Out of those, eight had been released from the camp with their mothers. Only 46 made it to liberation, out of which a few more died in the Red Cross hospitals at the former camp and in Brzeszcze."[328]

[327] Kubica H., *Dzieci i młodzież w KL Auschwitz*. In: *Auschwitz 1940-1950...*, op. cit., p. 209
[328] Ibidem, p. 190 i 211

MOTHER WITH CHILDREN WALKING TO GAS CHAMBER

JEWISH KIDS AT THE CAMP HAD PRACTICALLY ZERO CHANCE OF SURVIVAL.

A child was too small and too weak to work, so the Germans considered such prisoners useless. Thus they had to die. Most often the children were not even registered, but immediately sent to the gas chamber, or kept alive only so long as they were useful for medical experimentation. Afterward they were killed. Such was their fate.

152

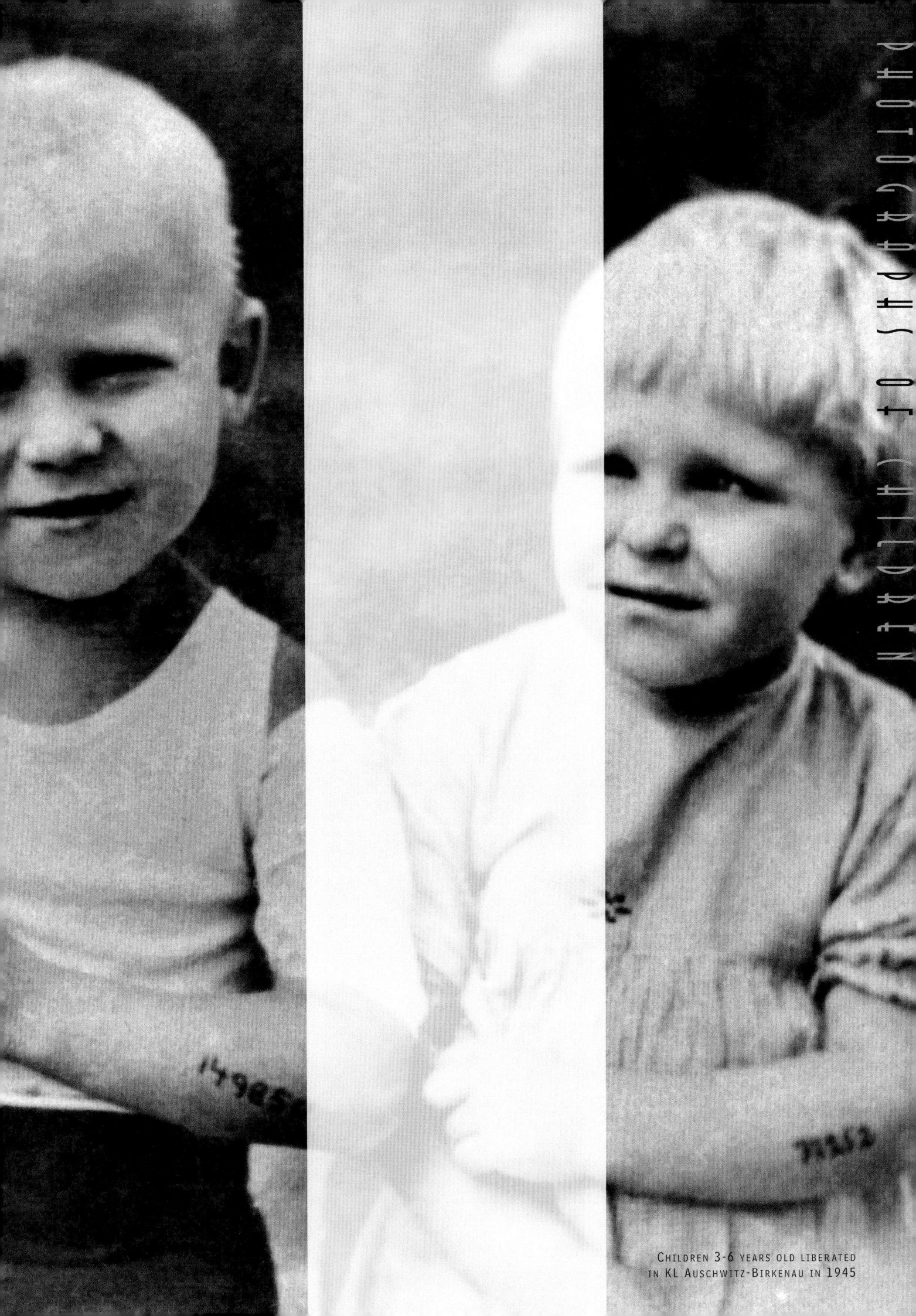

PHOTOGRAPHS OF CHILDREN

CHILDREN 3-6 YEARS OLD LIBERATED
IN KL AUSCHWITZ-BIRKENAU IN 1945

Mostly I had contact with the children who were subjects of experiments. They came were sent in by the doctors. It was important to me that the children in the atelier not be scared. I simply felt the tragic presence of their mothers. So I put a movable backdrop between us and the girls, the one I used for making SS portraits. The girls could undress behind it. I asked the nurses to tell them that no one would beat or threaten them here. I also did not want to touch them. I tried to interact as little as possible and only kindly and politely told them what to do. They were terrified by the mere sight of an SS man or woman. They calmed down some when the SS left. Sometimes they were brought in by female nurses.

There was one nurse, Ola Skalska[329] from Nowy Targ. I would instruct her how to position the girls. She would adjust them, moving them to the left or right. In all, there were about 250–300 of those girls.

I felt uneasy because among the kids there were thirteen to fourteen year old girls who experienced great shame, completely defenseless creatures about whom I knew only that they soon would die. They stood naked, one next to the other, and posed for the photo. There they were, completely exposed, facing a young man. I felt embarrassed. When males are together in a group, a woman is perceived differently. Under such circumstances, I could not look at them as a male. Instead, I experienced the tragedy of the child standing before me...

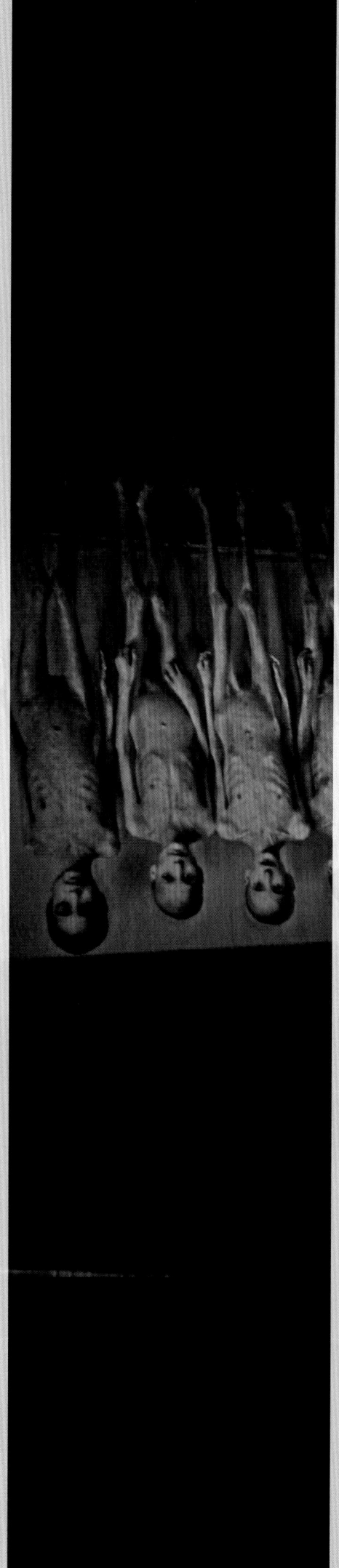

Sometimes they were very pretty. But there they stood maimed, disfigured, naked, with their hair not merely shaven but pulled out. I feared that

ALL THOSE CHILDREN WOULD BE EXAMINED AND THEN SENT TO THE GAS.

Later, by talking to the nurses and doctor Mengele I learned that my fears came true.

When I could, I would ask the kids where they were from. They would tell me that they were from Ružomberok in Slovakia or from Budapest. But they were actually scared of talking to me. Sometimes it was because of the presence of a block clerk. They were not permitted to talk without permission. They were very fearful, although the nurses tried to calm them down. They knew the kids and called them by name.
Sometimes I asked about their parents. They never said they had been taken to the gas, only that they had left in a car.
I did not speak much to them. Sometimes, while my comrade Jureczek was loading the film, I would ask him to give the child a piece of bread. Famished, they quickly tore it to pieces and ate it. But hunger was the normal condition at the camp: men incredibly wasted and weakened by work, women like walking skeletons, kids emaciated and uncared for.

---

[329] Aleksandra Skalska (Inmate No. 38103), b. Oct. 17th 1921 in Grodno. Brought to KL Auschwitz on March 9th 1943 in the Krakow transport. More → Biographies

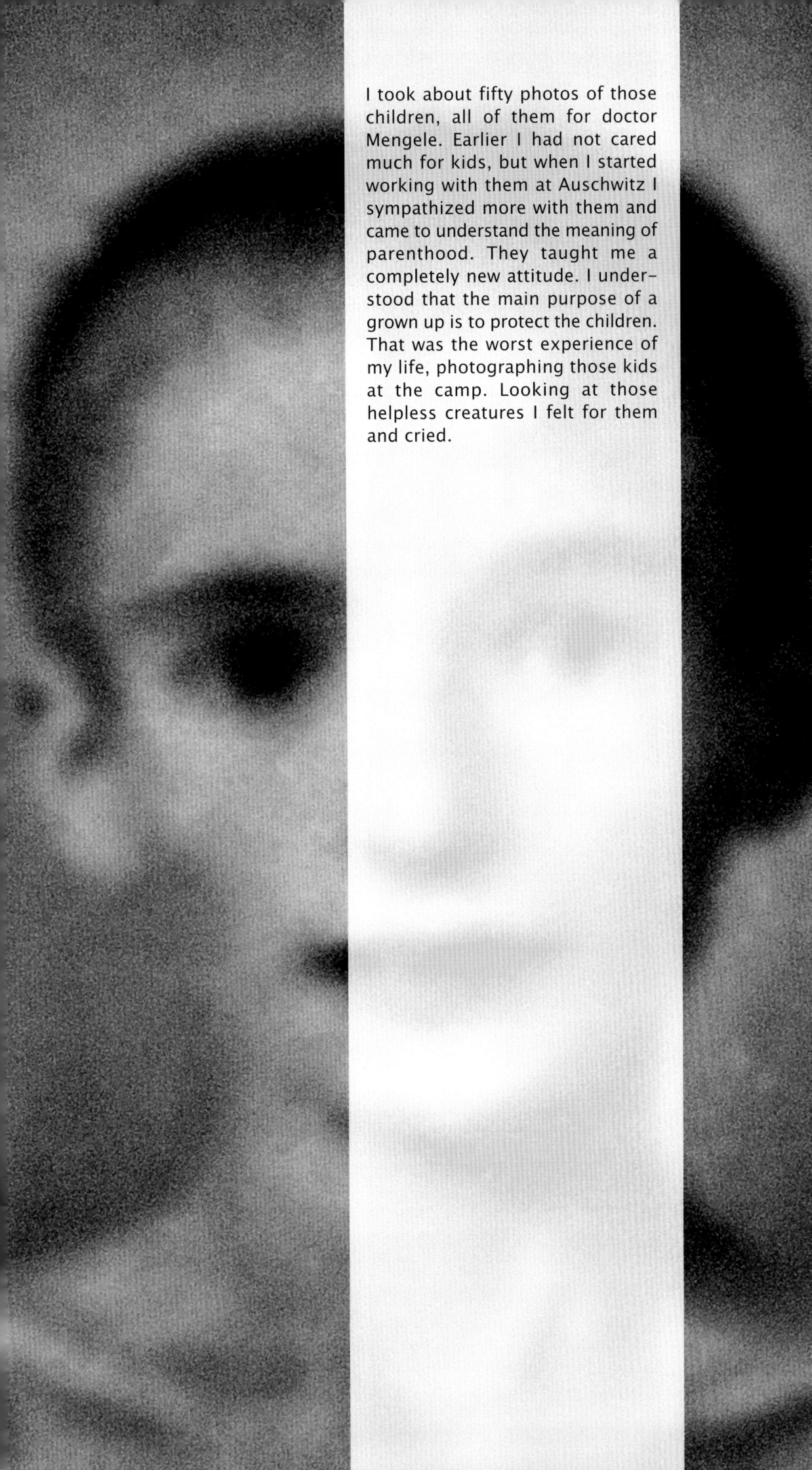

I took about fifty photos of those children, all of them for doctor Mengele. Earlier I had not cared much for kids, but when I started working with them at Auschwitz I sympathized more with them and came to understand the meaning of parenthood. They taught me a completely new attitude. I understood that the main purpose of a grown up is to protect the children. That was the worst experience of my life, photographing those kids at the camp. Looking at those helpless creatures I felt for them and cried.

The children from the ghetto in Łódź were liquidated in the cruelest way. This I heard about after the war.

"At the end of August 1943 the Łódź ghetto was liquidated in a manner similar to the ghetto in Zduńska Wola. Randomly selected people were transported to Auschwitz. The journey took place in enclosed boxcars, with 70 - 150 people in each one. Over 25% of the people died from thirst and exhaustion on the trains. Many suffocated. At the ramp in Auschwitz German officers implemented the segregation. Most of the women, all of the sick, and the children were gassed. Smaller children were loaded into trucks and hauled off to Brzezinka where they were dumped into pits, inside of which there were timbers that were drenched with kerosene and set aflame. The trucks backed up to the pits and dumped the living children into the flames."
SOURCE: Testimony no. 12[330]

I heard that Polish and Jewish female prisoners tried to rescue those children and that sometimes they were successful. They hid them away in the barracks. After liberation it turned out that thanks to these women a few dozen children survived.

"One example of such assistance was the rescue of a young mother and her child at Birkenau. Among one of my patients (I was a nurse) there was an eighteen-year old girl named Stefania Romik, from Zakopane. Secretly, she whispered to me that she was pregnant. This was around the end of 1942, when pregnant women and mothers with kids were being given lethal injections, or gassed. Young 'Funia', as I called her, received no care packages from outside and the man close to her heart, the father of her unborn child, had been executed at the infamous Wall of Death in Auschwitz. I decided to try to save her at all costs. During the selection (Sortierung) of the sick to the gas chambers I dressed 'Funia' in a large smock to hide her advanced pregnancy. I gave her a broom to simulate employment as a 'Putzer' (cleaner). On February 2nd 1943 she gave birth to a girl. (I remember that day because we named the newborn child Maria). During labor, amazingly, my 'Funia' did not make a peep, since she knew full well what would happen if she were discovered."
SOURCE: Janina Kałanczyńska's account[331]

"In the middle, for the full length of the barracks, ran a grooved heater made of bricks with furnaces on both ends. It was the only place for birthing, since there was no other even temporary facility for it. The heater would be turned on only a few times a year. (...) I had to provide the water for the woman in labor and her child. Bringing in a single bucket of water took 20 minutes."
SOURCE: Stanisława Leszczyńska's account[332]

"The little one needed to be washed, but in what? There was no water. And yet, even for that a solution was found. With another caregiver, Halusia Donarowska, we washed her at night in the so-called tisane, the herbal tea that was brought for the inmates in kettles. We even found some baby clothes for our little one. The Jewish women who sorted the clothes from the transports of the exterminated discovered that there had been babies in those transports and would give us the baby clothes in exchange for some soup. At each daily visit from the SS doctors and soldiers we were terrified that our little one would cry. But she never did!"
SOURCE: Janina Kałanczyńska's account[333]

330 Rajewski L., *Oświęcim...*, op. cit., p. 117-118
331 Auschwitz Museum [APMA-B, Zespół Wspomnienia, t. 95, k. 39]
332 Leszczyńska S., *Raport położnej z Oświęcimia*. In: *Przegląd Lekarski*, Nr 1, Kraków 1965, p. 104
333 Auschwitz Museum [APMA-B, Zespół Wspomnienia, t. 95, k. 40-41]

PHOTOGRAPHS OF CHILDREN

Naked Jewish women brought to gas chamber No. 5

Quite early we realized that the Germans were formulating a new method of efficient mass murder. It made the blood freeze in our veins…

In the fall of 1941[334] I saw SS men walking around the camp in gas masks. I did not know what it meant but I suspected the worst. In the event, they first ran an experiment in Block 1. They drove inside hundreds of Soviet POWs plus a sizable group, perhaps two or three hundred, from the camp hospital. Then they sealed all the doors and windows and tossed in canisters of Zyklon B.

"During my absence […] my deputy, Schutz–haftlagerführer Fritzsch, used gas for the killing, a preparation from prussic acid called Zyklon B that had previously been used at the camp for vermin control."
SOURCE: Pery Broad's account[335]

"Zyklon gas was used at the camp by Tesch and Stabenow Company to combat insects. That's why the administration always had numerous containers of it around."
SOURCE: Rudolf Höss's memoirs[336]

"On September 3rd [1941] at the order of the SS, the nurses brought about 250 sick prisoners from the hospital blocks and placed them in the bunkers of Block 11. Then about 600 Soviet POWs were also herded in."
SOURCE: Pery Broad's account[337]

"In the evening of that day a group of German military men came in, headed by some officers. The German delegation entered the room and, after putting on gas masks, threw around several cans of gas, observing its effect."
SOURCE: Witold Pilecki's report[338]

"On September 4th a Rapportführer with a gas mask on his head opened the door to the bunker and noted that some prisoners were still alive. So another dose of the gas was poured in and the door sealed again."
SOURCE: Rudolf Höss's memoirs[339]

"After my return Fritzsch reported the first procedure to me. They used that gas again on the next transport. The killing took place in the cells of Block 11."
SOURCE: Pery Broad's account[340]

The gas trial run was successful and after that the gas chambers in Birkenau started full operation. Everything changed after that. Human death seemed even more meaningless…

---

334 It happened on Sept. 3rd 1941
335 Oświęcim w oczach..., op. cit., p. 164
336 Höss R., Autobiografia, Warszawa 1989, p. 188
337 Oświęcim w oczach SS..., op. cit., p. 164–165
338 Cyra A., Ochotnik..., op. cit., p. 319

339 Oświęcim w oczach SS..., op. cit., p. 62
340 Ibidem, p. 164–165

Death was an inevitable stage of prison life that was all too easy to come by. An SS man could report a so-called insubordination or failure to carry out even the most stupid order, and send you to the Penal Company. If an SS man ordered you to move stones from one pile to another and back you had to do this, although it might seem pointless. Once we carried sand in a wheelbarrow from one end of the roll call square to another, poured it out; then other prisoners loaded it into their wheelbarrow and brought it back. The only point was to work us to death.

"Another time 50 prisoners were told to climb a frail tree. According to the order, they were supposed to get up into that little tree all together, which was physically impossible since the tree collapsed after the first few prisoners went up. That 'gymnastics' was a pretense for beating, first – for not being on the tree, and then for breaking it."
Source: Rudolf Höss's memoir[341]

We had to obey. If we didn't we got a licking. The more sadistic Germans, like Palitzsch or Plagge, would kill you for nothing. Everyone was terrorized by hunger, fatigue, beating, and the executions. The gassing operations were accompanied by—you might say—an eerie calm.

"Nobody screamed when the command was given to undress and fold their stuff. When all the prisoners were naked, they were marched inside, supposedly to bathe."
Source: Józef Paczyński's account[342]

"The challenge was how to fit 2000 people into one gas chamber. It took a full hour, not less. [...] It was impossible to move in there or to get out. It was just too crowded. They stood next to another, as if glued together, crammed like sardines."
Source: Josef Sackar's account[343]

"As you may know, the bigger the crowd the faster the gassing. The bodies [after death] would keep standing. The crowding was so extreme that they couldn't fall down."
Source: Henryk Mandelbaum's account[344]

"When there was no more room they picked up the small children and threw them onto the heads of the crowd. SS men kept beating people and shouting at them to squeeze inside even more tightly."
Source: Dov Pasikovic's account[345]

"At the end about thirty more big men were jammed into the chamber. [...]The men, beaten like cattle, passively jammed into the crowd, struggling to get inside to avoid the torture. It seems to me that many people died right there, even before they applied the gas."
Source: Shlomo Venezia's account[346]

"Inside the gas chamber family members would sometimes hug each other. [...] Yes, sometimes they held one another's hand."
Source: Josef Sackar's account[347]

"Then all the doors were closed tight and through a small window in the ceiling the gas was thrown in. The people locked inside could do nothing about it."
Source: Langfus Lejb's account[348]

"A moment later a horrible scream was heard. I thought it would burst through those thick walls. The Germans tried to drown it. They started up a couple of loud motors outside and someone drove around in a car but it didn't drown out the screaming."
Source: Józef Paczyński's account[349]

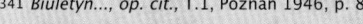

341 Biuletyn..., op. cit., T.1, Poznań 1946, p. 88
342 Paczyński J., Byłem fryzjerem..., op. cit.
343 Greif G., ...płakaliśmy bez łez..., L. Ulicka Trans., Warszawa-Oświęcim 2001, p. 252, 249
344 Bartosik I., Willma A., Ja z krematorium Auschwitz. Rozmowa z Henrykiem Mandelbaumem, byłym więźniem, członkiem Sonderkommando w KL Auschwitz, Warszawa 2009, p. 58
345 Setkiewicz P., Krematoria i komory gazowe Auschwitz, Oświęcim 2010, p. 87
346 Venezia S., Sonderkommando. W piekle komór gazowych, K. Szeżyńska-Maćkowiak Trans., Warszawa 2009, p. 82
347 Greif G., ...płakaliśmy..., op. cit., p. 264, 270
348 Langfus L., Rękopis. In: Zeszyty Oświęcimskie 14, Oświęcim 1972, p. 58
349 Paczyński J., Byłem fryzjerem..., op. cit.

KL Auschwitz. The first, temporary gas chamber created in 1941/1942

They coldly murdered the powerless crowd. The bodies were initially buried in the Birkenau meadows.

"We saw an enormous bonfire. The trucks were arriving filled to the brim. At the side of each truck stood the Sonderkommando prisoners. In pairs they took each body, by the arms and legs, and heaved it in a wide arc into the giant fire pit. When the body landed there was a huge cloud of sparks. The body flying through the flames looked like some fantastic, otherworldly bird."
SOURCE: Zofia Stępień-Bator's account[350]

„With more and more transports of Jews arriving from all over Europe, the Germans feverishly built new crematoriums and gas chambers in Birkenau."
SOURCE: Józef Paczyński's account[351]

"The equipment for this death factory was provided by specialized companies, such as Topf un Söhne from Erfurt, which Höss commissioned to build four gas chambers and the crematoriums in Birkenau, and also a firm from Dessau which produced Zyklon B."
SOURCE: Kazimierz Albin's account[352]

"After they expanded the camp into the whole of Birkenau in the spring of 1943, they constructed and started using the next four crematoriums. [...] The new ones had a total of 46 incineration chambers, each with the capacity of 3-5 bodies. The combustion of one load of the chamber took about half an hour and because it took one hour a day to clean the grills, the four crematoriums could burn about 12,000 bodies a day, or 4,380,000 a year.[353]"
SOURCE: Rudolf Höss's memoirs[354]

"In the large crematoriums from 1943-1944 the Sonderkommando crew varied in size. I think that the biggest manpower was used for the Hungarian transports. [...]. That kommando was made up of perhaps 900 prisoners."
SOURCE: Filip Müller's deposition[355]

It happened sometimes that even with the new crematorium they fell behind. Then they would burn the bodies en masse on pyres. The bottoms of them were wood, holding layers of corpses, over which gasoline or oil was poured and set aflame. The stench could be smelled even in Auschwitz, 3 kilometers away from Birkenau. It was a bittersweet smell. The smoke was a yellowish-black color. When the crematorium was burning at full capacity, the wind would carry an even more intense smell.
To photograph the cremating, Walter would usually go by himself or take Hofmann. The two of them photographed both at the ramp and at the crematorium.

"[Walter] was laconic and never talked about any subjects other than those connected to work and our kommando's operation. He was dark, slim, wiry and physically fit. He always came to work on his clattering motorcycle, which during the day he parked outside the office window. He liked military drills and would often come in with a small caliber sports rifle, which he used for the Wall of Death executions at Block 11. Walter was quite carefree about that activity. He acted like a sportsman fascinated with target shooting."
SOURCE: Janusz Karwacki's account[356]

"We had the impression that [Walter] was popular among his SS colleagues, as a martinet and a good pal. We knew from our observation that he took part in the reception of larger transports on the Birkenau ramp, and in their subsequent liquidation in the gas chambers.
Being of explosive temperament, Walter could be counted on to beat and kick any prisoner who crossed him. He considered it great fun and would later savor his feat. But we had never suspected him of taking part in the executions at block 11. Only in the summer of 1943, when about two hundred fifty prisoners were selected and marched to Block 11, did I notice that he went there too—without his camera. For a few hours there was

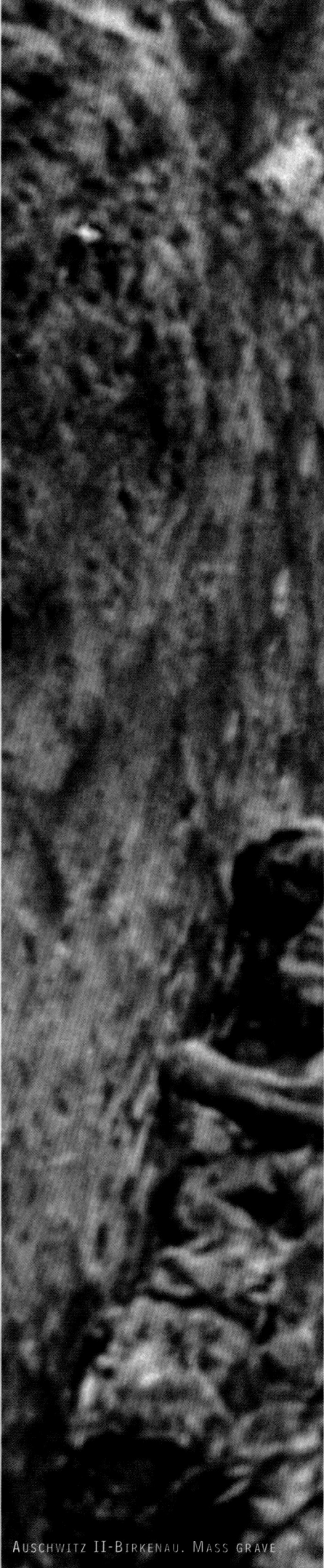

AUSCHWITZ II-BIRKENAU. MASS GRAVE

---

350 Auschwitz Museum [APMA-B, Zespół Oświadczenia, t. 68, k. 141]
351 Paczyński J., *Byłem fryzjerem..., op. cit.*
352 Auschwitz Museum [APMA-B, Zespół Wspomnienia, t. 149, k. 112-113]
353 According to the surviving documents from Topf and Söhne Erfurt, the company which designed and built the Birkenau crematoriums, the theoretical daily capacities were: for Crematorium I - 340 bodies, Crematoriums II and III - 1440 bodies, Crematoriums IV and V - 768 bodies each. The combined capacity was supposed to be at 4756 human bodies per 24 hours.
354 *Biuletyn..., op. cit.*, T.1, Poznań 1946, p. 125
355 Langbein H., *Auschwitz przed sądem..., op. cit.*, p. 101
356 Auschwitz Museum [APMA-B, Zespół Wspomnienia, t. 175, k. 61-62]

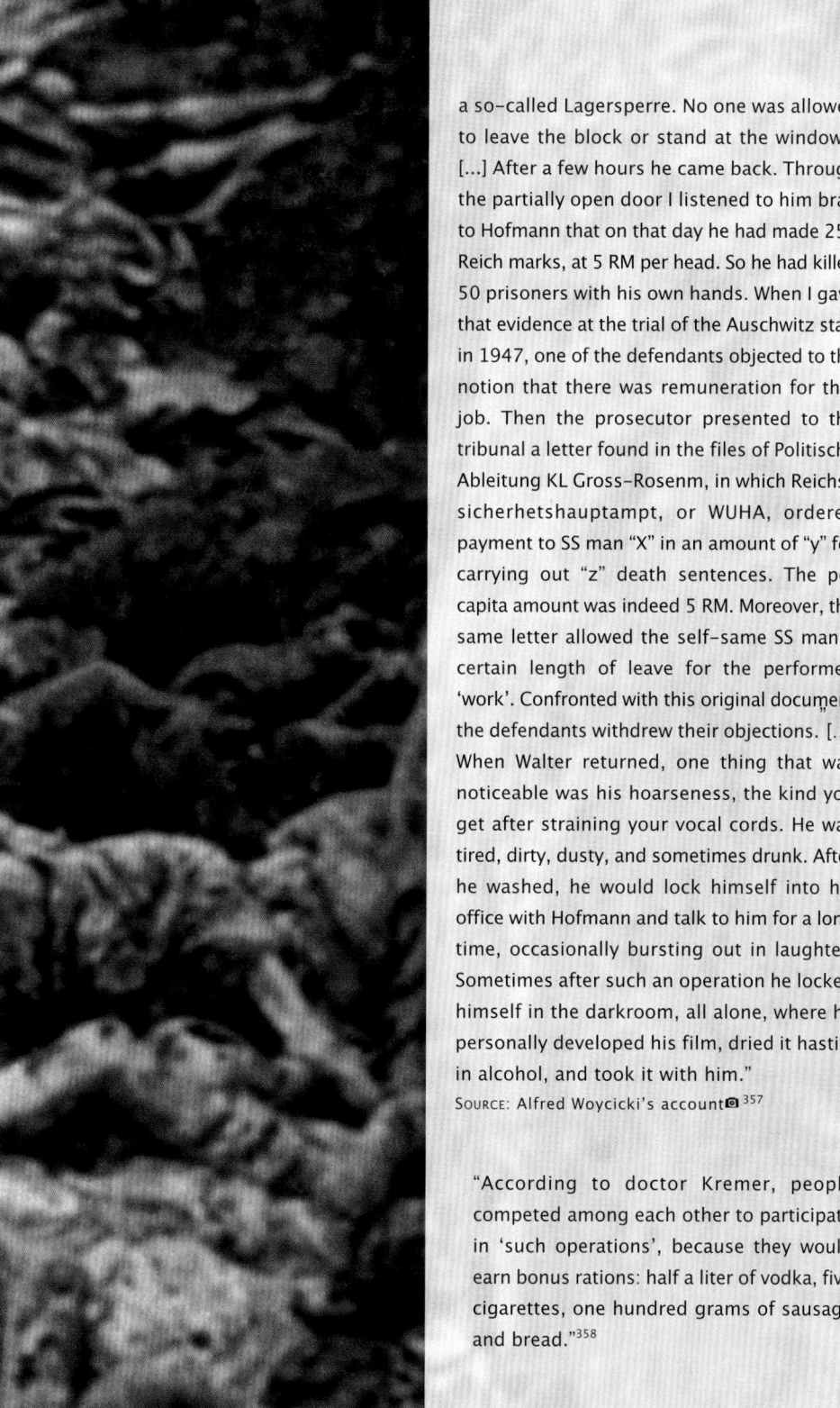

a so-called Lagersperre. No one was allowed to leave the block or stand at the windows. [...] After a few hours he came back. Through the partially open door I listened to him brag to Hofmann that on that day he had made 250 Reich marks, at 5 RM per head. So he had killed 50 prisoners with his own hands. When I gave that evidence at the trial of the Auschwitz staff in 1947, one of the defendants objected to the notion that there was remuneration for that job. Then the prosecutor presented to the tribunal a letter found in the files of Politische Ableitung KL Gross-Rosenm, in which Reichs-sicherhetshauptampt, or WUHA, ordered payment to SS man "X" in an amount of "y" for carrying out "z" death sentences. The per capita amount was indeed 5 RM. Moreover, the same letter allowed the self-same SS man a certain length of leave for the performed 'work'. Confronted with this original document the defendants withdrew their objections. [...] When Walter returned, one thing that was noticeable was his hoarseness, the kind you get after straining your vocal cords. He was tired, dirty, dusty, and sometimes drunk. After he washed, he would lock himself into his office with Hofmann and talk to him for a long time, occasionally bursting out in laughter. Sometimes after such an operation he locked himself in the darkroom, all alone, where he personally developed his film, dried it hastily in alcohol, and took it with him."
SOURCE: Alfred Woycicki's account [357]

"According to doctor Kremer, people competed among each other to participate in 'such operations', because they would earn bonus rations: half a liter of vodka, five cigarettes, one hundred grams of sausage and bread."[358]

[357] Auschwitz Museum [APMA-B, Zespół Oświadczenia, t. 9, k. 1315-1316]
[358] Struk J.,*Holocaust...*, op. cit., p. 154

I saw the pictures from the executions only when they gave them to me to work on.

Some pictures from the ramp that Walter took and that I processed in our darkroom can be found in Lili Jacob's[359] album. They show the unloading of the cars with newly arriving prisoners; the tossing of suitcases, bags and other personal items; other prisoners sorting those things at the camp warehouses, the so-called "Kanada"; the selections at the ramp in Birkenau; the passage to the gas chambers; whole families awaiting extermination in the woods next to the crematorium; and the entrance to the crematorium.

One day Hofmann showed me a picture of an older woman taken at the moment when the gas chamber was opened and she saw the unimaginable sight of strangely intertwined corpses. The face of the woman expressed horror and excruciating pain. I had never seen an expressionanything like it. I will never forget it.

"Erkennungsdienst developed negatives (over 200 pictures) taken by SS-hauptscharführer Walter and SS-Unterscharführer Hofmann. The photos were taken at the train ramp in Birkenau and show scenes of the arrival of the deportees, exiting from the cars, segregation according to gender, selection by SS-Ärzte (SS doctors) and SDG and the accompanying SS men, loading of the baggage onto trucks, leading people to the men's or women's camp, the wait before the gas chamber in crematorium V, male and female prisoner's work at sorting of the stolen property at "Kanada I" (Auschwitz) and II (BII) Birkenau. The photographs were taken from many view points, including from the main watchtower in Birkenau (from above). Analysis of the structures visible in the background (smokestacks of crematorium II and III, the roads and ditches in construction, and the barracks), suggests that the pictures were shot in mid-1944 and most probably show Jews from Hungary (as inferred from

[359] The album saved by Lili Jacob contains 189 pictures taken by the SS-men of Auschwitz-Birkenau in the spring of 1944.

the style of clothes and baggage. The variety of viewpoints and their number justify the hypothesis that they could not have been taken on a single day. It is hard to determine what the reason for permitting them to be taken was, and who commissioned them. Because the recovered collection was placed in an album, the first pages of which told (in handwritten capital characters) the history of Auschwitz (photos of sub-camps, visits of SS officials)—the whole thing suggests that it was some kind of souvenir album. The lettering in the album was made by the former prisoner-artist Tadeusz Myszkowski."[360]

---

[360] Smoleń K., "Erkennungsdienst". In: *Fotografie...*, op. cit., p. 21-22

When everything was over the Sonderkommando groups stripped the bodies of anything of value that could be found on them—gold or silver in their teeth and hair. Later they even found uses for the ashes. All the findings were meticulously segregated.

"In the archives of the Auschwitz Museum there are reports of pulling teeth made of gold and other precious metals from the bodies of deceased prisoners. The reports are very detailed. They contained the prisoner's number, often his name and surname, and especially the dental classification of the removed teeth. [...] In 1944, as determined by the Resistance activists, Auschwitz yielded monthly 10-12 kilograms of gold from the teeth of the victims of extermination. To clean them of the remains of bone and muscle they were soaked in hydrochloric acid. Later they were melted into bars weighing from 0.5 to 1 kilogram and sometimes into discs of 140 grams. The gold processed in this way was then transferred to the dental service and the 3rd Reich Bank.

The prisoners' hair also had monetary value: 0.5 RM per kilogram in 1943. This included both the hair shaven upon the prisoners' arrival at the camp (it had to be at least 5 centimeter long to be of use) and the hair cut off from the bodies of the gassed Jewish women. The hair was disinfected and then dried on the floors heated by the crematorium furnaces. Packed into paper bags it was then given away to private companies for further use. It was valuable, for instance, in making the soles of special stockings used by submarine crews. In January 1945, after the liberation of the camp, 7 tons of human hair was discovered. Estimating the weight of one person's hair at about 50 g, the discovered hair came from 140,000 victims."

"The bones and ashes of the victims also had profitable uses. In 1943-44 over 100,000 tons of bone aggregate was sent by Auschwitz authorities to 'Strem', a company making fertilizers. The Sonderkommando was in charge of the sorting out of body parts that could profitably be used. 'They worked in a factory-like way, in day and night shifts. Bonuses and penalties were given, just like in a regular work place. Only the materials were different. People. Human bodies and ashes', writes Israeli historian Gideon Greif."[361]

Open resistance in the gas chambers was extremely rare and was then excitedly discussed by the other prisoners.

"An unbelievable thing happened. On the night of the liquidation of one of numerous transports. Oberscharführer Schillinger[362], the Rapportführer from the men's camp in Birkenau and one of the most hated and cruel SS men, got shot. The news spread with lightning speed all over the camp, creating widespread joy. [...] Schillinger, ever dutiful, was on the ramp assisting at the reception of the night transport of Jews, in the company of his comrade, Hauptscharführer Emmerich[363]. Both of them drunk, they accompanied the transport all the way to the door of the crematorium. They even went into the changing room, either in hope of easy loot or to satisfy their sadistic instincts at the expense of frightened, vulnerable, stripped women about to die an excruciating death. The latter version seemed most likely given Schillinger's reputation, and especially since he was drunk. His attention was drawn to one of the young and reportedly very beautiful women who refused to undress in the presence of SS men. Enraged, Schillinger walked up to the woman and attempted to tear off her bra."

SOURCE: Wiesław Kielar's account[364]

"Schillinger turned around and yelled... "No, take everything off!" and pointed his gun at her brassiere. So the woman took it off and threw it at his face, but instead it struck his shoulder. The gun dropped on the floor. The woman grabbed it, pointed it at Schillinger and shot him. Bedlam broke out in the undressing room. The Germans feared that the woman would start shooting at them too, so they drove all the people outside and shot them. Only after that did they allow the Sonderkommando prisoners to return to the undressing room. On the floor next to Schillinger's body was the body of that woman. At the news of Schillinger's death the whole camp went berserk with joy. (...) There were rumors that [the woman] had been an actress, but we never found out who she was."[365]

SOURCE: Szlomo Dragon's account[366]

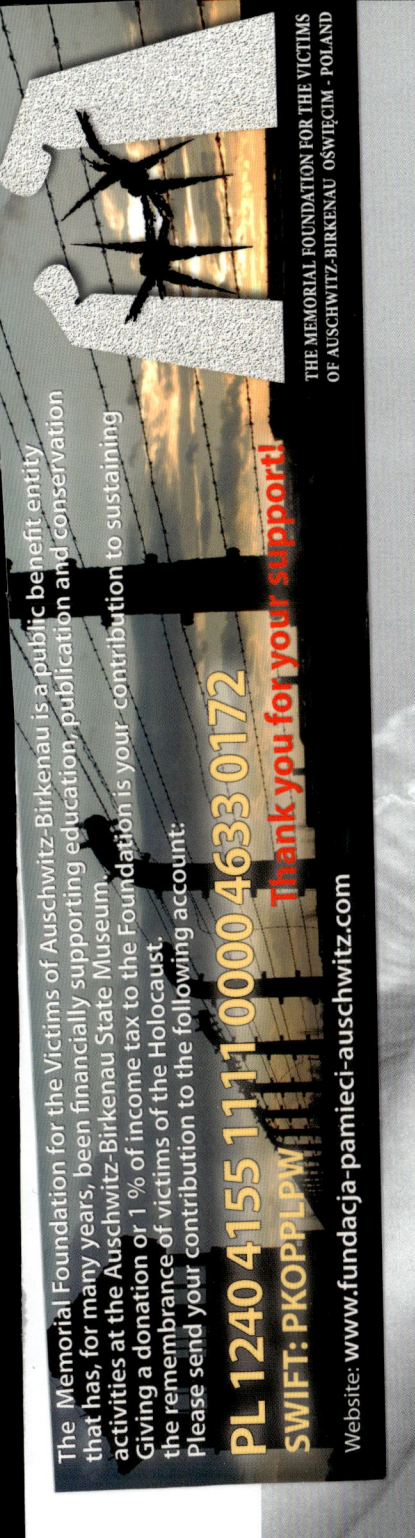

Those stories were moving, but there were not many of them. There were practically no witnesses of such events, since all who were present would die. I never heard of anyone surviving the gas chamber.[367]

---

361 Strzelecki A., *Kości i popioły*. In: *Auschwitz 1940--1950...*, *op. cit.*, p. 304

362 Josef Hermann Schillinger (SS-Unterscharführer), b. Jan. 21st 1908 in Oberrimsigen, cooper. In the active duty in the SS since Sept. 1st 1939. On March 3rd 1941 transferred to KL Auschwitz and assigned to Department III – the camp Head Office. Since April 25th 1943 a reporting NCO in MKL (men's camp) in KL Auschwitz II–Birkenau. More → BIOGRAPHIES

363 Wilhelm Emmerich (SS-Oberscharführer), b. Feb. 7th 1916 in Tiefenbach. Came to KL Auschwitz in 1940 from KL Sachsenhausen. Member of Department IIIa, including as deputy of the camp Labor Deployment office. More → BIOGRAPHIES

364 Kielar W., *Dzieła...*, *op. cit.*, p. 247

365 The actress was reportedly Franciszka Mann, b. Feb. 4th 1917, and the event probably took place on October 23rd 1943. Ms Mann was considered a collaborator of Group 13, also known as the Jewish Gestapo, which operated in the Warsaw Ghetto. In spite of her collaboration the actress is usually mentioned in the context of her heroic comportment in Auschwitz. Some sources describing the event mention also Lola Horowitz, but there is no likelihood of two identical happenings. Probably it was the same person and the other name was added by a misinformed witness. The situation occurred during the extermination of 1800 Polish Jews brought in from the Bergen-Belsen camp. The Warsaw Gestapo, at a high fee, promised to facilitate their departure to South America. The same woman shot also SS-Untrscharführer Wilhelm Emmerich. Enraged women seriously wounded a few other SS men.

366 Greif G., *...płakaliśmy...*, *op. cit.*, p. 149–150, 231

367 Dr. Nyiszli in his memoirs described one such case: „The girl has a violent coughing fit and spits out a thick, phlegmy liquid from her lungs. The little one opens her eyes and stares at the ceiling with a deadly gaze. (...) Her breathing becomes deeper. The lungs, ravaged by the gas gasp for air. After the injections her pulse becomes stronger. I wait patiently [...] knowing that in a few minutes she will regain consciousness. This is exactly what happens. Her delicate face regains color, her eyes become present. She looks at me in utter amazement. She closes her eyes, not yet knowing what has happened. [...] Her moves become more energetic. She raises her arms, head, looks around, some twitches cross her face. She catches my by the collar and holding tight tries hard to sit up. I want to lay her down, but she persists in her efforts. It is a serious nervous shock. Slowly she calms down, lies there exhausted. Huge tears sparkle in her eyes, but she doesn't cry. She starts to answer my questions. I don't want to torment her, I don't ask much. I find out that she is sixteen and that she came with her parents in one of the Hungarian transports. [...] Fifteen minutes later the girl was taken out, or more precisely carried out to the hallway and shot through the back of her head."
In spite of Nyiszli's efforts to save the girl's life, SS man Muhsfeldt decided to shoot her. Because she could have told "anybody she met about all she went through, where she was and what she saw."
SOURCE: M. Nyiszli, *Pracownia...*, *op. cit.*, p. 91–94

FRANCISZKA MANN, DANCER

ILLEGAL PHOTOGRAPHS

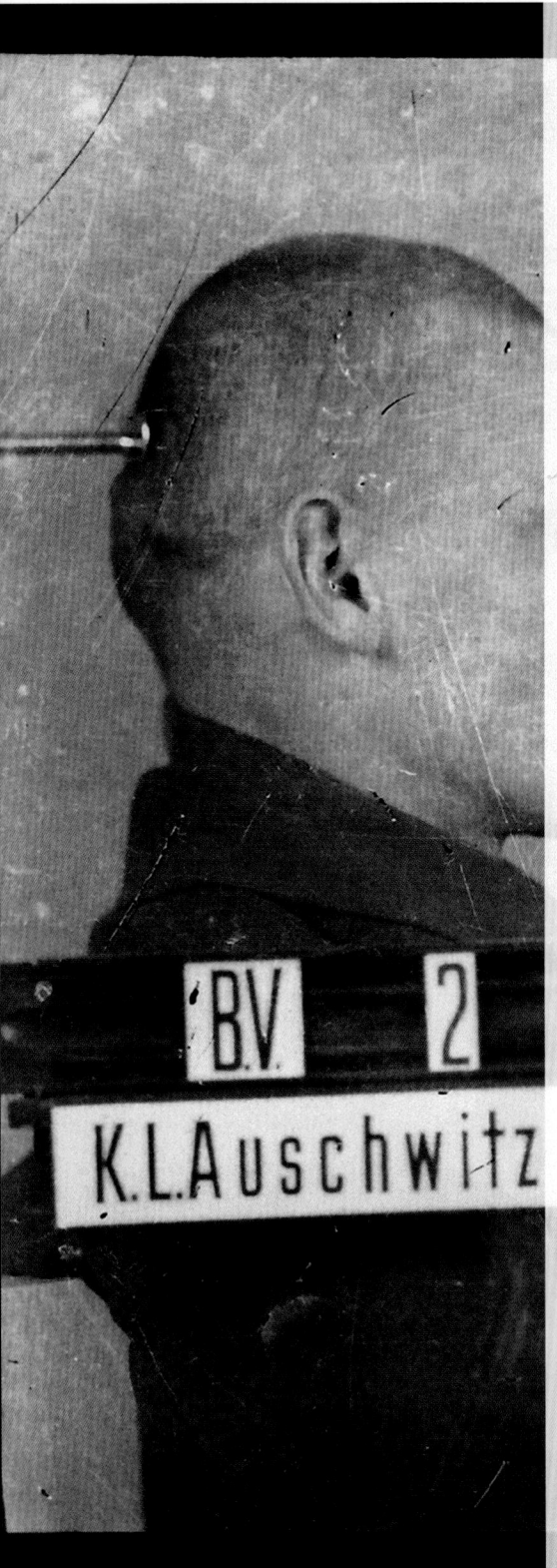

At the end of 1942, shortly before New Year's Eve, I made a new Polish friend, Mietek Januszewski,[368] – who was the deputy of Otto Küsel[369], prisoner no 2, chief of the employment office. One day that Pole came to me and said, "Listen. Otto Küsel needs a picture taken. He will have the permit."

The German prisoners would sometimes get a special permission from Headquarters to make a private ID photo, since at that time they might possibly get released to the Wehrmacht or Waffen SS forces of General Dirlevanger. Mostly criminals were recruited that way.

With Otto it was a different story. He was planning an escape and needed an ID photo for his fake papers. The Erkennungsdienst had a civilian jacket (it was official), which was sporadically used when the SS demanded it. I took a few pictures of Otto, but they were no good because the background was too dark. So he asked for another one with a light backdrop and with the possibility to draw something on the photo, such as a uniform. He mentioned that he was planning to flee. A graphic artist wanted to go with him—Baraś[370]

—but that was not his real name. It was he who painted a very convincing uniform on Otto's photograph. They found somewhere an empty ID pass, filled it out and then covered it with varnish in order to disguise the paint. Four of them flew the coop: Otto, Mietek Januszewski, Baraś and the dentist Kuczbara[371].

They took a horse and cart. Inside the horse cart Otto Küsel had

hidden an SS uniform and the good, fake ID, pretending to take the others to work.³⁷²

They left Auschwitz, went off the road, changed and fled. They went to Krakow and then got through to Warsaw.

"Otto took them out with a wagon, in an armoire, since he was not subject to SS inspection at the postenketta. He was known by the man who was working at that gate. Near Krakow, after they slept in a barn, he woke up and discovered that Mietek and Kuczbara had already gone. They left him all alone, with only a Polish address for a hiding place near Warsaw in Wilanów, and part of the money. All the dollars, in the amount of about 4,000 in cash and 800 in gold were taken. In that precarious situation he bought a violin with a case and pretended to be a deaf person on his way to Warsaw. He found the safe house of a professor who had been Surzycki's friend, and remained there until his re-arrest about 8 months later."
SOURCE: Edward Kiczmachowski's account³⁷³

One day in the summer of '44, one month into the Warsaw Uprising, I saw Otto Küsel escorted back to the the bunker as a prisoner. They had caught him in some restaurant. I learned that some that a Polish woman—an informer—had turned him in.

"The traitor was a Polish woman, who knew about his situation and whom he asked to find Kuczbara, who at the time was in Warsaw and didn't make much effort to stay hidden. He partied in clubs, wore German clothing—tall boots, leather jacket, hat—so he looked like a Gestapo man. Otto found out about his behavior through that Pole. That woman found Kuczbara in Warsaw and told him where Otto was living and suggested they meet. Three days later the Gestapo arrested Otto and the family which had sheltered him. […]."
SOURCE: Edward Kiczmachowski's account³⁷⁴

Unfortunately, the discarded clothes had been found and with them the forged ID with Otto's picture. There was a huge scandal. Grabner, the chief of Politische Abteilung, stormed into Erkennungsdienst and threatened, that if it was proved that the picture was made in our studio, he would deal with us appropriately.

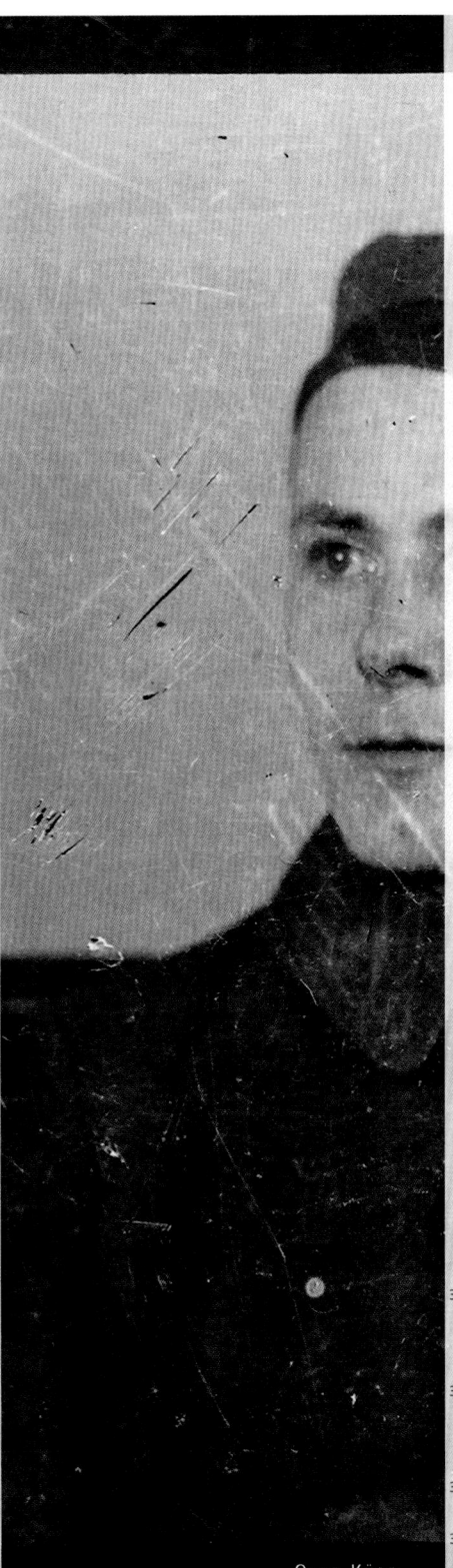

OTTO KÜSEL

It frightened me to the bone. If they started interrogating Otto about how on earth he had escaped, he would break and give us away. Walter became furious and repeated Grabner's threats, adding that we would all be executed. I was doubly scared, as it had been my work. Fortunately, I had friends at the Penal Block and learned that Otto was not as strictly isolated as Politische Ableitung was claiming. If there was a way to deliver a message to Otto, then there was some hope of clearing me from suspicion.

The Kupiec³⁷⁵ brothers worked there and I told them that I had to speak with Küsel. They helped me to see him while he was heading to the bath. I managed to whisper to him, "The picture was taken by kapo Malz. He's already dead."

Otto understood and nodded.

That version was completely believable, because Malz was the kapo who was in charge of Erkennungsdienst and he could have made the pictures for the fugitive. It was also likely, that no witness could have confirmed or denied that version. Later they took Otto in a penal transport to Flossenbürg. It was a very tough camp, in Bavaria, Upper Palatintinate, near Weiden, which was then almost at the Czechoslovak border. They worked in the quarry there. He was fortunate enough to survive the war.

368 Mieczysław Januszewski (Inmate No. 711), b. July 1ˢᵗ 1918 in Łódź. Brought to Kl Auschwitz on June 14ᵗʰ 1940 in the Krakow-Tarnów transport. More → BIOGRAPHIES

369 Otto Küsel (Inmate No.2), b. May 16ᵗʰ 1909 in Berlin. Came to KL Auschwitz in the May 20th 1940 transport of prisoners selected by Palitzsch in KL Sachsenhausen. More → BIOGRAPHIES

370 Jan Baraś-Komski (Inmate No. 4308), b. Feb. 3ʳᵈ 1915 in Bircza, artist. More → BIOGRAPHIES

371 Bolesław Kuczbara (Inmate No. 4308), b. Nov. 26ᵗʰ 1911, dentist. Brought to Kl Auschwitz on July 14ᵗʰ 1940 in the Warsaw transport. More → BIOGRAPHIES

372 Otto Küsel's escape took place on December 29ᵗʰ 1942

373 Auschwitz Museum [APMA-B, Zespół Oświadczenia, t. 111, k. 106]

374 *Ibidem*, t.111, k. 107

375 The Kupiec brothers came to Auschwitz in Krakow--Tarnów transports, four of them on June 20ᵗʰ 1940, and the youngest one on October 8ᵗʰ 1940. More → BIOGRAPHIES

At the end of 1943 I had a strong feeling that I should myself try to pass documentation of the Nazi crimes to someone outside. I tried to sneak out pictures of the SS men, among others, along with copies of Staś Trałka's[376] caricatures. Trałka was a prisoner from the first Polish transport who had drawn caricatures of members of our kommando. Unfortunately, each time we tried it, the courier was forced to destroy them to avoid the inspection on the train. It made no sense to risk it. But we did manage to send the caricatures of Commandant.

While I was still unable to send out illegal correspondence, I was able to write regular camp letters in German, according to a strict camp formula, to let them know I was well. The correspondence was censored by the Germans and sometimes even faked, in order to mask their real camp activities.

When I wanted to communicate something important, I added sentences in a kind of code. For instance, when my mother's brother—my uncle—died, I wrote at the bottom: "Uncle Staszek went to see uncle Wiktor and they are together." Uncle Wiktor had died of pneumonia a few years earlier, so my mom immediately understood what had happened to her other brother.

When I was able to write illegally, I wrote to her openly that Staszek died. But I did not say he had been gassed, because if such a letter was captured I would have had huge problems. If he died, he died…

"Prisoners' correspondence was going directly through the block clerks' office. The block writing clerks delivered the letters. Then they were packed and taken to the checkpoint, where they were censored by SS men (Zensurstelle). All the incoming correspondence addressed to the prisoners was also censored. It was only after that procedure that the letters got to the camp secretariat, where they were sorted according to the blocks and handed to the block writers, who then delivered them to the addressees. Letters addressed to deceased prisoners weree returned to the secretariat, where they were destroyed. It was forbidden to return them to the sender."[377]

I sent my parents a total of 54 legal letters from the camp. My mother preserved all of them meticulously for many years after the war. Unfortunately, my brother once took them out and sold them for 5 dollars apiece. He traded my camp letters for 270 dollars. I was mad at him, but I also understood. In PRL [Polish People's Republic] times, 270 dollars was a fortune.

During my whole time at the camp

I TOOK ONLY ONE UNAUTHORIZED, PRIVATE PHOTO TO KEEP FOR MYSELF.

It was in Birkenau in the hospital, where a beautiful girl worked for doctor Mengele as a nurse—Basia she was called, although her real name was Anna Tytoniak[378].

I went there to shoot pictures for Dr. Wirths, and I took the opportunity to take one clandestine photo of her. Then, in greatest secrecy, I developed it. When the war ended, all excited I gave her the copy, but she looked at it and said she didn't like herself in that picture. Then she tore it to pieces.

---

376 Stanisław Trałka (Inmate No. 660), b. July 14th 1921 in Wąbrzeźno. Brought to KL Auschwitz on June 14th 1940 in the Krakow–Tarnów transport. More → BIOGRAPHIES

377 Paczuła T., *Izby Pisarskie w KL Auschwitz*. In: *Księgi zgonów…, op. cit.*, p. 3

378 Anna Tytoniak (Inmate No. 6866), b. Jan. 4th 1920 in Jasło. Brought to KL Auschwitz on April 27th 1942 from Tarnów prison, from Nov. 1942 she work in the office of the women's hospital. At the camp known as Barbara Stefańska. More → BIOGRAPHIES

Leo für Dich liebe Luise die besten Grüße
u. Wünsche. Schade, dass ich von Nyna
u. Jacus keine Nachricht erhalte. Freue
mich, dass beide gesund sind. Besondere
Wünsche u. Grüße für Nyna zu ihrem Namenstag.
Für Frau Schirm u. allen Bekannten u. Verwandten
alles beste u. Gesundheit. Dich liebe Luise
küsse ich herzlichst u. danke für alles, bleibe
gesund u. schreibe auf jeden meinen Brief.
Für Tadek u. Frau ein gutes Neues Jahr. Dein Franz

PHOTOGRAPHS USED IN FORGING

Almost from the very beginning the Germans forged documents. For instance, they did not register those who were executed as dead but rather, as transferred. We knew when the prisoners were escorted out and you could see about how many of them there were. Later, when we got the lists of the deceased, everything became clear to us.

Cause of death was picked arbitrarily. Only sometimes did they check what had been written in the files when the prisoner arrived at the camp. If he happened to have a history of a serious disease, then that was entered as the cause of death. But I heard that it was mostly left to the fancy of the people filling the forms.

"My job consisted in filling out *Totenmeldungen*. The prisoner's disease description applied also to those who had been murdered at the camp. Executed by shooting, injected, gassed. Every deceased had to have his disease history, fictitious of course. That was what the camp authorities demanded and that's what I was in charge of. Initially, for the prisoners who were shot I wrote '*herzschlag*', but later I concluded that there would be too many of those 'heart attacks', which would reflect badly on me if Politische took notice. So I wrote *Totenmeldungen* in the way they wanted: if someone was shot I would put in: 'diarrhea', if they had diarrhea I wrote 'heart attack', if one got injected – 'nephritis', etc.".
SOURCE: Wiesław Kielar's memoirs
(Kielar W., Dzieła..., op. cit., s. 213)

The involvement of our kommando in the forgery consisted at first of copying various German documents for the SS men, mostly IDs, military service books and birth certificates.

Sometimes after making copies there were remaining bad prints or other rejects. The Germans didn't let us throw them out in the trash; we had to burn them.

"Our work was strictly supervised. Trial copies had to be destroyed and the carefully numbered prints were handed to Walter."
SOURCE: Tadeusz Krzysica's account [379]

BANK NOTES

A few times I noticed Alfred Woycicki pulling something out of

the trash, so I let him know that I could make him decent quality prints. With that one sentence I started cooperation with the camp resistance movement. From then on I made illegal photographs and their copies were smuggled to the Polish underground.

"Although all the photographs made in Erkennungsdienst were strictly confidential and Grabner frequently warned the prisoners that if they were to take anything out of the studio they would be shot, the workers smuggled materials outside through the camp resistance movement. Alfred Woycicki, who was arrested on February 18th 1942 for resistance activity in Krakow, at the camp continued to work for the Underground. Because of his fluent German he looked after the office paperwork and the photographic files, and regularly passed rejected prints or documents to the camp's resistance movement. Brasse was also involved in the preparation of false IDs for prisoners trying to escape. Also Myszkowski admitted to having been a member of, as he called it, 'a secret organization.'"[380]

After that memorable exchange with Alfred Woycicki I regularly made decent copies of various German documents. I gave them to Woycicki or Dr. Kłodziński. Dr. Kłodziński was from Krakow and worked as a nurse in Block 20. He was one of the few that passed information to the Home Army in Krakow. He would often meet with me, asking about the prisoners I photographed. I knew it was conspiracy, but I had great mutual trust in Alfred, and Dr. Kłodziński was my great friend. For illegal activity you could end up in the yard of Block 11, at the Wall of Death. Even for sending smuggled letters you would get the Penal Company, where they finished off a man in two-three weeks.

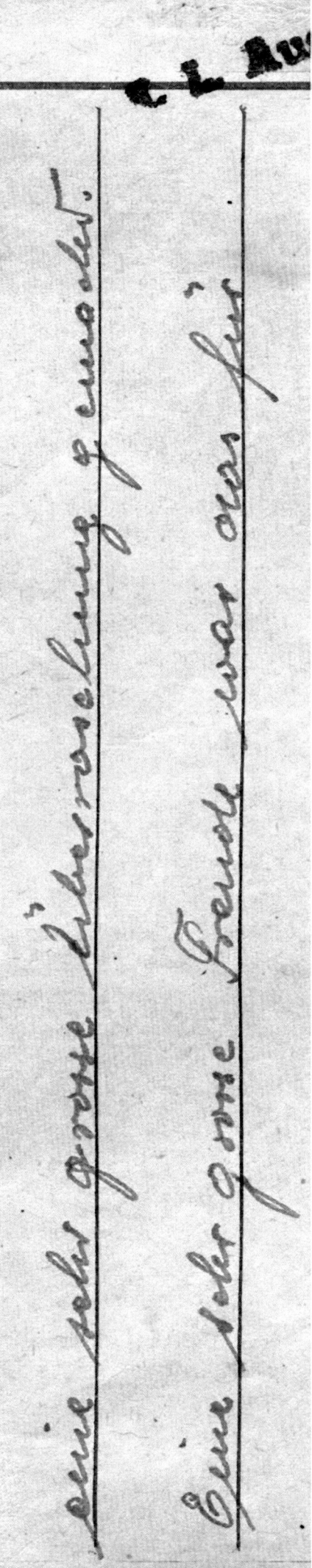

I realized I was risking my life, but it was too late. I was already into it. Initially I did just small things, later more serious ones. I still don't know how they were getting them out of the camp.

"THE LESS YOU KNOW, THE BETTER."
I thought.

"I personally gave the letters and the photograph to colleague Światłoch. He, on the other hand, somehow arranged with the Effektenkammer prisoners to take dirty laundry to the cleaners in Bielsko, where he would meet with his sister, to whom he handed the illegal packages."
SOURCE: Bronisław Jureczek's account [381]

379 Auschwitz Museum [APMA-B, Zespół Oświadczenia, t. 67, k. 118]
380 Struk J., *Holocaust...*, *op. cit.*, p. 153
381 Auschwitz Museum [APMA-B, Zespół Oświadczenia, t. 19, k. 30]

One day in 1944 my boss Walter brought me an underground paper, called "The Guardsman" (Gwardzista); for reproducing. From then on the Germans told me to reproduce falsified copies of that paper. On top of of a few original articles, they printed forged material in "Gwardzista" at the camp printing shop and distributed it in Silesia. A copy of that false left-wing leaflet was then recopied and circulated by the Germans. The effect of that provocation was the arrest of a very important PPR[382] activist, secretary of the local PPR unit from Sosnowiec or thereabouts. The arrested man was brought to KL Auschwitz, where he was interrogated personally by SS man Boger[383], a famous butcher. Those interrogations involved the most sophisticated torture techniques. I saw the effect with my own eyes, as my boss odered the PPR activist to be photographed at Erkennungsdienst. He was a man of middle height and stocky build. His buttocks were cut so badly that he could not sit for the picture.

In 1944 I took part in the "Bernhard" operation, a big effort at forging the Allies' currencies.

"The idea to forge bank notes reportedly came to the mind of SS man Naujocks.
[...] About that time Naujocks came across a book about the forgers in Hungary after WWI. The author mentioned, among other things, the counterfeiting of the first five-hundred Czechoslovak korona notes. The main part of the book was devoted to the forgery of one-thousand French frank notes.
[...] Naujocks was obviously interested in the book and he began to wonder if it was possible to use this method to finance Nazi intelligence abroad. So he persuaded his boss Heudrich to order a written paper on the history of counterfeiting 1000 FF bills with all the circumstances and particulars of that case. After he studied that, Naujocks became convinced that forging foreign currency could be successful, especially in the manufacturing of fake British pounds, which were then printed with black ink on white paper, with no background. He expected the successful counterfeits to be used as payments for spies and also for making purchases abroad. One could anticipate that the fake pounds in circulation would cause inflation in England and also erosion of trust in the British currency."
Source: Oskar Skála's memoirs[384]

Operation "Bernhard" was the code name of a secret German program, developed during WWII to destabilize the British economy by introducing into the British market a certain amount of counterfeit bills of 5, 10, 20 and 50 pounds sterling, face value.[385]

"Today it is known that from 1942 until the end of the war Germans circulated forged bills worth about 135 million pounds, which was equivalent to the whole gold reserve of the Bank of England."[386]

---

[382] PPR – Polish Workers' Party

[383] Wilhelm Friedrich Boger (SS-Oberscharführer), b. Dec. 19th 1906 in Stuttgart-Zuffenhausen; secretary at the political police. In Auschwitz since 1942, sentry. Later, beginning in 1942, in Department II, where he was the head of the investigative division.
More → Biographies

[384] Skála O., *Komando Fałszerzy*, Warszawa 1969, p. 21, 24-25

[385] The Germans carried out such operations mainly in KL Sachsenhausen.. Apart from Wilhelm Brasse's account there is no information of such activities in KL Auschwitz

[386] Wołkoński J. *Operacja Bernhard*, (audiobook), Warszawa 2006

One day Walter brought an epidiascope and a one dollar bill with President Washington on it and the words: "In God we trust." He had been ordered by the SS to make a perfect counterfeit of a dollar, which would be indistinguishable from the original. He told me to make the best copy of the note I could. This job was extremely important to him. He even brought in another prisoner, a Jew by the name of Haas. In time we got to know him a little better. Leon Haas[387] was a painter who did portraits and had studied at the German Academy of Fine Arts. For a few years he lived in Berlin, where he worked in a graphic design studio. So he spoke excellent German.

In 1926 Haas, then 26 years old, found himself in the Czech town of Opava and began to work for an advertising firm. He married a beautiful woman named Sophie and half of the town envied him that marriage. In time he became a portrait artist, renowned in Opava and environs. After the pogrom of Jews in that town in 1937, he and his wife moved to Ostrava to live with her parents. In 1942 Leon Haas was put into the Jewish ghetto in Terezin (Theresienstadt). He documented life in the ghetto in his drawings. In 1942 he was brought into KL Auschwitz and placed in Block 24. He said his "wife left in a car." Which I understood meant she went to the gas.

In Auschwitz Haas became the draftsman for Mengele. At his command he drew portraits of selected prisoners. This is how he made it to our atelier.

[387] Leo Haas (Inmate No. 199885) b. 1901 in Opava in 1901, artist. Arrested by the Gestapo in August 1942 and included in the transport to Terezin at the end of September 1942. Arrived in Auschwitz on Oct. 28th 1942 and was classified as a political prisoner. More → BIOGRAPHIES

[388] In fact the models for Salomon Sorowitsch - main character in „The Counterfeiters" – were Salomon Smolianoff and Adolf Burger, whose memoires were adapted for the movie. Smolianoff was a Russian Jew who even before the war was renowned for his talent in forgery of bank notes.

In our studio he did other things. Probably while in Auschwitz he was working on the top secret counterfeit operation, which he developed later on a larger scale in Sachsenhausen. I heard that he became the model for Salomon Sorowitsch[388], the main character in the movie "Counterfeiters".

I was the one who helped him in our lab.

WE BOTH APPLIED OURSELVES TO MAKING THE IMITATION DOLLAR BILL.

I took the photos, and then he made detailed drawings of parts of the bill in 20x magnification. He did it in three colors: black, green and red. It was all about making the negative, and I was the one who was an expert at that.

We asked for additional materials. We needed the color filters, then the zinc plates and, finally, the paper. We received all we asked for. It was the same kind of paper that was used for making dollars, with the watermarks. Somebody else had toiled over that part, but I had no contact with that person. I enlarged the particular parts of the bill 20x and connected them together, so that in the end I had a 1:1 reproduction. After I was done, Haas took over and drew everything. He was incredibly precise. He could imitate every detail and color. And indeed, he intricately transferred them to the paper. With such huge magnification you could immediately notice even a tiny line that was out of place.

The drawing of the note was compared with the original by parallel projection of both images. Later subsequent corrections to the drawings were made, until, after appropriate retouch, the results were satisfying. Then all the parts were reassembled, photographically reduced to the size of the original and printed in the camp print shop. That took a month and a half. Later, the results of our work were sent to Berlin.

Apparently, the final test was going to be—exactly like in the movie—sending the bills for verification to Swiss bankers. They asked if, by any chance, they were not counterfeits.

"No, they are not. These are originals." was the supposed reply of a Swiss bank. I did not know much about it at that time, but people said that the bills were assessed by the most important watercolor painter of the 3rd Reich, Adolf Hitler.

At that point, I stopped working with the forged bank notes. I returned to my routine occupations and Leon Hass was transferred to Sachsenhausen, where he got involved in forging money—this time, British pounds.

PHOTOGRAPHS OF PRISONERS' ART

In the beginning of my stay at the camp—in Block 3A—I lived in one dorm with Xawery Dunikowski[389]. At that time Dunikowski worked at the spoon workshop with camp interpreter Baworowski. I photographed Dunikowski's paintings and sculptures, mostly wooden, including figures of women. He made many works for SS-Obersturmführer Schwarz.
I also took pictures of works by Czesław Lenczowski[390], Czesław

Kowalski-Wierusz[391] and Bronisław Czech[392].

There are no precise statistics on the number of professional artists imprisoned in Auschwitz-Birkenau and in 40 Auschwitz satellite camps. But you can say with certainty that there were over 200 artists of many nationalities. The largest group consisted of over 150 Polish artists, arrested for their resistance activity or because they were members of Poland's intellectual and cultural elite. Some of them never had a chance to make any drawings in Auschwitz. A few did, but we will never be able to identify much of their art, as they are not signed, or have more than one signature. Moreover, some Polish artists were murdered directly on their arrival in Auschwitz, as for example the majority of the 198 artists arrested at Kawiarania Plastyków [Artists' Café] in Krakow, at 3 Łobzowska Street on April 16th 1942. They were murdered immediately after coming to Auschwitz I on May 27th 1942. 168 people from that group were put in front of the firing squad at Block 11 in the main Auschwitz camp."[393]

We photographed paintings in order to document them for the authors, as, since

THE ORIGINALS HAD BEEN TAKEN BY THE SS.

The originals disappeared but the photographed copies survived.

"[...] In spite of the strict supervision, thanks to Wacław Weschke (Höss's "kalifaktor") our kommando transferred many materials outside the camp. Weschke often came to kommando "Erkennungsdienst" and secretly picked up the materials prepared by me, Tadeusz Myszkowski and Alfred Woycicki. They were copies of some photographs as well as paintings, sketches and drawings made by the prisoners in the camp. Weschke gave them to his wife, who sometimes visited him from Chorzów. They were kept in her home."

SOURCE: Tadeusz Krzysica's account [394]

I remember nice portraits by Mieczysław Kościelniak[395] who often came to our kommando, and I remember beautiful, typically Polish landscapes, created in the camp by Czesław Lenczowski.

"The main recipient of my paintings was the aforementioned Untersturmführer Dr. Turek from Vienna, a man of medium height, aged about 38, handsome and always smiling. Arriving at the Museum he always greeted me by shaking hands—if no one was watching, of course. Once, in astonishment, he asked a question: 'Why did such cultured people get into such deep shit? (i.e. Auschwitz)' We answered: 'Because we are Polish.' Dr. Turek always brought sugar, salt pork and cigarettes. He mostly asked me to paint female nudes, or genre paintings with female nudes."

SOURCE: Czesław Lenczowski's account[396]

"In Auschwitz camp kapos, block supervisors and SS men would eagerly seize the opportunity to have a portrait or a custom 'painting.' Prisoners-artists, on the other hand, were getting a break, and, what's more important, were being protected from hard labor."

SOURCE: Mieczysław Kościelniak's account[397]

---

389 Xawery Dunikowski (Inmate No. 774), b. November 29th 1875 in Krakow; painter, sculptor, professor at the The Academy of Fine Arts in Krakow. Brought to Auschwitz on June 20th 1940 in the Krakow-Tarnów transport. More → BIOGRAPHIES

390 Czesław Lenczowski (Inmate No. 29553), b. March 13th 1905 in Świątniki Górne, artist. Brought to Auschwitz in the April 13th 1942 transport from Krakow. More → BIOGRAPHIES

391 No data

392 Bronisław Czech (Inmate No. 349), b. July 25th 1908 in Zakopane; skiing instructor, mountaineer, Olimpic champion. Brought to KL Auschwitz on June 14th 1940 in the Krakow-Tarnów transport. More → BIOGRAPHIES

393 Jagoda Z., Kłodziński S., Masłowski J., *Oświęcim...*, op. cit., p. 126

394 Auschwitz Museum [APMA-B, Zespół Oświadczenia, t. 67, k. 119]

395 Mieczysław Kościelniak (Inmate No. 15261), b. Jan. 28th 1912 in Kalisz, painter, graphic artist, sculptor. Brought to KL Auschwitz on May 2nd 1941 in the Łódź transport. More → BIOGRAPHIES

396 Auschwitz Museum [APMA-B, Zespół Oświadczenia, t. 47, k. 43-44]

397 Auschwitz Museum [APMA-B, Zespół Oświadczenia, t. 57, k. 85]

Reproductions of these paintings ended up in the *Lagermuseum* (camp museum).
At some point Franciszek Targosz[398] took inventory of the Museum and would send us batches of paintings to be photographed. There was an album made of those photos.

"The main and official institution was the museum in block 24, where various objects of artistic or historical value were stored. There you could find ceramics, glass, metal works, camp bank notes and coins and various currencies (there were over 1,000 numismatic coins). Other exhibits of the Museum were decorations or even uniforms (of the Soviet army), an old military casket from Napoleonic times, and even a velocipede. On a daily basis they stored vestments and liturgical accessories of various religions—tallits, Talmuds, prayer books—and also folklore exhibits and various technique paintings made by prisoners. There was a separate collection of old documents (such as nobility and knighthood titles, etc.) as well as pennants and standards, including church banners. There was a red standard with golden letters: 'PPR—Brzezinka' (Polish Workers' Party – Brzezinka/Birkenau). Today it is hard to name all the types of exhibits. They were delivered to the museum from Bekleidungskammer Effektenkammer and from the 'Kanada'."
Source: Franciszek Targosz's account[399]

„If I had to explain why camp Commandant Rudolf Höss ordered establishment of the so-called 'Museum in Konzentrationslager Auschwitz' I would name a few reasons. The Nazis planned the extermination of Jews and Slavs, as they were considered races of little value. The collection of exhibits was planned as a curiosity and at the same time to provide justification for ridicule of the traditions and customs of the exterminated."
Source: Mieczysław Kościelniak's account[400]

398 Franciszek Targosz (Inmate No. 7626) b. Sept. 7th 1899 in Lipnik. Brought to KL Auschwitz from Bielsko on Dec. 18th 1940. More → Biographies
399 Auschwitz Museum [APMA-B, Zespół Oświadczenia, t. 64, k. 51]
400 Auschwitz Museum [APMA-B, Zespół Oświadczenia, t. 73, k. 195]

PHOTOGRAPHS OF THE ORCHESTRA

The photographs of the orchestra were taken by Walter. He took the pictures in large format, and I helped, as usual, with the finishing. The first pictures were taken near the beginning when the orchestra was small, consisting of perhaps ten people. There's also a picture from a later period when the ensemble had grown to forty.

"The pictures were taken during at least two time frames. This conclusion can be reached on the basis of the number of orchestra members, their clothing, and the appearance of the square and size of the camp kitchen behind them, which in later years was enlarged. The quality of those photos is not the best, compared to others taken by the SS; probably they were taken illicitly by the prisoners working at Erkennungsdienst."[401]

"As early as January 1941 Franz Nierychło[402] from the kitchen—the former bandmaster of a Krakow orchestra—and 'Lager-Ältester' Bruno Brodniewicz had the idea of creating a camp orchestra. They gathered four of us musicians—accordions, violin and some other instrument—and held a rehearsal. They asked around for people who could play and began assembling the orchestra."
SOURCE: Jan Baraniok's account[403]

"[...] The rehearsals took place in one of the rooms on the ground floor of Block 24[404]. The first official concert took place in 1941 on New Year's Eve or on the Epiphany. The performance was attended by Lagerführer Fritzsch. They played some folk and German melodies. They did it to please Fritzsch, who then granted official permission for the establishment of the orchestra."
SOURCE: Kazimierz Smoleń's account[405]

"They are excellent musicians, gathered from every corner of Europe. Among them there are famed virtuosos, really renowned musicians, who had performed on many and the best stages in the world. This ensemble would be an asset to any symphony. And today they play in the strangest auditorium in the world, for the listeners in green uniforms with their skulls and bones, for the criminal prisoners

---

[401] Smoleń K., "Erkennungsdienst". In: *Fotografie...*, op. cit., p. 23
[402] Franciszek Nierychło (Inmate No. 994), b. Nov. 17th 1905 in Łagiewniki; musician. Brought to Kl Auschwitz in the June 14th 1940 transport from Krakow-Tarnów. More → BIOGRAPHIES
[403] Auschwitz Museum [APMA-B, Zespół Oświadczenia, t. 33, k. 59]
[404] Today it houses the Auschwitz Museum publications office
[405] Auschwitz Museum [APMA-B, Zespół Oświadczenia, t. 76, k. 174]

with kapo armbands, and for the human shadows—those who attended either in fear or out of a powerful need to listen to those eternally beautiful melodies, so heart wrenching under the present circumstances,."
SOURCE: Wojciech Kawecki's account[406]

They held both serious concerts and ones of lighter repertoire, such as Johann Strauss. There was classical music including arias from German operas and even Polish folk music. Most of the time, however, the orchestra was stationed at the camp gate, where they played marches as the prisoners went in and out.

"The orchestra played for us four times a day. In the morning when we were leaving for work, when came back for lunch, when we left after lunch and returned for evening roll call. [...] He felt the whole madness of it especially during the marching of the squads returning from work. The passing columns were dragging the corpses of those killed during work. Those corpses were horrifying. Accompanied by lively marches played at a fast tempo, reminding you more of a polka or an oberek, in came the beaten, staggering figures exhausted by hard labor. The columns made an effort to march in step, dragging behind them the often half-naked bodies of their friends as clumps of dirt, mud, and stones dragged off parts of their clothing. These columns of infinite physical human misery were surrounded by a ring of overseers, beaten with sticks, and forced to march to macabre tunes of joyful music. Whoever could not march in step was struck on the head until he too was being dragged by his friends."
SOURCE: Witold Pilecki's report[407]

WHEN THE GERMANS WERE WINNING ON THE EASTERN FRONT THEY MADE THEM PLAY BOMBASTIC MARCHING MUSIC.

Conductor Franz Nierychło even composed a special piece for the occasion, entitled "March to the East". He wanted to show off in front of his superiors. Who, I must say, appreciated it.

The camp orchestra played also each Sunday at the first crematorium. There they set up music stands and opposite, benches and chairs for the SS. Officers and non-commissioned officers sat in the front rows, regular soldiers in the back.

"On Sundays at 2-4 PM we played in the square in front of the house of camp Commandant Rudolf Höss[408]. Those concerts were for the SS and their families. The concerts consisted of light repertoire, mostly German hits."
SOURCE: Ludwik Żuk's account[409]

The SS men liked it. Once in a while I even heard them clap. The crematorium kept working as always, the smoke rising from the chimney.

THE CAMP ORCHESTRA IN FRONT OF THE "ARBEIT MACHT FREI" GATE

[406] Auschwitz Museum [APMA-B, Zespół Oświadczenia, t. 75, k. 244]
[407] Cyra A., Ochotnik..., op. cit., p. 308
[408] Rudolf Höss's villa is located in the area adjacent to the camp. From its windows one can see a watch tower and Crematorium I.
[409] Auschwitz Museum [APMA-B, Zespół Oświadczenia, t. 34, k. 61-62]

The musicians played because they were told to. It was their profession and it allowed them to live. They got extra food and were spared heavy labor. They played for an hour or two and returned to the barracks. The fact that behind the walls next to where they were sitting the bodies of their comrades were being incinerated was of lesser importance. The crematorium had become something normal. You wouldn't pay attention to it any more and you would not think much about it. The Germans especially treated it as something ordinary, banal. They sat still and content, listening to the music.

"One Sunday in March[410], during the morning, 'Lager-Ältester' Bruno invited 'Lagerführer' Fritzsch to a concert of our orchestra at Block 24. We played the 'Bayerishe Mädel' Waltz, on purpose since Fritzsch was a Bavarian. He liked it a lot. He approved the camp orchestra and declared that its members must be kept at work inside the camp, so that they could be available to play at any time in case of an inspection."
SOURCE: Jan Baraniok's account[411]

"Each arrival of an inspection committee had to be celebrated with a traditional welcoming march. The five fanfare chords, embellished with all kinds of 'winkels' gave the creeps to the inmates who, of course, wanted to know the purpose of the committee's visit which, more often than not, preceded new rounds of mass execution."
SOURCE: Adam Kopyciński's account[412]

"[...] Himmler, who entered the camp in a black limousine, with his entourage, was being showed round the camp by Commandant Höss. [...]
For the welcome the orchestra played the Generals' March and at the farewell other marches. Nierychło conducted with his back to the orchestra."
SOURCE: Ludwik Żuk's account[413]

The orchestra also gave private concerts in the camp. I liked those. Sometimes we asked them to play something for us—just like that— for friends. There was a very good violinist there, named Dottenberg[414] whom we nicknamed "Dotek". And the cellist was a colonel, head of the Bielsko military orchestra, Józef Sitko[415] by name. There was also Adaś Wysocki[416], from the former

revelers group "Chór Dana" (Dan's Choir)[417]. For a while we were neighbors at the dorm, so I knew him well. He played the violin and also arranged music for various instruments. The repertoire was quite wide ranging from classical and patriotic music to the light, popular tunes.

---

410 It was in 1941.
411 Auschwitz Museum [APMA-B, Zespół Oświadczenia, t. 33, k. 60]
412 Kopyciński A., *Orkiestra w oświęcimskim obozie koncentracyjnym*. In: *Przegląd Lekarski*, Nr 1, Kraków 1964, p. 114
413 Auschwitz Museum [APMA-B, Zespół Oświadczenia, t. 34, k. 61-62]
414 No data
415 Józef Sitko (Inmate No. 75906), b. Sept. 3rd 1887 in Dembno, Lieutenant Colonel of the Polish Army. Brought to Auschwitz on Nov. 11th 1942 from the Montelupich prison in Krakow. In the camp orchestra he played cello. More → BIOGRAPHIES
416 Adam Wysocki (Inmate No. 2985), b. July 23rd 1907 in Kopyńczyce. Came to KLAuschwitz on August 5th 1940 in the first Warsaw transport. More → BIOGRAPHIES
417 Chór Dana— Polish revelers group established in 1928 in Warsaw. The group as a chorus accompanied various artists including Adolf Dymsza, Stefcia Górska, Hanka Ordonówna, Zula Pogorzelska. They appeared in many Polish pre-war movies. They toured in Poland and abroad.

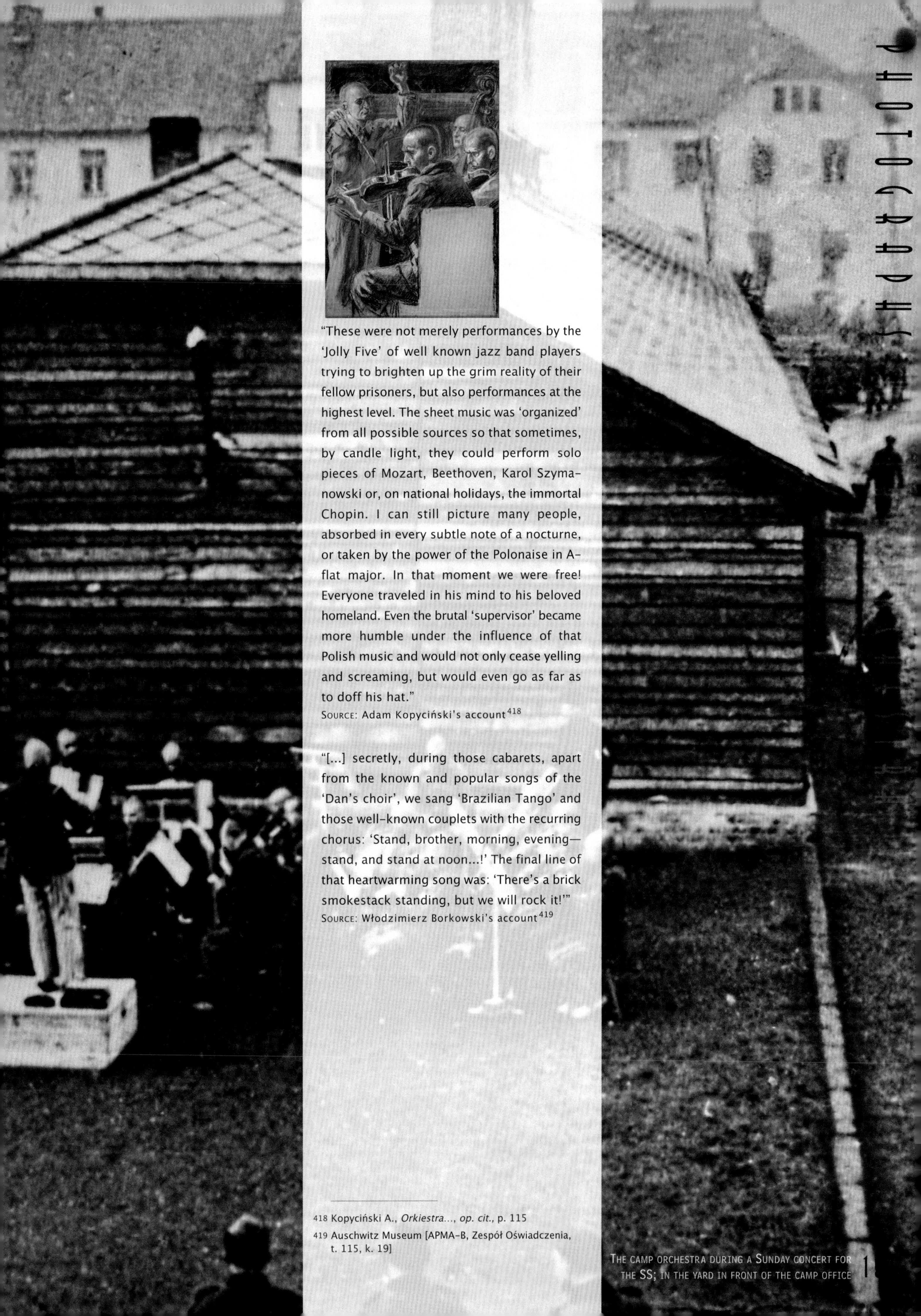

"These were not merely performances by the 'Jolly Five' of well known jazz band players trying to brighten up the grim reality of their fellow prisoners, but also performances at the highest level. The sheet music was 'organized' from all possible sources so that sometimes, by candle light, they could perform solo pieces of Mozart, Beethoven, Karol Szymanowski or, on national holidays, the immortal Chopin. I can still picture many people, absorbed in every subtle note of a nocturne, or taken by the power of the Polonaise in A-flat major. In that moment we were free! Everyone traveled in his mind to his beloved homeland. Even the brutal 'supervisor' became more humble under the influence of that Polish music and would not only cease yelling and screaming, but would even go as far as to doff his hat."
Source: Adam Kopyciński's account[418]

"[...] secretly, during those cabarets, apart from the known and popular songs of the 'Dan's choir', we sang 'Brazilian Tango' and those well-known couplets with the recurring chorus: 'Stand, brother, morning, evening—stand, and stand at noon...!' The final line of that heartwarming song was: 'There's a brick smokestack standing, but we will rock it!'"
Source: Włodzimierz Borkowski's account[419]

[418] Kopyciński A., *Orkiestra...*, op. cit., p. 115
[419] Auschwitz Museum [APMA-B, Zespół Oświadczenia, t. 115, k. 19]

The camp orchestra during a Sunday concert for the SS; in the yard in front of the camp office

HELPING OTHERS

I liked to listen to the orchestra, which brought me back to the best of times with my father. One summer I was able to help someone get into the camp orchestra. I received a smuggled message concerning a Jewish woman from Żywiec of the Springut[420] family, who was asking for help. Because she was working in the fields and was close to death, her situation was tragic. I had seen those Jewish women in Auschwitz. They worked in inhuman conditions and went to work in Soviet uniforms. This woman played the bass and had gotten word that they were creating a female orchestra in Birkenau. In the message I was asked if I would be able to help get her into that orchestra. She would have to be transferred to Birkenau for it to work. This had to be approved by Untersturmführer Zelt[421]. I recalled that a friend of mine, Franciszek Piela[422], was his tailor. The SS men were vain and appreciated Piela because he sewed very well. I spoke to him, so he took down the Jewish women's name and indeed, it worked. She got to play bass in that orchestra. She survived. I met her after the war, but never told her of the favor that I did her. She might have thought I was looking for gratitude.

I helped also to transfer some women from Birkenau to Auschwitz. The conditions at the latter were comparatively better. I remember Jadwiga Bartel[423]—a very good woman who wanted to join her younger brother.

"Jadwiga Bartel wanted to be moved to Auschwitz because her younger brother, Erwin Bartel[424], was there. She was only motivated by sisterly love. In Auschwitz she contacted her brother and they helped each other out. That contact was possible because, among other things, we were taken to be photographed by the Erkennungsdienst."
SOURCE: Janina Perun's account [425]

I had many more opportunities to help men than women. If someone asked me, and I could do something, I did it. Often I said, "Come tonight. You will get a piece of bread."
Most often my colleagues from Żywiec directed other Żywiec people to me. And they did come.
A few times I got the newcomers into relatively good kommandos. Others, especially those from the Żywiec area, I advised to avoid being scapegoated. Because if someone at the camp became a scapegoat he was particularly persecuted. If they wanted to get into a good kommando, working indoors, I told them to declare a useful skill. Under no circumstance say you are a student or an intellectual, and for sure not a professional soldier.

"Most intellectuals brought into the camp were whimps. They didn't realize that their scientific knowledge and degrees needed to be deeply hidden under the intelligence of a practical mind looking for ways to find a footing on the rocky, life threatening ground of the "koncentrak" [camp jargon: concentration camp]. You needed to forget your titles, and take on the existing circumstances. Don't request to work in the office because you are an engineer, or in the hospital because you are a doctor but try to fit into any opening that presents itself. Just find some job which might be useful to the authorities and is not dishonoring to a Pole. Don't act important because you are a lawyer, as such a profession is of no use. Foremost, be a good sport in your dealings with any fellow Pole, unless he is a scoundrel, and take advantage of any favor, being sure to pay it back. Because the only way you could survive was by creating bonds of friendship, helping one another out. Many never understood that... There were many egoists, as in the poem: 'He neither seeks the wave, nor it him'[426]. Such a one had no chance."
SOURCE: Witold Pilecki's report [427]

---

[420] Renata Springut (Inmate No. A-26594), b. April 18th 1921 in Żywiec. Brought to KL Auschwitz on Oct. 22nd 1944 in the transport from KL Kraków-Płaszów; she worked in the clothing workshop. More → BIOGRAPHIES

[421] No data.

[422] Franciszek Piela (Inmate No. 1258), b. April 24th in Cięcin. Brought to KL Auschwitz on Oct. 22nd 1940 transport from Katowice. More → BIOGRAPHIES

[423] Jadwiga Bartel (Inmate No. 21953) b. Oct. 6th 1913 in Oświęcim. Came to Kl Auschwitz in the Oct. 6th 1942 transport from KL Ravensbrück. More → BIOGRAPHIES

[424] Erwin Bartel (Inmate No. 17044) b. Feb. 3rd 1923 in Oświęcim, student. More → BIOGRAPHIES

[425] Auschwitz Museum [APMA-B, Zespół Oświadczenia, t. 11, k. 46]

[426] *Ode to Youth* [Oda do młodości] by Adam Mickiewicz

[427] Cyra A., *Ochotnik...*, op. cit., p. 313

I told the Żywiec people that if they could get into a good kommando, they would be able to carry on. That's exactly what I said:

YOU CAN SOMEHOW CARRY ON HERE.

Apart from that I advised them to lay low. I knew more than the newcomers and reassured them, for they were terrified by the situation. One time I heard from Gustaw Baron[428], who was from Pietrzykowice near Żywiec. He said he knew my brother Janek. His face was pale and shocked after what he had seen, so I told him to come and visit me the same evening. He asked me straight out what were the chances of survival. He could see others falling like flies, and I had been there already three years. It happened that he was an automobile electrician and that before the war he had worked as an electrician in a paper mill.

At that time I could find him a decent placement thanks to my friends at the Labor Deployment office. I went there, gave the number of the newcomer, and asked to place him somewhere: either in the carpentry shop or in some warehouse, or with the painters. I was also friends with two Austrian prisoners, the chief of the prison garages Vesely[429], and with Friemel[430], for whom I had recently made a wedding picture. Thanks to Friemel I could help especially a person who had skills in mechanical or electrical work. Rudolf helped me more than once by taking my acquaintances into his kommando.

The transport service, for which Friemel was a kapo, and then Oberkapo, was a good assignment. The work was relatively light, in a heated space. Although a kapo, he didn't yell or hit, which mattered a great deal.

So I went to him saying I had a true expert and asked him to employ him. I gave him the guy's camp number. Rudolf immediately said that he would find something for him, because an auto electrician was a good and necessary job at his kommando. Indeed, they employed Gustaw at the garages the next day and he survived the camp. After the war he went to school and became a vocational school teacher in Sosnowiec. One time he came with his wife and kids to thank me. He died in 1967.

---

428 No data

429 Ludwig Vesely (Inmate No. 38169) b July 5th 1919 in Vienna, mechanic. Brought to Auschwitz on April 15th 1942. More → BIOGRAPHIES

430 Rudolf Friemel (Inmate No. 25173) b. April 11th 1907 in Vienna, car mechanic. Brought to Auschwitz on Jan. 2nd 1942. More → BIOGRAPHIES

KL Auschwitz I. Inside the camp's forges

If I could I brought my friends into my kommando, but those opportunities were rare.

I helped Edward Josefsberg, who came to us thanks to Bródka. One day Tadzio stopped by and said that one of his colleagues from Lwów was a photographer's son and knew the trade. Because with time the amount of work kept growing, I had more justification to go to my boss and ask for extra help. We brought in Edek, my boss looked at him, and took down his name and number. Soon the matter was settled. Walter wrote him a note, ordered a bath, and directed him to get clean underwear and a good prison uniform. I took Edek to the bath house, which was at the back of our building and we went into the showers.

When Edek undressed

I WAS DUMBSTRUCK..

He was circumsized! I knew that if Walter found that out, we would both be doomed. Walter hated Jews; if Edek was discovered there would be no mercy.

Edek explained to me that it was because of a condition—phimosis—which was treated with circumcision, but before he could explain that to any German he would be dead. I could not imagine a solution. I told him that that while in the showers he always must hide behind the other prisoners so that no German would ever see him. That was his only chance. And so Edek stayed. He was a great find, as he was helpful and good at making prints. He was a fine colleague. A very good man. We worked together till the very end.

Edek survived the camp and went to live in Ystad, Sweden. After over fifty years I visited him there and we reminisced. We had a long talk and we both cried. We were supposed to meet the next day, but his wife called and pleaded with me to leave him alone. After our talk Edek had gotten very upset. He had run

outside and crouched in the bushes behind the house, searching for something by digging in the dirt. She also told me that Edek had been treated psychiatrically. He could not forgive himself that in the camp he had renounced his Jewishness. I never saw him again.

At the end of '42 or at the beginning of '43 a good colleague of mine came in and said he had a big favor to ask: his friend from Bielsko was wasting away, and because his sister was a photographer he knew a thing or two about photography as well. He had been sent to Auschwitz for a minor offence—he had writen a card to his friend near Bielsko in which he warned him of widespread arrests in town and some informant at the post office reported him, since he had put his address on the card. So they got him.
"Please, try and do something, otherwise he will die." said my good comrade.
So I told him to bring over the Bielsko boy; I would see what could be done. When I saw him I was shocked.
He was already a complete "Muselmann". His hands were covered with scabies. I thought to myself: "Jesus Christ! If my boss sees him he will kick him out on the spot, and I will get smacked."

But since my colleague had begged me, I took the risk. I went to my boss and said I needed an assistant, because Jureczek couldn't catch up with the enlargements and I had found someone who could help. He was an expert and spoke some German, I said. The boss agreed to speak with him. The next day I brought that prisoner—it was Józef Pysz, and I can still remember his

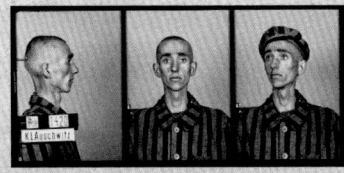

number: 1420. My boss took one look at him and cursed, but nevertheless wrote a note to get him a bath and a new uniform, and then bring him to work in our kommando. I took that boy to the bath—he was just a skeleton covered with skin. The bath assistant, a doctor by profession, took me aside and said it was hopeless to take that fellow as he would not last longer than two or three days. But we tried to help him anyway. We got ahold of some raw onion from the gardeners and some sugar. Lo and behold, after a time Józek began to walk normally again. Against all odds, he survived. Then I took him for an X-ray and it was discovered that he had a pus exudation in his lungs. Still, he hung on and even began to put on weight because we nourished him with whatever we could find and managed to bring him some extra portions of soup. After a time, he completely recovered.

In the summer of '44 Pysz was released from the camp because his mother signed the Volksliste. After the war we kept in touch, but the contacts were not frequent. Józek was a withdrawn man. He wouldn't talk at all about the camp. Although, I must say, he was always grateful toward me.

A similar scenario happened when Tadzio Bródka and Woycicki helped Tadek Krzysica:

"Because a longer stay in Krankenbau was becoming dangerous, colleagues: Marian Toliński, Michał Pieńkos, Alfred Woycicki (from 'Erkennungdienst' Kommando), Kazek Szelest (working in the camp kitcher) decided to find me a light employment under a roof, which would enable me to regain my health. Because I had been a professional chemical etcher and I was familiar with photography work, my colleagues considered the 'Erkennungsdienst' kommando. However, my physical appearance was a serious obstacle. I was riddled with disease, terribly emaciated—I looked like a typical 'Muselmann'. The chief of 'Erkennungsdienst' kommando was SS-hauptscharführer Bernhard Walter and his deputy was SS-Unterscharführer Ernest Hofmann. They had to find a person who had some leverage with Walter. [...]

Dressed in a decent, clean uniform I went to Block 26, where Walter had his office and where 'Erkennungsdienst' kommando was located. [...] Walter, after listening to the doctor's plea, called me in. In the office, in addition to Walter and the doctor, there was the 'Erkennungsdienst' kapo, Tadeusz Bródka. On seeing me, Walter exclaimed: 'Was, solche Muselmann, raus!' and then he kicked me out. But at the insistence of the doctor, whose name I unfortunately do not know as well as kapo Bródka and also Alfred Woycicki, Walter took into consideration that I was an expert and called me back, declaring to kapo Bródka in front of all the others,'Bródka, you watch out! If he shits on the stool you'll be eating it at the roll call.'
Those words meant that the efforts of my friends were successful. I was admitted to 'Erkennungsdienst' kommando and that fact saved my life."
SOURCE: Tadeusz Krzysica's account 📷 431

431 Auschwitz Museum [APMA-B, Zespół Oświadczenia, T. 67, k. 117-118]

We knew that a good trade and getting into a good kommando was essential. But what could be done for colleagues, whose professions were useless in the camp? One day, in the summer of 1943, I had a visit from a teacher whom I had known before the war. Such people usually automatically would end up in the gravel pit or the building kommando where the work went on all day without food, and where, on the way back to the camp, the prisoners had to carry bricks on their backs.

I wondered how to help that teacher. It was then that Otto Küsel helped me out shortly before his escape[432]. I was good friends with him. He was a very fine person. Otto was a kapo in a kommando which sought out and placed skilled prosiners in details where they could be useful. He was responsible for the efficient organization of prisoners' work.

"He was a good man, with a sense of humor. As much as he could he tried to help by placing the weaker or the endangered ones in kommandos where they had a chance to improve their health and survive. He liked to surround himself with Poles. He was learning Polish and spoke it reasonably well."
SOURCE: Stanisław Skibicki's account[433]

„I remember that, when after our arrival at the camp we were placed in the basement of the Tobacco Monopoly building, [Otto] was the only one who brought us some water. Later I spoke with him many times; he even told me the story of his life. Apparently, as a young boy he became involved with a gang of burglars. He did not steal himself, but kept a watch making sure his pals were safe. He got busted once, twice, and then, as a multiple offender, was put into a Nazi concentration camp. Many years in the camps did not temper his contrary nature. He was willful. His liking for the Poles was not the result of his political convictions, but but of his contrariness. Because all the kapos beat and tortured Polish prisoners, he, in his rebellious spirit did exactly the opposite. He helped and supported us whenever he could."
SOURCE: Kazimierz Szczerbowski's account[434]

Otto decided to place the teacher in the stove building kommando. Of course there was a risk that a teacher would not last there long either. However, as it turned out, other prisoners took to him and taught him how to mix the yellow clay they needed to build the stoves. In time, he became a real master at kneading clay. That teacher also survived the war and also came to see me to say thanks.

Once another of my colleagues, who came to the camp relatively late in 1943, asked my help to find him a good job. I managed to place him at the pantry. They sorted cheeses there, prepared all kinds of parcels, and served food. While he worked there the mass transports with Hungarian Jews were coming in, and they would bring a lot of bread and goose fat with them. He was in charge over there and often would bring me something. I did not need that food. I told him to give it to others, but he insisted. He wanted to reciprocate.

---

[432] Compare chapter „Illegal Photographs"
[433] Auschwitz Museum [APMA-B, Zespół Oświadczenia, t. 149, k. 109-110]
[434] Auschwitz Museum [APMA-B, Zespół Oświadczenia, t. 67, k. 67]

My comrades and I supported one another in the most tragic moments. At one time

I BECAME A CONFESSOR TO MY FRIEND

Roman Karwat, a block clerk from

Chorzów in Upper Silesia. We became close, because he tutored me in German. He went to good German schools before World War I and so his German was as fluent as his Polish. Often I would ask him how to formulate a German sentence.

Karwat was not very much older than I. At our kommando his job consisted of writing summons for the prisoners. He ran the prisoner records with both the files and the photographs. The file archive was divided into three parts: for the living, the dead and those transferred from the camp. If the file in the archive did not have a picture Roman prepared a summons to Schreibstube, or the camp office, with the number of the summoned prisoner.

One evening Roman got word that the next day he would be executed, because as the block clerk he was the one who got the list of numbers to be called and saw among them his own: 5959. He whispered to me then, "Come. I need to talk to you." He told me his life story, from beginning to end, up to the last days before the arrest. It was a kind of confession, as we did not have a priest. He urged me to behave honorably, as he had tried to. He was a member of a secret organization in Silesia, but he did not regret what had happened. He was tormented by something else—an infidelity. He was married, but just before the arrest when he was in hiding he had met a woman. It bothered him. He wanted to confess, to tell everything at the end of his life... He was very calm, taking everything very mildly, and he wished me to survive.

The next day he was taken to Block 11. Walter tried to help him. When Tadziu Bródka and I reported that Karwata was taken, our boss went to Block 11 and brought Karwat back to the kommando. He asked him to prepare various reports, accounts for various funds received from SS men. All day he kept making up all those tasks hoping that the problem would fade away. Unfortunately, it did not help. Karwata was called again.

"Give me some hot tea"—that was his last request before going to his death.

He went back to Block 11 where he was executed by shooting.

Sometimes there was someone who might have helped but they didn't. We had a colleague from Żywiec who was a block clerk and had plenty of opportunities, but never helped anybody. His colleagues told him that he better not return back home, as they would smash his face if they found him there. Indeed, after he left the camp he never went back to Żywiec. He lives somewhere in Canada and when he comes to visit his family he meets them in Krakow.

CAMP LIFE

Camp life had its rhythm. You can say that my privileged position in our kommando enabled me to have a social life. That life consisted simply of meeting with friends, regularly and on special occasions. I cherish the memories of the times when I was intimate with other prisoners, as was the case on Christmas. We then felt a great solidarity.

"Sadness and depression prevailed until a great Christmas tree arrived at the camp. It started with the singing of a German Christmas carol, followed by a resounding song: 'Bóg się rodzi, moc truchleje' ('God is born, the power trembles') and other tunes, finished by the 'Dąbrowski Mazurka'—'*Jeszcze Polska*'[435]. Everybody was hugging and crying long, deep, and loud. There were some whose hearts stopped beating."
SOURCE: Józef Jędrych's account[436]

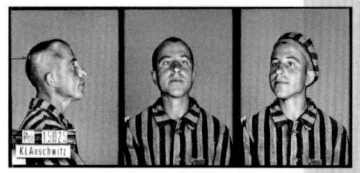

It happened on occasion that those who had money would give it to those who had none. Some fellows from our kommando never received any parcels, so those of us who had something pitched in from our parcels and divided them equally among everyone.

The first Christmas at the camp was very cold. That Christmas Eve luckily we took no photographs, but I have a vivid memory of it. The German kapos put up a Christmas tree in front of the kitchen and decorated it with a few electric bulbs. There was an evening roll call at Christmas Eve and that was when we saw a terrible scene: under the tree the Germans arranged a number of Jewish corpses. Next to it three kapos played a Christmas carol. Kapo Markus played the bandoneon[437], another one the guitar, the third one sang *Heilige Nacht*[438].

---
435 Polish national anthem.
436 Auschwitz Museum [APMA-B, Zespół Oświadczenia, t. 101, k. 21]
437 Bandoneon - kind of accordion
438 "*Stille Nacht, heilige Nacht*"

SS-OFFICER KARL HOECKER LIGHTS CANDLES ON A CHRISTMAS TREE

"One of the SS climbed the podium and conducted the German carol 'Stille Nacht, Heilige Nacht'. Although there were several thousand gathered in the square the singing was not very loud. The sight of the bodies spread out under the tree and that of our dying fellows was more conducive to a mood of silence and reflection."
SOURCE: Karol Świętorzecki's account[439]

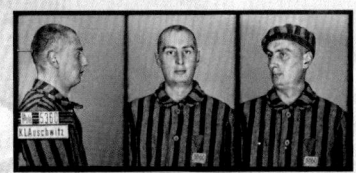

The following year the Germans organized another Christmas Eve. When the Soviet kommandos that built KL Auschwitz II Birkenau were returning to the camp, the Germans murdered anyone who couldn't stand on his own feet. That day about 300 people were massacred. I saw also other transports, which were mercilessly tortured during that holiday period.

I was ordered to take photos just before one of the camp Christmas Eves, when there was a so-called Jew hunt. A transport of Jews came in, out of which the camp doctor pulled an extremely fat man. He was first sent to our atelier to be photographed. He was imposing and tall. I took his nude picture. I recall that he was named Chairman Feivel[440].

The next day I watched him march to work outside the camp. I went out to get something and saw him behind the wires. In the place where those prisoners worked, there was a pit from which they were digging out gravel. The German kapos mistreated that huge Jew in the most horrible way, beating him with sticks and pushing him down into the pit. The kapo and the SS men were in stitches with laughter. He struggled to get out, but as soon as he managed to scramble out, they shoved him back with their legs and beat his head with wooden batons. You could hear those blows 50-70 meters away. That cruel picture stayed deeply embedded in my memory. I keep seeing him getting beaten without mercy. They made a comedy show of it. At the end they murdered him.

CHRISTMAS EVE, WŁADYSŁAW SIWEK

CHRISTMAS EVE IN OŚWIĘCIM, JERZY POTRZEBOWSKI

[439] Auschwitz Museum [APMA-B, Zespół Oświadczenia, t. 86, k. 234]
[440] No data

Apart from evil images of those Christmas Eves, which keep coming back to me, I can recall a few beautiful memories from those times.

I had, for instance, one very abundant Christmas Eve (the second one in the camp, in 1942). We owed it to Marian Studencki[441] from Żywiec. He worked as a butcher and twice

a week he went to the train station to fetch cattle and pigs. That Christmas, he brought all sorts of fresh and smoked meats. We anticipated getting alcohol, bread and other delicacies. We prepared a fine Christmas Eve dinner. There were twelve of us, including the kapo. On Christmas day we had another feast.

On my third Christmas Eve at the camp everybody in our kommando decided to observe the Christmas fast, so we agreed not to eat any sausage. With my friend I made some pasta and syrup. We cooked the pasta sweet style, because we had the sugar, and thus made a meal of it. We broke and shared the Christmas wafer, which we had gotten from the civilian workers. There was no fish, but we made sautéed potatoes with bouillon. We had a little vodka.

Christmas Eve 1944 I spent with friends at the camp hospital in Block 28. It was the vegetable-sorting kommando. They invited me for pasta and vegetables which could be had from the gardeners even in winter. I was able to obtain some sardines that had been brought into Auschwitz by transported Greek and Dutch Jews. That Christmas Eve dinner was quite opulent. We had wonderful cheese, sautéed potatoes as the main dish, and raisins and figs for dessert.

In those better moments

WE COULD EXPRESS, AGAINST THE ODDS, A SENSE OF HUMOR.

Of course, we did not play jokes on the SS men. That was too risky. But on ourselves we did. We would, for instance, take a sponge from Tadzio Myszkowski, the draftsman, dip it in water and hide it under a thin blanket. He would sit on it and quickly jump to his feet, wet and cursing. It did happen one time, though, that our boss's deputy, Ernst Hofmann, happened to sit on that sponge. He "verfluchted"[442] some, but fortunately that was all it came to.

Once I made a special kaleidoscope. I removed the crystals from inside and replaced them with photos of half-naked girls. The Jews from Greece often had those sorts of pictures; sometimes even in color. That was a popular toy and then I got the notion of smearing the eyepiece with soot. When someone put his eye to it, his face got smeared up and everybody laughed.

The SS men sometimes bought those kaleidoscopes from us for cigarettes. Occasionally, the Blockführers[443] visited us to chat. Mostly we talked about ordinary subjects: food, commandos—who worked where and so on.

---

441 Marian Studencki (Inmate No.5822), b. Nov. 14th 1907 in Żywiec. Came to KL Auschwitz on Oct. 8th 1940 in the Krakow-Tarnów transport. More → BIOGRAPHIES

442 Verfluchen — curse angrily
443 Blockführers — „Block leaders"; Pol. „blokowy"; SS man, block supervisor in Nazi concentration camps.
444 Auschwitz Museum [APMA-B, Zespół Wspomnienia, t. 175 k.50]
445 Auschwitz Museum [APMA-B, Zespół Oświadczenia, t. 101, k. 93]
446 Jagoda Z., Kłodziński S., Masłowski J., Oświęcim..., op. cit., p. 113-114

"Camp life was at its most intense in the evening between roll call and the gong which signified curfew. During that time of day you met up with your friends or made new ones. This was also the time for bartering and preparing foods that required cooking."
Source: Janusz Karwacki's account 444

"As early as in the fall of 1940 it became the fashion among friends to go from block to block in the evenings and tell stories about events, interesting people and things they had come across during their lives. Quite often these were intriguing tales, yes, highly interesting. We found out about things which for many of us had been completely unknown heretofore. One of my colleagues, whose name unfortunately escapes me, a former diplomat and an older man, enlightened us about diplomatic protocol and various occurrences at embassies and ministries of exotic countries."
Source: Andrzej Rablin's account 445

"In the never-ending tales of natural born storytellers, whether simple folks or intellectuals, reality was subject to true literary transformation. Imagination ran free and the narrators told not just of their experiences, but sometimes even of their unconscious dreams. I think it had a psychotherapeutic component for both the narrators and the listeners alike, a quality which was lacking in the popular bedtime stories of retold novels and movies. (...) An important role was played by poetry, written not by professional poets but by ordinary people. (...) These were not bombastic patriotic odes, but on the contrary, mostly very personal lyric verses expressing the longing for freedom and family, or despair and pain or—mostly in irony—self description. Tales of a more general appeal expressed the feelings of the many, and these circulated around the camp. Indeed, there was a strong urge to express the reality of Auschwitz, to create an alternate identity for a man in a striped uniform and to answer the fundamental question: What has become of Man?"
Source: Tadeusz Hołuj's account 446

WE DID NOT TOUCH UPON FORBIDDEN SUBJECTS. DOING SO OPENLY WAS VERY DANGEROUS.

One day I was in the food storage room when an SS man started asking me how I imagined the end of the war. He had a friendly attitude towards prisoners, but still I was wary of expressing what I really thought.

I had a similar conversation with SS man Schumacher[447]. He was from Frankfurt-on-Main, 32 years old, and one of the managers of the food warehouses. He was liked by his workers. I went there often, so he chatted with me. He asked where I was from, who my father was, what was my offence. He also asked how I imagined the end of the war. I did not care to talk about that, but he assured me more than once that I had nothing to fear from him. I subtly suggested that probably Germany would lose, but possibly would make a deal with the Brits. Various rumors were going around at that time. It was the end of 1943 and Germany was being heavily bombed. Later that SS man took a leave of absence. He came back completely devastated. His house had been bombed out and his wife, child and parents killed. He began to drink heavily. Then he volunteered for the front and was never heard of again.

For a time I lived in a dorm with a German of about 45 years of age. He worked at the canteen. A very quiet, decent man. After a few months I learned that he was a pastor. He had been sent to the camp because in a sermon he had mentioned that he had heard rumors of the murdering and gassing. Even the words "I heard

---

447 Hans Schumacher (SS-Unterscharführer)), b. Aug. 31st 1906 in Düsseldorf. In KL Auschwitz since 1942, deputy manager of the food storage rooms.
More → Biographies

"Organizing"

get you arrested. In the camp we would tell the rumors or jokes only in the company of our most trusted friends, for there were informers everywhere.

"The jokes that came from outside the camp and took a satirical view of the Germans, especially of their leaders, were especially popular. This is one of many examples: "What does a true Nazi look like? Answer: Blond as Hitler, slim as Göring, tall as Goebbels, virile as Röhm, and his name is Rosenberg."[448]

Speaking negatively of the Germans invariably led to tragic consequences.
Kapo Malz once told our kommando his dream. In the dream he saw all of Germany surrounded by barbed wire, outside of which Hitler, Himmler and Goebbels were taking a walk. Later he told it to other prisoners around the block. I warned him: "Franz, keep your mouth shut or you might lose your head!"
But he waved me away and kept on telling that story until, eventually, it came to the attention of the manager of the camp canteen, Unterscharführer Jakob Raith[449], a Bavarian and a dedicated Nazi. Raith reported Malz to the Political Department. The next day they ordered our kapo to the gate, from where he was taken to the Political Department. They say he was interrogated by a guy named Kirchner[450]. When Malz realized that his situation was dire he attempted to run towards his friend, the camp informer Kauer[451], but they caught him by the crematorium, pulled him inside and murdered him.

In my opinion he was harmless, although many prisoners spoke against him. In the beginning, yes, he had been nasty and taken things out on us. But overall he was harmless.
I don't even know if it was a true dream or whether he had just made it up. Malz despised National Socialism. He was from Stettin and had gotten arrested soon after Hitler came to power because he was an active Communist. Apart from that, he was a simple minded fellow. I will not even repeat how vulgar he could be. And his physical behavior was no better. He liked to eat cabbage, get bloated and fart loudly. He would then get up, take a bow, and sit again. Same thing again in a minute or two. He got such "inspirations."
For all that, many of us felt sorry for Malz, and terrified by what happened to him. After all, Malz was a native German, and still got brutally murdered by his own.

---

448 Jagoda Z., Kłodziński S., Masłowski J., *Oświęcim...*, op. cit., p. 153
449 Jakob Raith (SS-Unterscharführer), b. May 22nd 1909 in Bittenkirchen. In KL Auschwitz from Feb. 1st 1941 until Dec. 2nd 1941; manager of the SS canteen and the canteen for the inmates. More → BIOGRAPHIES
450 Kurt Paul Kirchner (SS-Hauptscharführer), b. Oct. 23rd 1913 in Eckstartsberg. In KL Auschwitz from Sept. 1944. More → BIOGRAPHIES
451 Rudolf Kauer (Inmate No. 15592), b Jan. 24th 1902 in Teschen; construction engineer. Came to KL Auschwitz in May 16th 1941 in a transport. More → BIOGRAPHIES

Any contacts with Polish workers who had jobs at the camp but were not prisoners were prohibited. A prisoner could get sent to the Penal Company and the outside worker could end up in detention, sometimes even put in the camp. There were such cases and so those workers were extremely terrorized. Once I went with my boss Hofmann to photograph some workers for their IDs. They lived in a separate building. I set up the camera, got everything ready, and started taking photos. Among those workers was an acquaintance from Żywiec. I asked him to send greetings to my family. He was so scared that he demanded I say nothing to him. A similar thing happened with another man from Żywiec, a so-called correction prisoner. Those would be sent to the camp for six weeks for some small offence or missing work and had a separate numbering system.

SS OFFICER KARL HOECKER RESTING IN FEMALE COMPANY IN SOLAHUETTE, 1944

That first correction prisoner acquaintance of mine was being released from the camp and was dressed in civilian clothes. I met him in a hallway, and since we were alone I asked him to visit my parents. He told me to shut up and go away.

As for the "social life"

THERE SEEMED TO BE TWO DISTINCT REALITIES.

One, as I have just described, was where people avoided contact out of fear. But there was another reality which was quite remarkable and hard to imagine when you consider nature of the camp. There were certain situations that were purely social in nature. For example, playing sports. There was more than one memorable game like one I recall between the Poles and the kapos.

"The playing of sports, such as soccer, boxing, gymnastics, and swimming can be definitely counted among the peculiarities of the concentration camps."[452]

"Soccer was hands-down the most popular sport at the camp. It not only had the most fans and spectators among both the prisoners and SS officers, but also the largest number of prisoners who actively played. The first matches took place in Auschwitz I near Block 11. [...] They also played at the crematorium."
SOURCE: Stanisław Głowa's account[453]

"It often happened that matches were held immediately following public executions, in the square freshly swept of blood stains. On one end there was a goal made of... the portable gallows, the other goal was the Wall of Death where mass executions were held. We played in spite of the stench from the crematorium".
SOURCE: Stefan Świszczowski's account[454]

"[...] Most often there were matches between kommandos. That meant it became a camouflaged competition between the various nationalities. Or there were matches between prisoners and kapos, between prisoners and 'Krankenbau', DAW[455] versus TWL[456], youngsters versus 'old boys' etc. Polish prisoners often played in matches of 'international' character, i.e. against Austrian, French, German, Soviet and Jewish teams. The teams were typically made up of prisoners-functionaries, block supervisors and kapos. Some of the more important matches were watched also by the SS officers.

[...] Apart from prisoners-amateurs who had enough energy for playing, some European-class soccer players also took part. In some accounts, former prisoners remember games taking place as early as 1942, but later, in 1943-1944, soccer was played much more frequently. It was during that time that many of those memorable international games were held. [...]

The Polish team was characterized by an unparalleled competitive spirit. Cheering from prisoners was fervent and the Poles dominated with their chanting: 'Polska gola!' [Go Poland!]. But sometimes things were awkward. During one particular match, when the Polish team began to win, one of the SS men stood behind the Polish goalie with a gun in his hand and threatened to kill him if he continued to block the balls kicked by the German players. Needless to say, the Germans won that one. "I don't remember the score—says one of the respondents—but for us, who watched that Sunday match, it was big. We realized that in spite of the Nazi plans we were still a unified nation."
SOURCE: Julian Kiwała's account[457]

---

452 Ryn Z., Kłodziński S., *Patologia sportu...*, op. cit., p. 109
453 Ibidem, p. 110
454 Ibidem, p. 112

455 DAW - Deutsche Ausrüstungswerke - multiple trade camp workshops, mostly for arms production. They employed a large number of prisoners' kommandos.
456 TWL - Truppenwirtschaftslager - SS supplies depot at the camp.
457 Ryn Z., Kłodziński S., *Patologia sportu...*, op. cit., p. 110-111

"After soccer, boxing was the second most popular sport at the camp. [...]
In 1941-1942 boxing matches were held in the Block 2 bath and in the square by the kitchen. They were mostly between Polish prisoners. [...] In 1942 boxing matches were held every Sunday." [458]

"I remember the fight between Pietrzykowski, who before the war had the moniker "Teddy", and the kapo of the 'Fleischerei' slaughterhouse. The kapo had a bodybuilder figure with huge muscles, probably Heavyweight class, and "Teddy" was a Bantamweight at most. He was small, quick, agile and had been a pre-war member of the Polish boxing team. Such a fight could never have taken place in any professional ring, for they were probably four weight classes apart, a colossus against a small skinny guy. Anyway that bodybuilder lost, even though he had a little boxing experience. The disproportion in weight was not the only reason why this fight shouldn't have taken place. There was 'Teddy's' professional advantage. I have never seen a fighter in the ring demolish his opponent like that. Blood from the broken nose, lacerated lips and eyebrows covered the torso of that butcher as the fight continued. Such a spectacle could have happened only at Auschwitz".
SOURCE: Andrzej Rablin's account [459]

„The Pole is in the ring, and the Pole is pummeling a German criminal who even a day before had beaten and murdered our comrades. The atmosphere around the ring, the emotional climate among the haggard and emaciated Polish prisoners, was of a transfusion of faith, a spiritual uplift reminding us that 'Poland has not yet perished'."
SOURCE: Tadeusz Sobolewski's account [460]

It was almost as unbelievable that in 1944 they opened a movie theater for us regular prisoners. The screen was set up next to the crematorium and so we didn't want to go, scared that it was some kind of ruse.

"A civilian in a Tyrolean hat operated the projector, and the SS men sat around him. The show began. It was some movie with Marika Rück. I did not see much because those in front obstructed my view, nor did I understand the dialogue. The light music had an enervating effect on me, especially, since I thought I could hear cars pulling up outside. At times when the dancing Marika Rück showed her shapely thighs a murmur of approval was heard in the room, accompanied by smacking lips and deep sighs. It was similar to the reaction one remembered from pre-war B movies. Maybe even louder now, so that at one point an annoyed Blockführer yelled: Ruhe da! (Silence!) —and the excited racket obediently piped down."
SOURCE: Wiesław Kielar's memoirs [461]

"They showed us science movies and comedies of the lowest sort. There were some traveling reviews and cabarets in German. It is not worth talking about. They did it only to erase any remainder of morality and higher spirit from our human hearts."
SOURCE: Wanda Tarasiewicz's account [462]

„[...] An interminable propaganda movie recounted the story of the Russian GPU. It depicted the internal and foreign operations of the Soviet security apparatus, so there were all sorts of provocative scenes. It was typical anti-Soviet propaganda."
SOURCE: Kazimierz Smoleń's account [463]

I know that in Birkenau twice they showed a musical about the German singer Erna Sack.
In Auschwitz they once showed a film about the destruction of the Warsaw Uprising. It was done to break our spirit.

"The showing of movies began as late as 1944 and took place temporarily in larger spaces in the dorms or in the baths. [...] The titles of the movies are forgotten, but usually they were propaganda or romantic-adventure films, all of them German productions." [464]

TADEUSZ PIETRZYKOWSKI

SOCCER MATCH ALEKSANDER KOŁODZIEJCZYK

---

[458] *Ibidem*, p. 112
[459] Auschwitz Museum [APMA-B, Zespół Oświadczenia, t. 101, k. 97]
[460] Cyra A., *Boksował by przeżyć*. In: *Kronika*, Nr 24, Bielsko-Biała 1988, p. 6
[461] Kielar W., *Dzieła...*, *op. cit.*, p. 241
[462] Auschwitz Museum [APMA-B, Zespół Wspomnienia, t. 19, k. 29]
[463] Auschwitz Museum [APMA-B Zespół Oświadczenia, t. 114, k. 69]
[464] Iwaszko T., *Kontakt ze światem zewnętrznym*. In: *Auschwitz 1940-1950...*, *op. cit.*, p. 320

TRADE

You traded, you lived. Trading at the camp was part of everyday life. I traded too.

"Starving prisoners were always trying to satisfy their hunger. Most often the only solution what was called 'organizing', or the procurement of food during work hours, by cultivating vegetables in the garden for instance or getting something during the transfer of foodstuffs to the SS warehouses. The greatest demand was for fresh vegetables and fruits, which were totally lacking in the camp diet. In spite of the ruthless punishment of prisoners caught at 'organizing', the behavior was widespread not only in KL Auschwitz but in all the concentration camps. The illegally obtained food, including various objects 'organized' from the warehouses where the property of the exterminated was stored, was traded on the camp's 'black exchange'."[465]

I had friends who often dropped something by for me. Sometimes they wanted to pass me some margarine or a can of meat. Trading went on among practically all who did not give in to death. They did not wait for help; they acted. And they were ingenious in many ways, since the camp had so many nationalities...

I did not so much trade in food as I "organized" it. I found ways to get good stuff because I was a photographer. That's the truth!

I SUPPLIED FOOD FOR OUR WHOLE KOMMANDO,

starting in mid-1942.

Some time in the summer Schebeck[466] from Vienna, a manager at the storage rooms, came to me to be photographed. Later on he also wanted an enlargement. He did not go my boss for it, but rather came directly to me. He asked how it could be done. He wanted enlargements of

---

[465] Iwaszko T., *Zakwaterowanie, odzież i wyżywienie więźniów*. In: *Auschwitz 1940-1950 Auschwitz 1940-1950...*, op. cit., p. 47

[466] Franz Schebeck (SS-Unterscharführer), nicknamed "Schweik" by the inmates, in KL Auschwitz from 1940 to 1944; worked at the food storage rooms. More →Biographies

his whole family. And yes, I made them. I also made sure the portraits were of excellent technical quality, using soot for corrections and fixing it later with matte varnish. Tadek Myszkowski helped me with the drawing. As a result I had some very nicely finished photos.

The SS man was pleased indeed with the results of our work. I said I would gladly make more for him, but... and I stressed that last word... and then in a joking tone said:

"I could use some margarine for the developer and some bread for the fixative."

"If you come back tomorrow, you'll get it.", he replied.

And so he started bringing me food daily. He would give me a couple of loaves of bread and a bar of margarine in addition to normal rations. My friends from the pantry would drop in with another two, sometimes three loaves and two or three margarines instead of one. Sometimes they would even come up with a little marmalade.

"Willi was an expert in attracting clients and fulfilling their fancies. Thus he won over many SS men in various positions within the camp. In this way our kommando became a permanent client of the kitchen manager and the chief of Krankenbau, which was what they called the camp hospital.

[...] From his daily afternoon trips to the kitchen Willi would bring margarine, bread, sugar and sometimes sausage, and from the hospital soup made with milk, sometimes even sweetened with real sugar."

SOURCE: Janusz Karwacki's account 467

From then on I went back almost every day. My task was to get things and share them with my colleagues. It brought me joy. I had a number of people who were, in a way, my charges. They came in the evening, stood by the building and waited for me to give them food. It was risky, but since I could offer some comfort I did so. And they returned the favor.

Those who traded with me asked simply for "half and half," and I would always agree.

THE MIDDLEMAN ALWAYS TOOK HALF.

This rule was observed throughout the camp.

In early autumn of '44 I went to the warehouse for my share and the prisoner in charge of distributing food told me there was a whole thirty bar box of margarine to be had.

"Do you take "half and half?" he asked.

"Of course," I answered.

So I took out the first load of the lot, walking from the kitchen to my kommando, which was quite a distance. I carried it in a bucket covered with a kitchen towel. I had almost made it to the block when I was spied by an SS man at the gate. I could not go back, so I approached him, took off my cap as per regulations and recited the formula:

"I ask for permission to pass."

The SS man replied, "Go in."

But as I passed him, he lifted the towel. He was speechless, for he had never seen so much margarine in his life. He asked me in German where I got it.

And I, resigned in the knowledge that I faced six weeks of Penal Company, replied in the most natural way imaginable:

"Stolen."

He thought for a second and said: "Man, what am I to do with you?" Suddenly I realized that he was not a German, but a Croat, by his accent. So I had the cheek to answer him in German:

"Come tonight sir, and you'll get your half."

And come he did. I gave him four bars of margarine, rather less than I had promised, but he went away happy.

467 Auschwitz Museum [APMA-B, Zespół Wspomnienia, t. 175, s. 63]

197

Some friends from Żywiec worked in the slaughterhouse, and I always returned from visiting them with a heavy load. I would lug four sausages on my back with sides of smoked bacon tucked into my belt in front. I always let that Croatian SS guy know when I was headed to the slaughterhouse. When I returned he would be waiting at the gate. He would approach me as required by regulations. I would report to him: "Number so and so returns to camp." And he would check me on the list, pat me down, or "feel" me, as we called it, and ask quietly how many pieces. I would answer:
"Four."
"Half for me." – he would reply.
That routine lasted until the end of November '44, when the Croatian got transferred.

THINGS WEREN'T ALWAYS THAT EASY.

I recall one time when disaster over the food was all but inevitable. The boss wrote me a pantry note addressed to the food storage manager, Schebeck, and sent me over for two cans of meat. Those were one-kilogram cans of ground pork, by the way, very tasty.
I picked up my ration of bread and margarine at the same time but the prisoner who worked there—Adolf Maciejowski[468] from Chorzów—told me there was a whole crate of those cans of pork available. Again I heard, "You take half and half?"
"Sure!"
I loaded those cans into a bucket, covered them up, and left. I had only walked a few steps when I was seen by the kitchen chief, Egersdörfer. He looked like a good-natured fellow, but he wasn't. He stopped me and asked what I had in there. Cans of meat, I answered.
"Where from?"
I said I got them from the pantry manager.
"Let's go and ask."
I was all in a cold sweat. When I entered the office of the pantry manager I left the bucket by the door, purposely not bringing it in. Eckersdorfen asked Schebeck if he had given me any meat cans, but he did not ask how many. Schebeck answered:
"Sure, I did. He got them."
And to me he hissed, "Run!"
"If the pantry manager says so, then it's time to make myself scarce," I thought. I scooped up those cans and ran off holding them close. I returned a couple more times to fetch the rest and in this way brought in thirty cans. A magnificent feast! And there was plenty to share with friends.

---

[468] Adolf Maciejewski Inmate No. 1130), b. Feb. 9th 1910 in Chorzów-Batory. Brought to KL Auschwitz June 25th 1940 in the Katowice transport. More →Biographies

"Willi's connections helped provide for our other basic needs such as shoes and clothing. Here also we were taken care of by our bosses, since by being in personal service to the SS we were expected to be clean and neatly dressed."

SOURCE: Janusz Karwacki's account 📷 469

There were many prisoners in need. They kept coming to me for bread, margarine, or something warm. And if there was a piece of canned meat, the feast could be quite wonderful. Looking at it from today's perspective I can see I was endangering myself. But that was in the nature of things there. I got used to it. I had to go for that food, because I had my deal with Schebeck and it would have been stupid not to use it.

---

469 Auschwitz Museum [APMA-B, Zespół Wspomnienia, t. 175, k. 64]

When the Jews started coming to the camp in mass transports there were many items confiscated from them, all sorts of things like Dutch cheeses and raisins and figs... So sometimes I got this kind of stuff. Once, among the raisins, I found 20 dollars worth of gold. I traded it for alcohol and a meal at the canteen.

There were partly funny, partly scary moments. Once, when I was leaving the pantry I saw an SS man at the gate by the name of Kaduk[470] from Siemianowice Śląskie near Katowice. He spoke in  Silesian German dialect but he also spoke decent Polish. He started to search someone and found a bar of margarine tucked into his belt. I heard him demand in German, "Where did you get that?"

And the prisoner answered, "I don't understand."

Because there was always an official translator at the gate, the SS man called him over[471]. The translator asked the prisoner in Polish, and he answered in the most natural manner:

"Tell the prick I found it." [Polish Silesian dialect]

The SS man of course understood the answer and smacked him in the face. But that was the end of it. If he had reported him, the guy would have gotten the Penal Company and 25 lashes.

THE "HALF AND HALF" RULE WAS UNIVERSALLY OBSERVED.

One day I had an opportunity to get some food into the women's camp. One of my colleagues from Żywiec, the one who worked in the slaughterhouse, asked me to arrange to sneak some sausage in to his wife. It worked, sort of. It turned out that out of the four pieces I sent in she received only a single half-piece, since everyone in between had taken their half.

The same thing with money. They also took half.

I remember a story, which began back in February 1939 during my stay in Zakopane. I went with my friends to a girl's school prom and met a girl from Warsaw—Krysia. We danced, I liked her, and we started writing cards back and forth. It wasn't some great romance, but it was definitely a friendship. After the invasion when I ended up in the camp, I lost touch with her. I had her Warsaw address—she lived somewhere in Chmielna Street—but in the camp I was only allowed to write once a month to one address, so since I was writing to my parents, I couldn't write to anyone else. However, it turned out that the girl kept in touch with my mother.

In 1944 after the Warsaw Uprising started, my mother sent me an illegal message that Krysia was in a transit camp in Pruszków and begging for any possible financial help that could be offered; even 50–100 German marks would be appreciated.

> "After the outbreak of the Uprising in Warsaw, in August and September of 1944, over 13,000 people from Warsaw were sent to the camp—men, women and children."[472]

> "Most of the people from those transports were transferred after a few weeks as part of the preliminary evacuation of KL Auschwitz, to camps within the Reich where they were put to work in the armaments industry. Many died in those camps."[473]

I wanted to help Krysia, because for me at the time getting hold of money was no problem. Although some people were dishonest and took the money and then claimed there had been an inspection on the train and they had been forced to toss everything, I believed that with the proper calculation things could work out. I calculated that in order to get her one thousand marks I had to send out at least five thousand. I knew that the person who would go to Żywiec would take half, and the one who would go to General Government a half of that half. I went to the Jews and told them upfront that I needed money. After two or three days everything was in place. In return I gave the Jews four sausages, a loaf of bread and margarine. The sausages I procured from the slaughterhouse and the rest from the pantry. I made a deal with one guy, that I would give two sausages up front and the rest in a day or two. And that is exactly what happened. I had to be honest or else the next time I would get nothing. The Jew was pleased and so was I. I sent the money out on a Friday via the workers who were going home to Żywiec. The next day that same colleague brought me a letter from my mom saying she got 2.5 thousand and that she had sent it on to Krakow with a railway man. From there another railway employee took it to Warsaw, and still another to Pruszków. The girl received only 500 marks but she still thanked my mom wholeheartedly since she hadn't expected nearly such a sum. In the General Government original marks were very valuable.

---

[470] Kaduk Oswald (SS-Unterscharführer), b. Aug. 26th 1906 in Chorzów; butcher, fireman. In KL Auschwitz from July 1941; after December 1941 employed as sentry. Then he was in Department III as the block manager and reporting NCO of Auschwitz I. More →Biographies

[471] The translator (*Dolmetschel*) was always available for the camp manager or any reporting officer. In everyday situations the translation was probably done by any bilingual persons near at hand.

[472] Piper F., *Ilu ludzi zginęło w KL Auschwitz*, Oświęcim 1992, p. 23

[473] Albin K., *Księgi Pamięci. Transporty Polaków z Warszawy do KL Auschwitz 1940-1944*, vol. 3, Warszawa-Oświęcim 2000, p. 1293

CAMP VALU

In the camp, the values of goods were completely different from those of the outside world.

THE MOST PRECIOUS OF ALL WAS FOOD, ESPECIALLY SAUSAGE.

For that "currency" you could get just about anything. Some prisoners received sausage or other durable smoked meats in parcels. I remember the case of a famished colleague, who managed to get into a transport of newly arrived prisoners and started shouting from within their midst, "Guys, great fortune! Sausage, they have it, fat, they have it. They have the greatest treasure—sausage!"

The butchers sold four SS sausages for a hundred dollars. In other places you could get sausage cheaper, but that was for the inferior stuff. Normally, we got a twice weekly ration of 5 dekagrams of inferior horse sausage, which was red and tough. Sometimes they would give us beef. Compared to that real pork sausage was something wonderful.

Second in value was bread and third, margarine. Two breads and a bar of margarine were worth 100 American dollars. For 5 dollars you could buy only half of a small portion of bread. Soup was lower on the list.

Cigarettes always held their value. You could buy them in the camp canteen, mostly French or Croatian ones, but occasionally the really good German ones. Of course those French cigarettes were really strong.

"The vocabulary connected to stimulants, which were of course hard to obtain at the camp, is noteworthy. The addicts—smokers and coffee drinkers—searched for those items in the exchange market, sometimes boying them in the canteen, receiving them in parcels, or obtaining them in some other, creative way. Smoking was tolerated at the camp only in designated hours and places. However, prisoners smoked furtively in various circumstances and times, hastily passing one lighted cigarette from one person to the next. In such a circumstance even one puff was a pleasure, and the promise of getting a few more later kept hope alive. There were very few brands of cigarettes at the camp, mostly the cheap German ones like Haudegens (Pol. "junaki") and Junos. There were also Ballerinas, Zorkis and a few others. For a while, after the Nazi takeover of Yugoslavia, the canteen had Bregavas, Dravas and Sava tobacco. During the most intense period of extermination activities, the privileged few smoked all kinds of often excellent cigarettes from the countries under Hitler's heel—for instance the famous, very strong Gauloises."[474]

You could get cigarettes for German marks but only prisoners from Silesia, Pomerania and Poznan had those marks, because those areas had been incorporated into the Reich. They would usually get them from their families and could use them to buy in the canteen. Prisoners from the General Government area had it harder. They had to figure out other ways to get cigarettes because they seldom had the money for them.

[474] Jagoda Z., Kłodziński S., Masłowski J., *Oświęcim...*, op. cit., p. 45–46

"I remember, probably in 1940, toward the end of the fall, a famished Muselmann, his nose blue as a beet and long as a carrot, was walking unsteadily from Block 4. He was so weak he wobbled. His eyes were swollen in the typical way, so all you could see of them was just little slits. He walked as if strangely happy because he had a long tube in his mouth, rolled from piece of cement bag. In the funnel of that paper he had put a bit of tobacco. The blue smoke was more a product of the burning paper than tobacco and he walked on, smoking, only to drop dead after perhaps ten more steps while still smoking his final treasure."
Source: Krzysztof Hofman's account [475]

I too tried to get as many cigarettes as possible, although I was not a smoker. My colleagues knew that and kept sniffing around for my cigarettes. Like Tadek Myszkowski, for instance...

I hid my cigarettes in the bellows of the camera. I stashed them because they were easy to barter. Once, there came a time when there were no cigarettes anywhere in the camp, not even in the canteen. Tadek, that rascal, had figured out where I had hid them and helped himself to two packets out of that bellows. I came in and saw him puffing away. I asked him, "Where in hell did you get that cigarette?!"
And he said, "I... I organized it..."
Suspicious, I ran into the atelier, and looked inside the bellows, and thought to myself, "Jesus Christ! The cigarettes are gone!"
"You rat," I thought to myself, "You might at least have saved them for the ladies!"
Sometimes women prisoners asked for cigarettes. To whom would I be giving them if not to my Polish women?

"On April 28th 1942, when women occupied a few blocks in Auschwitz I, we were taken to the men's camp to Erkennungsdienst, in order to be photographed for the political criminals' album. It was there that we first established contacts with the Polish prisoners who worked there and who supplied all the smokers with cigarettes. Until the end of Auschwitz-Birkenau, cigarettes were provided for us by those men."
Source: Anna Tytoniak's account [476]

Unfortunately Tadek noticed somewhere that I was giving cigarettes away and chided me for sucking up to the ladies. But all in all he was a nice guy. His life dream was to die one day while inside a woman... or so he would say. Anyway, his nickname "Nase" was no accident. His "nose" was enormous... He was a short man, with bow legs that he had supposedly broken while skiing. But his "nose"... quite a guy. He was an incredible ladies' man.

POSSESSIONS BROUGHT BY THE DEPORTEES: SUITCASES

[475] Jagoda Z., Kłodziński S., Masłowski J., *Więźniowie ...*, op. cit., p. 164
[476] Jagoda Z., Kłodziński S., Masłowski J., *Oświęcim...*, op. cit., p. 182

Smokers sold their bread for cigarettes. I myself saw smokers give away a whole portion of bread—one third of a loaf, or about one kilogram—for a single cigarette. During some other periods, you could get four or five cigarettes for a portion of bread.

Of course there were those wise guys who hollowed a loaf with a knife, leaving only the outside crust. They ate the inside, stuck a little bit of it back into the crust and then, after they had perfected that empty shell they would trade it. Similar cheating was going on with margarine. You could buy a small stick of margarine for a cigarette. It usually weighed 2 dekagrams, but sometimes it was less than 1.5 dekagrams. Someone would carve out a bar from a potato, case it nicely in margarine, and exchange for a cigarette. That was what the trading looked like sometimes.

"There were places at the camp popularly known as exchanges. Such an exchange [...]commonly happened between blocks 18 and 19 and the approaches to them. There, in the outside space, flourished the barter of whatever was available, with bread as the basic currency. The exchange rates depended on the supply of cigarettes in the camp. There were different values for the 'canteen' cigarettes, as opposed to the 'organized' ones, and still different values for those from 'freedom'—(i.e. from parcels)."
SOURCE: Ludwik Kozakiewicz's account[477]

If someone had marks, he could buy razor blades or shaving cream in the canteen, although there were barbers at the camp who shaved the prisoners and shaving was obligatory. Moreover, the canteen sold beets—sliced and fermented in a barrel—or portions of snails. A portion of salted escargots from the barrel cost two marks. They were incredibly salty and there was nowhere to soak them. Yet if you managed somehow to rinse and sauté them, they were not bad. A few times I bought them myself, but only in the beginning of my time at the camp up till 1942, when I got a few marks from my mom.

They also sold other small items in the canteen, such as a postage stamp once a month. That was a necessity, for without a stamp you could not mail a letter. There was practically nothing else at the canteen. Ah, very rarely—condoms.

"Prisoners were allowed to shop in the canteen only on specific days, and only if they had marks in their account, deposited during registration or sent by money order from their families. In fact the canteens did not play any positive role because of the poor selection of foodstuffs they offered."[478]

[477] Ibidem, p. 176–177

[478] Iwaszko T., Zakwaterowanie. odzież i wyżywienie więźniów. In: Auschwitz 1940-1950..., op. cit., p. 46

ANOTHER HIGHLY PRIZED ITEM WAS ALCOHOL.

The spirits were smuggled in from the General Government. The smugglers sold it to the workers who labored around the camp in the area of the large watchtowers, the masons and carpenters. They brought booze into the camp and passed it to the prisoners. There were arranged spots at the building sites where the SS man's eye couldn't reach. One would bring alcohol, another one dollars. Later that alcohol had to be secreted into the camp. As I recall, the largest scale trafficking was done by the sweepers kommando. They had brooms with long brushes and when they were entering the camp they carried those brooms on their shoulders like shovels. In with the brushes they hid a bottle and attached its neck to the handle. One time, a bottle fell out and broke at the gate. The SS men searched the whole kommando and found twelve bottles. All the prisoners of the kommando were sent down for penal exercises and some got twenty five lashes.

Auschwitz II-Birkenau. Shaving brushes taken from the deportees

The vodka was also smuggled via the cesspool. The turds were pumped out from the camp latrines and dumped somewhere, but not all. They sank the bottles in the remainder and brought them into the camp that way. Later those bottles were pulled out, washed and the liquor went into trade. People bought it, because after work they just wanted a nip—especially the prisoner-functionaries: the kapos, block chiefs and clerks.

"The Krakow liquor was trafficked into the camp in various ways, for instance in bottles stuck into brooms or into the shafts of a cart pulled by prisoners (the shaft was a metal tube, screwed tight and painted in a faux wood pattern). I saw a few suitcases filled with bottles of the 'Krakow' vodka, which were brought in by an SS man—the ambulance driver of the car that carried off the sick to the gas chamber."
SOURCE: Dr. Tadeusz Orzeszko's account [479]

"Comrades from the iron workshop told me that they smuggled alcohol to the camp in water pipes. They took their tools and went out ostensibly to repair the waterworks."
SOURCE: Józef Osika's account [480]

"Offering a quarter liter of vodka to the block chief made the donor a block celebrity. He could lie in bed, smoke in the room etc."
SOURCE: Józef Brodnicki's account [481]

Sometimes the SS found out about a drunken prisoner and caught him red-handed. If he was German, he spent a few days in the bunker and, at most, lost his job in a good kommando.
But a drunk Pole first went to the bunker and then for six weeks to the Penal Company.

"The desire for a momentary intoxication and forgetfulness was so strong that people risked their lives for a sip of liquor. The Germans would torture a prisoner caught drinking to obtain the identities of people who provided the vodka."
SOURCE: Dr. Tadeusz Orzeszko's account [482]

---

[479] Jagoda Z., Kłodziński S., Masłowski J., *Oświęcim...*, op. cit., p. 198
[480] *Ibidem*, p. 197–198
[481] *Ibidem*, p. 199
[482] *Ibidem*, p. 190

Once I hustled some vodka myself and we had a party. It was in '42 or '43 I think. We drank to forget. It helped for a moment. If one had a drink, I mean not got drunk, but just a drink, the world seemed not so terrible. Then you sobered up, returned to reality and again tried to organize a bottle. Half a liter of spirits made about a liter and a quarter of vodka. We burned sugar and diluted the spirits. In that way we obtained mock-brandy: "zapalanka". To that we added an appetizer, for instance a piece of cheese, and that would make for a celebration. Not only us, but other colleagues as well. Sometimes we invited each other over.

At Christmas '43 a friend's slipper came unglued and he found inside it a hundred dollar bill. For that much you could get two half-liter bottles of vodka if the exchange rate was favorable. We gathered at the kommando, because we were allowed to go there even on a Sunday or a holiday. The master of diluting spirits into drinkable liquor was an older photographer from Ostrów Mazowiecka: Gienuś. He begged me for this task claiming to be an expert. He poured half a liter of spirit into one bowl, then the water for diluting it into the other. Then, absent mindedly, he poured one of the bowls down the sink drain. He had poured out the wrong bowl! He was so upset, he ran off in despair towards the electric wires. He wanted to kill himself!

We caught ahold of him at the last moment and asked what the hell he was doing; there was still another bottle. He replied in despair, "But I destroyed one. Such precious treasure..."
He tormented himself about it for a long time after.

Dollars and gold appeared at the camp with the mass Jewish transports. Today it might seem strange,

BUT MONEY HAD NO VALUE IN THE CAMP.
Gold, diamonds, marks, dollars or British pounds were not objects of desire for an average prisoner, although some SS men made deals with inmates, even Jews, to get gold and diamonds and later took them to their families. The Jews, especially the Dutch or Belgian ones, brought a lot of diamonds.

So the money was no longer valuable, but for food you could get just about anything. Getting dollars, marks, gold and diamonds for food—in Auschwitz it was easy. All it took was having access to food or the proper connections.

I personally hustled food, but did not hustle gold or other valuables because I had had bad experiences. Soon after the New Year, at the beginning of '43, Marian Studencki

—who had supplied all those delicacies for our second Christmas Eve— got in touch with his wife who lived nearby, in Maków near Sucha Beskidzka, and started trafficking. He had paid off some SS guy. One day they announced that anybody who wanted could go to the train station. It was a trap. A colleague came to me and told me to let Marian know. I did so. Marian swore not to go, but on the second day he went anyway. He got searched and they found gold and cash on him. He went straight to the bunker. It was Sunday; on Monday he was shot at the Wall of Death at Block 11.[483]
Another fellow worked at searching the suitcases of the Jews, in "Kanada". One day he came to me and brought a whole pile of cash, all hundred dollar bills, about 10 thousand in all. I showed him the open stove and told him to toss it in there. He first looked at me, and then burned the whole parcel. That money had zero value for either him or me.

"The belongings of the murdered people were sorted by the 'Kanada' kommando. It had everything. [...] Most came in with the Dutch Jews. Cash was sewn into their collars, jewelry hidden in heels. Their clothes contained every precious item imaginable."
Source: Józef Paczyński's account [484]

"Kanada was: gold, diamonds, jewelry, foreign currencies, watches, furs, clothes and shoes, elegant bedding, comforters, pillows, childrens' toys and other personal items. Kanada was also high calorie food, which rich Jews brought to the camp thinking they were going to Eastern Europe where, according to the assurances of Nazi authorities, they would find a peaceful existence. Ham and meat in cans, salami, excellent Dutch or Danish cheeses, cans of condensed milk, sardines, sugar, chocolate, wine, bread, tobacco and cigarettes."
Source: Kazimierz Albin's account [485]

„Loaded with trunks, suitcases and bundles, the cars left one by one to the warehouses at the Effektenlager, where all that property was subject to further, more thorough selection. A large part of those things, food and jewelry in particular, found its way by various routes into the camp."
Source: Wiesław Kielar's memoirs [486]

The temptation to take a large sum of money or valuables was, if at all, momentary. In the late spring of 1944 the French Jews started coming. On the other side of the corridor, opposite our atelier, was the space where they confiscated property. The prisoners walked along the hall and handed over everything they had.
They had already been selected. Some had already gone to the gas, and the others were brought here.

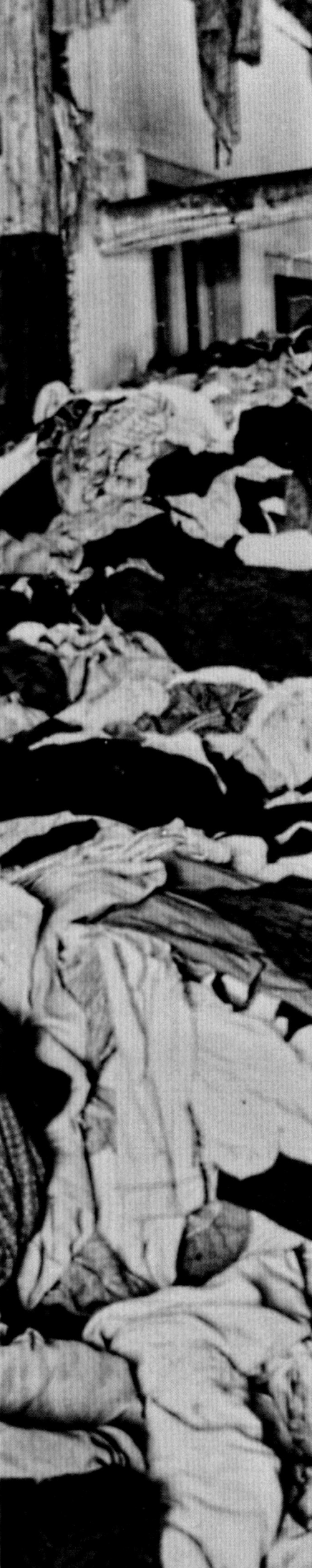

[483] It happened on January 25th 1943
[484] Paczyński J., *Byłem fryzjerem...*, op. cit.
[485] Auschwitz Museum [APMA-B, Zespół Wspomnienia, t.149, k. 112-113]
[486] Kielar W., *Dzieła...*, op. cit., p. 241

They were supposed to receive their numbers and relinquish their precious items. There was a crowd of them outside the atelier waiting in line. We regular prisoners were not allowed to remain there at that time, but were at least allowed to step out into the hallway. I opened the door and at that moment an older man about fifty years old spoke to me. He had on a cap full of gold, some coins and diamonds. He spoke in broken Polish:

"Take it, it will last you till the end of your life. I have no more use of this fortune."

I was never greedy for such things, as I knew it was a rotten business which usually ended badly. I thanked him and left him there. I resisted the temptation and did right, as that stuff would have given me nothing. At most, I could trade it for another half-liter of spirit, which I hardly drank anyway.

One time, I stopped by to see some friends who lived in a separate room, because one of them was a block clerk and another—comrade Andrzej Rablin[487]—worked in

a Kommando with access to Kanada. He pulled out a cloth sack and threw it on the table. A few diamonds fell out. They were the size of peas, maybe even larger.

"Fuck," he said, "I have a fortune in my pocket but can't even get a drink of vodka."

---

[487] Andrzej Rablin (Inmate No. 1410), b. Jan. 1st 1914 in Krakow. Brought to KL Auschwitz on July 18th 1940 in the Krakow-Tarnów transport. More→Biographies

Clothes collected in the storage depot „Kanada" near Auschwitz I

LOVE IN THE CAMP

Intimate contact with a woman was nearly impossible in the camp.[488] In spite of that sometimes, rarely, the canteen sold condoms.
I was approached by some women —German—often quite pretty, and although those were only professional encounters, you must remember that before the camp I had been with girls. Not much, but I had normal sexual needs. I considered these feelings quite understandable, especially since my work put me in touch with women. Young, reasonably well-nourished men had to find ways to deal with their sex drive. I had to release that tension somewhere.
We men sometimes had wet dreams, but that did not give particular satisfaction. Some masturbated. That was very frequent and completely understandable. There were also irregular encounters with other men. I myself had physical revulsion for that. I never heard of such cases in our kommando. But I did hear of such cases elsewhere in the camp.

"At work we were tormented by rocks, in the camp—by homosexuals. There were some Germans that raped serially, whenever they felt like it. They would just come up to someone and say, 'Today you stay on the block!'
You protest, 'But why? I'm going to work!'
A short reply, 'Out of the question. You shall stay.'
Hell can wait! The whole barracks is empty. I remember Piotruś. He got raped on the kitchen table in front of other prisoners. Unfortunately I witnessed that with my own eyes. I curled up in a corner, closed my eyes, covered my ears. It didn't help. The first one, the second, the third... They gang raped him and then tossed him on the ground. It was too much for Piotruś. He got up and went straight to the wires. A few spasms. Fog in his eyes and then the end."
SOURCE: Józef Skrzypek's account[489]

I was well fed so once or twice a month I went to the Puff. I went for temporary respite.

"Eventually, brothels were created in ten camps in the Reich and on the occupied Polish territories. One of them opened in Auschwitz I in August 1943; 20 women worked there. In November of the same year another one opened in Auschwitz III - Monowitz, where 10 women worked. The original kommando was located in Block 24. It was the first building on the left behind the gate with the sign 'Arbeit macht frei'"[490]

However, the older comrades condemned such behavior. The majority, in protest against the German system, did not use the brothel. They said it was unethical and dishonorable.

"No self-respecting Pole would ever disgrace himself by going there. We considered ourselves political prisoners, who were illegally detained and suffer for our country. Using such a facility provided for us by the enemy was beneath our dignity. We treated it as an abomination."
SOURCE: Józef Stós's account[491]

"Not true. Everybody went there. The Poles, the Germans—everybody. A man who had spent several years behind the wires doesn't think of his country at those times. He wonders if he will live another day."
SOURCE: Jerzy Bielecki's account[492]

---

[488] The women's camp was located 3 kilometers away in Auschwitz II-Birkenau. The female prisoners stayed in a designated part of the main camp only between March and August 1942 and then from 30th of October 1944 until the evacuation. There were instances of sexual intercourses between male and female prisoners, but they were certainly very rare.

[489] Skrzypek J., *Różowi*. In: *Dziecko szczęścia...*, op. cit., s.12

[490] Weseli A., „Puff w Auschwitz." Nov. 4th 2009 *Polityka*. http://www.polityka.pl/historia/260561,1,puff-w-auschwitz.read

[491] Zychowicz P., *Domy publiczne w Auschwitz*: 21st July 2007 Rzeczpospolita

[492] *Ibidem*

DUBLOSAN GUMMI SCHUTZ — ALUMINUM CONDOM CAN

For good work, such as completion of a particular project, prisoners-experts were sometimes given by their Kommandoführer a token of 2-3 marks. They could take this token to the brothel to pay for their pleasure; the entry fee was 2 camp marks.

Also those who were well nourished went when they had the desire and health for it. And, of course, if they had the money. A wasted Muselmann would not go there, what would be the point? And of course the Jews were excluded. The brothel was available to all Arians except the Russians.

You could pay your way in with regular money, paper money that is, since we never got any coins. Nobody cared where we you had gotten the money. Usually we traded it from the Jews; and sometimes our families sent some.
I did use the brothel. But like the other inmates I knew that the cathouse was another element of the humiliating motivational system, which rewarded us for compliance. That system intensified after May 1943.[493]

The Germans commonly called it:

"FRAUEN, FRESSEN, FREIHEIT" (WOMEN, GRUB, FREEDOM)

and awarded special prizes for particular productivity at work: the right to more frequent correspondence, food bonuses, permission to buy cigarettes or even release from the camp—that last option for German prisoners only.

"The 'institution' created by Höss was not just a work of cynicism and sophistication, but also of careful planning. It was supposed to be the propaganda rebuttal to accusations of starvation, terror and murder."
SOURCE: Władysław Fejkiel's memoirs[494]

"How did the Puff get established? I lived in Block 24, when one day the block leader Oksy came in and said we were moving to Block 3a, bacause here is where the Puff will be. Nobody wanted to believe it. A Puff in the camp? Impossible! But soon it became reality.
Builders and painters went into Block 24 to make certain adjustments. Large rooms were changed into several smaller ones. The work was quickly completed and one day on our way back from work we saw women in the windows of that block."
SOURCE: Józef Paczyński's account[495]

Visits to the Puff had precisely defined rules. Downstairs at building 24 stood a designated prisoner-functionary, to whom you handed the token. You were given a ticket and went upstairs. The use of condoms was included in the price of the visit. Every girl had her own space which was furnished like a room in a regular home. A bed, a table, lace curtains.

---

[493] The motivational system used one mark bonus vouchers "Premienschein" which could be exchanged for tickets to Block 24.
[494] Fejkiel W., *Więźniarski szpital...*, op. cit., p. 161
[495] Auschwitz Museum [APMA-B, Zespół Oświadczenia, t. 100, k. 107]

"At the designated hour we gather at the entrance to the block. Everyone is spruced up, clean and fresh. We go upstairs. A 'schwanzparade' takes place in front of a male nurse. Everyone has to pull down his pants and allow for a detailed inspection of his penis. Everything has to happen according to the principles of hygiene. After the parade we go to individual rooms…"
SOURCE: Janusz Karwacki's account [496]

I tried to get the girl that I liked. I waited until she invited me in. I stayed there for the prescribed time. At the sound of a bell all guys had to leave the rooms and the next ones would enter. If you had the money you could buy yourself a double session, or half an hour but that rarely happened. I seldom heard of someone being so extravagant.
After the visit a nurse disinfected your penis and you went back to your barracks.

There were quite nice looking girls working at the Puff. No one who hasn't spent a few years behind wires can understand how impressed we were at their appearance.

"[As I lay in the hospital block] I observed one day a young girl with her hair made up, her eyes and lashes defined with henna, in a beautiful blue night shirt with black lace and a blue dressing gown folded on her arm. On her feet were high heeled slippers. (…) With a nonchalant stride she walked along the block following a female block leader who was taking her to her bed. For us it was a phenomenon."
SOURCE: Zofia Stępień-Bator [497]

Compared to regular prisoners the girls working in the brothel looked like birds of paradise. They had real feminine, nicely styled hair and they were very neat. They bathed daily and dressed well. They did not wear prison uniforms, but civilian dresses. And they were well nourished.

"The SS authorities took very good care of the Puff staff. They got white bread from the dietary kitchen of Krankenbau and for the money they earned they bought mineral water, cigarettes and perfumes from the prisoners' canteen."
SOURCE: Władysław Fejkiel's memoirs [498]

I knew the women from the Puff because I took their ID pictures. One day they came in, laughing and relaxed. Very pretty. They joked and giggled in front of the camera. At the time there were eight Poles and seven Germans. I spoke with them. They were glad to talk once given a chance. The Germans had promised them that after six months they would be released to freedom.

The women were recruited from among the prisoners. Some of them were forced to do it and some, most likely professional prostitutes, volunteered. Many of the women had they not made that choice would have been condemned to immediate extermination. The German promises were however all false. It was just a deferred death sentence. Hardly any of them made it through.[499]

"There was a known case around the camp, where a young girl declared to the Commandant of the female camp Hessler that she was ready to work at the brothel. Hessler, who in this case decided to be humane, asked her age. She answered that she was 17 and that she had never been with men; but that, however, she wanted to save her life, and since she did not see any other solution she volunteered for the brothel in the hope of better conditions and survival. It seems that Hessler sent that girl to another, less brutal labor kommando."
SOURCE: Alfred Woycicki's deposition [500]

"At one point they announced they were looking for candidates for light work. She volunteered (…) not knowing what was involved. She was received by an SS man. (…) After he examined her, he asked: 'Do you know where you are going?' She said, 'No, I don't, they told me to some light work, where there will be plenty of bread.' So he said to her: 'Listen, the work will consist of you dealing with men and there also will be a procedure which will deprive you of a chance of motherhood. Think about it; there are other ways to survive the camp. You are young, you will want to be a mother and after this it will be completely impossible'. But she kept saying: 'A mother, a mother… who cares? I need bread.'"
SOURCE: Zofia Stępień-Bator's account [501]

My favorite was a Pole named Krysia, from Ostrołęka. She was a pretty, statuesque blond. And also Basia from Warsaw. Of the Germans, Helga and Sonia.

EVEN IN THE BROTHEL THE SS FOLLOWED THE NUREMBERG LAWS.

"The guards looked through the spy-hole to make sure everything was going by the rules.
It was because the prisoners were only allowed to satisfy their needs in the 'missionary' position. All deviation from the standard was treated by the SS as a perversion. Prior to intercourse they also had to take off their shoes."[502]

---

[496] Auschwitz Museum [APMA-B, Zespół Wspomnienia, t. 175, k. 74]
[497] Auschwitz Museum [APMA-B, Zespół Oświadczenia, t. 68, k. 51-52]
[498] Fejkiel W., Więźniarski szpital…, op. cit., p. 161-162
[499] German historian Rober Sommer indentified 230 women who had worked in the brothels within the Nazi labor camps. The majority were German. There were 49 Poles. There were a few Ukrainians, Belarusians and a Dutch woman. In Auschwitz a few dozen girls were employed for this purpose.
[500] Auschwitz Museum [APMA-B, Höss's Trial, t. 7, k. 7]
[501] Auschwitz Museum [APMA-B, Zespół Oświadczenia, t. 68, k. 52]
[502] Sommer R., Das KZ-Bordell, Paderborn 2010

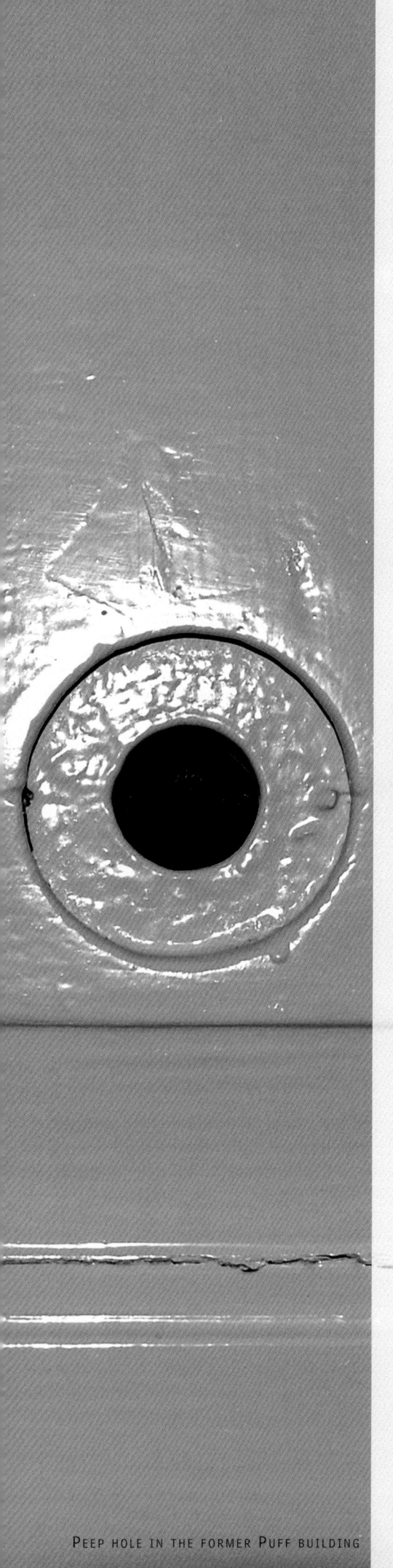

PEEP HOLE IN THE FORMER PUFF BUILDING

The Germans could go to bed with the Germans, Poles with the Poles or other Slavs. But that was just in theory, since in practice prisoners traded their tickets. Especially the Germans were keen on such switcheroos. The Polish girls were prettier. If I wanted a particular girl, even a German, I would trade. But I had to have a ticket to the right Pole, one that the German would want.

There were cases when I got a bad number, could not switch it with anybody, and it all went to naught—a wasted fee. There were some ugly, even repellant women there, among them three Poles. They had volunteered, so they were accepted. And there were also two disgusting German women which were used by the German men by default if they could not exchange their ticket. But the Germans were not particularly choosy. Almost any female body was good enough for them.

Going to the brothel was a pleasure for me. I always got good service. I was fully satisfied and from the girl's behavior I could tell that she was too.

The women there had their favorite men, for whom they waited. Such was the case with "The Nose"—or Tadek Myszkowski—one of the biggest supporters of the Auschwitz brothel.

Tadek Myszkowski made paintings, caricatures and other kinds of graphic works for SS men. A caricature is what got him sent to Auschwitz. He drew a German woman spreading her legs with soldiers in helmets jumping out of her vagina and he pinned it up in a toilet at his uncle's restaurant in Zakopane. Somebody informed and he and his uncle were both arrested.

Our boss liked Tadek, so he would often give him brothel tokens. Once in mid-'44, then-Lagerführer Schwarz came to see Tadek and told him they wanted him to make caricatures of SS officers. They organized a stag party for somebody and decided to decorate the room with the caricatures.

"I remember colleague Myszkowski received the order to create decorative pictures on Bristol paper with grotesque SS themes. I saw those pictures. One of them was called 'Grabner watches bathing ladies through binoculars'. I think there was a dinner in the SS casino[503], or maybe a party, and those pictures served as decorations."
SOURCE: Franciszek Targosz's account[504]

I know that when our boss called Myszkowski and asked him to do that he replied in his halting German that he lacked inspiration. Lagerführer asked when his inspiration was going to come back.
"If you locked me up in the brothel, it would come back fast," replied Tadek without hesitation.
Indeed, they locked him up in the brothel for three days with his easel, papers and crayons. After three days the caricatures were done to SS satisfaction. Tadek commented on his stay concisely: "Boys, I got fucked all over!"

---

[503] SS canteen
[504] Auschwitz Museum [APMA-B, Zespół Oświadczenia, t. 113, k. 64]

TRUE LOVE

It's amazing, but in the nightmare world of Block 24 true affections could be born. I watched a few times as my colleagues fell head over heels in love.

"One of my friends, a Pole, worked at the camp's fire brigade. He spent all his money on visits to one of the girls, Irka. He really fell in love. Apparently, after the war they got married and left together for Canada or Australia."
SOURCE: Jerzy Bielecki's account [505]

Those in love with the girls from the Puff went to see them after roll call. They circled the building and climbed the walls with a ladder. Or sometimes the girls pulled them up with ropes.

They brought vodka and had drinking parties with those girls. Romance blossomed. Sometimes there were screw-ups. I remember a musician, Zygmunt Wojszczyk[506], who had a soft spot for one of those girls. She was so vulgar that she really was suitable for that kind of work. Once she pulled him up on a rope and half way up she asked, "But Zygmunt, do you have the vodka?"
And he, jokingly, replied that he did not. She let the rope go. He fell, the bottle broke, and he cut himself badly on the glass. They had to take him to hospital and stitch him up.

I also recall the love story of a certain actor. Before the war I had seen him in a movie about a seventeenth-century warrior. He worked near the women's kommandos. He was caught in flagrante with a Jewish woman. I heard from a physician, Dr. Rudolf Diem, who worked in at the operating room in block 28, that as punishment he was castrated without anesthesia.

The most famous affair was the love between Edek Galiński[507] and a Jewish woman called Mala Zimetbaum[508].
I knew Edek personally. He was a very cheerful man as you can tell from his mug shot.

Edek said they would try to escape. And indeed he dressed up as an SS man, took Mala and walked her out of the camp. But unfortunately in Jeleśnia near Żywiec they were stopped by German border guards and escorted back to the camp.

The couple escaped from the camp on June 24th 1944. Edek wore an SS-Rottenführer uniform. He escorted Mala, who had on a work suit. He showed the guard a forged pass and explained that he and the prisoner, who carried a washbasin on "his" head (not a toilet bowl as pictured in the sketch), were going to the Auschwitz apartment of a certain German. From there, they walked away unobtrusively, without Mala being recognized. But on July 7th they were picked up by a German patrol, which captured them and brought them back to Auschwitz.

---

505 Zychowicz P., *Domy publiczne w Auschwitz*. In: *Rzeczpospolita*, 21st of July 2007
506 Zygmunt Wojszczyk (Inmate No. 5482) b. Jan. 10th 1910 in Częstochowa. More →BIOGRAPHIES
507 Edward Galiński (Inmate No. 531), b. Oct. 5th 1923 in Więckowice. Brought to KL Auschwitz on June 14th 1940 in the Kraków-Tarnów transport. More →BIOGRAPHIES
508 Mala Zimetbaum (Inmate No. 19880), b. Jan. 26th 1918 in Brzesko. Came to KL Auschwitz on Sept. 3rd 1942 in the transport from Malines, Belgium. At the camp she worked as an interpreter and courier. More →BIOGRAPHIES

MALA ZIMETBAUM

"Mala Zimetbaum was an extraordinary person. She had a solid, influential position at the women's camp but she never abused her power. She always was helpful, with a strong personality. They said at the camp that her escape with the Pole Edek Galiński was no ordinary one. It was said that they took along documents to inform the world about Auschwitz"
SOURCE: Raya Kagan's deposition [509]

After the war I found out that Bolesław Staroń [510] spent 70 days in the cell with Edek. He told their story:

"They arrested her [Mala] when she was leaving a store to join Edek who waited nearby. They had made a promise never to separate and never to leave each other. So Edek did not run and when ordered by the German guard he performed the 'Mützen ab!' routine, removing his cap from his head and exposing his shaven skull, betraying that he was a camp escapee."
SOURCE: Bolesław Staroń's account [511]

They had been interrogated and awaited their sentence.

"I wondered at Edek's behavior. After the evening roll call which like the morning roll call took place in the cells, he would stand by the slanted window and sing the beautiful Italian song 'Serenata in Messico'. [...] Even today I can hum and play that melody, not remembering the words, which Edek sang during almost all the prison nights at the Death Block. In the quiet of the night his singing, or sometimes just his whistle, echoed through the bunker. I did not realize he was signaling Mala and his many friends around the camp that he was alive."
SOURCE: Bolesław Staroń's account [512]

[509] Langbein H., *Auschwitz przed sądem...*, op. cit., p. 98
[510] Bolesław Staroń (Inmate No. 127829) b. May 9th 1919 in Berlin-Adlershof, building technician. More → BIOGRAPHIES
[511] Auschwitz Museum [APMA-B, Zespół Oświadczenia, t. 137, k. 238]
[512] Ibidem
[513] Langbein H., *Auschwitz przed sądem...*, op. cit., p. 99
[514] "Poland is not yest lost" (*Jeszcze Polska*). Beginning of the Polish national anthem.
[515] Auschwitz Museum [APMA-B, Zespół Oświadczenia, t. 8, k. 1172]

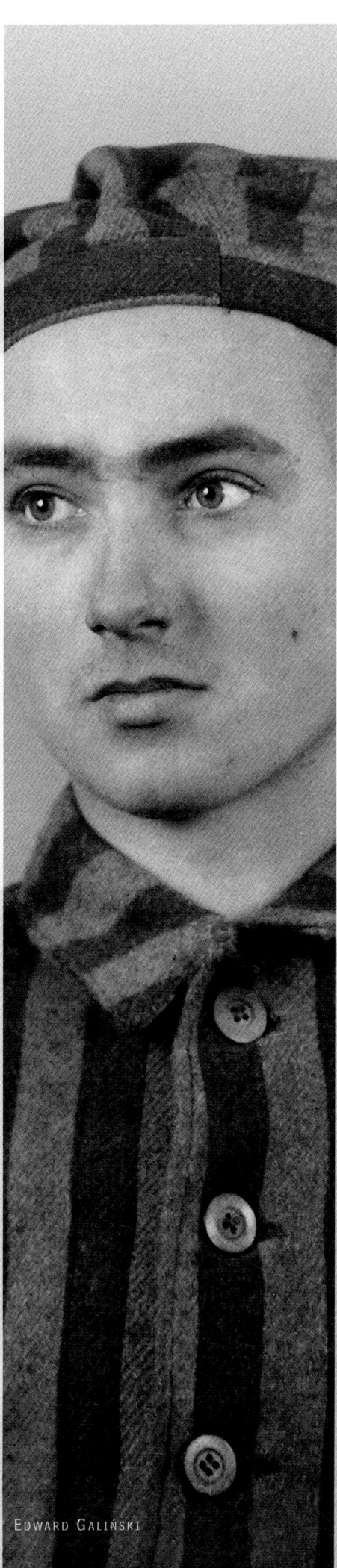

EDWARD GALIŃSKI

Finally the sentence came down. They were condemned to death.

EDEK WAS HANGED AND MALA SLASHED HER OWN WRISTS.

Someone smuggled a razor blade to her, so there was no one left to hang. That was a famous story.

"The camp manager Mandel wanted to make a big show out of Mala's execution and called a general roll call. [...] SS officer Ritter tried to take that razor blade away from her but she hit him on the face with her bloody hand. She cried: 'I will die like a hero, and you will die like a dog!' And so they carried her off in a wheelbarrow, still alive, to the crematorium."
Source: Raya Kagan's deposition [513]

"Before they finished reading out the sentence Galiński put his own head into the noose and kicked away the stool. Lagerkapo 'Jup' instantly ran to him, releasing the noose and repositioning the stool. They continued on reading the sentence. The last words were still sounding in the air when Galiński started to shout 'Poland is not yet...' [514] and then they hung him. Suddenly, from the gathering of prisoners-fitters someone commanded in Polish: 'Hats off!' In silence, thousands of prisoners' hands performed the familiar gesture. It was their last farewell and homage to the executed."
SOURCE: Władysław Kielar's account [515]

MALA'S PORTRAIT WAS DRAWN BY INMATE ZOFIA STEPIEŃ-BATOR. MALA HAD AN INFLUENTIAL POSITION OF A COURIER (LÄUFERIN). SHE WAS VERY POPULAR AMONG OTHER PRISONERS. MALA THANKED ZOFIA WITH AN AMPLE MEAL AND ARRANGED FOR THE ARTIST TO BE TRANSFERRED TO THE STEIKEREI (EMBROIDERS') KOMMANDO, WHERE THE LABOR WAS LIGHT AND INDOORS. EDWARD GALIŃSKI PASSED MALA'S PICTURE TO HIS FRIEND WIESŁAW KIELAR, WHO AFTER THE WAR DONATED IT TO AUSCHWITZ-BIRKENAU MUSEUM, TOGETHER WITH MALA'S AND EDEK'S LOCKS OF HAIR.

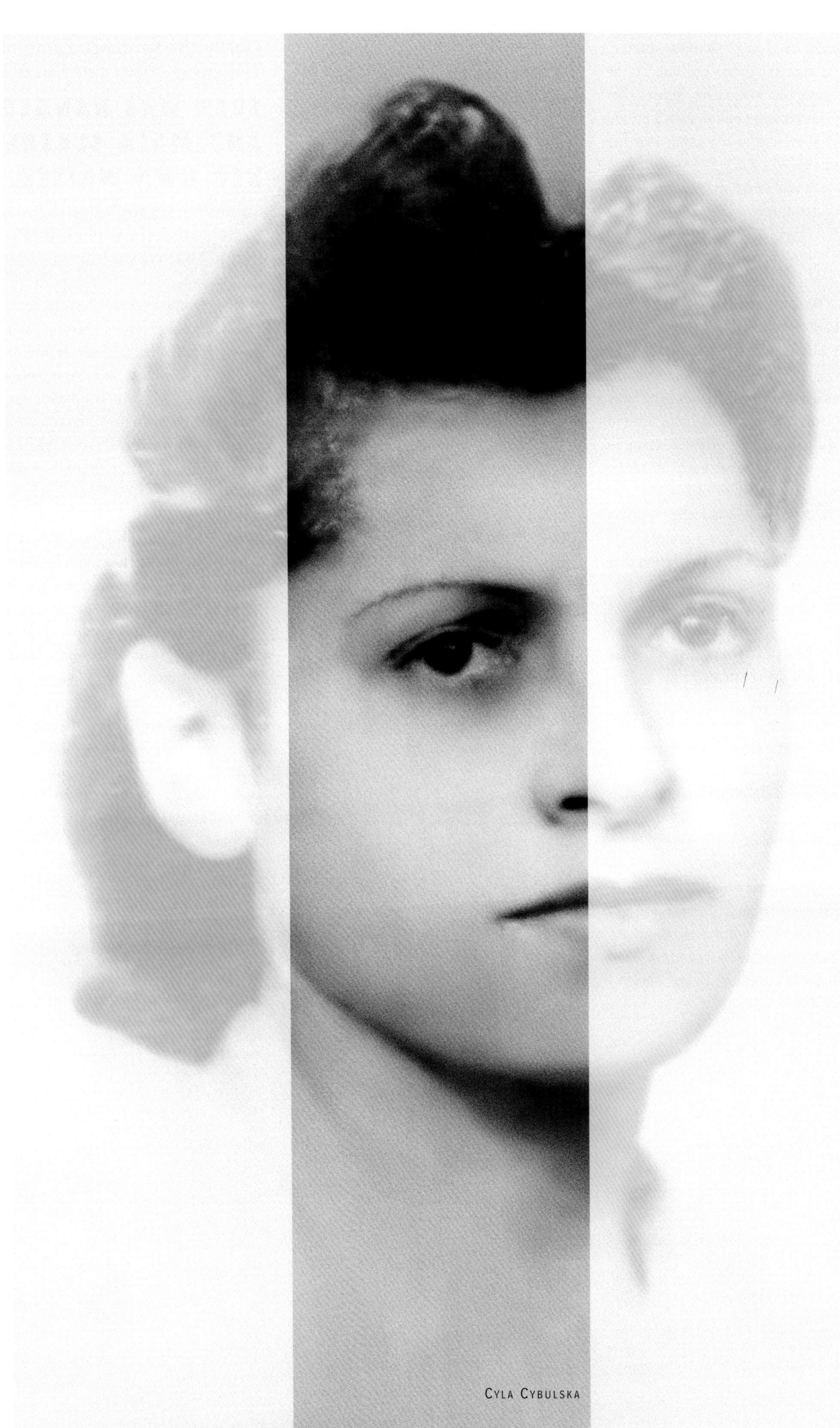

Cyla Cybulska

TRUE LOVE

Another spectacular escape of a couple took place on July 21st 1944. The lovers were Jerzy Bielecki[516], a Pole from the first transport with number 243 and a Polish Jew named Cyla Cybulska[517].

Jerzy met Cyla in the sack room and in the face of great risk they managed to see each other there. They fell in love.

Bielecki, suspecting all the Jews would be murdered during the camp evacuation, decided to save Cyla. Using his long experience of camp realities he procured an SS uniform and on July 21st 1944 took Cyla out of the camp 'for interrogation'. The escape succeeded. The runaways made it to Bielecki's family near Kielce. Soon after, however, they had to separate for safety reasons.

Bielecki went into hiding and started working with a Home Army squad where his brothers served. Cyla waited long for Jerzy's return but eventually, in April 1946, she married someone else and left for Sweden. She kept in touch with the Czerniks, Jerzy's relatives, who had sheltered her. She even sent some pictures from a hospital where she was in treatment. Jerzy's friends told him that she had fallen sick and died. He didn't believe it, but in the fall of 1946 he too got married, although he kept looking for her. In 1949 Cyla left Europe for the USA. In 1975 she was widowed. Up until then her husband had forbidden her to mention Jerzy or to look for him.

Finally in 1983, in the middle of the night, he was awakened by the telephone: 'Juracek, it is me, your Cytulka'.

Up until 1989 she visited him 11 times, although she became disenchanted with Communist Poland. Then she broke off all communications for 10 years, although Jerzy traveled to the US and tried to stay in touch. A breakthrough came at last in 1999, during the filming of a documentary about them. Afterwards, they kept in contact until the very end.

Cyla died in 2002 in New York and Jerzy on October 20th 2011 in Nowy Targ.

JERZY BIELECKI

[516] Jerzy Bielecki (Inmate No. 243) b. March 28th 1921 in Słaboszów, student. More →BIOGRAPHIES

[517] Cyla Cybulska-Stawiska (Inmate No. 29558), b. Dec. 29th 19920 in Łomża. Came to KL Auschwitz on Jan. 21st 1943. More →BIOGRAPHIES

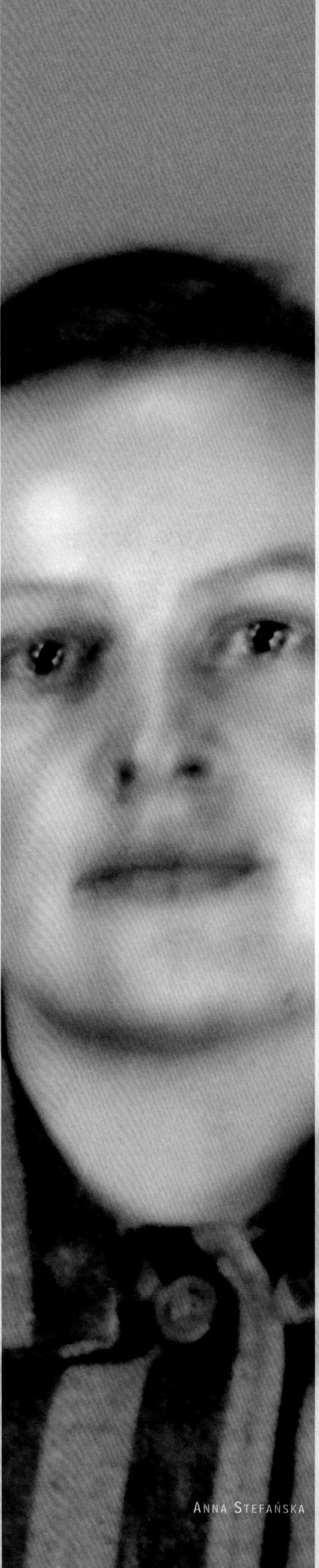

I also had a girlfriend in the camp. Often a group of prisoners was brought in by a block clerk from the women's hospital, from doctor Mengele. She was Anna Stefańska, or Baśka. As I mentioned, she did

not like her name. She was a pretty girl. I was head over heels about her. I felt it particularly strongly in 1943.

We were happy together whenever we could manage to meet and talk. She spoke excellent German. We sent each other all kinds of illegal letters. Then she came to work closer to the men's camp and so I could meet her sometimes. A certain affection was born. I admired her a lot. She was close to my heart. But it wasn't sexual.

I remember one time I got some carnations for my Basia and offered them to her with chivalry. And in 1944 I managed to find a pot of nice azaleas and sent them to her with Jurek's help. That was a most unusual thing at the camp. Flowers—apart from those famous pansies for the postcards—were a very rare sight. Maybe the gardeners brought a few blooms into the camp, but hardly anyone ever got to see them.

APART FROM THAT, THERE WERE NO FLOWERS IN THE CAMP

We were able spent some short times together only when she was there for her work. There were few other opportunities. Leisure time was not scheduled until after roll call—and at that time of day I was typically with my comrades. Moreover, I often had to work late into the evening because that was when the SS-men and other clients were available to come in.

Most of the time I chatted with Basia about our families, what they had written, and generally how they were doing. An SS man or woman would look away indulgently from these private conversations, so under those awkward conditions we were able to exchange a few words. Naturally, with the Germans present, we would avoid talking politics. We just shared our feelings and plans for the future. Sometimes, when the SS left for a bit, we whispered a few thoughts about the war and the prospects for its ending.

In 1943 I got yet another offer to leave the camp if I signed the Volkslist. I was called by the camp manager, who was then Lagerführer Aumeier[518], and asked in an official manner first about my family, and then about my intentions if I were to leave the camp. I knew the correct answer was "I would join the German military", but I did not say so. I said, truthfully, that I wanted to work in my profession, because it is a good one. Answering that way, I was ensuring the extension of my sentence. Never, neither before nor later when it got much worse, did I feel more Polish than at that moment.

I remained at the camp and kept on feeling affection for Basia. I knew the feeling was mutual because she told me so. She wrote illegal letters in which she expressed her affection. I am not talking about love, but of liking; of true friendship.

We both knew that our chances of leaving the camp were minimal. It was hard to make concrete plans for the future but we imagined that if we were to survive she would become a teacher and I would open a photo studio. We did not yet think about a future together.

After the war Basia got married and I visited her as a friend.

---

518 Hans Aumeier (SS-Sturmbannführer), b. Aug. 20th 1929 in Amberg in Bavaria; turner, office worker. Manager of KL Auschwitz from Feb. 1942 till July 1943. More →Biographies

WILHELM BRASSE

WEDDING IN AUSCHWITZ [519]

I have an especially nice memory of a very atypical event: taking a family photo of my close friend, Rudolf Friemel, a student who was a little older than me. He wore a red triangle, meaning that he was a political prisoner; in his case, an Austrian Communist. During the Spanish civil war in 1936-39 he had fought in the international Communist brigades. He told me about his Spanish girlfriend, some professor's daughter, who bore him a boy child. When the war ended they escaped to France where they were interned. That girl followed him, got a job, and lived with his family. Sadly, in February 1942 Rudolf got taken to Auschwitz. He had a privileged position at the camp. As a mechanic—a Diesel engine specialist—he got into Fahrbereitschaft, part of the transportation service, where he was appreciated even by the Germans.

"In KL Auschwitz there was a privileged group of prisoners, the so-called *Bezorzugte—Häftlinge*. Theoretically those ought to have been prisoners of impeccable conduct throughout their stay. But in practice things were different. [...] 'Bezorzugte—Häftling' was allowed to wear long hair, could have a watch, and was not required to wear the triangle next to the number on his shirt. [...] Some were permitted to go for Sunday walks outside the camp (supervised by an SS man), wearing civilian clothes. Those cases were rare, but they happened."
SOURCE: Erwin Olszówka's account [520]

"Car mechanics had better food, probably from the SS kitchen. Friemel looked well fed, as did Vesely, a cheerful boy doing office work, acting as a kind of adjutant to Friemel. They were considered inseparable and I think Friemel felt somewhat responsible for the youngster who maybe reminded him of his own youth. Friemel was upbeat and full of good humor. He was a strong man and convinced there was a way to survive that hell. A sworn Marxist of solid moral principles, he had joined the Party not out of calculation but because he consciously broke away from the socialists and opted for the Communist party. When that change occurred, I don't know. Probably in 1941, after Germany's attack on the Soviet Union."
SOURCE: Recollection in: *Wesele w Auschwitz* [521]

I became friends with Friemel since we lived in the same block. He told me a lot about his Spanish girl and his little son.

"My friend worked in the censorship office and sometimes had a chance to read Friemel's letters to the Spanish woman. She was able to quote whole paragraphs from memory. [...] So many cares, dreams, terms of endearment. My brave, poor wife! My dear Spaniard! My beloved, beloved Margo! Dear little pet! How beautiful our life will be. Don't get discouraged, be patient. I am proud of you and Eduardito. He takes after me but has your eyes, and in their look—your sunny homeland. [...] I know, wrote Rudi, that you want to break free from that misery and I am sad thinking that you want to leave with our son and be far away from me. But I can't do anything other than tell you, 'Be brave and fight with me for our future together. This is the hardest part of the road, but also the last one before reaching our goal.'"
SOURCE: Recollection in: *Wesele w Auschwitz* [522]

MARGARITA FERRER

---

519 Erich Hackl (b. 1954 in Steyr), one of the leading Austrian writers, published a book devoted to that event entitled „A wedding in Auschwitz". The book was published in Poland in 2006.
520 Auschwitz Museum [APMA-B, Zespół Oświadczenia, t. 72, k. 135]
521 Hackl E., *Wesele w Auschwitz*, Kraków 2006, p. 87
522 *Ibidem.*, p. 107-109

Rudi told me that his family in Vienna kept looking for ways for him to marry the girl even while in Auschwitz. They wrote to the chief of SS, Heinrich Himmler. Rudolf very much wanted to marry her. And so on the last Saturday of March 1944[523] a rare event took place.

THE SPANIARD CAME TO AUSCHWITZ,

where she was first taken to the secretariat.

"One day news broke out: a Spanish woman is coming to visit us, a civilian, to marry Rudi Friemel. Soon after she was brought in by one of the SS men. She looked just like you would imagine a typical Spaniard: a slender face, black hair, black eyes. She wore a dark suit and a white blouse, and on her head she had a white hat with flowers. Somebody invited her to sit but she kept standing. She was embarrassed and nervous and did not speak a word."
SOURCE: Recollection in: *Wesele w Auschwitz*[524]

"The civil registry office had three departments: births, marriages and deaths. The birth department had a book and a card index of children born in the camp. The birth book was the basis for issuing documents sent to the admission office. That, in turn, was the basis for assigning a number to a child and creating its file in the registry (register of the living).
[...] Of course, the most developed of all was the department of death certificates."[525]

"When we were leaving the office the band played another march and it seemed that the prisoners were looking at us in a more friendly way, as if the enemies of their enemies had achieved a victory. Then we went to the dining room where we found a table especially for us and the prisoners who were serving whispered to me how happy they were about this exceptional wedding."
SOURCE: Margarita Ferrer Rey's account in: *Wesele w Auschwitz*[526]

Margarita had coal-black eyes and was really beautiful. We looked at Rudi with envy but also with warmth, because he was very much liked by the Poles. My colleagues knew that he would have a wedding ceremony, so they arranged for the orchestra. The orchestra positioned itself nearby in the bath and the musicians played a song entitled: 'Long Live Love', which is kind of our Happy Birthday. A minute later everybody was under the showers and some rascal played a prank by turning on the water, so we quickly scattered. He did it for a laugh. And indeed it was funny, at least for a moment.
Rudolf Friemel and Margarita Ferrer were married in the SS head office because that's where the civil registry office was, although normally it was used for other purposes such as recording the flow of prisoners and preparing death certificates.

[523] "On March 18th Austrian inmate Rudolf Friemel (25173) married in a civil ceremony Margarita Ferrer Rey, a Spaniard of French citizenship. It was the only case of a camp inmate getting married."
SOURCE: Paczuła T., *Izby Pisarskie w KL Auschwitz*, In: *Księgi zgonów...*, op. cit., p. 32
[524] Hackl E., *Wesele...*, op. cit., p. 124
[525] Paczuła T., *Izby Pisarskie w KL Auschwitz*, In: *Księgi zgonów...*, op. cit., p. 32
[526] Hackl E., *Wesele...*, op. cit., p. 107-109

After the wedding the couple was permitted to have a picture taken with their child. I took that picture and I was most happy to do it, for he was a true friend. The child wasn't frightened and held his mom's hand.

I EXPERIENCED INCREDIBLE JOY SEEING THAT FREE LITTLE BEING.

"That was the single instance of a camp prisoner getting married. On the day of the wedding he got his civilian clothes and the couple was escorted to the Auschwitz Civil Registry. After the wedding they were brought back to the camp and lodged on the upper floor of Block 24, which was the site of the brothel. The day beore the regular occupants had been moved from their apartments."
Source: Jan Dziopek's account [527]

"After the meal we looked over the rooms assigned to us for the night, one for my father and brother in law, another one for the three of us. When we were climbing upstairs Rudi said not to get upset that they had put us up in this place that was normally occupied by prostitutes. On the upper floor, in a long corridor, we were greeted by numerous political prisoners. They congratulated us, joked and also presented us with drawings they made especially for the occasion."
Source: Margarita Ferrer Rey's account in: *Wesele w Auschwitz* [528]

"The newlyweds remained there till the next day. The prisoners gave the spouse, leaving her husband, a farewell cheer with music."
Source: Jan Dziopek's account [529]

That event was exceptional. Such things never happened although by that time in 1944 the camp rigor had softened a bit.

"In spite of frequent transports to the gas chamber and selection of the sick and even the healthy, generally speaking the conditions at the camp improved. The change generated various conjectures. The Auschwitz people attributed it to the new Commandant Liebehenschel, the successor of Höss. [...] Others maintained, having some news from the 'well informed' sources that the change of policies was caused by the reports on London radio, which alleged to know everything that was happening here."
Source: Wiesław Kielar's memoirs [530]

We learned that things would be better when the new Lagerführer, Liebenschel, abolished the death penalty for attempted escape. From then on the punishment was twenty five lashes or transfer to the Penal Company.

Still, better treatment was mostly an illusion. We found that out when two months after the wedding Friemel tried to escape with other prisoners but was caught and sent to the bunker.

On October 27th 1944 an attempted escape took place of five prisoners from the leadership of the camp resistance network. The escapees, with the help of a bribed SS man, planned to be driven out of the camp in a truck taking laundry to Bielsko. As a result of SS-Rottenführer Johann Roth's betrayal, the attempt failed. Zbigniew Raynoch (no 60746) and Czesław Duzel (no 3702) took poison upon their arrest. Bernard Świerczyna, Piotr Piąty (no 130380) and Austrian Ernst Burg (no 23850) went through investigation, as did two other Austrian organizers of the escape, Ludwig Vesely (no 38169) and Rudolf Friemel.

We were shocked when we heard that that Freimel got a death sentence. On December 30th 1944 he and the others were put under the gallows in the roll call square. [531]

"Pale as ghosts, but with their heads held high, those unfortunate fellows entered the roll call square, brightly illuminated with floodlamps. All the way they shouted political slogans. They kept getting beaten, but that did not stop their shouts. [...] Ernst Burger called out, 'Down with National Socialism! Long live free, independent Austria!' and Rudi Friemel raised his tied hands over his head and called, 'Down with the brown shirts! Long live...'"
Source: Recollections in: *Wesele w Auschwitz* [532]

Rudi managed to shout:
"Hoch Österreich, es lebe Freiheit— Long live Austria, long live freedom."

"[...] they wore old pants and worn out shirts. All except Rudi. Heinz Dürmayer, a block elder, ordered them to give Rudi the shirt in which he was married. I don't know if it was his last wish. I only know he was hanged in his wedding shirt with embroidered roses. His Spanish wife never found out about that."
Source: Recollections [in:] *Wesele w Auschwitz* [533]

It was the last execution by hanging carried out in the men's camp in Auschwitz. [...] Those were the last executions before the camp evacuation. And to think that freedom was just around the corner... The Red Army troop liberated KL Auschwitz on January 27th 1945.

---

[527] Auschwitz Museum [APMA-B, Zespół Oświadczenia, t. 10, k. 27-28]
[528] Hackl E., *Wesele...*, op. cit., p. 124
[529] Auschwitz Museum [APMA-B, Zespół Oświadczenia, t. 10, k. 27-28]
[530] Kielar W., *Dzieła...*, op. cit., p. 273
[531] Friemel was hanged in a public execution in Stammlager - the main camp - on December 30th 1944
[532] Hackl E., *Wesele...*, op. cit., p. 183
[533] Ibidem

Friemel's wedding greeting card

WEDDING IN AUSCHWITZ

RUDOLF FRIEMEL WITH WIFE AND SON EDI

POSTCARD PHOTOGRAPHS

BY THE END OF THE WAR WE HAD TWO PHOTOGRAPHY STUDIOS AT AUSCHWITZ.

That opened new possibilities.

In front of the building where I worked there was a grassy patch. Our colleague Gienuś Dembek obtained from the gardeners some pansy seeds and planted them there. When the flowers blossomed I picked them, for I yearned for something pretty, and there was certainly nothing else that could be called pretty anywhere at the camp. I had a notion to photograph them, to no particular purpose. I put the flowers into a glass container, which looked more like a medical tube than a vase, and shot a postcard picture. The next day someone gave a print to Walter and he took it home, home to show his wife. Walter soon after told me to make a hundred copies of that postcard. He took them and sold them, maybe at the canteen. He said that everybody loved my flowers. Apparently the SS bought them and sent home to Bavaria or Saxony as greeting cards. They did the same with prisoner graphic postcards made by the prisoner graphic artists and painters.

"The demand for those cards was great and our comrade artists made them, mechanically and 'on demand', not particularly engaging their talents. Still, sometimes they succeeded in producing some nice small form graphics."
SOURCE: Franciszek Targosz's account [534]

Walter himself valued those pansies; he told us this straight out. We began copying that photograph by the thousands. Apparently he got some financial gain out of it.

I even tried to color the pansies using watercolor crayons. Unfortunately, that was not durable. I was quite familiar with the technique of coloring photographs and I knew that the emulsion requires aniline paints that blend with it, together forming an indelible surface. I asked the boss to get such paints and we made few color copies. That part was directed by Tadziu Myszkowski. The color version of the postcards was even more to Walter's liking and so he ordered another two thousand copies. He had to "organize" some photographic materials from Katowice. We needed a lot of those.

I made a slightly different sort of postcard for Walter's deputy, Hofmann, a teacher who once had taught in Witkendorf.

"Before joining the SS Hofmann was a village school teacher and so he had a precise mind, suited for thorough and detailed problem solving, and accomplishing things in an efficient and practical way."
SOURCE: Janusz Karwacki's account [535]

"As a former teacher he was a little more educated, although he didn't possess deep intelligence or knowledge. Sometimes while talking with a prisoner he had to resort to evasive answers or even avoid discussion altogether. He treated his SS service as protection from going to the front and as more financially rewarding than other postings. He felt entitled to use prisoners' gifts, assistance and private time. He did not object when offered opulent food parcels, either from our families or from the camp warehouses. Some of them he sent home to Germany, a fact of which he made no secret, asking us to wrap up the parcels for him. Since our kommando had an artist named Tadeusz Franciszek Myszkowski, (called Nase), Hofmann ordered him to make various wood sculptures and enlargements in oil of various paintings, mostly in color postcards. Those items he also sent or personally carried to Germany. He was conscientious about his job at the kommando, but was less harmful [than Walter] and thus less dangerous than other members of Politishe Ableitung."
SOURCE: Alfred Woycicki's account [536]

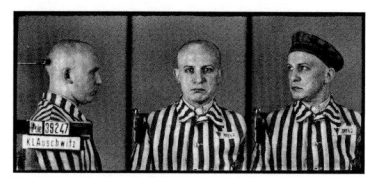

Some time after the successful pansy experiment Hofmann asked me to bring along the postcard camera with normal film and a tripod. He took me to a bridge with a view of the whole town of Oświęcim and ordered me to take a good picture of the place. While on the bridge, he displayed his pistol so that I wouldn't try to run away. There were cat tails growing on the riverbank and I suppose some daredevil could have escaped by jumping into them.

I took a picture of the bridge and the Oświecim castle and made it into a postcard. Tadek Myszkowski prepared a caption in German: "View of the Bridge and the Castle in Auschwitz" (Blick auf die Brücke und die Burg in Auschwitz). That landscape we mass reproduced by the thousands. Later deputy chief Hofmann went to Porąbka near Żywiec. He took a picture, brought it, and we produced postcards with a view of the lake in Porąbka. The postcards with landscapes were nice enough, but

NOTHING COULD BEAT MY PANSIES.

That was the postcard we printed the most, in massive amounts.

---

534 Auschwitz Museum [APMA-B, Zespół Oświadczenia, t. 64, k. 58]
535 Auschwitz Museum [APMA-B, Zespół Wspomnienia, 175, s. 61]
536 Auschwitz Museum [APMA-B, Zespół Oświadczenia, t. 9, k. 1317]

VIEW OF DOWNTOWN OŚWIĘCIM

SAVING THE PHOTOGRAPHS

Already in mid-December 1944 our boss Walter was ordering us to pack a whole lot of pictures and negatives into crates. Those were mostly photos from Birkenau—the unloading of Jewish transports and the march to crematorium. At that time the packing up of photos and other materials was still being done slowly and deliberately.

While I putting the pictures into giant suitcases I came across photos of the liquidation of Soviet POWs. Those pictures, which were being destroyed, showed atrocious things.

Among the hastily destroyed materials was also movie footage shot by both our bosses with a 16mm Agfa camera. Our atelier was not capable of developing those materials but the boss would take them to RSHA in Berlin, and then I would get copies of them. I watched the films in a special cinema projector which Erkennungsdienst had. In one of the movies you could see several thousand Soviet Prisoners of War in the square of Block 11 at first dressed, then naked, probably just before execution. Another movie had scenes of thousands of Soviet POWs being murdered with axes, shovels and sticks.

I also saw pictures taken during the construction of Birkenau. We did not take those pictures. A separate photography group was created for that purpose and I heard there was a showing of those films at the camp.

"[...] The photo documentation of the construction of Auschwitz II-Birkenau survived. The department was under the direct supervision of Karl Bischoff, chief of Zentralbauleitung (Central Construction Bureau), and was led by SS-Sturmmann (corporal) Uscha Dietrich Kamann. The idea of a separate photo studio was suggested to Kamann by Polish political prisoner Ludwik Lawin, whose job was to prepare photo albums documenting the progress of construction work. Kamann, who wanted to avoid being

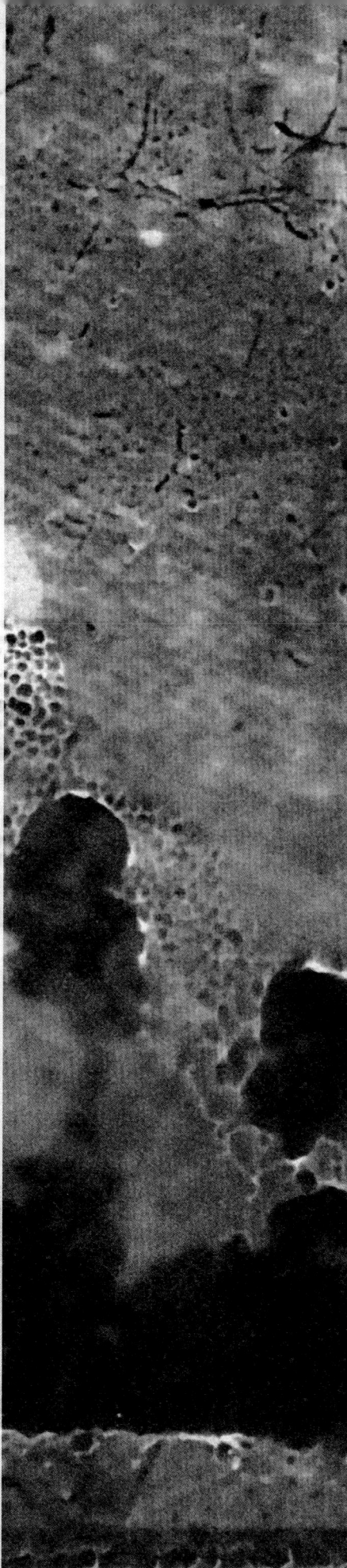

sent to the front, thought it an excellent idea and got permission to oversee it. [...] The majority of the pictures was from the Construction Bureau and taken in 1943, when the construction work in Birkenau was in full swing. All the work stages were recorded on film, including drainage of the area and construction of the barracks, gas chambers and crematoriums."[537]

"The central management of the construction of the Auschwitz concentration camp was so proud of their achievement that in the lobby of their office they publicly displayed a series of crematorium pictures. They did not pay much attention to the fact that civilians who walked in and out and saw the giant photos of fifteen incineration chambers put side by side would not so much admire the technical aptitude of the building site managers as wonder about the sinister purpose of those 3rd Reich facilities."
SOURCE: Pery Broad's memoir[538]

537 Struk J., *Holocaust...*, op. cit., p. 149
538 *Oświęcim w oczach...*, op. cit., p. 176

One day—either the 19th or 20th of January 1945, in the evening—Walter rushed in (Hofman was already gone) and told us to burn all the pictures. The Germans had not expected liberation to come so soon.
They didn't want to leave evidence of their crimes.

"During the evacuation of Polish prisoners from Auschwitz the personnel make up of our kommando changed. Of the previous employees only Brasse and I remained. I knew that we also would be evacuated, at the last moment. I prepared my camp pictures with their negatives and also some smaller photographs in order to hide and take them with me. The chaos of the evacuation made this possible.
Apart from Brasse and me there were probably 7 Jewish prisoners at Erkennungsdienst, of whom 3 were Hungarian, 3 Czech and one a German who said he was an attorney by profession. That was our team at the time."
Source: Relacja Bronisława Jureczka [539]

Walter ordered us to empty the cabinets of negatives and prints and throw them into the stove. He mostly cared about the destruction of mug shots. We started to toss them in but the fire immediately died out because the films were made of fireproof material. Curiously, Walter did not know that it was his compatriots who invented that fire resistant material which made our task harder.
The boss stood over us for nearly half an hour, then answered a phone call and left. The room contained also files of the deceased and executed which we were able to decipher. I considered myself a conscious political prisoner so it was important to me to preserve those things. Same with my colleague, Jureczek. So at first we purposely packed the films too tight to make it harder for them to burn. As soon as Walter closed the door we stopped the burning and poured water into the stove.

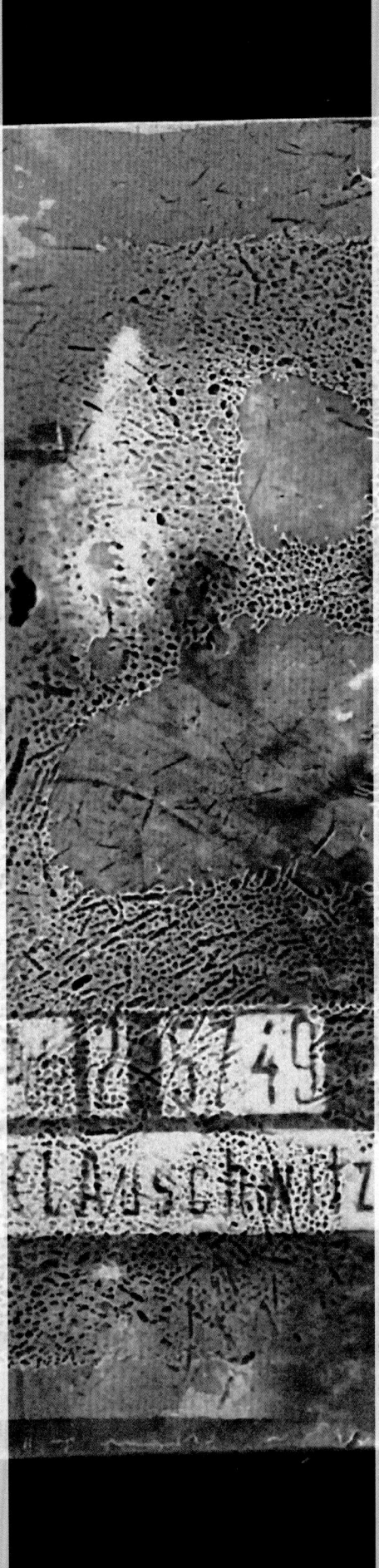

"First we put wet photographic paper and photographs into the tile stove and then lots of pictures and negatives. The huge amount of materials that we jammed into the stove blocked the chimney. When we lit the fire we were confident that only a small portion of materials would burn, just a bit by the stove door, and that the fire would die out for lack of air."
Source: Bronisław Jureczek's account [540]

As soon as Walter's steps could no longer be heard we pulled out the partly burned materials and tried to protect them so that no one would destroy or steal them. We were aware that if Walter came back he would shoot us. In such cases the Germans acted very quickly. So we found two or three solid planks and nailed them across the door. No one could enter that room then.

"I deliberately scattered some pictures and negatives around the rooms, faking a diligent rush. I was quite sure that in the chaotic evacuation no one would have time to pick everything up and that at least some would be saved.
[...] As I found out after the war, things happened exactly as we had believed they would and a large percentage of the photos and negatives ended up in the right hands. I don't know exactly what and how much survived, but certainly the negatives of the three-pose prisoners' IDs which are now at the Auschwitz Museum."
Source: Bronisław Jureczek's account [541]

"The photographs of prisoners of camp Auschwitz-Birkenau have been in the archives of the Auschwitz/Oświęcim State Museum since 1947. [...] The collection consists of 38,916 photos, including 31,969 of men and 6,947 of women, usually taken in three poses."[542]

---

539 Auschwitz Museum [APMA-B, Zespół Oświadczenia, t. 19, k. 30-31]
540 Ibidem
541 Ibidem
542 Parcer J., Zdjęcia więźniów KL Auschwitz ze zbiorów PM w Oświęcimiu. In: Fotografie..., op. cit., p. 3
543 Those photographs had not been taken at the camp, but rather were private family photos brought by the Jews from Zagłębie Dąbrowskie [the Dąbrowa Basin], who got deported to KL Auschwitz in summer of 1943, mostly from the Będzin and Sosnowiec ghettos. That these photographs survived is amazing, for the photos and personal documents of incoming Jews were burnt in special incinerators in Crematoriums II and III in Birkenau simultaneously with the cremation of their murdered owners.
544 Struk J., Holocaust..., op. cit., p. 161

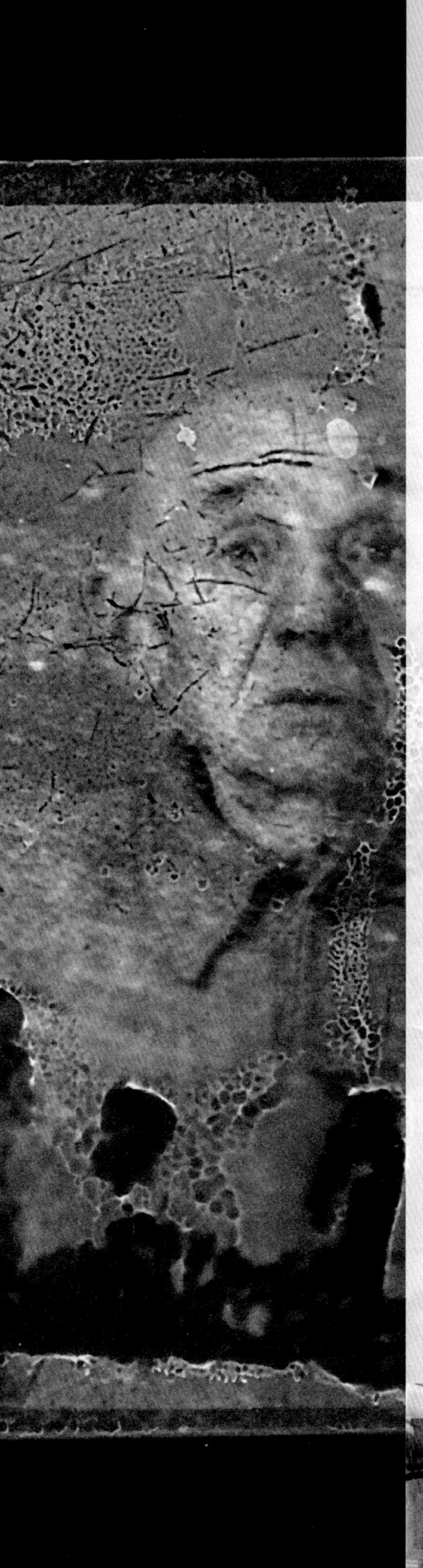
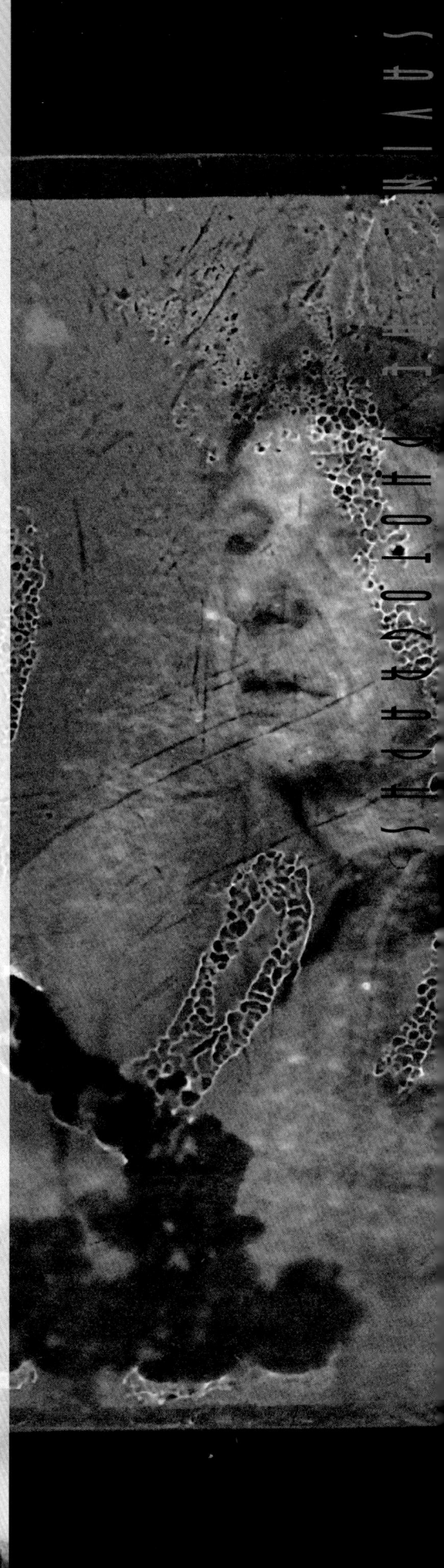

"FORTY THOUSAND ID PICTURES WERE SAVED THANKS TO BRASSE'S AND JURECZEK'S INGENUITY. THEY WERE THE ONLY PHOTOGRAPHS FOUND AT THE TIME OF THE LIBERATION.

During the next twenty years other photos taken in the camp gradually surfaced. On September 25th 1946 Ludwik Lawin returned to Auschwitz to retrieve fifty-three photographs of the Bauleitung department which he had secretly buried in a sealed bottle in the winter of 1944. The photographs were still where he had buried them—fourteen paces from the third Bauleitung barracks—and were well preserved. [...] At the end of the 1940s thirty eight photographs of medical experiments which doctor Kaschub had made on prisoners' limbs were used as evidence in the trial of Auschwitz criminals in Krakow. [...] In 1958 a museum employee returned a suitcase to the archive containing about 2,500 family photographs, probably brought to the camp by the deportees[543]. The name of this person has not been noted."[544]

I KNEW THE GERMANS WOULD WANT TO ELIMINATE ME, SINCE I WAS A "GEHEIMNISTRAGER"

(a bearer of secrets). I had worked at the kommando of the Identification Service of the Political Department, and so posed a threat to the SS. The Germans were liquidating such prisoners.
I will tell you of two kapos, both horrible butchers. One was called Krankenmann, the other Siegruth. I have already told the stories of Krankenmann, the priests and the roller. The other one, Siegruth, was also a figure known in the camp for his sadism. He had only one arm; he had lost the other one in World War I.

Both Krankenmann and Siegruth were privileged prisoners. Like Friemel those two, supervised by an SS guard, could go to the movies in Oświęcim, outside the camp. But because it was the camp, the wheel of their fortunes could change in the blink of an eye, particularly for someone who knew too much. That was the case with Siegruth and Krankenmann. One day they had privilege and the next their colleagues threw them in with the cripples who supposedly were leaving for treatment in Dresden.
We later learned both of them were murdered on the train.

"[...] We found out that kapo Krankenmann was hanged in the train car by Lagerällteste Brunon Brodniewicz with the help of a group of German kapos while Oberkapo Siegruth went on under the escort of SS guards. In Dresden he was gassed along with all the sick. The lynching of Krankenmann was authorized by Commandant Höss, Lagerführer Fritzsch and the Chief of Politische Abteilung Grabner, allegedly for revealing to the prisoners, albeit in a cynical and scary manner, the true destination and fate of the transported sick."
SOURCE: Adam Stapf's account [545]

In the first year of the camp's operation, I I had believed thought it would be a miracle if I survived. I knew that what I did at the camp was far from safe. Now, at the end, with liberation approaching, I kept having premonitions and memories, made scarier by the fate of Siegruth and Krankenmann.

At the end of the war there were were many examples examples of the SS getting rid of inconvenient people. Some of them got their just deserts, as in the case of Palitzsch.

"Palitsch's career ended in Matzkau. The mass murders he had committed—of course for the glory of Great Germany and prompted by his deeply held Nazi and racist ideology— did not prevent him from engaging in intimate relations with enemies of the state, among them Jewish ones, especially if those enemies happened to be female, young and pretty. His threats that he would finish them off if they started talking were of no help to him. His fate was sealed. His relationship with one Jew remained, luckily for him, undiscovered[546]. However, his sexual liaison with the Latvian prisoner Vera Lukans and his part in the widespread Auschwitz custom of appropriating valuables from the newcomers for one's own financial gain resulted in a long prison sentence for him."
SOURCE: Pery Broad's memoir [547]

One of the crematorium staff— Mietek Morawa, my colleague from

Krakow—tried to escape from his Sonnderkommando. He wanted to leave with a transport, but he got caught. The head of the political intelligence unit told him, „Morawa, we need you and so you can't go."

---

[545] Auschwitz Museum [APMA-B, Zespół Oświadczenia, t. 148, k. 101]
[546] It refers to his relationship with a Slovakian Jew— Katja Singer— which Brasse mentions in the chapter "Photographs of Women".
[547] Oświęcim w oczach..., op. cit., p. 164

Mietek did not leave then, but 2 months later, in mid-December 1944, he was removed to the Mathausen camp. There he was shot along with his whole crew. We found out about it from the SS.

"It seemed so certain to the SS that all the members of Sonderkommando had been exterminated that when Rapportführer Kaduk, at his trial in Frankfurt, was shown evidence by one of the Survivors of that kommando he jumped up, most offended, and cried, 'It is impossible that the witness survived the camp as a member of Sonderkommando. I know for a fact that members of Sonderkommando were liquidated without exception.'"
SOURCE: Hermann Langbein's account [548]

"They put us, the members of the Sonderkommando, in a separate barracks. They wanted to kill us without a trace. I told my colleagues: 'Something is not right, why are they locking us in?' They kept us in the barracks with no possibility of contacting anybody. We heard some noises outside. We saw all the prisoners leave the barracks and begin the evacuation march. So we escaped from the barracks and blended in with the crowd of prisoners. We went on the road with everybody else because we hoped that this way we might survive. When we got to Mathausen two guards from Crematorium II were searching for us. They kept asking, 'Who worked at Sonderkommando?' During that long evacuation march with almost no food we slimmed down some and it was no longer possible to distinguish us from all the other prisoners. [...] They looked and looked, but they never found us. They were on our heels all the way to Mauthausen! Can you imagine? They looked for us up to the last moment, intending to kill us!"
SOURCE: Shaul Chasan's account [549]

I was infected by the fears of my boss Walter who kept saying in private conversations:

"BRASSE, I HAVE A DARK FEELING ABOUT YOUR FUTURE..."

[548] Langbein H., Ludzie..., op. cit., p. 216
[549] Greif G., ...płakaliśmy..., op. cit., p. 306

EVACUATION

The German newspapers were now reporting on the approaching front. We read the "Kattowitzer Zeitung"[550], borrowing it from a Katowice German who was allowed to receive newspapers. Moreover, the SS were themselves saying that when the Ruskis got too near they would flee and the rest of the prisoners would be moved further into Europe. About the 10th or 12th of January we found out that the Soviet offensive had begun. In a great rush they began evacuating the camp. The first large transports left on January 17th 1945.[551] They departed almost daily, shipping prisoners west.

"We were divided into marching groups (Marschkolonnen), each of about 2000 prisoners. I don't know how many of those groups there were. Each of them left the camp at precise intervals. At the same time the rumble of Red Army cannons from the Krakow side heralded the quick approach of liberation; we were not permitted to wait for it in the camp."
SOURCE: Walter Fajnzylberg's account[552]

The SS men rushed people out of the camp. Jureczek had disappeared a few hours earlier. They caught him and added him into the transport. I hoped to hide away somewhere and stay behind. But later on neither I nor anybody else wanted to stay when we learned that during the evacuation of the concentration camp in Majdanek, the Germans shot all who remained—15 or 16 thousand Jews and Poles.

"The whole process of liquidation of the concentration camps and other detention centers was another series of atrocities against the prisoners. It included massacres in Maly Trostenets, Belarus (about 6,500 victims), Klooga in Estonia (about 2,200 victims), Radgoszcz[553] (about 2,000 victims), Słońsk by Kostrzyń (800 victims), Isenschnibbe by Gardelegen (over 1000 victims) and Kaufering (one of Dachau sub-camps, at least a few hundred victims.) In accordance with the 'scorched earth' policy observed by the German troops and the order that 'No prisoner should be found alive by the Enemy'

('Kein Häftling darg lebendig in die Hände des Feindes fallen'), the SS killed all prisoners that they could not evacuate, or saw no advantage to themselves or the 3rd Reich in evacuating."[554]

I WENT IN TRANSPORT ON JANUARY 21ST 1945.

It was Sunday. For the road we got a loaf of bread and a bar of margarine. We were a bit frightened. There were hundreds of bodies scattered in disarray all round the camp. The Germans had no time to cover their tracks.
I saw Józef Cyrankiewicz[555] and Dr. Fejkiel also leaving the camp. Dr. Kłodziński stayed behind. As it turned out, after the columns of prisoners left the camp the panicking Germans tore down the watchtower posts so there were no guards. My colleague from Żywiec, Janusz Baut[556], took the risk and stayed behind. Later, he simply walked out of the camp. We did not dare try that.

"In the Auschwitz complex there were over 8000 sick and completely exhausted male and female prisoners left behind without food or medical care, including a few hundred children. As a result of the Vistula-Oder offensive by the main forces of the Soviet Army, undertaken eight days ahead of schedule, Auschwitz came within the scope of the First Ukrainian Front.
On the memorable day of January 27th 1945 soldiers of the 60th Army of the 1st Ukrainian Front entered Auschwitz and liberated about 1,200 prisoners of the main camp, 4,000 women and 1,800 men-prisoners in Birkenau, and 650 prisoners in Monowice."[557]

We were formed into columns along with everybody else and set out. I had on civilian clothes, a decent jacket, and quite a bit of money given to me by my Jewish friends. They gave me a packet of US dollars, over 10 thousand in various bills. I hoped that after escaping I could exchange it for zlotys, buy a professional camera and open my own photographic shop. Before the war a dollar cost 4.50 zloty, so I possessed some 45,000 zlotys, and to open a shop I needed only 5-6 thousand. From my colleagues who had access to the Jewish possessions in the Kanada I got a backpack. I put in a good camera, which before the war had cost about 1,200 zlotys and accessories for it, a telephoto and a wide angle lens worth 1,500 zlotys. I also took the Agfa Mofik 16mm movie camera. It had been used exclusively by Walter; I was never permitted to use it. Besides, I didn't know how. The movie camera specialist was Bródka. Still, I knew it was valuable, worth maybe 1,800 or 2,000 zlotys, so I took it along. I also brought my prison ID photo and a picture of my uncle. I was ready to flee. I intended to escape along the way.

[550] Trans. "The Kattowitz Newspaper"

[551] The final evacuation of the camp took place between 17th and 23rd January 1945. Then began the death march for about 58,000 inmates, men and women.

[552] Auschwitz Museum [APMA-B, Zespół Oświadczenia, t. 114, k. 15]

[553] Radogoszcz is now part of Łódź's district Bałuty.

[554] Strzelecki A., *Likwidacja obozu*. In: *Auschwitz 1940--1950: węzłowe zagadnienia z dziejów obozu. Tom V. Epilog*, W. Długoborski, F. Piper, op. cit., p. 8

[555] Józef Cyrankiewicz (Inmate No. 62933), b. April 23rd 1911 in Tarnów; lawyer. Later Prime Minister of the Polish People's Republic. Brought to KL Auschwitz on Sept. 9th 1942 in the Krakow transport; worked as a nurse at the hospital in block No. 20. More→Biographies

[556] Tadeusz Baut (Inmate No. 1529), b. Aug. 14th 1921 in Żywiec. Brought to KL Auschwitz on June 26th 1940 in the Katowice transport. More→Biographies

[557] Czech D., *Konzentrationslager Auschwitz - zarys historyczny*, op. cit., p. 38

They marched us from Auschwitz to Pszczyna. I had hoped that in Pszczyna I'd be able to slip out unnoticed. But I was scared, because there were lots of evacuated bauers—German farmers—around. They screamed if any prisoner tried to approach their carts. We camped under the open sky near Jastrzębie at a large German farm. We slept in the frosty fields, standing up or lying down. I had no idea where they were taking us but I still hoped to be able to get away into the forest somewhere along the way. It wasn't so easy. The SS men escorting us were about 8-10 meters apart, each holding a gun ready to shoot, and the distance to the forest was simply too great.

"The parade was enclosed by a few SS men. They never put their pistols in their holsters. Whoever fell behind or sat down from fatigue got a bullet in his head right in front of our eyes. The only food was melting snow."
SOURCE: Józef Paczyński's account [558]

We walked to Wodzisław, about 80 km[559] from Auschwitz, and there we were loaded into open coal cars. It snowed; it was a few degrees below freezing. We were being taken via Morawska Ostrava toward somewhere south.
I was lucky enough to have brought from Auschwitz a very warm, woolen Canadian blanket. I wrapped it around me and went practically the whole way in a kind of half-sleep.

"It was late at night when the transport moved forward, but it did not go far. Soon it stopped, then after a few hours went in the opposite direction. The next day the train did not move a single kilometer. At night the same thing happened again. And again the following day."
SOURCE: Lech Szawłowski's account [560]

"The cars were terribly overcrowded. Practically no prisoner could move or change his initial position. (...) Today it is hard for me to describe what was going on during that ride. With no protection against the cold the prisoners were getting weaker. Infernal scenes took place. Everyone fought for the little space they occupied. The weakest prisoners slid down to the bottom of the car while dying. Their excruciating moans were mixed with the cries of some prisoners who were losing their minds. Biting, kicking and scratching their neighbors, they grew dangerous."
SOURCE: Józef Tabaczyński's account [561]

"We were conscious of our tragic circumstances. Many of us did not have even a bite of bread. The SS walked by the cars asking, 'How many dead?' (*Wieviel Tote?*) We wondered if it was maybe better to jump out of the train and be killed by a bullet than starving to death. Finally, at night, the train started moving and in the morning, on the seventh day of our evacuation it stopped at a larger train station in Czechoslovakia (Bogumin). There the local people threw some loaves of bread into our car which greatly refreshed our energy."
SOURCE: Lech Szawłowski's account [562]

When people from the viaducts started throwing us bread and cigarettes the SS men started shooting at them.

---

[558] Paczkowski J., *Byłem fryzjerem...*, op. cit.
[559] The distance is 63 kilometers.
[560] Szawłowski L., *Z przeżyć warszawskich dzieci w obozach hitlerowskich*. In: *Przegląd Lekarski*, Nr 1, Kraków 1972, p. 161
[561] Auschwitz Museum [APMA-B, Zespół Oświadczenia, t. 44, k. 26]
[562] Szawłowski L., *Z przeżyć...*, op. cit., p. 162

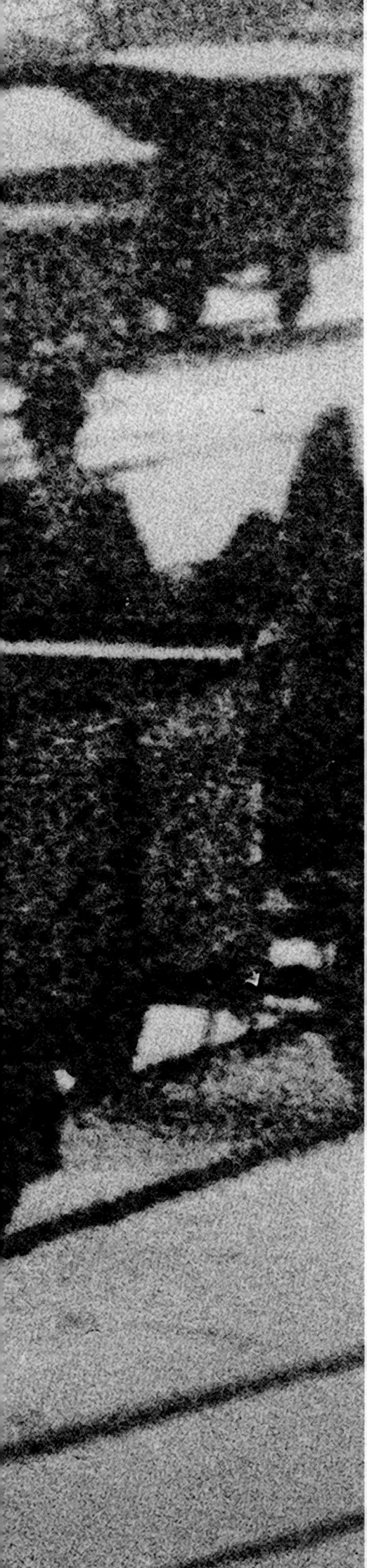

We arrived at Mauthausen. I had to get rid of my dangerous baggage so on a train bridge I threw the backpack with my photographic and film equipment into the Danube. I regretted that for many years, but I could not see any other way.

In Mathausen we waited again for a few hours in the frost. Later we stood naked in front of the bath and waited while they took down our personal data.

I DID NOT SAY I WAS A PHOTOGRAPHER, BUT CLAIMED TO BE AN IRONWORKER.

My father was a mechanic so I knew a little about iron work. But, that did not help me. I knew they had me. There was no escape.

We spent a week at a so-called quarantine and then I was transferred to Melk. It was a Mauthausen subcamp, the so-called Inner Kommando Melk, in a beautiful town in central Austria on the Danube. I got a new number—116588—since they had a different registration system there. You got the numbers of prisoners who had died.

Melk was a sizeable camp which produced ball bearings and tank parts. We were put to work constructing an underground factory. The factory in Melk had about twenty five kilometers of underground corridors and gigantic hangars of 25 x 50 m. We dug out tunnels in sandstone. I worked at the jackhammer. It was dreadful. Then I was employed for the construction of the barracks and the fence. I spent two and a half months there, from February till mid-April. I was famished all the time and got skinny as a rail. The conditions were wretched. We lived in former stables of the Austrian cavalry. There were so many of us that water dripped from the ceiling— human breath condensing.

In Melk I got stuck in a terrible kommando but I had excellent comrades to whom I owe my life.

Once I was poisoned by some bad bread and my colleagues took me with them to work. You had to travel eight kilometers by train to reach the mountain where we were digging the tunnels. We arrived, but I was unable to walk let alone work. My colleagues decided to let me lie down somewhere hidden and covered me up. Surprisingly, the SS man who was the kommando leader agreed to hide me in the barracks. It was March, and outside was cold and rainy. Six colleagues took off their prison coats. They covered me with them and left for work in their indoor clothes. I warmed up and got better. In the afternoon I got up and went to thank them. Such was our solidarity.

I stayed in Melk until April 16th 1945.

I BECAME A MUSELMANN, AND WAS AT DEATH'S DOOR.

Around that time the Soviet Army entered Vienna[563]. A few days later, on April 13th 1945 we watched the civilian population flee—whole families, with loaded carts. It reminded me of September 1939 in Poland. Complete panic. The next day we went to work, but there was no more work. They ordered a general roll call and return to the camp. At the camp: evacuation. The whole camp marched out in one giant column. On the way there was an air raid. They were Soviet planes. The pilots probably thought we were a marching army. They shot like hell. I was so wasted that I had no energy to run. Some prisoners were killed in the raid. They were left there and the rest of us marched to the station.

They loaded us into various freight and passenger cars and then moved us to the Mauthausen sub-camp in the beautiful Alpine town of Ebensee. There we met our previously transferred colleagues. We were a horrifying sight, emaciated to the worst degree. Walking skeletons.

The conditions in Ebensee were the most awful I had ever experienced. I believed my death there was certain. There was almost no regular food. They gave us only boiled potato peels and water.

"The daily ration was a scoop of soup made from potato peels which the prisoners' kitchen received from the SS kitchen, plus 1/10, and then just before the liberation only 1/12 of a prison loaf of bread, which was just one third of the Auschwitz portion."
Source: Józef Ciepły's account [564]

They drove me to cleaning up a train junction in a neighboring town. It had been bombed by the Americans, most likely to disrupt railroad communications and disable operations of the German Army. The civilians were terrified after that raid. As soon as they heard a car engine, they panicked and ran for cover. The Germans wanted to free up at least one track. The station was a mess. The rails were twisted like thread and tangled up with the cars. To our joy, we discovered the cars contained food—rice and pasta. During the bombing it had all gotten mixed up with dirt but we managed to pick out a little something.

EVACUATION

We were watched over by both SS troopers and regular Wehrmacht soldiers. When they brought us our soup one of those soldiers approached me and asked if that was all our food. I confirmed it and added that back at the camp we got only herbal tea or coffee. He looked into the pot and stirred the ladle... He looked shocked, but that was the end of our conversation.

I worked three days at that train station and came down with phlegmon; I started oozing pus. This condition is caused by lack of vitamins and nourishment. I had seen cases of it in Auschwitz. Then I had escaped it, but this time I was already feeling very sick and I reported that I could not work. I went to the hospital. I did not know those doctors at all. One of them, also a prisoner, looked me over and sent me to ambulatory. I sat in the procedure chair and the doctor, a French Jew, tried to cut through the oozing spot. He was so exhausted he could barely stand on his legs. He didn't have the energy to work and on top of that the lancet was dull. I got angry and I pushed that man. He fell, poor guy. Although I treated him so brutally he stood up to me again and finally managed to cut me open. The pus leaked out and he bandaged me and ordered me to stay at the hospital. I went into a ward filled with the sick. I spent a week there. They did not really treat me there; just wrapped my wound up in paper dressing and that was it. There were no medications.

The sick that could walk were encouraged to hide from the American raids in a mine shaft. But I heard that someone had warned the civilian workers that the shaft was mined. Things became chaotic.

We knew the Americans were approaching. We could hear the artillery firing. Some of the German prisoners got dressed in military uniforms and were incorporated into the Wehrmacht. Even before the Americans came, the lynching started.

There was one block supervisor who sucked up to the Germans, a Ukrainian from Kiev, a very brutal guy—a murderer who had executed people with his own hands. I once saw him bludgeon a prisoner with a metal rod. On the last day the prisoners—mostly Russians and other Ukrainians—threw him into the firefighting reservoir and did not let him out. Later they stoned him there. Various kapos got beaten up. I could hear the sounds of beating and screaming. In some cases they got stabbed. I was unable to get up and watch them getting their just desserts, since I could barely stand on my feet.

EBENSEE SHORTLY AFTER LIBERATION

563 The Red Army entered Vienna on April 2nd 1945.
564 Auschwitz State Museum [APMA-B, Zespół Wspomnienia, t. 165, k. 15]

On Sunday about two in the afternoon the Americans entered the camp.

THEY FREED EBENSEE ON MAY 6TH.

By the time that they came in, all the SS crew was gone. In the morning they had moved out the SS guards and replaced them with Wehrmacht soldiers, older draftees. The Americans disarmed them. I watched as they took the gun from one and pushed him away.

From the window of the room where I lay I could see the piles of corpses at the crematorium. People starved to death in scores and they couldn't catch up with burning the bodies. They were stacked in layers, one on top of the other, up to the level of the second floor. I had thought I would end up in such a pile. I was too seasoned a prisoner not to realize the danger of phlegmon: progressive gangrene reaches the heart, and that's it. But, to be honest, I was no longer scared. I was reconciled to my fate. Fortunately the Americans came and everything changed.

A few hours after the liberation of the camp the Americans brought to the crematorium some twenty German officers, among them two generals in beautiful uniforms with trouser stripes, although without guns or belts. They walked them through the whole camp to show them those piles of cadavers. I went a few steps outside the hospital barracks because I wanted to watch it. Apparently those guys were claiming they knew nothing.

In the afternoon I noticed prisoners carrying bread from the camp bakery. I ran over there half naked, wearing nothing but a shirt, because they didn't give you drawers. I managed to steal a piece of bread and hide it in the bed. Later the Americans brought canned meat, the same good ham I had known in Auschwitz. The Spanish Communist prisoners, whom the Germans had arrested and sent to the camp, helped unload the truck. They chased prisoners away but fortunately or not, I managed to pinch a can.

I went into the woods near the hospital barracks, hid in the bushes and opened it enough with a nail to get at some of the meat. I knew I shouldn't eat it, but a starving human doesn't think logically. I was emaciated, weighing at most 40 kilograms. I remembered from Auschwitz how some prisoners got parcels of lard from home and died after eating it. But I could not resist. I ate a few spoonfuls including, of course, the fat, and got very sick. At first I threw up and then began the torment of diarrhea. I ran to the toilet every half an hour, then every fifteen minutes, then every ten minutes, and finally I lived there. I spent the whole night in the bathroom. People started fighting for that spot, but I sat on the toilet seat and would not be pushed away. The next day I was so exhausted that someone simply knocked me off that seat and dragged outside. I got transferred to the hospital. There I met a comrade from Auschwitz— Janusz Müller, also known as Młynarski[565], who had worked at the camp hospital as a nurse's assistant. He was from Poznań. In order not to attract attention with a German sounding name he had changed his name to Młynarski at the beginning of the war. Then he became a resistance activist in Catholic Church circles. Interestingly, after the war he took back the name Müller.
But now, he took me under his wing. First he berated me: what was I thinking to eat such fatty pork? He brought some medicinal charcoal

---

[565] Janusz Młynarski (Müller) (Inmate No. 355), b. August 14th 1922 in Poznań. Brought to Kl Auschwitz on June 14th 1940 in the Krakow-Tarnów transport; worked as a lab assistant at the hospital in block No. 20. More → BIOGRAPHIES

[566] Grenda J., Wspomnienia z pracy w szpitalu PCK w Oświęcimiu po wyzwoleniu obozu. In: Okupacja i medycyna: trzeci..., op. cit., p. 272

[567] Strzelecki A., Likwidacja obozu. In: Auschwitz 1940--1950: węzłowe zagadnienia z dziejów obozu. Tom V. Epilog, W. Długoborski, F. Piper ed., op. cit., p. 39

and tannalbin which helped a bit. The hospital had been taken over by the Americans. On the second day came American doctors and military nurses—girls in uniforms. I was registered as a stomach patient. I was completely wasted and could not move.
They put me on a strict diet. They were very rigorous about it.

Młynarski got hold of some dried apple chips and fed me those. He also brought some biscuits. Apart from that I was permitted only unsweetened tea and some pills. After a few days I improved and began to eat normally. We patients still on the strict diet were very unhappy watching the recovered ones get stew, real stew. They had it great while we had to fast.

"Neither the prisoners nor anyone among those who freed them realized that excessive food for a starving, dehydrated organism that was unable to assimilate it could prove fatal. The ingested nourishment passed through the digestive tract in a few minutes. The dehydration intensified and the deproteinization progressed. The liberated prisoners began dying en masse. My most tragic memories are of my conversations with prisoners who rejoiced at the prospect of going back to their families not realizing that those were often their last words. Although I was just a student at the time, there were some experienced doctors there who were taken by surprise at those developments. In spite of hard war experience the medical world did not have procedures for such cases as they encountered here for the first time. Those who gave the prisoners excessive amounts of food out of sympathy did not know it either. So people who wanted to help these unfortunates had to rely only on their own energy, ideas and knowledge." [566]

"The patients were reintroduced to regular diet by ingesting food almost as medicine; for instance they would take one spoonful of mashed potato soup three times a day. After a while they got a few spoonfuls. For many weeks following the liberation, the nurses kept finding bread hidden under the pallets and mattresses, tucked away by some prisoners, because they didn't trust that they would get another meal." [567]

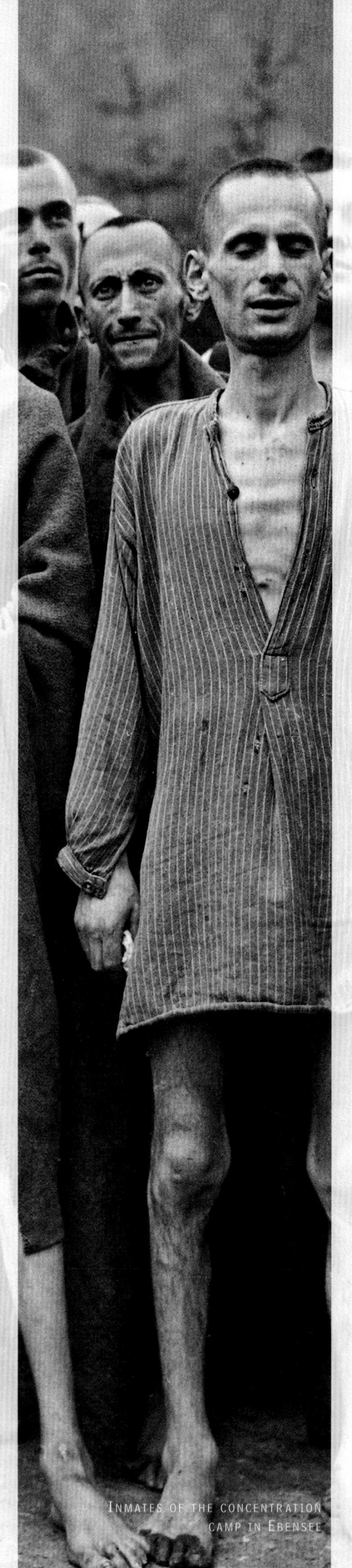

Inmates of the concentration camp in Ebensee

EVACUATION

In Ebensee I met a few Auschwitz pals. For instance Leon Haas. Haas told me he had been required to counterfeit British pounds while there. I never met him again. I found out he died in 1983.

I also came across the Croatian with whom I had shared my stolen margarine. Sometimes the Americans would take us around the Alps in their military cars. Every few kilometers there were checkpoints and we had to stop. They checked out the travelers more thoroughly than their documents. We stopped at one of those points. I noticed a group of young men in civilian clothing. One of them carried a bundle on a stick. That was him—the Croatian SS man from Auschwitz. He recognized me, too. He became mortally scared. I didn't have it in me to report him to the Americans. At the camp he had behaved humanely. He could have very easily reported my stealing of food and I would have ended up in the Penal Company. I did not give him to the Americans. Let somebody else do it, I thought. When I was leaving he gave me a look of gratitude.

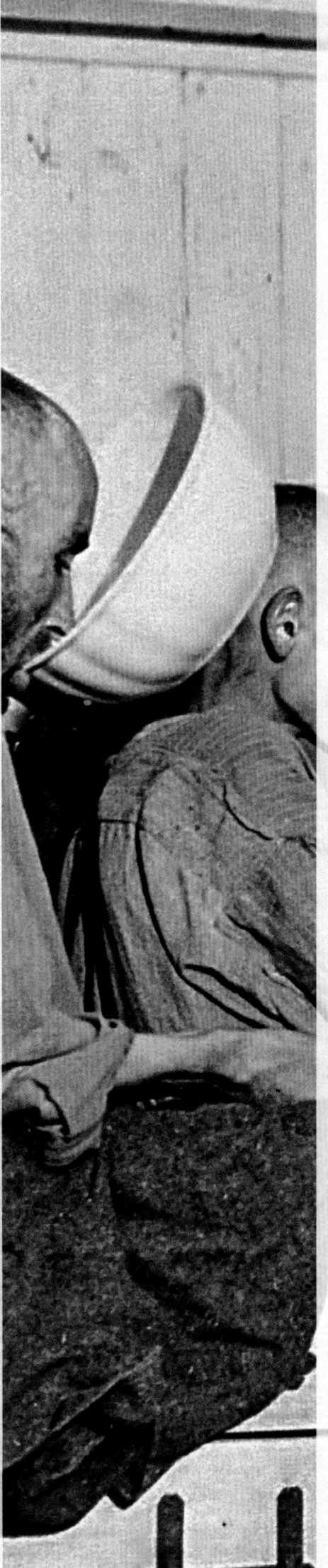

Some time later the Americans established a hospital. It was divided into wards: internal diseases, skin diseases, soft surgery, hard surgery. They brought a portable X-ray machine and other wonderful things. They gave me a thorough exam, a blood transfusion and an IV drip for strengthening. I felt better and started to walk.

When I became strong enough I volunteered as a technician for the X-ray apparatus. You got a uniform and four dollars a day. I did not like that work as it involved contact with the sick. I kept getting really serious cases, for instance people who needed to have their badly healed bones re-broken. I left that work after a week. I was moved to the convalescing ward in another barracks of the former camp.

There we finally got real food! For breakfast

YOU COULD GET AS MUCH BREAD AS YOU WANTED,

real butter, slices of sausage or ham as well as thick rice pudding with milk. I must say that in those days I was able to eat a few liter bowls full of that rice. And for lunch they had wonderful soup. I grew stronger with each passing day.

Almost daily we also got food parcels from the Jewish organization "Joint" from USA. Each one contained a bar of margarine, biscuits, canned jam, slices of preserved ham, raisins, chocolate and two packets of Camel cigarettes. I did not smoke so I gave the cigarettes to my colleagues.

We were grateful to the American Jews for sending us such things. They insisted that everybody should get them, regardless of nationality. Even the German prisoners got parcels from "Joint".[568] No exceptions. The food must have been coming in huge amounts, for there were about three hundred sick and each one got a daily parcel. Apart from that, once a week both the convalescents

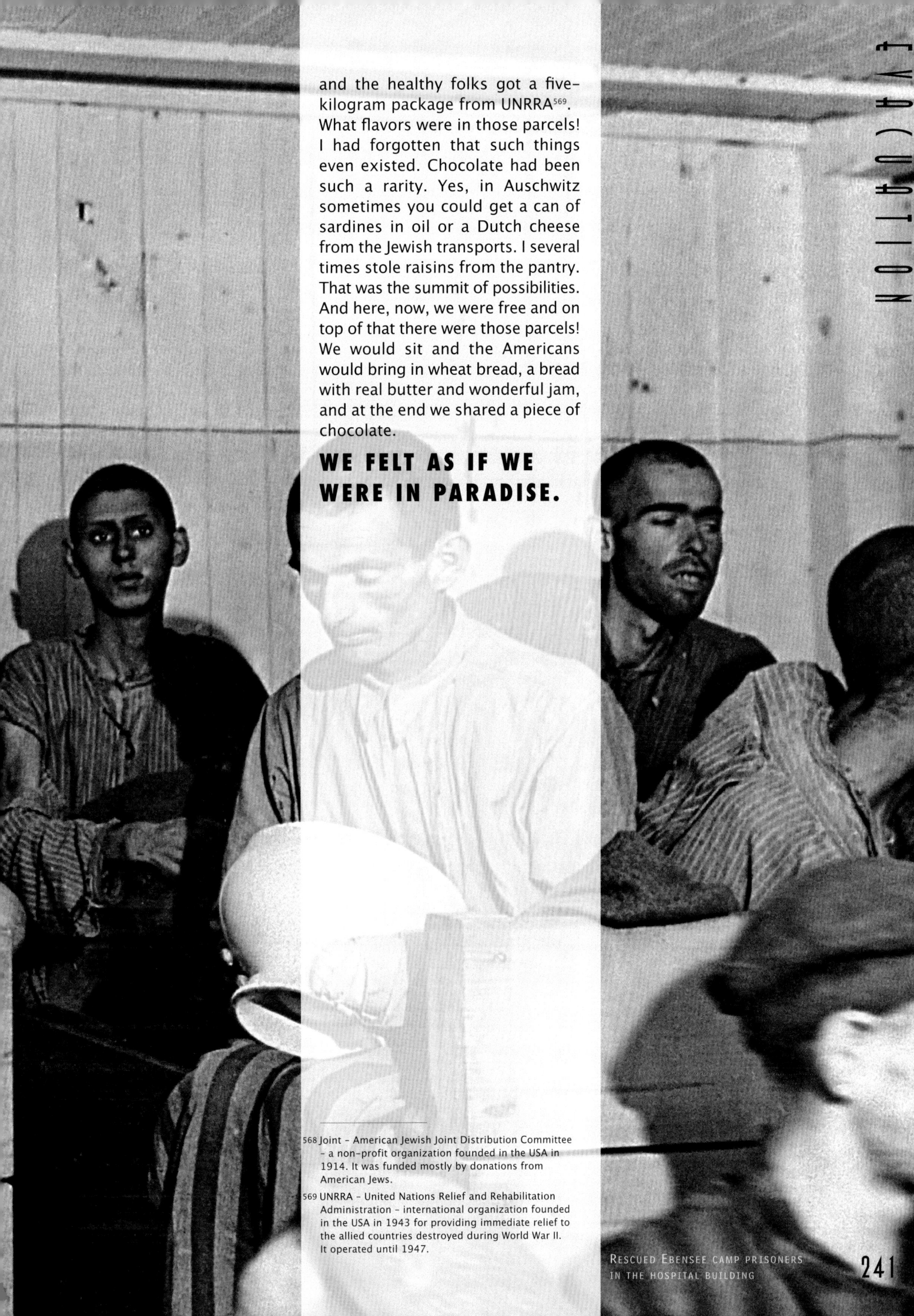

and the healthy folks got a five-kilogram package from UNRRA[569]. What flavors were in those parcels! I had forgotten that such things even existed. Chocolate had been such a rarity. Yes, in Auschwitz sometimes you could get a can of sardines in oil or a Dutch cheese from the Jewish transports. I several times stole raisins from the pantry. That was the summit of possibilities. And here, now, we were free and on top of that there were those parcels! We would sit and the Americans would bring in wheat bread, a bread with real butter and wonderful jam, and at the end we shared a piece of chocolate.

WE FELT AS IF WE WERE IN PARADISE.

[568] Joint – American Jewish Joint Distribution Committee – a non-profit organization founded in the USA in 1914. It was funded mostly by donations from American Jews.
[569] UNRRA – United Nations Relief and Rehabilitation Administration – international organization founded in the USA in 1943 for providing immediate relief to the allied countries destroyed during World War II. It operated until 1947.

RESCUED EBENSEE CAMP PRISONERS IN THE HOSPITAL BUILDING

END OF PHOTOGRAPHY

I did not have to return to Poland. The Americans offered immigration and transportation to everybody who had even some acquaintances in the USA. Those who spoke English could go there easily. Or I could have stayed in Germany.

"Stay here. The Bolsheviks are already here. If you want you can be German, English or American", they said.

I heard that those interested were going to Hamburg and then by ship to the States. But I decided not to take advantage of that offer. When I was near dying I thought only of home. That was when I most wanted to return to my country. It never occurred to me that I ought to go to some other land, never. In our home we spoke only Polish and my father had been in the Polish-Bolshevik war. How could I now be a German or an American? On demand?! Forgetting my honor?!

I asked to return to Żywiec.

After my recovery at the American hospital I came home. It was July 9th 1945. I walked on the same street I had taken on that doomed day, in the spring of 1940, leaving home. No one was there. Then I was noticed by my youngest brother, born while I was away. He ran to mom and cried, "Mom, mom, a gentleman is coming to see us!"

My mom stepped out, saw me, and burst into tears.

"My God, after six years!", she cried. "Dear God, my child!"

A year later on July 6th 1946 I married a beautiful girl, Stasia, five years my junior.

I started my life anew. I was twenty-eight, healthy and strong. I even wanted to be a photographer again. Although I had thrown out everything and I did not have any equipment I felt I could eventually get it. I took a job as an assistant in a photo shop in Żywiec. From Soviet soldiers I bought a Kodak Retina, a decent camera for rolled film. The problem was that as soon as I started shooting pictures, especially of women and children, I began to see before my eyes the images from Auschwitz—especially of those girls of doctor Mengele[570]. I would be taking a picture of an ordinary woman and would see before me a naked Jew from the camp. Those images kept coming back. I kept seeing the children, the disabled, the retarded...

---

[570] Brasse's photograph, which became known around the world, is a picture of four Gypsy children, two pairs of twins affected with noma - gangrenous stomatitis - which occurs in cases of serious malnutrition. The disease eats into parts of the flesh of the face and into the bone.

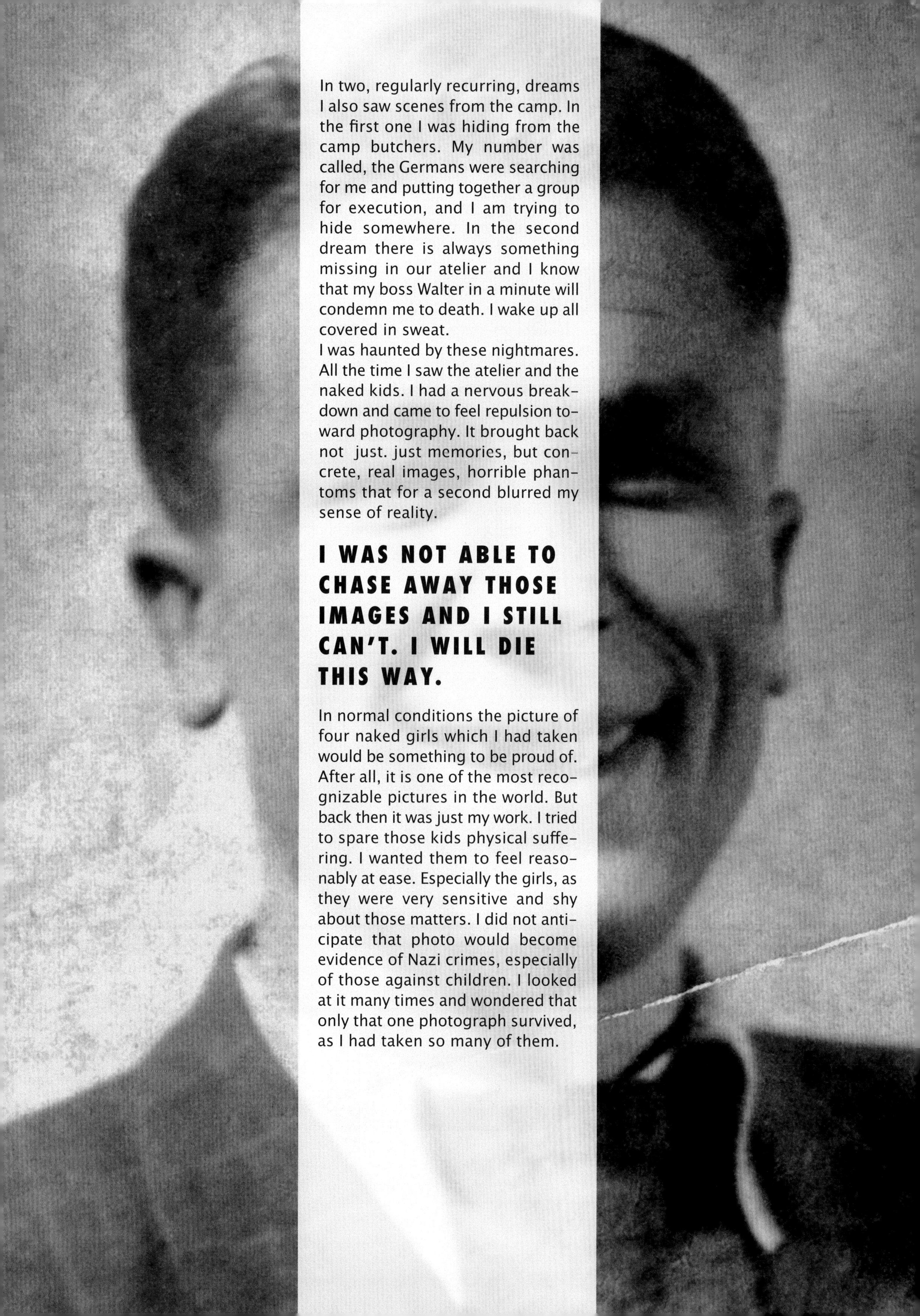

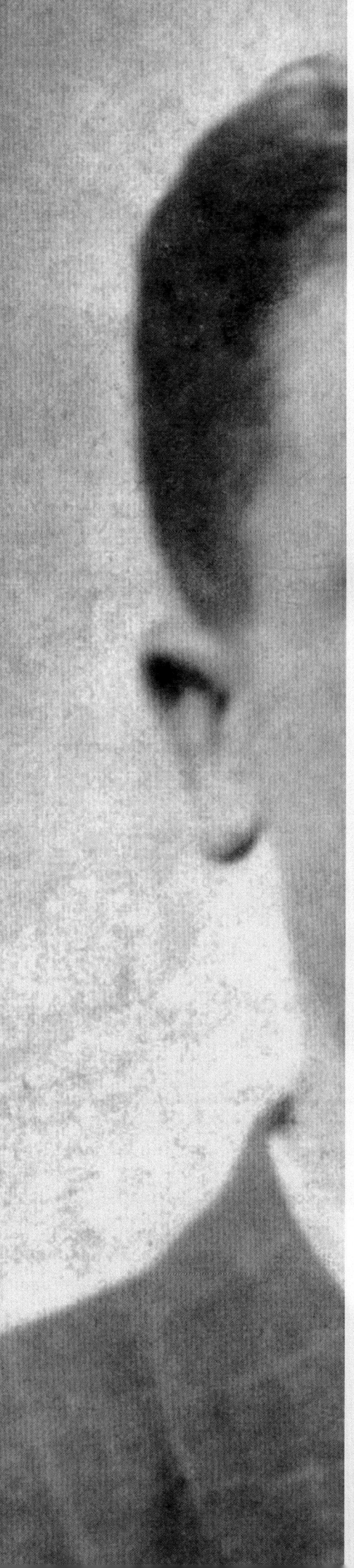

In two, regularly recurring, dreams I also saw scenes from the camp. In the first one I was hiding from the camp butchers. My number was called, the Germans were searching for me and putting together a group for execution, and I am trying to hide somewhere. In the second dream there is always something missing in our atelier and I know that my boss Walter in a minute will condemn me to death. I wake up all covered in sweat.

I was haunted by these nightmares. All the time I saw the atelier and the naked kids. I had a nervous breakdown and came to feel repulsion toward photography. It brought back not just. just memories, but concrete, real images, horrible phantoms that for a second blurred my sense of reality.

I WAS NOT ABLE TO CHASE AWAY THOSE IMAGES AND I STILL CAN'T. I WILL DIE THIS WAY.

In normal conditions the picture of four naked girls which I had taken would be something to be proud of. After all, it is one of the most recognizable pictures in the world. But back then it was just my work. I tried to spare those kids physical suffering. I wanted them to feel reasonably at ease. Especially the girls, as they were very sensitive and shy about those matters. I did not anticipate that photo would become evidence of Nazi crimes, especially of those against children. I looked at it many times and wondered that only that one photograph survived, as I had taken so many of them.

Until the movie "The Portraitist"[571] by Irek Dobrowolski I never told my wife about my work and experiences at the camp. As soon as I started talking about it I would get very upset. After all, photographs like that one put me entirely off of the photographic profession. I abandoned photography.

After a time I found another occupation. My wife and I opened a little business making artificial casings for sausage.

In 1976 I received a veteran's pension. Since then my wife and I have traveled around Western Europe a lot with our trailer. It happened that up until 1992 the sausage casings continued to be a good business. I was happy with Stasia until she died in 2008.

Sometimes I ask myself, "Did you really go through all that?" If not for the documents and the photographs, you might think that nothing ever happened. The only thing that remains is that even to this day,

I CANNOT HOLD A CAMERA IN MY HAND.

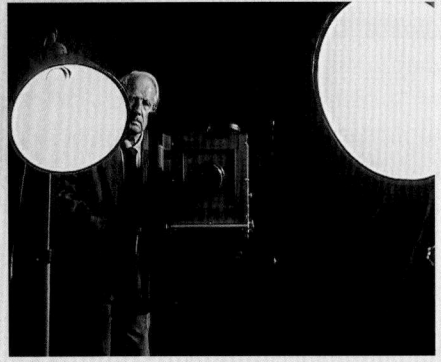

---

[571] The movie premiered in January 2006.

"After the war the surviving members of Erkennungsdienst returned to their ordinary lives. Bernhard Walter after serving his sentence became a projectionist in Bavaria. Hofmann disappeared soon after the war; according to Brasse he never returned to his family home in Germany. Bródka went to live in Sweden; Myszkowski remained in Auschwitz and became the director of the Auschwitz-Birkenau State Museum until 1950, when he immigrated to Israel. Woycicki went back to his job at a repertory theatre in Krakow and Jureczek found employment at the Bytom steelworks, a few kilometers from Oświęcim. Former professional photographer Brasse returned to his native Żywiec and never took another picture."[572]

---

[572] Struk J., *Holocaust...*, op. cit., p. 164

WILHELM BRASSE

– a descendant of Austrian settlers, was born in a Polish family in Żywiec on December 3rd 1917. He was a promising portrait photographer. For refusal to claim German nationality he was sent during World War II to the Auschwitz concentration camp where he was assigned a job at the photo Identification Service. He survived Auschwitz but at the end of the war he went through other harrowing experiences, after which he returned home completely burned out. He never photographed again. Instead he became an artisan producer of sausage casings. He spent the rest of his life in Żywiec. He left numerous depositions at the Auschwitz-Birkenau State Museum and the majority of the pictures he helped preserve enrich the Museum collection and publications.

For Wilhelm Brasse, Żywiec is a special place. His grandfather, who spoke three languages (French, German and Polish) settled there and this is where the family put down its roots. Three times during ninety-five years of his long life he refused to reject his Polish heritage although to do so would have bought him peace and security. Twice the offer was made by the Germans, who were astonished by the fact that someone with a German name, surname and Austrian ancestry remained faithful to his Polish identity.

Brasse remained in Auschwitz almost until the end, but he did not experience its liberation. In the last days of the operation of the death factory he was evacuated from KL Auschwitz to other camps in Germany and Austria. There he lost hope for salvation. Terminally exhausted after dangerous infections, he nearly died. From the Americans who liberated the camp he got one more offer to change his citizenship. Instead, he asked them to be returned to Żywiec.

Wilhelm Brasse knew that his testimony was historically priceless, so he cooperated with Museum researchers collecting witness evidence of the extermination activities. It has never been easy for him. It is enough to say that in spite of his good command of German acquired in school and later developed at the camp, after the liberation he did not speak another word of German for 20 years. Even Mr. Brasse's wife—Stanisława—did not realize he spoke German. She found that out during a trip to Krakow, when he assisted a German tourist.

That was his way of clearing his mind from the memories of pain and humiliation.

Wilhelm Brasse died on October 23rd 2012 in his home town of Żywiec. Until his final days he was helping with the creation of this book. Unfortunately, he did not live to see it in print.

AFTERWORD

I came to Poland for the first time with my family, arriving by train in Krakow late one Christmas night. For the next two days we strolled Market Square, toured Wawel Castle, walked the banks of the icy Vistula. And on the third morning we made the trip to Auschwitz. Time seemed to slow as we followed our guide through the gate, over the hard frozen ground, in and out of block after sooty brick block. We listened and looked and yes we looked away, trying to absorb the enormity.

Of all the exhibits—the piles of shoes, hair, suitcases, glasses—there was one that I had not foreseen. Along the central corridor of Block 6 we passed between hundreds of framed black-and-white photographs. In each, sharply focused and wearing rough prisoner stripes, a man, a woman, a girl or a boy stared back through the decades, unblinking. The living eyes in each portrait seemed to search out mine, and the effect was dizzying. As we neared the block exit our guide was saying something about how the photographer still returned to tell the story of his imprisonment...

Back home in Los Angeles the strangeness of the guide's remark stayed with me. One night I was teaching a class at the university when I found myself veering off topic to describe the vertigo of that walk between those portraits. How could the man who had made them keep returning?

The next night after class one student stayed behind to hand me a scrap of paper. There was a documentary film about the Auschwitz photographer, she said, and here was the director's name and address.

Soon I was in touch with Irek Dobrowolski. From Warsaw he sent me a copy of his award-winning film The Portraitist, about the young Polish photographer Wilhelm Brasse and his five-year ordeal as a political prisoner at Auschwitz, where he was forced to put his professional skills to work for the SS.

Dobrowolski's film made me want to know more. I began reading everything I could find about the Nazi camp experience, eyewitness reports by Primo Levi, Elie Wiesel, Victor Frankl, Eugen Kogon, Miklos Nyiszli, Jorge Semprun, and others. Inevitably, it seemed, these accounts led me to Regarding the Pain of Others and Susan Sontag's latter-day challenge to "Let the atrocious images haunt us."

After repeated viewings of The Portraitist I began to see how Dobrowolski was fulfilling this challenge by turning his lens on the man who had taken those portraits now hanging in the corridor of Block 6. Face to face with atrocity and the photographic evidence of same, neither man's camera blinked.

A year later I returned to Warsaw to interview Irek Dobrowolski. When he had finished answering my questions he asked one of his own: Would I like to meet Mr. Brasse?

In one day we drove more than 600 kilometers to and from Mr. Brasse's hometown of Żywiec, in southern Poland. Over dinner and throughout a long evening of conversation I saw the friendship that Irek and Mr. Brasse shared, never more so than when they made each other laugh.

Mr. Brasse survived Auschwitz, it was true. Afterwards, however, whenever he peered through a camera's viewfinder, ghostlike images of the people he had photographed there would return to him. The pain of seeing those images forced him to abandon his profession and find another way to live. And yet at the end of our long evening together, when I asked if he would take a picture of his visitors, Mr. Brasse did not hesitate. He took my miniature digital in hand, raised it to his eye, and snapped Irek and me smiling back.

Mr. Brasse died in October 2012 at age 95. For more than half a century he had kept his wartime experiences a secret. But in his last years, thanks to The Portraitist, he had become one of Auschwitz's main witnesses. Now, thanks to Anna Dobrowolska—Irek's wife, producer, and closest collaborator—Mr. Brasse's legacy still resonates.

Trained as a journalist and driven by novelistic instincts, Anna considers Auschwitz one of the world's great narratives. And yet, as she also knows, we live in a time when great narratives have vanished. Anna is working to change that. In a post-graduate course on documentation taught on the grounds of Auschwitz by University of Warsaw Professor Marek Miller, Anna came to embrace the lessons of Russian language philosopher M.M. Bakhtin. "Truth is not born nor is it to be found inside the head of an individual person," Bakhtin reminds us; "it is born between people collectively searching for truth, in the process of their dialogic interaction."

In the midst of this two-year course Anna spent two summer weeks living with classmates on the grounds of the former Nazi death camp while doing research in the archives of the Auschwitz-Birkenau Museum. It was there that she determined to apply Bakhtin's literary lessons of dialogism and polyphony to the archival materials at hand. Using Miller's methods of documentary reconstruction, she wanted to deepen our understanding of the Auschwitz narrative by illustrating it with the memories of many individuals who had their own perspectives on shared episodes of camp life. And so, starting with the 18 hours of video recordings that Irek had made of Mr. Brasse, she set out to arrange his trove of stories amidst multiple parallel accounts by others—victims and perpetrators alike—together with a wealth of photographic evidence. She calls the outgrowth of her work, the book you now hold in your hands, a documentary novel.

"Everyone who has had contact with great narrations has the impression that everything connects," she says. "Love and death, faith and hopelessness, joy and sadness—all the nobility and lowliness of a man." After reading innumerable testimonies and discovering how they overlapped and interpenetrated, she felt that the speakers were coming to know each other. In The Portraitist Irek had focused on the voice of Mr. Brasse alone. In The Photographer of Auschwitz Anna would orchestrate a chorus of voices centered around Wilhelm Brasse speaking for himself in his clear, simple, and direct way.

Enter into the interweaving text and imagery of Dobrowolska's book and you will find yourself growing intimate with the most alien of subjects, daily life in mankind's most productive death factory. No matter how widely you have read on the subject, this book may be the first to convey a sense of the camp's moment-to-moment realities as lived by those on the killing ground, from the nightmare logic of Nazi violence to the absurdities of human warmth and even humor. If God is in the details then so too, as Anna Dobrowolska shows us, is God's absence.

Nor is she yet finished. In addition to placing The Photographer of Auschwitz in schools throughout Poland and beyond in order to educate young people, Anna aims to create a virtual atelier that will replicate the one at Auschwitz. When this project is completed we will be able to enter that room as if through the eyes of the young Wilhelm Brasse leaning over to peer into his camera. We will be able to see what he saw in the eyes of countless fellow prisoners as he photographed them on the way to their fates.

Against our urge to look away, those of us who come later must now turn to his photographs and listen to his stories. Like no other witness he stands in for us.

STEPHEN COOPER
California State University,
Long Beach

Stephen Cooper, Wilhelm Brasse and Irek Dobrowolski

KL AUSCHWITZ II-BIRKENAU. THE MAIN WATCHTOWER, CALLED THE GATE OF DEATH

AUSCHWITZ CHRONOLOGY

1939

▼ September 1st: Nazi Germany attacks Poland. The outbreak of World War II.

▼ End 1939: due to mass arrests of Poles and the overcrowding of prisons in Upper Silesia and in the Dąbrowa Basin, the Higher Office of the SS and Police Commander in Breslau/Wrocław devises a plan to create a concentration camp for the Poles.

1940

▼ April 27th: After having inspected a range of locations Heinrich Himmler, the head of SS, issues an order to establish a concentration camp in the former Polish artillery barracks in Oświęcim, called Auschwitz under the Nazi rule.

▼ June 14th: Nazi authorities sent to Auschwitz the first transport of political prisoners—728 Poles, including a small number of Polish Jews. This is considered the first day of the camp's operation. Between 1940–1945 there were around 405 thousand registered prisoners, 270 thousand of them men.

▼ June 19th: First relocation of local people to maintain secrecy of the crimes, isolation of prisoners and to limit the possibilities of escapes. Subsequent evictions are due to the planned expansion of the Auschwitz camp. In all, over 5 thousand Poles were displaced from Oświęcim and the surrounding villages. The whole Jewish population of the town—about 7 thousand—got deported to the ghettos in the area. Eight villages got destroyed and over a hundred Oświęcim buildings in the direct proximity of the camp got demolished.

▼ July 6th: The first escape of a prisoner, Tadeusz Wiejowski. During the camp operation, for over a million people imprisoned there were a few hundred attempts of escape. The most were undertaken by the Poles, Soviet POWs and Jews. Less then 150 prisoners managed to flee. Most of the

others were shot during the attempt or captured and murdered afterwards.

▼ The fall: Polish Resistance informs the Polish Government in Exile in London about the camp.

▼ November 22nd: The first execution by shooting. 40 Poles killed.

1941

▼ March 1st: The first Auschwitz inspection by SS Commander Heinrich Himmler. He orders the camp to be expanded and allows IG Farbenindustries to use 10 thousand prisoners in the construction of their industrial plant.

▼ April 23rd: In retaliation for a prisoner's escape, Camp Commandant Rudolf Höss for the first time condemns 10 prisoners to death by starvation.

▼ June 6th: The first transport of Czech political prisoners. The beginning of non-Polish deportations to Auschwitz.

▼ September 3rd: The first mass gassing of people using Zyklon B. About 600 Soviet POW and 250 Poles die.

▼ The Fall: The first gas chamber in Auschwitz I starts operation.

▼ October: A camp for Soviet POW established in Auschwitz I.

▼ October: Beginning construction of the second part of the campl, Auschwitz II—Birkenau on the site of the demolished village of Brzezinka.

▼ November 11th: In the first execution at the Death Wall the Nazis shoot 151 Polish prisoners.

1942

▼ Early in the year: Beginning of mass extermination of Jews in the gas chambers.

▼ March: Beginning of mass deportation to Auschwitz of Jews from France—69 thousand and Slovakia—27 thousand.

▼ March 1st: Auschwitz II–Birkenau begins operation.

▼ March 26th: First women imprisoned in Auschwitz, 2 thousand of about 130 thousand female prisoners registered during the existence of the camp.

▼ March-June: Temporary gas chambers established outside Auschwitz II-Birkenau.

▼ Spring: Opening of the so-called Judenrampe, the area between Auschwitz I and Auschwitz II-Birkenau where transports of Jews, Poles, Roma and other nationality prisoners were received.

▼ May: Beginning of Auschwitz deportation of Jews - 300 thousand from Poland and 23 thousand from Germany and Austria.

▼ May 4th: The first selection by SS in Birkenau. The selected prisoners get murdered in the gas chamber.

▼ June 10th: Mutiny and attempted mass escape by about 350 prisoners from the Penal Company in Birkenau. Only 7 of them made it, over 300 got killed.

▼ July: Beginning of deportation to Auschwitz of 60 thousand Jews from Holland.

▼ July: Sub-camp Golleschau starts operation at the cement plant in Goleszów near Cieszyn—the first of about 50 satellite camps of Auschwitz.

▼ July 29th: Edward Schulte, a German industrialist and anti-Nazi passes to the Allies information that Heinrich Himmler visited Auschwitz in July and was present at the gassing of 499 Jews with Zyklon B in the so-called Bunker 2. This is the first precise message from German sources about the extermination of Jews in the Auschwitz gas chambers. Beginning in the fall of 1940 the Allies are being regularly informed about what is going on in Auschwitz. The information comes mostly via the Polish Government in Exile in London, which is in close communication with the Polish Resistance, active both in the camp and around it.

▼ August: Beginning for deportation to Auschwitz of 25 thousand Jews from Belgium and 10 thousand from Yugoslavia.

▼ October 30th: The sub-camp of Buna is created at the plant of synthetic rubber owned by IG Farbenindustrie; later to be renamed Auschwitz III-Monowitz. Between 1942-1944 there will be 47 of similar sub-camps and external kommandos of KL Auschwitz. Their prisoners work mostly in German industrial companies.

▼ October: Beginning of Auschwitz deportation of 46 thousand Jews from the Protectorate of Bohemia and Moravia.

▼ December: The first transport of Jews from Norway. Almost 700 people arrive in two transports.

▼ December 13th: The first transport of Poles from the Zamość region; part of Nazi "Generalplan Ost"— the General Eastern Plan. The Plan envisioned deportation and extermination of about 50 million Slavs (Poles, Russians, Belarusians, Ukrainians and others) and of German settlers colonizing Central and Eastern Europe, beginning with Poland.

▼ End of year: SS doctors begin sterilization experiments on male and female prisoners.

1943

▼ February 26th: The establishment of the so-called Gypsy Family Camp for Roma people in Birkenau.

▼ March: Beginning of deportation of 55 thousand Jews from Greece.

▼ March 22nd– June 25th: Four new crematoriums with gas chambers begin operation in Auschwitz II-Birkenau.

▼ June 7th: civilian workers of the Krupp factory begin installing machinery in the hall leased from the camp authorities. Hundreds of German companies are involved in the establishment of Auschwitz; many—like IG Farbenindustrie or Siemens—draw profits from slave labor provided by the prisoners.

▼ July 19th: The largest public execution. In retaliation for an escape of a few prisoners and for contacting civilian population SS men hang 12 Polish prisoners.

▼ September 9th: Establishment at Birkenau of the so-called Family Camp Theresienstadt for the Jews from the Theresienstadt ghetto.

▼ October: Beginning of deportation of 7,5 thousand Jews from Italy.

1944

▼ May: First Allies' planes flying over Auschwitz take aerial photos which show the gas chambers and smoke from the burning pits. Three months later the Americans and the British bomb the synthetic rubber and liquid fuel plant belonging to IG Farbenindustrie, located a few kilometers from Birkenau.

▼ May 16th: First use of inner ramp, which enabled direct access of train transports to gas chambers II and III of Auschwitz II-Birkenau. First arrivals of 438 thousand Jews from Hungary.

▼ July 10-12: Liquidation of the so-called Family Camp Theresienstadt. The Nazis murder in gas chambers about 7 thousand Jews.

▼ August: Beginning of deportation to Auschwitz of 67 thousand Jews from Litzmannstadt (Łódź).

▼ August 2nd: Liquidation of the Gypsy Family Camp—SS men murder in gas chambers almost 3 thousand Roma.

▼ August 12th: Start of deportation to Auschwitz of 13 thousand Poles from the mass arrests at the outbreak of the Warsaw Uprising.

▼ October 7th: Sonderkommando mutiny. During the mutiny 3 SS men and 450 prisoners of Sonderkommando die. Jews were forced to incinerate the bodies of the murdered.

▼ November: Mass murder of Jews in gas chambers stops.

1945

▼ January 6th: the last execution of about 70 Poles tried by a summary court. Four Jewish women condemned for helping to prepare the Sonderkommando mutiny die in the last public execution.

▼ January 17th: Beginning of the the Death Marches—SS men evacuate almost 60 thousand prisoners from Auschwitz.

▼ January 21st-26th: The Nazis blow up the gas chambers and crematoriums in Birkenau.

▼ January 27th: 7 thousand prisoners survive to the camp liberation by the Soviet Army troops.

www.auschwitz.org

PRISONER BADGES

▼

Coding of main prisoner categories in KL Auschwitz

Red triangle – political prisoner

Red triangle over a yellow one – Jew

Black triangle – "asocial element"

Green triangle – criminal prisoners

Purple triangle – Jehovah's Witness

Pink triangle – homosexual

SU – Soviet POW

EH – Correctional prisoner

PH – Police prisoner

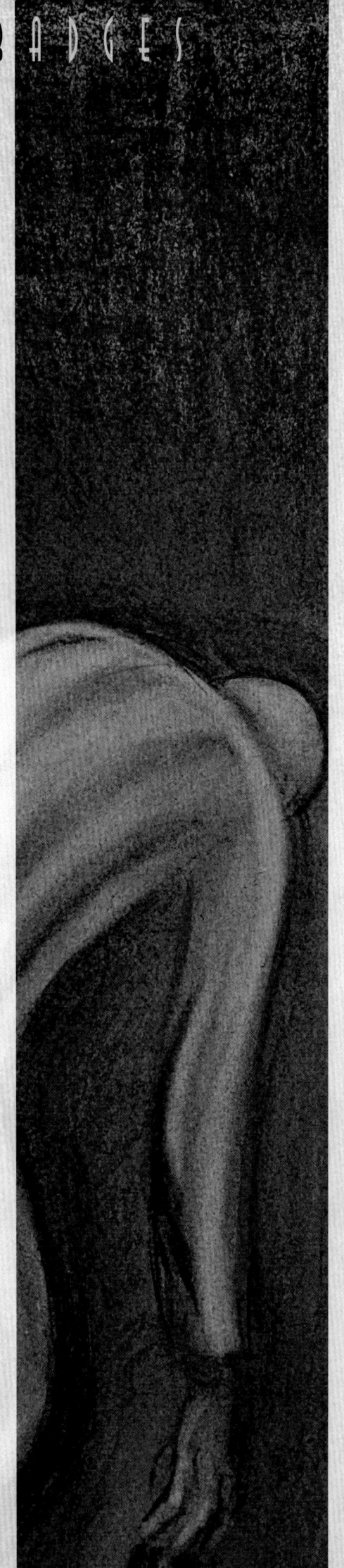

SS Ranks

German Rank		English Equivalent
SS-Mann		Private
SS-Sturmmann		Lance corporal
SS-Rottenführer		Corporal
SS-Unterscharführer		Sergeant
SS-Scharführer		Staff Sergeant
SS-Oberscharführer		Sergeant 1st Class
SS-Hauptscharfuhrer		Master Sergeant
SS-Stabscharführer		Staff Squad Leader
SS-Untersturmführer		2nd Lieutenant
SS-Obersturmführer		Lieutenant
SS-Hauptsturmführer		Captain
SS-Sturmbannführer		Major
SS-Obersturmbannführer		Lieutenant Colonel
SS-Standartenführer		Colonel
SS-Oberführer		Senior Leader/Brigadier
SS-Brigadeführer		Brigadier General
SS-Gruppenführer		Major General
SS-Obergruppenführer		Lieutenant General
SS-Oberstgruppenführer		General
Reichsführer SS		Marshal

With each step, Jerzy Adam Brandhuber

PRISONERS

of KL Auschwitz whose accounts were quoted in this book:

Kazimierz Albin

Arnold Andrunik

Jan Baraniok

Jerzy Bielecki

Włodzimierz Borkowski

Józef Brodnicki

Mieczysław Brożek

Shaul Chasan

Józef Ciepły

Edward Cieśliński

Szlomo Dragon

Alojzy Drzazga

Stanisław Dubiel

Jan Dziopek

Walter Fajnzylberg

Władysław Fejkiel

Stanisław Głowa

Franciszek Hillmann

Krzysztof Hofman

Tadeusz Hołuj

Czesław Jaszczyński

Józef Jędrych

Bronisław Jureczek

Adam Jurkiewicz

Raya Kagan

Janina Kałanczyńska

Janusz Karwacki

Wojciech Kawecki

Edward Kiczmachowski

Wiesław Kielar

Julian Kiwała

Ruth Klüger

Stanisław Kłodziński

Adam Kopyciński

Mieczysław Kościelniak

Ludwik Kozakiewicz

Artur Krzetuski

Tadeusz Krzysica

Erich Kulka

Szymon Laks

Hermann Langbein

Langfus Leib

Czesław Lenczowski

Stanisława Leszczyńska

Primo Levi

Jan Liwacz

Henryk Mandelbaum

Filip Müller

Michał Mysiński

Tadeusz Myszkowski

Josef Neumann

Moshe Ofera

Jan Olbrycht

Erwin Olszówka

Józef Osika

Tadeusz Orzeszko

Jan Otrębski

Tadeusz Paczuła

Józef Paczyński

Dov Paisikovic

Wiktor Pasikowski

Janina Perun

Zofia Pohorecka

Józef Putek

Andrzej Rablin

Josef Sackar

Stanisław Skibicki

Józef Skrzypek

Kazimierz Smoleń

Tadeusz Sobolewski

Adam Stapf

Bolesław Staroń

Anna Stefańska – Tytoniak

Zofia Stępień – Bator

Józef Stós

Adam Stręk

Franciszek Stryja

Lech Szawłowski

Kazimierz Szczerbowski

Janina Szczurek

Jan Szembek

Anna Szyller

Józef Światłoch

Karol Świętorzecki

Stefan Świszczowski

Józef Tabaczyński

Jerzy Tabeau

Wanda Tarasiewicz

Franciszek Targosz

Kazimierz Tokarz

Roman Trojanowski

Helena Tyrankiewicz

Shlomo Venezia

Jan Weiss

Alfred Wetzler

Edward Wieczorek

Alfred Woycicki

Ludwik Żuk

Paweł Żur

BIOGRAPHIES OF PRISONERS

JAN BARAŚ-KOMSKI (Inmate No. 564)
b. Feb. 3rd 1915 in Bircza, artist. On December 29 1942 escaped from the camp. After the escape he got recaptured and sent back to KL Auschwitz, where he did not get identified as a fugitive. He survived.

JADWIGA BARTEL (Inmate No. 21953)
b. Oct. 6th 1913 in Oświęcim. Came to KL Auschwitz on Oct. 6th 1942 from KL Ravensbrück. Later transferred to KL Bergen-Belsen and liberated there on April 15th 1945.

ERWIN BARTEL (Inmate No. 17044)
b. Feb. 3rd 1923 in Oświęcim, student. Survived KL Auschwitz.

TADEUSZ BAUT (Inmate No. 1529)
b. Aug. 14th 1921 in Żywiec. Brought to KL Auschwitz on June 26th 1940 in the Katowice transport. Escaped from the camp on January 21st 1945.

JERZY BIELECKI (Inmate No. 243)
b. March 28th 1921 in Słaboszów, student. Escaped from KL Auschwitz on July 21st 1944. Survived.

WŁADYSŁAW MARIA AGENOR, COUNT BAWOROWSKI FROM BAWOROWO; "PRUS" COAT OF ARMS. (Inmate No. 863)
b. Aug. 10th 1910 in Germakówka, landowner. Brought to KL Auschwitz on Aug. 20th 1940 in the Kraków-Tarnów transport. Died in Auschwitz on June 1st 1941.

TADEUSZ BRÓDKA (Inmate No. 245)
b. Jan. 1st 1920. Came to KL Auschwitz in the June 14th 1940 transport from Kraków-Tarnów. In 1944 transferred to KL Sachsenhausen. Survived.

CYLA CYBULSKA-STAWISKA (Inmate No. 29558)
b. Dec. 29th 1920 in Łomża. Transported to Kl Auschwitz with her whole family on Jan. 21st 1943. At selection only Cela was directed to join the labor force on the right. Her mother and 10 year old sister were taken to the gas chamber. Her father and brother were murdered after a few days. Cyla escaped from the camp with Jerzy Bielecki on July 21st 1944.

JÓZEF CYRANKIEWICZ (Inmate No. 62933)
b. April 23rd 1911 in Tarnów, lawyer. Brought to KL Auschwitz on Sept. 4th 1942 in the Kraków transport. Employed as a nurse in the hospital block 20. In 1945 evacuated to KL Mauthausen and liberated there. Later Prime Minister of the Polish People's Republic.

BRONISŁAW CZECH (Inmate No. 349)
b. July 25th 1908 in Zakopane, skiing instructor, Alpine climber, three times member of the Olympic team. Brought to KL Auschwitz on June 14th 1940 in the Kraków-Tarnów transport. Died on June 5th 1944 in the camp hospital.

EUGENIUSZ DEMBEK (Inmate No. 63764)
b. 1900. Brought to KL Auschwitz in the Sept. 15th 1942 transport from Warsaw. His later fate unknown.

RUDOLF DIEM (Inmate No. 10022)
b. August 23rd 1896 in Hermanów, physician, Major of the Polish Army. During the Polish Campaign of September 1939 he was the sanitary chief of the capitals' defense command; after the capitulation he took active part in the resistance, providing medicines and dressings to the inmates of Pawiak prison. He survived KL Auschwitz.

STANISŁAW DUBIEL (Inmate No. 6059)
b. Nov. 13th 1910 in Chorzów. Brought to KL Auschwitz in the Katowice transport on Nov. 6th 1940. Employed for a time as a gardener of the Camp Commander Rudolf Höss. He survived.

XAWERY DUNIKOWSKI (Inmate No. 774)
b. Nov. 29th 1875 in Kraków, sculptor, painter, Professor of the Academy of Fine Arts in Kraków. Brought to KL Auschwitz on June 20th 1940 in the Kraków-Tarnów transport. Liberated in KL Auschwitz on Jan. 27th 1945.

ARMIN ENOCH (Inmate No. 27148)
b. April 27th 1900 in Petroutz in Romania, chemist. Died in KL Auschwitz on April 7th 1942.

WŁADYSŁAW FEJKIEL (Inmate No. 5647)
b. Jan. 1st 1911 in Krościenko Wyżne, physician, Professor of the Kraków Medical Academy. In August 1940 he got arrested by the Gestapo; on Oct. 8th taken to KL Auschwitz. Famished, he got admitted to the inmate hospital (Häftlingskrankenbau). After recovery he worked there for four years in various capacities – from a night warden to the elder of the hospital block – Lagersälter. In 1945 he was evacuated to KL Mauthausen, where he got liberated.

RUDOLF FRIEMEL (Inmate No. 25173)
b. April 11th 1907 in Vienna, car mechanic. Brought to Auschwitz on Jan. 2nd 1942. On March 18th 1944, in a civil ceremony, he married Margarita Ferrer Rey – a Spanish woman with French citizenship. It was the only instance of an inmate marriage at the camp. On Oct. 27th 1944 he was taken to the bunker of Block 11 as a co-organizer of an unsuccessful escape, planned by members of the camp resistance. He was sentenced to death. His execution took place on Dec. 30th 1944.

EDWARD GALIŃSKI (Inmate No. 531)
b. Oct. 5th 1923 in Więckowice. Brought to KL Auschwitz on June 14th 1940 in the Kraków-Tarnów transport. On June 24th 1944 he escaped with Mala Zimetbaum; apprehended. Taken to the camp prison cell and condemned to death. Hanged in September 1944 in the men's camp Bild in Birkenau.

LEO HAAS
(Inmate No. 199885)
b. in in 1901 in Opava, Czechoslovakia. Artist. He moved to Karlsruhe in Germany for studying art and he also studied piano and voice in addition to painting. In 1929 he married Sophie Hermann and became a well-known portrait painter in Opava. Haas was arrested by the Gestapo in August 1942 and included in the transport to Terezin, at the end of September 1942. Haas arrived in Auschwitz on October 28th 1942 and was classified as a political prisoner. In November 1944, Haas was transferred to Sachsenhausen camp where he was given a new number: 118029. After a few days he was sent to blocks 18 and 19, which were separated from the rest of the camp. At the end of February 1945 he was transferred to Mauthausen. He survived. He passed away in 1983.

MIECZYSŁAW JANUSZEWSKI
(Inmate No. 711)
b. July 1st 1918 in Łódź, Lieutenant in the Polish Navy, ship mechanic. Brought to KL Auschwitz on June 14th 1940 in the Kraków-Tarnów transport. Escaped on Dec. 29th 1942. Arrested, died on the way to KL Auschwitz.

BRONISŁAW JURECZEK (Inmate No. 26672)
b. July 13th 1920 in Brzozowice Kamień. Brought to KL Auschwitz on Jan 23rd 1943 in the Kraków transport. In 1944 transferred to KL Flossenbürg, then again to Auschwitz, then to KL Buchenwald. Liberated in KL Sachsenhausen.

JANUSZ MIECZYSŁAW KARWACKI
(inmate no. 93186)
b. July 22ns 1925 in Ostrowiec. Came to KL Auschwitz in the Jan. 23rd transport from Krakow. In 1944 transferred to KL Flossenbürg and then back to Auschwitz and Buchenwald. Liberated in KL Sachsenhausen.

ROMAN KARWAT (Inmate No. 5959)
b. Nov. 11th 1904. Brought to KL Auschwitz on Oct. 10th in the Katowice transport. Executed by firing squad on June 14th 1942.

RUDOLF KAUER (Inmate No. 15592)
b. Jan. 24th 1902 in Teschen, building engineer. Brought to KL Auschwitz in a group transport on May 16th 1941. Transferred on Sept. 14th 1944 to KL Flossenbürg. He survived.

STANISŁAW KŁODZIŃSKI (Inmate No. 20019)
b. May 4th 1918 in Kraków. Brought to KL Auschwitz on Aug. 12th 1941 in the Kraków transport. In 1945 evacuated to Mauthausen; survived.

BOGDAN KOMARNICKI (Inmate No. 3637)
b. July 28th 1913 in Synowodzko. Brought to KL Auschwitz on Aug 30th 1940 in the same transport as Brasse – the 2nd Tarnów transport. In 1945 taken to KL Mauthausen, he survived.

MIECZYSŁAW KOŚCIELNIAK (Inmate No. 15261)
b. Jan. 28th in Kalisz, graphic artist and painter. Brought to Auschwitz on May 2nd 1941 in the Łódź transport. Author of many paintings depicting life in the camp. Evacuated to Mauthausen in 1945, liberated there.

ERNST KRANKEMANN (Inmate No. 3210)
b. Dec. 19th 1895. Brought to Auschwitz on August 29th 1940 in the Sachsenhausen transport; kapo of the Penal Company. On July 28th 1941 he was added to the transport of 575 disabled prisoners who were sent to Sonnenstein near Pirna in Saxony. There they got murdered in the gas chamber as part of the euthanasia program under code name "Action 14/f13". There were rumors at the camp that other inmates lynched him during the journey.

TADEUSZ KRZYSICA (Inmate No. 120557)
b. Oct. 22nd in Kraków. Brought to KL Auschwitz on May 8th 1943 in a group transport. In October 1944 transferred to KL Sachsenhausen, sub-camp Barth. Liberated during the evacuation march on May 1st 1945.

STANISŁAW KUCHARSKI (Inmate No. unknown)
b. April 26th 1918 in Żywiec, son of Karol and Karolina née Ertel, single. Official couse of death – Darmkatarrh bei Körperschwäche – enteritis during body exhaustion (!); sick with typhus. Date of death: Sept. 7th 1942

BOLESŁAW KUCZBARA (Inmate No. 4308)
b. Nov. 26th 1911, dentist. Brought to KL Auschwitz on Sept. 22nd 1940 in the Warsaw transport. Escaped from the camp on Dec. 29th 1942.

JAN KUPIEC (Inmate No. 790)
b. Feb. 17th 1904 in Zakopane, building technician. Brought to KL Auschwitz on June 20th 1940 in the Kraków–Tarnów transport. He survived.

JÓZEF KUPIEC (Inmate No. 791)
b. Feb. 17th 1904 in Zakopane, building technician. Brought to KL Auschwitz on June 20th 1940 in the Kraków–Tarnów transport. He survived.

BOLESŁAW KUPIEC (Inmate No. 792)
b. July 12th 1913 in Poronin, sculptor. Brought to KL Auschwitz in the June 20th 1940 transport from Kraków–Tarnów. Transferred from the camp to the Palace prison in Zakopane where he died on March 4th 1943.

WŁADYSŁAW KUPIEC (Inmate No. 793)
b. Aug. 13th 1907 in Zakopane, carpenter. Brought to KL Auschwitz in the June 20th 1940 transport from Kraków–Tarnów. Survived.

KAROL KUPIEC (Inmate No. 794)
b. Jan. 27th 1909 in Zakopane, merchant. Brought to KL Auschwitz on June 20th 1940 in the Kraków–Tarnów transport. Executed by firing squad in KL Auschwitz on Sept. 21st 1942.

ANTONI KUPIEC (Inmate No. 5908)
b. Jan. 19th 1919 in Poronin, sculptor. Brought to KL Auschwitz on Oct. 8th 1940 in the Kraków–Tarnów transport. Transferred to KL Sachsenhausen. Survived.

OTTO KÜSSEL (Inmate No. 2)
b. May 16th 1909 in Berlin, office clerk, thief convicted for stealing cars. Brought to KL Auschwitz on May 20th 1940 in the transport of prisoners selected by Palitzsch in KL Sachsenhausen. On Dec. 29th 1942 escaped from the camp with three other inmates: Jan Baraś (564), Mieczysław Januszewski (711) and Bolesław Kuczbara (4308). He was hiding in Warsaw, got arrested and brought back to KL Auschwitz and was tried in the bunker of Block 11. On Nov. 23rd 1943 he was released from the bunker and in 1944 transferred to KL Flossenbürg. Survived.

CZESŁAWA KWOKA (Inmate No. 26964)
b. Aug. 15th 1928 in Wólka Złojecka. Brought to KL Auschwitz on Dec. 13th 1942 in the Zamość transport. Died in Auschwitz on March 12th 1943.

JULIAN LACHENDRO (Inmate No. 265)
b.Sept. 14th 1895 in Wieprz, Doctor of Law, judge of the county court. Brought to Kl Auschwitz on April 13th 1940 in the Kraków–Tarnów transport. His death date in the camp records: Feb. 13th 1941.

CZESŁAW LENCZOWSKI (Inmate No. 29553)
b. March 13th 1905 in Świątniki Górne, artist, painter. Brought to KL Auschwitz in the Kraków transport on April 13th 1942. In 1944 transferred to Kl Flossenbürg. Survived.

JAN LIWACZ (Inmate No. 1010)
b. Oct. 4th 1898 in Dukla, blacksmith. In 1944 transferred to KL Mauthausen. Survived.

ADOLF MACIEJEWSKI (Inmate No. 1130)
b. Feb. 9th 1910 in Chorzów Batory. Brought to KL Auschwitz on June 25th 1940 in the Katowice transport. Escaped during the evacuation march out of Auschwitz.

FRANZ MALZ (Inmate No. nieznany)
b.Sept. 25th in Brandenburg, photographer. Before his arrest he lived in Stettin. His death record of Feb. 5th 1943 states Plötzlicher Herztod (heart attack) as the cause of death. Such cause of death was given in case of an execution.

JANUSZ MŁYNARSKI (MÜLLER)
(Inmate No. 355)
b. August 14th 1922 in Poznań. Brought to KL Auschwitz on June 14th 1940 in the Kraków-Tarnów transport. Employed as a lab technician in the hospital Block 20. In 1945 evacuated to KL Mauthausen. Survived.

MIECZYSŁAW MORAWA (Inmate No. 5730)
b. March 19th 1920 in Kraków. Brought to KL Auschwitz on Oct. 8th 1940 in the Kraków-Tarnów transport. Employed as a kapo in the crematorium; first in the original camp, later in Birkenau. Executed by firing squad on April 3rd 1945.

FRANCISZEK TADEUSZ MYSZKOWSKI
(Inmate No. 593)
b. Sept. 25th 1912 in Zakopane, graphic artist. Graduate of the State School of Decorative Arts in Kraków. On May 6th 1940 arrested in Zakopane and placed in the Palace prison. Later in Tarnów prison, from which he was taken to KL Auschwitz on June 14th 1940. He worked in the carpentry shop, sculpture workshop and "Erkennungsdienst". He drew portraits and caricatures of inmates and SS-men, painted and made sculptures. In September 1944 he was moved to Oranienburg (sub-camp of KL Sachsenhausen), and later to Barth (sub-camp of Ravensbrück). On May 1st 1945 he escaped from the evacuation transport. He died on June 21st 1980 in Jerusalem.

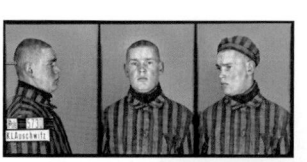

FRANCISZEK NIERYCHŁO (Inmate No. 994)
b. Nov. 17th 1905 in Łagiewniki, musician. Brought to KL Auschwitz on June 14th 1940 in the Kraków-Tarnów transport. On May 29th 1944 he was released from the camp.

KAZIMIERZ PIECHOWSKI (Inmate No. 918)
b.Oct. 3rd 1919 in Rajkowy, ironworker, soldier in the Home Army (AK). Arrested in 1939, he was sent to KL Auschwitz in the June 20th 1940 Kraków-Tarnów transport. He escaped from the camp on May 20th 1942

FRANCISZEK PIELA (Inmate No. 1258)
b.April 26th 1916 in Cięcin. Brought to KL Auschwitz in the June 26th 1940 transport from Katowice. In January 1945 walked in the evacuation march and was moved to KL Mauthausen; liberated there.

JAN PILECKI (Inmate No. 808)
b. April 27th 1913 in Warsaw. Brought to KL Auschwitz in June 20th 1940 in the Kraków transport. He worked as a clerk in Block 11. Transferred to KL Sachsenhausen in 1944; survived.

WITOLD PILECKI (Inmate No. 4859)
b. May 13th 1901 in Ołoniec, officer of the Polish Army, the "Auschwitz Volunteer" and organizer of camp resistance. Came to KL Auschwitz in the second Warsaw transport on Sept. 21st 1940. Escaped on April 26th 1943. Condemned to death by the Communist authorities of the Polish People's Republic and executed on May 25th 1948.

ARTUR POPIEL (Inmate No. 951)
b. May 25th 1885 in Warsaw. Brought to KL Auschwitz on June 20th 1940 in the Kraków-Tarnów transport. Moved to KL Mauthausen on July 7th 1942.

JÓZEF PUTEK (Inmate No. 829)
b. July 4th 1892 in Wadowice, doctor of law, attorney, Member of the Polish Parliament representing the Peasant Party. Taken to KL Auschwitz in the June 20th 1940 transport from Kraków-Tarnów. Transferred to KL Mauthausen on July 7th 1942. Survived.

JÓZEF PYSZ (Inmate No. 1420)
b. March 9th 1915 in Dresseldorf, photrapeher. Brought to KL Auschwitz on July 29th 1940 in the Katowice transport. Note in the records says he was released from the camp on Feb. 2nd 1944.

ANDRZEJ RABLIN (Inmate No. 1410)
b. Jan. 1st 1914 in Kraków. Brought to KL Auschwitz on July 18th 1940 in the Kraków-Tarnów transport. Transferred to KL Sachsenhausen, then to Kl Ravensbrück. He escaped during the evacuation march in the village of Malhof.

MAX SAMUEL (Inmate No. 62907)
b. Sept. 15th 1880 in Franchen near Cologne, physician. Brought to KL Auschwitz on Sept. 2nd 1942 in the transport from Drancy. Employed in Block 10 in sterilization experiments conducted by Dr. Clauberg. He died in the camp in 1944, no exact date known; the last mention of him in the records is from May 1944.

JOHANN SIEGRUTH (Inmate No. 26)
b. March 24th 1903 in Katowice. Brought to KL Auschwitz on May 5th 1940 in the transport from KL Sachsenhausen, worked as a kapo. On July 28th 1941 he was taken to Sonnenstein with a group of 575 prisoners. Anticipating his fate, he hanged himself on the train.

JÓZEF SITKO (Inmate No. 75906)
b. March 9th 1887 in Dembno, county Brzesko, Lieutenant Colonel of the Polish Army. Arrested in Kraków on Nov. 13th 1942 for listening to the radio and for anti-Nazi activities in Bielsko. Placed in the Montelupi prison in Kraków. Brought to Auschwitz on Nov. 11th 1942. Played cello in the camp orchestra. Transferred to KL Sachsenhausen. Survived.

ALEKSANDRA SKALSKA (Inmate No. 38103)
b. April 18th 1921 in Żywiec. Brought to KL Auschwitz in Oct. 22nd 1944 in the Kraków-Płaszów transport, worked in the clothes workshops. Transferred to KL Ravensbrück; liberated in Neustadt-Glewe.

BOLESŁAW STAROŃ (Inmate No. 127829)
b. May 9th 1919 in Berlin-Aldershof, building technician. In 1944 moved to KL Fossenbürg. Survived.

MARIAN STUDENCKI (Inmate No. 5822)
b. Nov. 14th 1907 in Żywiec. Brought To KL Auschwitz on Oct. 8th 1940 in the Kraków-Tarnów transport. Executed at the Wall of Death on Jan. 25th 1943.

JÓZEF SZAJNA (Inmate No. 18729)
b. March 13th 1923 in Rzeszów. Brought to KL Auschwitz on July 25th 1941 in the Kraków transport. In 1944 transferred to KL Buchenwald. Survived.

WACŁAW SZYMBORSKI (Inmate No. 1976)
b. 1913 in Warsaw, finish painter. Brought to Auschwitz on Aug. 15th 1940 in the Warsaw transport. He was an assistant block leader. Died in KL Auschwitz on Aug. 3rd 1942.

FRANCISZEK TARGOSZ (Inmate No. 7626)
b. Sept. 7th 1899 in Lipnik. Brought to KL Auschwitz from Bielsko on Dec. 18th 1940. Transferred to KL Mauthausen on Jan. 21st 1945, and later to Melk, where he got liberated on May 5th 1945.

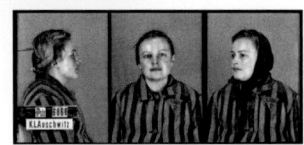

FRANZ TERESIAK (Inmate No. 3231)
b. Jan. 23rd 1914. A German brought to the camp from Sachsenhausen on Aug. 27th 1940. His later fate unknown.

STANISŁAW TRAŁKA (Inmate No. 660)
b. July 14th 1921 in Wąbrzeźno. Brought to KL Auschwitz in the June 14th 1940 Kraków-Tarnów transport as a political prisoner. His death is marked in the camp records on Oct. 2nd 1942.

ANNA TYTONIAK (Inmate No. 6866)
b. Jan. 4th 1920 in Jasło. Brought to the camp on April 27th 1942 from the Tarnów prison. Since November 1942 she worked in the office of the women's hospital. She was known in the camp as Barbara Stefańska. She escaped during the evacuation march from KL Auschwitz. Survived.

LUDWIG VESELY (Inmate No. 38169)
b. July 5th 1919 in Vienna, mechanic. Brought to Auschwitz on April 15th 1942, a member of Austrian resistance group in the camp. Hanged on Dec. 30th 1944 with other prisoners involved in assisting an escape.

FELIX WACHSBERGER (Inmate No. 31504)
b.Sept. 29th 1889 in Tvrdošin. Murdered/died in Auschwitz in 1942.

ZYGMUNT WOJSZCZYK (Inmate No. 5482)
b. Jan. 10th 1910 in Częstochowa. Survived. After the war played in an orchestra.

ALFRED WOYCICKI (Inmate No. 39247)
b.June 21st 1906 in Lwów. Brought to KL Auschwitz on June 11th 1942 in the Kraków transport. Went in the evacuation march to KL Gross-Rosen. Survived.

ADAM WYSOCKI (Inmate No. 2985)
b. July 23rd 1907 in Kopyńczyce. Brought to KL Auschwitz on Aug. 15th 1940 in the first transport from Warsaw. In 1944 transferred to KL Sachsenhausen, liberated there.

MALA ZIMETBAUM (Inmate No. 19880)
b. Jan. 26th in Brzesko. Brought to KL Auschwitz on Sept. 3rd 1942 in the transport from Malines, Belgium. Employed as a translator and courier. She escaped with Edward Galiński, was captured and after interrogation sentenced to death and executed.

SS-STAFF IN KL AUSCHWITZ

HANS AUMEIER (SS-Sturmbannführer)
b. Aug. 20th 1906 in Amberg, Bavaria, turner, clerk. NSDAP member since Dec. 1929, in the SS since Aug. 1929. From July 1930 in the professional SS force. Beginning Aug. 1934 on the staff of the Reichsführer's office. Later in guard squads in concentration camps: KL Dachau, KL Esterwegen, KL Lichtenburg, KL Buchenwald. Later transferred to KL Flossenbürg, Department III. Commander of that camp till February 1942. Feb. 1942 – July 1943: Head of the camp. In October 1943 became Commandant of KL Vaivara in Estonia, in February 1945 Commandant of KL Mysen near Oslo, Norway. Tried in Krakow before the Supreme National Tribunal, sentenced to death on Dec. 22nd 1947, hanged Jan. 28th 1948.

RICHARD BAER (SS-Sturmbannführer)
b. Sept. 9th 1911. Member of NSDAP No. 454991 and the SS No. 44225. First post in concentration camps in 1933 in KL Dachau; guard. In 1939 he joined Death Head Units. Following an injury, he became an adjutant in KL Neuengamme in 1942. Later in KL Auschwitz. After three days there he was recalled to become an adjutant to Osvald Pohl. In Nov. 1943 he became the head of Department D I (Political Division) in the Inspectorate for Concentration Camps. On May 11th 1944 he became the last commandant of KL Auschwitz. At the end of the war Commandant of KL Mittelbau-Dora. After the war till December 1960 he lived near Hamburg as Karl Neumann. There he got arrested and put in prison, where he died awaiting trial on June 17th 1963.

WILHELM FRIEDRICH BOGER
(SS-Oberscharführer)
b. Dec. 19th 1906 in Stuttgart-Zuffenhausen, secretary of the political police. From March 1922 till October 1930 in Hitlerjugend. From July 1930 member of NSDAP and Allegemeine-SS. In KL Auschwitz since 1942, initially a guard. Later the head of Department II, the interrogation and investigation unit. After the evacuation of the camp moved to KL Buchenwald. Tried in the Frankfurt Auschwitz Trial on August 20th 1965 he was sentenced to life. He died in 1977 in the Bietigheim-Bissingen prison.

MARGOT ELISABETH DRECHSLER
(SS-Aufseherin)
b. May 11th 1908 in Neusdorf, Saxony. Transferred to KL Auschwitz in early October 1942 from FKL Ravensbrück. Till the end of June 1944 she was an SS overseer in women's camp in KL Auschwitz II-Birkenau. Tried by the Soviets, sentenced to death and hanged in May or June 1945.

KARL EGERSDÖRFER (SS-Unterscharführer)
b. July 20th 1902 in Rosenberg n. Nuremberg, butcher. NSDAP member since Jan. 1934, in SS since Jan 1933. In SS active duty since March 30th 1941, in Auschwitz. Since August 1941 member of Department IV - Administration, as the manager of the prison kitchen. In January 1945 moved to KL Bergen-Belsen. Tried in 1945 by the Allies, acquitted.

WILHELM EMMERICH (SS-Oberscharführer)
b. Feb 7th 1916 in Tiefenbach. Member of NSDAP and the SS. Arrived in KL Auschwitz on July 22nd 1940 from KL Sachsenhausen. Member of Department IIIa - Labor Deployment, where he was deputy chief. After the camp evacuation he went to KL Mittelbau-Dora. He died on May 22nd 1945 in hospital in Schwarmstedt.

FRIEDRICH KARL HERMANN ENTRESS
(SS-Hauptsturmführer)
b. Dec. 12th 1914 in Poznań, physician. Member of the SS since Nov. 1939. Medic in the SS medical battalion since December 1940, since December 1941 in KL Gross-Rosen and KL Sachsenhausen. Camp doctor for the SS in KL Auschwitz since October 1943. Transferred to KL Mauthausen where he was the head doctor of the SS Garrison. At the end of the war he went to the front as a member of Waffen-SS. In the Mauthausen crew trial he was condemned to death and executed on May 25th 1947.

KARL FRITZSCH (SS-Hauptsturmführer)
b. July 10th 1903 in Nassengrub in the Sudetes. Roofer. Skipper of the Danube river inland waterway service Donauschifffahrtgesellschaft. In NSDAP since July 1930, in Allegemeine SS since July 1933. Until Sept. 1939 served as officer of guard units in concentration camps. In KL Dachau in Department I. Since June 1940 manager of KL Auschwitz and deputy Comandant under Rudolf Höss. In 1942 moved to KL Flossenbürg. Tried for corruption in the SS court. Later served in 18th SS grenadier regiment. Died on May 2nd 1945.

MAXIMILIAN GRABNER
(SS-Untersturmführer)
b. Oct. 2nd 1905 in Vienna, criminal police employee. Member of NSDAP since August 1932, in the SS since Sept. 1939. Nov. 1939 - June 1940 policeman in Katowice. From June 1940 till Dec. 1st 1943 in KL Auschwitz as Chief of the Political Department (Gestapo). Arrested and tried for corruption by the SS. Captured by the Allies in 1945, extradited to Poland and tried in Kraków by the Supreme National Tribunal. Sentenced to death on Dec. 22nd 1947, executed January 28th 1948.

ELISABETH HASSE (SS-Aufseherin)
b. Dec. 14th 1917. Came to Kl Auschwitz on October 7th 1942 from KL Ravensbrück. in 1944 promoted to Rapportführerin, in this rank until 1945. She took part in the selections, was present when female inmates were taken from the Death Block (No. 11 in Birkenau) to the gas chambers. After the war she was arrested in the British Zone of Occupation, her later fate is unknown.

ERNST HOFMANN (SS-Unterscharführer)
b. Nov. 11th 1901 in Witkendorf. In Auschwitz from May 16th 1941 till Sept. 14th 1944 as the deputy manager of the identification service of Gestapo - Department II (Erkennungsdienst). Later fate unknown.

RUDOLF HÖSS (SS-Obersturmbannführer)
b. Nov. 25th 1900 in Baden-Baden, rural clerk. Volunteer in the World War I. Member of NSDAP since November 1922 (No. 3240) For participation in the murder of Walter Kadow sentenced to 10 years of heavy prison. Member of Allegemeine-SS since Septemter 1933. Active duty in KL Dachau since Dec. 1934. In 1934 promoted to adjutant of the camp manager in Sachsenhausen, in Jan. 1940 he became the camp commandant. May 1940 Nov.- 1943 he was the Commandant of KL Auschwitz and head of the SS Garrison. Later transferred to WVHA (Economic and Administrative Department of the SS) and was deputy inspector of concentration camps. When the extermination program of the Hungarian Jewswas initiated he returned to KL Auschwitz as a coordinator and the head of the SS Garrison. He worked in those positions till late Summer 1944. Tried in Warsaw by

the Supreme National Tribunal, sentenced to death on April 2nd 1947. The sentence was carried out in Auschwitz on April 16th 1947.

OSWALD KADUK (SS-Unterscharführer)
b. Aug. 26th 1906 in Chorzów; butcher, fireman. In KL Auschwitz from July 1941; after December 1941 employed as a sentry. Then in Department III as a block manager and a reporting NCO of Auschwitz. Sentenced to life for murders, he was released in 1989 due to poor health. Died on May 21st 1997 in Langelsheim.

EMIL KASCHUB
physician in the rank of ensign. He came to Auschwitz in the summer of 1944. Carried out pseudo-medical experiments on inmates. Later fate unknown.

KURT PAUL KIRCHNER
(SS-Hauptscharführer)
b. Oct. 23rd 1913 in Eckstartsberg. In KL Auschwitz from Sept. 1944 till Jan. 20th 1945, manager of sub-camp "Charlottengrube" in Rydułtowy. Tried in Poland, sentenced to death.

JOSEF KLEHR (SS-Oberscharführer)
b. Oct. 17th 1904 in Langenau; carpenter, nurse. The SS member since 1932. Part of the SS crew first in KL Buchenwald, later in KL Dachau. Since September 1941 SS nurse at Department V - medical orderly of the SS garrison in KL Auschwitz and the head of the disinfections kommando, which poured Zyklon B into the gas chambers. Known for murdering inmates with phenol injections. In January 1945 after the evacuation of the camp he went to KL Gross-Rosen. During the denazification process he spent 3 years in a labor camp. After the Frankfurt Trial he served life imprisonment. In January 1988 he was released on probation due to ill health and died later that year.

JOHANN PAUL KREMER
(SS-Obersturmführer)
b. Dec. 26th 1883 in Stelberg; PhD in philosophy and medicine, professor at the Münster University. Member of NSDAP since Aug. 1932 and of Allgemeine-SS since Dec. 1934. In June 1941 in active SS duty, worked at the SS hospital in Dachau, later in Prague. At the end of August 1942 transferred to KL Auschwitz as an SS physician. He conducted experiments on the atrophy of liver and on

starvation. In mid Nov. 1942 he returned to the SS hospital in Prague and took an official leave to return to the Münster University. Sentenced to death by the Supreme National Tribunal in Kraków on Dec. 22nd 1947; the sentence was commuted to life imprisonment. He was released by the Polish court in Bydgoszcz in 1958 and extradited to West Germany. He was tried again, stripped of his academic titles and sentenced to 10 years of hard labor but he walked out free since he had served ten the years in Polish prisons. He died in 1965.

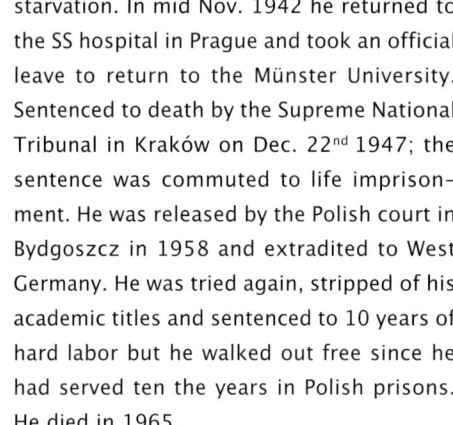

ARTHUR LIEBEHENSCHEL
(SS-Obersturmbannführer)
b. Nov. 25th 1901 in Poznań, tax office employee. Member of NSDAP and Allgemeine-SS since 1932.
Since August 1937 in active duty in the SS as an adjutant in KL Lichtenburg. Since May 1940 Chief of Staff of the inspectorate of concentration camps in Berlin and in WVHA (Office of Economic Policy of the SS). In November 1943 he became commandant of KL Auschwitz. In May 1944 he was named Commandant of Kl Lublin. In July 1944 held administrative posts in the Higher Command of the SS and Police in Trieste, Italy. Arrested by the Americans and extradited to Poland. He stood trial in Kraków and was sentenced to death on Dec. 22nd 1947. He was hanged on January 24th 1948.

ERICH MALISCH (SS-Unterscharführer)
b. Aug. 23rd in Świętochłowice, worked as a driver at the main Auschwitz camp and in the sub-camp in Jaworzno. In the Auschwitz Trial in Poland he was sentenced to 6 years in prison.

MARIA MANDEL (SS-Oberaufseherin)
b. Jan. 10th 1912, office clerk. Member of NSDAP since 1942. In 1938 joined the staff of KL Lichtenberg; since Sept. 1939 in FKL Ravensbrück. Oct. 1942 - Nov. 1944 head SS supervisor at the women's camp in KL Auschwitz. Tried in the Auschwitz Trial in Krakow. Sentenced to death on Dec. 22nd 1947 and executed on Jan. 24th 1948.

JOSEF MENGELE (SS-Hauptsturmführer)

b. March 16th 1911 in Günzburg; PhD in humanities and a medical doctor. Member of NSDAP and Allgemeine SS since April 1938. Oct. 1939 - July 1940 served in Wehrmacht. Later assigned to Waffen-SS as a medical officer. Nov. 1940 - July 1942 he worked in the Race and Resettlement Main Office in Pozen (Poznań). Later in active front duty in the 5th SS Panzer Division "Wiking", wounded. May 30th 1943 transferred to Auschwitz. Physician in the Gypsy camp at KL Auschwitz II-Birkenau and in the women's camp. From August till November 1944 head SS doctor at the camp. After the merging of KL Auschwitz II-Birkenau and KL Auschwitz I into one administrative unit he was a doctor at the SS hospital. In KL he conducted experiments on multiple pregnancy, "water cancer" (noma) and heredity of traits in twins and dwarfs. After the war he lived in the American Zone of Occupation, from which he emigrated to Argentina in 1949. Avoiding capture, since 1960 he lived in Urugway and other South American countries. He died on Feb. 7th 1979 in Brazil from a stroke.

GERHARD MAX ARNO PALITZSCH (SS-Hauptscharführer)

b. June 17th 1913 in Grossopitz-Therandt near Dresden; farmer. Member of NSDAP and the SS since March 15th 1933. Initially served as a guard in KL Oranienburg, KL Lichtenberg and KL Sachsenhausen, in the last camp attaining the rank of a reporting NCO. In KL Auschwitz since May 1940. In Department III initially as a reporting officer of KL Auschwitz I and KL Auschwitz-Birkenau II.
June-Aug. 1942 camp manager at the Gypsy Family Camp in Birkenau, since Oct. 1st head of KL Auschwitz III-Brünn (sub-camp in Brno in Moravia). Due to corruption and maintaining relations with Jewish female prisoners he was arrested and imprisoned in the penal camp for the SS in Danzig-Mackau (Gdańsk-Maczki), and later moved to the penal front units of Waffen SS. Further fate unknown.

LUDWIG PLAGGE (SS-Oberscharführer)

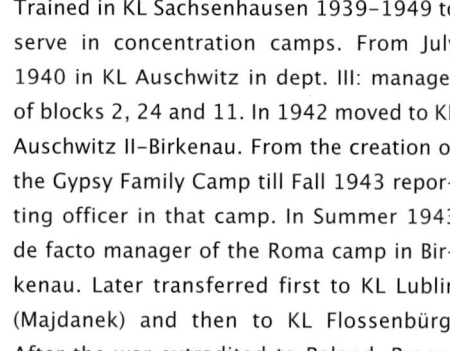

b. January 13th 1910 in Landesbergen; farmer. Member of NSDAP since 1931, in Allgemeine-SS since 1934.
Trained in KL Sachsenhausen 1939-1949 to serve in concentration camps. From July 1940 in KL Auschwitz in dept. III: manager of blocks 2, 24 and 11. In 1942 moved to KL Auschwitz II-Birkenau. From the creation of the Gypsy Family Camp till Fall 1943 reporting officer in that camp. In Summer 1943 de facto manager of the Roma camp in Birkenau. Later transferred first to KL Lublin (Majdanek) and then to KL Flossenbürg. After the war extradited to Poland. Prosecuted by the Supreme National Tribunal in Kraków he was condemned to death on Dec. 22nd 1948 and executed on Jan. 22nd 1948.

JAKOB RAITH (SS-Unterscharführer)
b. May 2nd 1909 in Bittenkirchen. In KL Auschwitz from Feb. 1st 1941 until Dec. 2nd 1941; manager of both the SS and the inmate canteens. Also employed in Erholungsheim Porombka (resort for the SS on leave). Fate unknown, probably died in 1944.

FRANZ SCHEBECK (SS-Unterscharführer)

b. Sept. 15th 1907 in Vienna, ironworker. Member of NSDAP since Jan. 1931, in the SS since May 4th 1934. In KL Auschwitz from 1940 to 1944; worked at the food storage rooms. Nicknamed "Schweik" by the inmates. On Dec 28th 1944 transferred to a unit of Waffen-SS. After the war stood trial in Vienna and was sentenced to 10 years.

JOSEF HERMANN SCHILLINGER (SS-Unterscharführer)
b. Jan. 21st 1908 in Oberrimsigen, cooper. In active SS duty since Sept. 1st 1939. On March 3rd 1941 transferred to KL Auschwitz and assigned to Department III - the camp head office. Since April 25th 1943 a reporting NCO in MKL (men's camp) in KL Auschwitz II-Birkenau. Shot dead on Oct. 23rd 1943 by a Jewish female prisoner in the changing room at the gas chamber.

HANS SCHUMACHER (SS-Unterscharführer)
b. Aug. 31st 1906 in Düsseldorf, factory worker. In KL Auschwitz since 1942, deputy manager of the food storage rooms. On Dec. 22nd 1947 sentenced to death in the Auschwitz Staff Trial in Kraków. Hanged in Montelupich prison in Kraków on Jan. 24th 1948.

HEINRICH SCHWARTZ (SS-Hauptschturmführer)
b. June 14th 1906 in Munich, chemical engraver. NSDAP member since Dec. 1931, in Allgemeine-SS since Nov. 1931. Before Oct. 1941 in KL Mauthausen, later in the Budget and Construction Bureau of the SS. Since end of September 1941 in Kl Auschwitz, Department III - manager of the Labor Deployment. Since April 1942 chief of the newly established Dept IIIa. From August till November 1943 manager of the main camp. Later, until evacuation, Commandant of Kl Auschwitz III-Monowitz. From Feb. 1945 Commandant of KL Natzweile. Tried by the French occupation authorities and sentenced to death. Shot by a firing squad on March 20th 1947.

MAX SELL (SS-Obersturmführer)
b. Jan. 8th 1893 in Kiel, tradesman. Soldier in WW I. Member of NSDAP and Allgemeine-SS since Nov. 1931. In active SS duty since April 1932. In Sept 1939 in FKL Ravensbrück; later in KL Auschwitz as deputy chief and since 1943 chief of Department IIIa. At this post till the camp evacuation. Declared dead on Oct. 2nd 1950.

FRIEDRICH STIEWITZ (SS-Unterscharführer)
b. May 15th 1910 in Sobernheim, Pfalz; locksmith and turner. Member of Waffen-SS since Oct. 1940. In 1941 in Auschwitz first as a sentry, since July as a block chief; later deputy of the Kl Auschwitz reporting NCO and in Department IIIa. After the camp evacuation in KL Buchenwald, sub-camp Ohrdruf and in KL Mauthausen. Declared dead on Oct. 30th 1957.

BERNHARD WALTER (SS-Hauptscharführer)
b. April 27th 1911 in Fürth, Frankonia; plasterer. Since May 1933 member of NSDAP AND Allgemeine-SS. From 1943 in Waffen-SS. Guard in KL Dachau and KL Sachsenhausen. In KL Auschwitz from Jan. 1941 to Jan. 1945. Member of Dept. II, manager of the photography and identification service. (Erkennughsdienst). Later in the front duty in Waffen-SS, finally in KL Mittelbau-Dora. Prosecuted by the Regional Court in Kraków, sentenced to 3 years in prison.

EDUARD WIRTHS (SS-Sturmbannführer)
b. Sept. 4th 1909 in Würzburg, physician. Member of NSDAP since May 1933, in the SS since Oct. 1934. In Sept. 1941 he became the physician to the SS in KL Dachau, later in KL Neuengamme. Since Sept. 1942 till Jan. 1945 the head doctor of the SS Garrison in KL Auschwitz. He did experiments on malignant cancers and conducted drug tests. After the camp evacuation he was in KL Mittelbau-Dora, KL Bergen-Belsen and KL Neuengamme. In September 1945 he committed suicide.

GLOSSARY

BARAK/BLOK (Germ.) – housing building for the inmates. Auschwitz I had mostly brick blocks, Birkenau and Monowitz consisted mostly of wooden buildings.

BLOCKFÜHRER – SS man overseeing one or several blocks

DURCHFALL – bloody diarrhea, dysentery

EFFEKTENKAMMER – deposit room for prisoners' personal possessions, taken away at registration

ERKENNUNGSDIENST – ID service of the Political Department (the camp Gestapo)

FUNKSTELLE – phone exchange at the camp headquarters

GESTAPO (Geheime Staatspolizei) – secret state police created in Nazi Germany

HÄFTLING – concentration camp inmate

"KANADA" – storehouses for goods stolen from the victims, located near the main camp (Kanada I) and in Birkenau in the B II section (Kanada II).

KAPO – "prisoner functionary" (Funktionshäftling) – prisoner assigned by the SS to supervise others and assist in the management of a work unit (Kommando)

KOMMANDO – labor unit (detail) of prisoners

LAGERMUSEUM – camp museum created by Commandant Rudolf Höss It housed various artifacts including Jewish ceremonial objects of art.

OBERKAPO – a kapo supervising a large kommando made up of several work details.

"PINNING" (Pol. 'szpilowanie')" – murder via intracardiac phenol injection

POLITISCHE ABLEITUNG – (Ableitung II) – Political Department, the camp Gestapo

POSTENKETTE – the security perimeter

RAMP – rail siding where the transport of deportees was unloaded

RAPPORTFÜHRER – SS NCO who received Blockführers' reports and controlled the number of prisoners at roll calls.

SELECTION – sorting out procedure at the arrival of Jews destined for extermination. People fit for labor were separated from the rest and registered at the camp as prisoners. Also selecting the sick or the disabled for lethal injections or the gas chambers.

"SPORT" – in the camp jargon specific kind of torture consisting of forcing prisoners to perform exhausting physical exercises.

SCHREIBSTUBE – camp office

UNTERKAPO – a deputy kapo

WALL OF DEATH – black wall in the yard between blocks 10 and 11 of the main camp (Auschwitz I), the site of mass executions by shooting

WASCHRAUM – prisoners' communal bathing facility

ZUGANG – new camp inmate(s)

FOTOGRAFIE I REPRODUKCJE

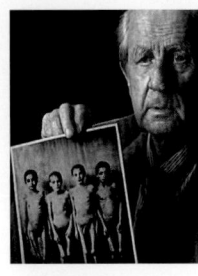

COVER:
Wilhelm Brasse,
Still from Irek Dobrowolski's documentary
„The Portraitist)
(cinematography J. Taszakowski)

p. 2-3
Wilhelm Brasse in Katowice, 1937

p. 4-5
Wilhelm Brasse soon after the war.

p. 6-7
Brasse with younger brothers

Wilhelm Brasse's grandfather—Albert Karol Brasse.

Brasse's mother, Helena, in traditional Żywiec costume.

p. 8-9
Right—Wilhelm Brasse's father

Wedding picture of Brasse's parents.

Brasse with mother, Helena, and his brothers.
(Pictures on pages 2-9 come from private albums of the Brasse family; further pictures: family archive)

p. 10-11
View of Żywiec and Zabłocie between the wars. The train and wooden bridges on the Sola river did not survive.

p. 12-13
Prewar view of Żywiec from the Cementary Hill. Town square on a market day.

p. 14-15
Kościuszki Street in Żywiec, before WW II

St. Florian's well in Żywiec town square, before WW II

Town Square in Żywiec before WW II

Maidens in traditional Żywiec costumes in front of the parish church, before WW II

Krakowska Street (today Sienkiewicza St.) in Żywiec; view towards the town square, before the war.

Garbarska Street (today Sempołowska St.) in Żywiec, view towards Kościuszki Street with Siejba buiding and church tower. Before WW II.

Żywiec parish church before WWII

p. 16-17
Brasse in Katowice, 1937 (family archive)

p. 18-19
Brasse in Katowice, 1937 (family archive)

p. 24-25
W. Brasse – post war picture
(family archive)

Still from „The Portraitist" by I.Dobrowolski

p.26-31
2nd Tarnów transport that took Brasse to Auschwitz

Still frrom „The Portraitist" by I. Dobrowolski

p.32-33
Welcome to the Newcomers, Władysław Siwek
Auschwitz State Museum (APMA-B-I-1-109)

Wilhelm Brasse after the war (family archive)

p.34-35
KL Auschwitz II-Birkenau. Jews during camp registration, after selection
(SS picture, 1944)

p. 20-21
Still from „The Portraitist" by I. Dobrowolski

p. 36-37
Beginnings of the agon— the bath,
Władysław Siwek
Auschwitz State Museum (APMA-B-I-1-110)

Polish armored train No. 54—„Groźny"
(A. Jońca's photo collection)

p. 38-41
KL Auschwitz II-Birkenau. A group of Jews directed to the camp after selection.

Fingerabdruck—German document certifying nationality in occupied Poland.
(ph. Nowis, Dec. 12th 2006)

At night, Jerzy Potrzebowski
Auschwitz State Museum (APMA-B-I-1-71)

Brasse in Katowice, 1937 (family archive)

p.42-43
Inmate uniform.
(Auschwitz State Muzeum exhibit)

p. 22-23
Wilhelm Brasse before the war.

Personal record of inmate Kazimierz Andrysiak, arrested for suspected resistance activity.

Wilhelm Brasse before leaving for Hungary
(family archive)

p. 44-47
KL Auschwitz I. The first crematorium which operated since 1940. Initially used for incinerating bodies of prisoners killed during labor, dead from starvation and from other causes. From late 1941 used also for burning bodies of people gassed with Zyklon B.
(ph. L. Foryciarz, 1968)

KL Auschwitz I. Barracks of Schutzhaftlager-weiterung, storage depot for the property taken from people sent to the gas
(ph. S. Łuczko, May 1945)

KL Auschwitz I. Section of the main street, left: blocks 22 and 23.
(ph. S.Łuczko, 1945)

p.48-51
KL Auschwitz II-Birkenau. The camp latrine in the wooden building of section BIIb. Before 1954
(ph. T. Kinowski)

KL Auschwitz II-Birkenau. Primitive latrines that the inmates could use only for a few minutes before and after their work day.
(ph. O. Kulka, 1941, Yad Vashem)

p. 52-53
KL Auschwitz I, Block 11. To prevent communication with prisoners in the standing cell metal shields were installed over the air vents. In winter frozen snow caused complete blockage of the airflow and death of the prisoners.
(ph. T.Kinowski, 1954)

Request to punish an inmate with whipping for attempting suicide.

Whipping penalty, Władysław Siwek
Auschwitz State Museum (APMA-B-I-1-92)

Whipping horse. Whippings were not supposed to exceed 25 lashes, but in practice inmates could receive as many as 70.
(ph. S.Koralowiec, 1945)

p.54-59
KL Auschwitz I. Main gate „Arbeit macht frei"
(ph. S.Łuczko, Spring 1945)

KL Auschwitz I. Section of fencing with the building of Theatergebaude on the left.
(photographer unknown)

Kl Auschwitz II-Birkenau. A corner pole separating section BIIb from Crematiorum II.
(ph. S.Korolowiec May 29th 1945)

Hans-Jürgen Höss and his airplane, picture taken by an inmate.
(Reiner Höss & IFZ Munich)

p. 60-61
KL Auschwitz II-Birkenau. Inmates digging a drainage ditch.
(ph. SS, D. Kamann)

p. 62-63
Potato kitchen at the main kitchen building.
(ph. Z. Klawender, Winter 1945/46)

p.64-65
Oświęcim. Inmates employed at tearing down buildings.
(photographer unknown, 1941)

p. 66-67
Auschwitz II-Birkenau. Building drainage ditches by Crematorium II.
(ph. SS, D. Kamann)

Building storage for cabbage and potatoes near Auschwitz II.
(ph. SS, 1943)

Member of the SS Garrison. Still from "The Portraitist" by I. Dobrowolski.

p. 68-69
A guard in KL Auschwitz. Still from "The Portraitist" by I. Dobrowolski.

SS-man "Perełka" with dogs.
Władysław Siwek
Auschwitz State Museum
(APMA-B-I-1-0090)

p.70-71
A camera such as this one was used by Brasse to take pictures at the camp. Still from "The Portraitist" by I. Dobrowolski. (cinematography J. Taszakowski)

p.72-73
Photographic camera. Still from "The Portraitist"
(ph. J. Taszakowski)

p.74-75
The Exchange Waldemar Nowakowski.
Auschwitz State Museum (APMA-B-I-1-196)

s.76-77
Prisoner's bowl and spoon.
(ph. Tomasz Pielesz)

p. 78-79
Chaim Nüssen (Inmate No. 25449),
b. Sept. 17th 1890 in Mielec, trader.
Died March 2nd 1942 in KL Auschwitz.

p.80-81
Benjamin Freuer (Inmate No. 21880)
b. May 20th 1910

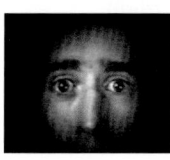
p.82-83
Israel Moses Pasyrman (Inmate No. 25503)
b. April 30th 1916

Jan Filipek (Inmate No. 25280),
b. Sept. 6th 1914 in USA. Cleric.
Died on Feb. 6th 1942 in KL Auschwitz

p. 84-86
Helena Wójcik (Inmate No. 24207)
b. in Trębaczów. Transferred from Auschwitz in 1944. Survived.

p. 86-87
Inmate (No. 45218) marked as a criminal prisoner.

Marcel Balteillard (Inmate No. 45203)
b. June 23rd 1912

David Israel Brül (Inmate No. 25372),
b. Sept. 1st 1901

p. 90-91
Stanisław Kwaśny (Inmate No. 25215),
b. Jan 13th 1909. Died April 28th 1942 in KL Auschwitz.

Salomon Israel Reichel (Inmate No. 25508)
b. May 25th 1920

p. 92–93
Józef Grzybowski (Inmate No. 21525),
b. March 1st 1922 in Dziesławice, farm worker. Died in Auschwitz on March 19th 1942.

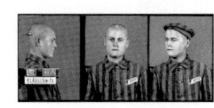

Iwan Androczienko (Inmate No. 63352)
b. Nov. 14th 1926

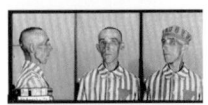

Jan Niewczas (Inmate No. 12948),
b. July 15th 1898 in Tychów, farmer.

Kazimierz Budziński (Inmate No. 21686)
b. Feb. 23rd 1899 in Żyrardów, iron worker. Died June 8th 1942 in KL Auschwitz.

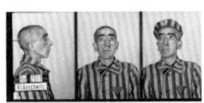

Polish political prisoner (Inmate No. 2911), came to the camp in the Warsaw transport on Aug. 15th 1940

Wasil Biszko (Inmate No. 21801)
b. Jan. 21st 1901. Transferred from KL Auschwitz in 1942. Did not survive the war.

Eugeniusz Siewierski (Inmate No. 630),
b. Sept. 4th 1917 in Sambor. Died in Oct. 1940 in Auschwitz.

Wasyl Borszcz (Inmate No. 62122)

Henryk Krajewski (Inmate No. 12451)
b. Nov. 26th 1920 in Warsaw, iron worker. In 1942 moved to KL Mauthausen, liberated there.

Ludwik Żurawski (Inmate No. 579)
b. Feb. 2nd 1915 in Charzewice. Died in Auschwitz on Dec. 28th 1940.

Piotr Grabski (Inmate No. 12840)
b. Jan. 6th 1906 in Kraków, office worker. In 1942 transferred to KL Gross-Rosen. Survived.

Prisoner No. 22661

p. 94–95
Bronisław Pawłęga (Inmate No. 494)
b. January 6th 1906 in Krakow

Stanisława Kozerawska (Inmate No. 24190)
b. November 11th 1909 in Opoczno.
Died April 22nd 1943 in KL Auschwitz.

Chaim Orner (Inmate No. 44568)
b. Dec 15th 1913 in Kutno, factory worker.
Died on July 29th 1942 in KL Auschwitz

Alina Jasińska (Inmate No. 24188)
b. June 14th 1920 in Warsaw, gardener.
Transferred to KL Bergen-Belsen, liberated.

Czesław Sawicki (Inmate No. 680)
b. July 5th 1909 in Warsaw. Died in 1941 in KL Auschwitz.

Irena Przesmycka (Inmate No. 24471)
b. April 17th 1925. Evacuated to KL Ravensbrück, survived.

Henryk Staniewski (Inmate No. 17531)
b. Feb. 2nd 1915 in Skaryszew, shoemaker.
Died Feb. 16th 1942 in KL Auschwitz.

Maria (Bronisława) Nistenberger
(Inmate No. 24167) b. Sept. 19th 1905
in Stanisławów, office clerk.
Died May 1st 1943 in KL Auschwitz.

Prisoner listed as antisocial
(Inmate No. 61931)

Prisoner No. 23605

Inmate No. 1730

Prisoner No. 25040

Edward Matysik (Inmate No. 541)
b. Sept. 19th 1914 in Nawojowa Góra.
Died Setp 7th 1942 in KL Auschwitz

Prisoner No. 26469

Maria Śledź (Inmate No. 22208)
b. Oct. 26th 1919 in Łuków.
Died Nov. 20th 1942 in Auschwitz.

Irena Kowalska (Inmate No. 23523)
b. Jan 8th 1920. Mentioned in camp records
Sept. 8th 1944.

Olga Stańczyk (Inmate No. 24476)
b. Sept. 2nd 1916 in Orsza. Transferred
to KL Flossenbürg in 1944, liberated.

Prisoner No. 24442

p. 96-97
Photo camera. Still from "The Portraitist"
by I. Dobrowolski.
(ph. J. Taszakowski)

The house of Commandant Rudolf Höss.
(ph. Around 1946)

p. 98-99
Maximilian Grabner (SS-Untersturmführer),
in Auschwitz from June 1940 till Dec 1st
1943; chief of the camp Gestapo.
(photo taken before 1945)

p. 100-101
Standgericht in Block 11/Summary court
in Block 11, Władysław Siwek
Auschwitz State Museum (APMA-B-I-1-97)

Rudolf Höss (SS-Obersturmbannführer),
camp Commandant 1940-1943
(photo taken before 1945)

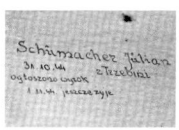
KL Auschwitz I. Block 11, ground floor, wall
inscription in correctional prisoners' cell.
(ph. L.Grabowska, Nov. 23rd 1965)

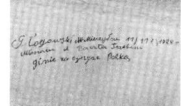

p.102-103
Ludwig Plagge (SS-Oberscharführer), since
July 1940 in KL Auschwitz, Dept. III - blocks
2, 24 and 11.
(Yad Vashem)

p. 104-105
Gerhard Palitzsch (SS-Hauptscharführer) In
KL Auschwitz from May 1940 till Nov. 1943,
member of Dept. III
(ph. before 1945)

p. 106-107
Soviet POWs
(undated photograph)

p.108-109
Bruised prisoner. Still from "The Portraitist"
by I. Dobrowolski

p. 110-111
Bogdan Komarnicki (Inmate No. 3637)
b. Jully 28th 1913 in Synowodzko, merchant.

KL Auschwitz I. The yard at Block 11,
portable gallows.
(ph. S.Łuczko 1945)

Welcome to the fugitives Jan Komski
Auschwitz State Museum (APMA-B-I-1-615)

At the shovel Władysław Siwek
Auschwitz State Museum (APMA-B-I-1-105)

p. 112-113
Witold Pilecki (Inmate No. 4859), b. May 13th
1901 in Ołoniec, Army officer. Escaped from
KL Auschwitz on April 27th 1943.

Escape from HWL Waldemar Nowakowski
Auschwitz State Museum (APMA-B-I-1-698)

p. 114-115
Auschwitz II-Birkenau arrival of a transport
of Jews. Rail tracks go across the main gate
of the camp and further to the gas chambers
and Crematorium II and III.
(ph. SS 1944)

p.116-117
At the Roller Władysław Siwek
Auschwitz State Museum
(APMA-B-I-1-0534)

p. 118-119
The first Tarnów transport which brought in 728 Polish political prisoners.
(auth. Unknown, June 1940)

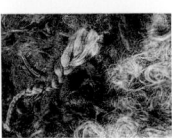
p.120-121
Hair cut from murdered women were sold to German company Alex Zink at 50 pfennig per kilogram. Still from "The Portraitist" by I. Dobrowolski. Source: "Chronicle of Camp Liberation" 1945

P. 122-123
The sick getting loaded into a car
Jerzy Potrzebowski.
Auschwitz State Museum (APMA-B-I-1-077)

p. 124-125
The fence in Auschwitz I visible from inside the camp. Electric wires and watchtowers increased the atmosphere of isolation and prevented escapes.
(ph. S. Mucha, 1945)

Inmates made many attempts to escape. Most of them ended in death. The photo shows a prisoner killed at the fence.
(ph. SS, 1940-1944)

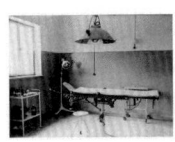
p.126-127
Birkenau. Hospital operation room.
(ph. SS, 1941, Yad Vashem)

Tattoo. Still from "The Portraitist" by I. Dobrowolski. (reconstructed photo)
(ph. J. Taszakowski)

p. 128-129
Dwarf - one of Dr. Mengele's research subjects.
(ph. SS, 1944)

KL Auschwitz I. Inscription above the entry of one of the hospital blocks (Block 21 - surgery). The camp hospital was called by the inmates the gateway to the crematoriums. The SS doctors carried out many criminal experiments and murdered the sick and the weak with phenol injections.
(photo taken after the camp liberation in 1945)

KL Auschwitz II-Birkenau. Crippled Jew photographed at the ramp in Birkenau.
(ph. SS 1944)

p. 130-131
Dr. Joseph Mengele experimented on twins, dwarfs and people crippled from birth.
(photographer unknown)

Selection of the sick to the gas
Jerzy Potrzebowski
Auschwitz State Museum (APMA-B-I-1-068)

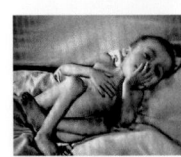
One of 600 rescued children from Auschwitz II-Birkenau.

Chronicle of the Camp Liberation, 1945
(Kronika wyzwolenia obozu)

p. 132-133
Preparation B-1034, manufactured by IG Farben, tested by the SS doctors on prisoners. (ph. L.Foryciarz, 1968)

p. 134-135
Auschwitz I, gynecological chair inside Block 10. (author unknown)

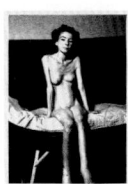
p. 136-137
Ewa Muhlrad (Inmate No. A-13160)
b. Oct 13th 1924

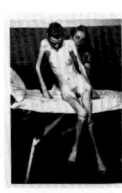
Betty Spinoza (Inmate No. A-27858)
b. Oct. 10th 1908

Pictures taken at the Red Cross Hospital in former KL Auschwitz I during inspection by the Commission for the Investigation of Nazi Crimes in Poland.
(ph. S. Łuczko, 11-25.5.1945)

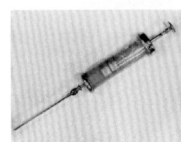
p. 138-139
Syringe used by the SS for lethal phenol injections.
(ph. L. Foryciarz, 1968)

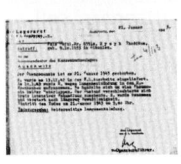
p.140-141
Camp document confirming the death of 9-year old Tadeusz Rycyk from Zamość region.

The Koch family from Zamość region.

The Koch brothers from the Zamość region.

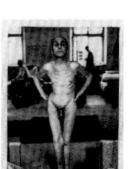
p. 142-143
Enrico Morpurgo (Inmate No. 192901)
Photograph taken at the Red Cross Hospital in the former KL Auschwitz I during the inspection by The Commission for the Investigation of Nazi Crimes in Poland.
(ph. S.Łuczko 11th-25th May 1945)

14 year old Jewish boy (Inmate No. B14615) from Hungary.
(photo taken during medical examination after the camp liberation)

p. 144-145
Members of female SS auxiliary team traveling by bus to an SS resort near Auschwitz.
(photo from the United States Holocaust Memorial Museum)

p. 146-147
Czesława Kwoka (Inmate No. 26947) Polish political prisoner. Taken to Auschwitz on Dec. 13th 1942 from Zamość. She died on March 12th 1943.

p. 148-149
KL Auschwitz II-Birkenau. A buiding for 52 horses was adapted as living quarters for a hundred prisoners.
(Chronicle of Camp Liberation 1945)

KL Auschwitz II-Birkenau. Wooden building No. 8 in the BIIa section.
(ph. April 9th 1963)

KL Auschwitz II-Birkenau. Inside of wooden building No. 16 in the BIIa section.
(ph. L. Forynciarz Nov. 11th 1974)

p. 150-151
KL Auschwitz II-Birkenau.
Jews walking to the gas chamber.
(ph. SS, 1944)

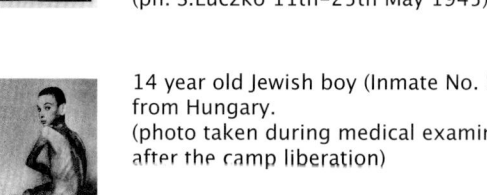
KL Auschwitz II-Birkenau. Mother with children walking to gas chamber No. IV or V on the road between camps BIIc and BIId.
(ph. SS, 1944)

p. 152-153
Children 3-6 years old liberated in KL Auschwitz-Birkenau in 1945.
(photo taken probably in Bucze Harcerskie in 1945)

p. 154-155
Four naked girls, subjects of medical experiments.
(Dr Mengele's collection).
Still from "The Portraitist" by I. Dobrowolski
(ph. J. Taszakowski)

p. 156-157
KL Auschwitz II-Birkenau. Women and children after selection waiting in the woods before being taken to the gas chamber.
(ph. SS 1944)

Two prisoners of KL Auschwitz during medical examination, showing frostbite of their feet.
(Chronicle of Camp Liberation 1945)

p. 158-159
Naked Jewish women brought to gas chamber No. 5
(photo probably by Alex - a Greek Jew, 1944)

p. 160-161
KL Auschwitz. The first, temporary gas chamber created in 1941/1942 in the mortuary of Crematiorum I.
(ph. A. Kaczkowski, 1970)

Entering Block 11 Władysław Siwek
Auschwitz State Museum (APMA-B-I-1-79)

Auschwitz II-Birkenau, arrival of a transport of Jews. Rail tracks go across the main gate of the camp and further to the gas chambers and Crematoriums II and III.
(ph. SS 1944)

Transport of Jews from Hungary. Many of them came from Slovakia and Transylvania, annexed by Hungary at the beginning of the war.

p. 162-163
Auschwitz II-Birkenau. Mass grave photographed by the Soviet Army after the camp liberation.
Chronicle of the Camp Liberation, 1945
(Kronika wyzwolenia obozu)

p. 164-165
Zyklon B in the form of granules of diatomaceous earth saturated with hydrogen cyanide was produced in cans of various sizes. It was manufactured by Degesch company and supplied by Testa company.
(ph. Z. Łoboda, 1968)

p. 166-167
Zyklon B manufacturer's information flyer. Still from "The Portraitist" by I. Dobrowolski.

Franciszka Mann, dancer.
(Publicity photo, Polish National Digital Archive)

p.168-169
Otto Küsel (Inmate No. 2) b May 16th 1909, survived.

p. 171
The Three Magi Adam Bowbelski
Auschwitz State Museum
(APMA-B-I-5-0041)

p. 172-173
Gardener Bronisław Czech
Auschwitz State Museum (APMA-B-I-5-110)

Children (artist unknown)
Auschwitz State Museum (APMA-B-I-5-429)

p. 174-175
One dollar bill
(ph. Jacek Szymczak)

p. 176-177
Portrait of Xavery Dunikowski Marian Ruzamski
Auschwitz State Museum (APMA-B-I-2-619)

Photograph of an oil painting of a winter mountain landscape, work lost.
Bronisław Czech
Auschwitz State Museum (APMA-B-R1-68)

Photograph of Spring, from the Four seasons series. Artwork lost. Czesław Kaczmarczyk.
Auschwitz State Museum (APMA-B-R1-228)

Caricature Album, cover. Stanisław Trałka
Auschwitz State Museum
(APMA-B-1-2-444)

Caricature of Wilhelm Brasse Stanisław Trałka
Auschwitz State Museum
(APMA-B-I-2-444/4)

p. 178-179
The camp orchestra in front of the "Arbeit macht frei" gate.
(ph. Summer 1941)

p. 180-181
The camp orchestra during a Sunday concert for the SS; in the yard in front of the camp office.
(ph. date unknown)

Inmate orchestra at KL Auschwitz.

p. 182-187
KL Auschwitz I. Inside the camp's forges.
(ph. SS, 1942-1943)

KL Auschwitz. Inside the camp iron workshop, left: SS-man Lubusch, right: inmates Pluta and Zając.
(ph. SS, 1942-1943)

p. 188-189
SS-Officer Karl Hoecker lights candles on a Christmas tree just week before the camp liberation.
(ph. from the United States Holocaust Memorial Museum)

Christmas Eve Władysław Siwek

Auschwitz State Museum (APMA-B-I-1-107)

Christmas Eve in Oświęcim Jerzy Potrzebowski
Auschwitz State Museum (APMA-B-I-1-669)

p. 190-191
Kantownia (Cheat-Canteen) Tadeusz Myszkowski
Auschwitz State Museum
(APMA-B-I-1-0431)

p. 192-193
"Organizing" (artist unknown, initials MM)
Auschwitz State Museum (APMA-B-I-2-417/17)

Caricature of SS-men Stanisław Trałka
Auschwitz State Museum
(APMA-B-I-2-444/6)

p. 194-195
SS officer Karl Hoecker resting in a deck chair in female company during vacation in Solahuette, 1944.
(ph. of The United States Holocaust Museum)

Tadeusz Pietrzykowski (ph. E. Szafran)

Soccer match Aleksander Kołodziejczyk
Auschwitz State Museum (APMA-B-I-1-251)

p. 196-197
"Organizing" artist unknown, initials MM.
Auschwitz State Museum (APMA-B-I-2-417/17)

p. 198-201
Evening Exchange Jerzy Potrzebowski
Auschwitz State Museum (APMA-B-I-1-066)

p. 202-203
Auschwitz II-Birkenau. Possessions brought by the deportees: suitcases.
Chronicle of the Camp Liberation, 1945
(Kronika wyzwolenia obozu.)

Piles of property belonging to the Jews deported to Auschwitz, collected in front of the camp storage depot "Kanada".
(ph. SS, 1944)

The prisoners from "Kanada" (ph. SS, 1944)

p. 204-205
Auschwitz II-Birkenau. Shaving brushes taken from the deportees.
(photo taken during inspection after the camp liberation)

SS officers, including a few doctors, having a drink after a visit to a coal mine. 1-10th Sept. 1944
(photo: United States Holocaust Memorial Museum)

Smokers Jan Komski
Auschwitz State Museum (APMA-B-I-1-606)

p. 206-207
Auschwitz II-Birkenau. Schoes of the deportees.
(photo taken during camp inspection after the liberation, 1945)

p. 208-209
Clothes collected in the storage depot „Kanada" near Auschwitz I.
(ph. S. Mucha, Feb./March 1945)

p. 210-211
Dublosan Gummi Schutz - aluminum condom can.
(ph. M. Tuza, GRH Festung Breslau)

p. 212-213
Peep hole in the former Puff building (now offices of the Auschwitz Museum)
(ph. M. Obstarczyk)

p. 214-215
Mala Zimetbaum (Inmate No. 19880)
b. Jan, 26th 1918 in Brzesko. Employed as an interpreter and courier.
(photo taken before deportation to the camp)

Mala's Escape, Waldemar Nowakowski
Auschwitz State Museum (APMA-B-I-2-694)

Edward Galiński (Inmate No. 531)
b. Oct. 5th 1923 in Więckowice.
(camp ID picture)

Mala's Portrait Zofia Stępień-Bator
Auschwitz State Museum
(APMA-B-I-2-0415)

p. 216-217
Cyla Cybulska-Stawiska (Inmate No. 29558),
b. Dec. 29th 1920 in Łomża. Came to KL
Auschwitz on Jan. 21st 1943.
(photo taken after 1945)

Jerzy Bielecki (Inmate No. 243),
b. March 28th 1921 in Słaboszów, high
school student. On July 21st 1944
escaped from KL Auschwitz, survived.
(photo taken after the escape, in Oct. 1944)

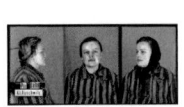
p. 218-219
Anna Stefańska (Inmate No. 6866)
b. Jan. 4th 1920 in Jasło. Escaped during
camp evacuation, survived.

Wilhelm Brasse before departing for Hungary
(family photo)

p. 220-221
Margarita Ferrer.

Rudolf Friemel (Inmate No. 25173)
(photo taken by W.Brasse on Friemel's
wedding day, March 18th 1944)

p. 222-223
Friemel's wedding greeting card.

Rudolf Friemel with wife and son Edi.
(photo taken by W.Brasse at Friemel's
wedding on March 18th 1944)

p. 224-225
Pansies—reconstructed postcard. Still from
"The Portraitist" by I. Dobrowolski.
(ph. J. Taszakowski)

View of downtown Oświęcim.
(photographer unknown, 1939)

p. 226-229
Ignac Jakubowski (Inmate No. 25749)
b. Feb. 2nd 1877 in Pułtusk, laborer.
Died March 22nd 1942 in Auschwitz.

One of the camp spaces photographed after
the liberation. Still from "The Portraitist" by
I. Dobrowolski.

p. 230-231
KL Auschwitz I. Scattered documents and
other items found after the camp liberation
in one of the buildings.
(ph. S.Łuczko 1945)

p. 232-233
KL Auschwitz I. Scattered documents and
other objects found after the camp
liberation in one of the camp rooms.
(ph. S.Łuczko 1945)

p. 234-235
An evacuation transport photographed at
departure at Kolin (Czechoslovakia) train
station.
(ph. J. Kremer, Jan. 24th 1945)

p. 236-237
Ebensee shortly after liberation.
(ph. 1945)

p. 238-239
Inmates of the concentration camp
in Ebensee, Austria.
(ph. Lt. A.E. Samuelson, 1945, Archival
Research International/Double Delta
Industries Inc.)

p. 240-241
Rescued Ebensee camp prisoners in the
hospital building drinking special light soup
prepared by the US Army.
(ph. J. Heslop, May 5th 1945, United States
Holocaust Memorial Museum)

p. 242-243
Wilhelm Brasse after the war

p. 288
Wilhelm Brasse
(Brasse family archive)

COVER:
Wilhelm Brasse
(Brasse family archive)

Wilhelm Brasse's wedding picture,
May 6th 1946
(Brasse family archive)

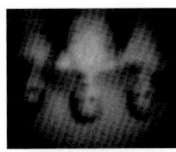
p. 244
Photo of the four girls. Still from
"The Portraitist" by I. Dobrowolski
(ph. J. Taszakowski)

Photographic atelier – reconstruction for the
movie "The Portraitist" by I. Dobrowolski.
(ph. J. Taszakowski)

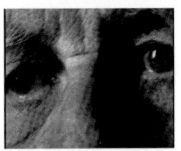
p. 246-247
Wilhelm Brasse's eyes. Still from "The
Portraitist" by I. Dobrowolski.
(ph. J. Taszakowski)

p. 248-249
Standing from left: Stephen Cooper,
Wilhelm Brasse and Irek Dobrowolski, 2007

p. 250-253
KL Auschwtiz II-Birkenau. The main
watchtower, called the Gate of Death, and
the train siding built in1944 for the
incoming trains with deported Jews.
(ph. S. Mucha, 1945)

p. 254-255
With each step Jerzy Adam Brandhuber
Auschwitz State Museum (APMA-B-I-1-368)

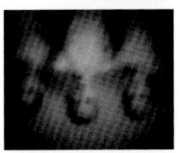
p. 257, 269
Photo of the four girls. Still from
"The Portraitist" by I. Dobrowolski
(ph. J. Taszakowski)

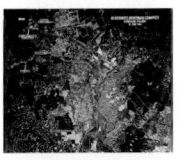
p. 284-285
KL Auschwitz II-Birkenau. Aerial photo taken
by the Allies. Showing Auschwitz I, II and III
on June 26th 1944

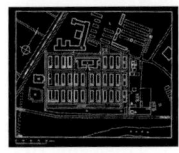
p. 286-287
Map of Auschwitz I.

BIBLIOGRAPHY

APMA-B – the Archives of the Auschwitz-Birkenau Memorial and State Museum

Albin Kazimierz, *Księga Pamięci. Transporty Polaków z Warszawy do KL Auschwitz 1940—1944* [Book of Remembrance. Transports of Poles from Warsaw to KL Auschwitz], Vol. 3, Warszawa – Oświęcim 2000

Auschwitz 1940-1950: węzłowe zagadnienia z dziejów obozu. Więźniowie -życie i praca. [Auschwitz 1940-1950: Key Issues from the Camp History. Inmates – life and labor.] Vol. 2, W. Długoborski, F. Piper ed., Oświęcim 1995

Bartosik Igor, Willma Adam, *Ja z krematorium Auschwitz. Rozmowa z Henrykiem Mandelbaumem, byłym więźniem, członkiem Sonderkommando w KL Auschwitz,* [I Come from the Auschwitz Crematorium. Conversation with Henryk Mandelbaum, Former Inmate, Member of the Auschwitz Sonderkommando]. Warszawa 2009

Bielecki Jerzy, *Kto ratuje jedno życie, ratuje cały świat,* [Who saves one life saves the whole world].Oświęcim 1999

Biuletyn Głównej Komisji Badania Zbrodni Niemieckich w Polsce [Bulletin of the Main Commission for the Investigation of Nazi Crimes in Poland,] Vol.1, Poznań 1946

Biuletyn Głównej Komisji Badania Zbrodni Niemieckich w Polsce. [Bulletin of the Main Commission for the Investigation of Nazi Crimes in Poland,] Vol. 7, Poznań 1951

Camon Ferdinando, *Rozmowa z Primo Levim.* [Conversations with Primo Levi].(E. Kabatc, Trans.). Oświęcim 1997

Cyra Adam, „Boksował by przeżyć" [He boxed to survive]. *Kronika Beskidzka* 24 (1988), Bielsko-Biała

Cyra Adam, *Ochotnik do Auschwitz. Witold Pilecki 1901-1948.* [The AuschwitzVolunteer. Witold Pilecki 1901-1948]. Oświęcim 2000

Czech Danuta, *Kalendarz wydarzeń w KL Auschwitz.* [The Auschwitz Chronology]. Oświęcim 1992

Czech Danuta, „Konzentrationslager Auschwitz – zarys historyczny". [KL Auschwitz – a historical outline]. In W. Michalak ed. *Oświęcim: hitlerowski obóz masowej zagłady.* Warszawa 1984

Death Books from Auschwitz, Vol. I, *Reports.* Munich: K.G. Saur.1995

Dziopek Jan, *Walka o życie. Pamiętniki nauczycieli z obozów i więzień hitlerowskich 1939–1945* [Struggle to survive. Memoirs of teachers who went through Nazi prisons and concentration camps.] K. Bidakowski, T. Wójcik ed., Warszawa 1962

Fejkiel Władysław, *Pamiętniki lekarzy* [Memoirs of doctors].Warszawa 1964

Fejkiel Władysław, *Więźniarski szpital w KL Auschwitz* [Inmate hospital in KL Auschwitz]. Oświęcim 1994

Giza Jerzy, Morasiewicz Wiesław, „Poobozowe zaburzenia seksualne u kobiet jako element tzw. Kz-syndromu" [Post-camp sexual dysfunctions in women as part of the KZ-syndrome]. In: *Przegląd Lekarski,* 1 (1974) Kraków

Greif Gideon, *...płakaliśmy bez łez...* [...We wept with no tears...]. L. Ulicka Trans. Warszawa-Oświęcim 2001

Grenda Józef, „Wspomnienia z pracy w szpitalu PCK w Oświęcimiu po wyzwoleniu obozu" [Recollections from work at the Red Cross Hospital in Oświęcim]. In: *Okupacja i medycyna. Trzeci wybór artykułów z „Przeglądu Lekarskiego – Oświęcim" z lat 1963–1976.* Warszawa 1977

Gutman Yisrael, Krakowski Shmuel, „Żydzi w KL Auschwitz" [Jews in KL Auschwitz]. In: *Księgi zgonów z Auschwitz. t. 1 Relacje.* Munich K. G. Saur, 1995

Hackl Erich, *Wesele w Auschwitz* [The Wedding in Auschwitz]. A. Buras Trans. Kraków 2006

Hitler Adolf – fragment of the Obersalzberg speech, Aug. 22nd 1939 r. In: *Nuremberg-Documents* nr *798* – PS

Höss Rudolf, *Autobiografia,* W. Grzymski Trans. Warszawa 1989

Höss's trial, Vol. 5a, k. 92 Archives of the Auschwitz-Birkenau State Museum,

Iwaszko T., „Kontakt ze światem zewnętrznym" [Contact with the outside world]. In: *Auschwitz 1940-1950: węzłowe zagadnienia z dziejów obozu – więźniowie – życie i praca.* Vol. 2, W. Długoborski, F. Piper ed., Oświęcim 1995

Iwaszko Tadeusz, „Przyczyny osadzania w obozie i kategorie więźniów" [Reasons for incarceration and categories of prisoners]. In: *Auschwitz 1940-1950: węzłowe zagadnienia z dziejów obozu – więźniowie – życie i praca.* Vol. 2, W. Długoborski, F. Piper ed., Oświęcim 1995

Iwaszko Tadeusz, *Więźniowie* [The Prisoners] In: *Oświęcim: hitlerowski obóz masowej zagłady,* W. Michalak ed., Warszawa 1984

Iwaszko T., „Zakwaterowanie, odzież i wyżywienie więźniów" [Inmates' lodging, clothing and alimentation]. In: *Auschwitz 1940-1950: węzłowe zagadnienia z dziejów obozu – więźniowie – życie i praca.* Vol. 2, W. Długoborski, F. Piper ed., Oświęcim 1995

Jacewicz Wiktor, Woś Jan, *Martyrologium Polskiego Duchowieństwa Rzymskokatolickiego pod okupacją hitlerowską 1939-1945.* [Martyrology of the Polish Roman Catholic Clergy under Nazi Occupation 1939-1945].Vol. 1, Warszawa 1977

Jagoda Zenon, Kłodziński Stanisław, Masłowski Jan, *Oświęcim nieznany* [Oświęcim unknown]. Kraków 1981

Jagoda Zenon, Kłodziński Stanisław, Masłowski Jan, *Więźniowie Oświęcimia* [The Prisoners of Oświęcim]. Kraków-Wrocław 1984

Kajzer Abraham, *Za drutami śmierci,* [Behind the wires of death].Wałbrzych 2008

Kielar Wiesław, *Dzieła zebrane 2. Anus mundi* [Collected Works vol. 2.]Wrocław 2004

Klee Ernst, *Auschwitz. Medycyna III Rzeszy i jej ofiary* [Medicine of the 3rd Reich and its victims]. E. Kalinowska-Styczeń Trans. Kraków 2001

Klüger Ruth, *Żyć dalej...,* [Keep on living]. M. Lubyk Trans. Wrocław 2009

Kłodziński Stanisław, „Fenol w KL. Auschwitz-Birkenau" [Phenol in KL Auschwitz-Birkenau]. In: *Przegląd Lekarski,* 1a (1963), Oświęcim

Kopyciński Adam, „Orkiestra w oświęcimskim obozie koncentracyjnym" [The orchestra in the Auschwitz concentration camp]. In: *Przegląd Lekarski,* 1 (1964) Kraków

Kubica H., „Dzieci i młodzież w KL Auschwitz" [Children and Youths in Auschwitz]. In: *Auschwitz 1940-1950: węzłowe zagadnienia z dziejów obozu. Więźniowie – życie i praca.* Vol. 2, W. Długoborski, F. Piper ed., Oświęcim 1995

Kubica Helena, „Dr Mengele i jego zbrodnie" [Mengele and his crimes]. In: *Zeszyty Oświęcimskie 20,* Oświęcim 1993

Laks Szymon, *Gry oświęcimskie* [Oświęcim games]. Oświęcim 1998

Langbein Hermann, *Auschwitz przed sądem. Proces we Frankfurcie nad Menem 1963-1965. Dokumentacja,* [Auschwitz Trial. Documentation].V. Grotowicz Trans. Wrocław-Warszawa-Oświęcim 2011

Langbein Hermann, *Ludzie w Auschwitz* [People in Auschwitz]. J. Parcer and H. Jastrzębska Trans. Oświęcim 1994

Langfus Leib, *Rękopis* [Manuscript_] In: *Zeszyty Oświęcimskie 14,* Oświęcim 1972,

Leszczyńska Stanisława, „Raport położnej z Oświęcimia" [Report of an Auschwitz midwife]. In: *Przegląd Lekarski,* 1 (1965) Kraków

Levi Primo, *Czy to jest człowiek,* [If this is a man]. H. Wiśniewska Trans. Warszawa1996

Nyiszli Miklós, *Pracownia doktora Mengele. Wspomnienia lekarza z Oświęcimia* [Dr Mengele's workshop. Memoirs of an Auschwitz doctor] T. Olszański Trans., Warszawa 1966

Okupacja i medycyna. Czwarty wybór artykułów z „Przeglądu Lekarskiego – Oświęcim" z lat 1963–1978, [Occupation and Medicine. 4th collection of articles from Doctors' Review].Warszawa 1979

Oświęcim: hitlerowski obóz masowej zagład [Auschwitz – Nazi mass extermination camp]. W. Michalak ed., Warszawa 1984

Oświęcim w oczach SS. Höss, Broad, Kremer [Auschwitz in the eyes of the SS.] I. Polska ed., E. Kocwa and J. Rawicz Trans. Katowice 1972

Paczuła Tadeusz," Izby Pisarskie w KL Auschwitz" [Camp offices in Auschwitz] In: *Death Books from Auschwitz Vol. I. Reports.,* Munich 1995

Paczuła Tadeusz, „Obóz i szpital obozowy w Oświęcimiu we wczesnych okresach istnienia" [The camp and the hospital in Auschwitz in the early years]. In: *Przegląd Lekarski,* 1a (1963), Oświęcim 1963

Parcer Jan, „Zdjęcia więźniów KL Auschwitz ze zbiorów PM w Oświęcimiu" [Photographs of Inmates in the Auschwitz State Museum]. In: *Fotografie więźniów z Obozu Auschwitz-Birkenau,* Vol. 1, J. Parcer ed., Oświęcim 1993

Piper Franciszek, Eksploatacja pracy więźniów [Exploitation of inmate labor]. In: *Auschwitz 1940-1950: węzłowe zagadnienia z dziejów obozu. Więźniowie - życie i praca.* Vol. 2, W. Długoborski, F. Piper ed., Oświęcim 1995

Piper Franciszek, *Eksterminacja* [The Extermination]. In: *Oświęcim: hitlerowski obóz masowej zagłady* W. Michalak ed., Warszawa 1984

Piper Franciszek, *Ilu ludzi zginęło w KL Auschwitz*, [How many people died in Auschwitz]. Oświęcim 1992

Proces ZO, [The Auschwitz Trial]. Archives of Auschwitz-Birkenau State Museum

Rajewski Ludwik, *Oświęcim w systemie RSHA*,Warszawa 1946

Raporty uciekinierów z KL Auschwitz, [Reports of the Auschwitz fugitives]. Henryk Świebocki ed., Oświęcim 1991

Ryn Zdzisław, Kłodziński Stanisław, *Patologia sportu w obozie koncentracyjnym Oświęcim—Brzezinka* In: *Okupacja i medycyna. Czwarty wybór artykułów z „Przeglądu Lekarskiego - Oświęcim"* z lat 1963-1978, Warszawa 1979

Ryn Zdzisław, Kłodziński Stanisław, „Z problematyki samobójstw w hitlerowskich obozach koncentracyjnych" [Suicides in Nazi concentration camps]. In: *Okupacja i medycyna. Trzeci wybór artykułów z „Przeglądu Lekarskiego - Oświęcim" z lat 1963-1976*, Warszawa 1977

Sehn Jan, *Obóz koncentracyjny Oświęcim—Brzezinka/Auschwitz-Birkenau*, Warszawa 1964

Setkiewicz Piotr, *Krematoria i komory gazowe Auschwitz* [Crematoriums and gas chambers in Auschwitz]. Oświęcim 2010

Setkiewicz Piotr, „Sonderkommando Zeppelin - Volager Auschwitz" In: *Łambinowicki Rocznik Muzealny*, Vol. 29 (2006) Opole

Skála Oskar, *Komando Fałszerzy*, [The forgerers' unit]. W. Kaniewski Trans. Warszawa 1969

Smoleń Kazimierz, „Erkennungsdienst" In: *Fotografie więźniów z Obozu Auschwitz--Birkenau*, Vol. 1, J. Parcer ed., Oświęcim 1993

Smoleń Kazimierz, „Sowieccy jeńcy wojenni w KL Auschwitz" [Soviet POWs in Auschwitz] In: *Death Books from Auschwitz. 1. Reports.*, Munich 1995

Sommer Robert, *Das KZ-Bordell. Sexuelle Zwangsarbeit in nationalsozialistischen Konzentrationslagern.* Paderborn 2009

Struk Janina, *Holocaust w fotografiach* [The Holocaust in photography]. M. Antosiewicz Trans. Warszawa 2004

Strzelecka Irena,"Eksperymenty" [The Experiments] In: *Auschwitz 1940-1950: węzłowe zagadnienia z dziejów obozu. Więźniowie - życie i praca.* Vol. 2, W. Długoborski, F. Piper ed., Oświęcim 1995

Strzelecka Irena, „Kary i tortury" [Punishments and tortures]. In: *Auschwitz 1940-1950: węzłowe zagadnienia z dziejów obozu. Więźniowie - życie i praca.* Vol. 2, W.Długoborski, F. Piper ed., Oświęcim 1995

Strzelecka Irena, „Kobiety w KL Auschwitz" [Women in Auschwitz]. In: *Auschwitz 1940-1950: węzłowe zagadnienia z dziejów obozu. Więźniowie - życie i praca.* Vol. 2, W. Długoborski, F. Piper ed., Oświęcim 1995

Strzelecka Irena, „Szpitale obozowe w KL Auschwitz" [Camp hospitals in Auschwitz]. In: *Auschwitz 1940-1950: węzłowe zagadnienia z dziejów obozu. Więźniowie - życie i praca.* Vol. 2, W.Długoborski, F. Piper ed., Oświęcim 1995

Strzelecki Andrzej, „Kości i popioły" [The bones and the ashes] In: *Auschwitz 1940-1950: węzłowe zagadnienia z dziejów obozu. Więźniowie - życie i praca.* Vol. 2, W. Długoborski, F. Piper ed., Oświęcim 1995

Strzelecki Andrzej, „Likwidacja obozu" [Camp liquidation]. In: *Auschwitz 1940-1950: węzłowe zagadnienia z dziejów obozu.* Vol. 5. *Epilogue*, Oświęcim 1995

Szawłowski Lech, „Z przeżyć warszawskich dzieci w obozach hitlerowskich" [Warsaw children in the Nazi camps]. In: *Przegląd Lekarski, Nr 1*, Kraków 1972

Świebocki Henryk, „Ucieczki z obozu" [Escapes from the camp]. In: *Auschwitz 1940-1950 węzłowe zagadnienia z dziejów obozu. Ruch oporu.* Vol. 4, W.Długoborski, F. Piper ed., Oświęcim 1995

Venezia Shlomo, *Sonderkommando. W piekle komór gazowych* [Inside the gas chambers]. K. Szeżyńska-Maćkowiak Trans., Warszawa 2009

Wołkoński Jurij, *Operacja Bernhard*, Warszawa 2006 [audiobook]

ELECTRONIC MEDIA AND PUBLICATIONS:

Albin Kazimierz, „W Oświęcimiu i konspiracji" [In Auschwitz and in the Resistance] 25 Sept.1984 *Rzeczpospolita*

Kołodziejczyk Marcin, 18.6.2010 http://www.polityka.pl/spoleczenstwo/reporta ze/1506442,2,pierwszy-transport-do-uschwitz.read#ixzz1pPetNA00

Dańko Ireneusz „Byłem fryzjerem Hössa" [I was the Höss's barber. Interview with Józef Paczyński] 29 Jan.2010 r. *Gazeta Wyborcza - Kraków*

Skrzypek Józef, „Jak przeżyć?" [How to survive?] In: Dziecko szczęścia, A. Morawska, http://www.fpnp.pl/swiadkowie/materialy/dziecko-szczescia.pdf

Skrzypek Józef, „Różowi" [The Pink Triangles] In: Dziecko szczęścia,A. Morawska, http://www.fpnp.pl/swiadkowie/materialy/dziecko-szczescia.pdf

Tylus, Ewa „Bóg ocalił nielicznych" [God saved just a few. Interview with Adam Stręk] 30 Jan.2009, http://fakty.interia.pl/wiadomosci/podkarpackie/news/bog-ocalil nielicznych 1251240,3328

Szembek Jan, „Obozowe wspomnienia Auschwitz-Birkenau. Zugang - Block" [Camp recollections]. 27 July 2012 http://www.auschwitz88369.republika.pl/

Weseli Agnieszka, „Puff w Auschwitz" 4 Nov. 2009 *Polityka*, http://www.polityka.pl/historia/260561,1,puff-w-auschwitz.read

Zychowicz Piotr, „Domy publiczne w Auschwitz" [Brothels in Auschwitz] 21 July 2007 *Rzeczpospolita*

KL Auschwitz II-Birkenau. Aerial photo taken by the Allies on June 26th 1944

AUSCHWITZ-BIRKENAU COMPLEX
OSWIECIM, POLAND
26 JUNE 1944

PRZEMSZA RIVER

VISTULA RIVER

ENLARGED FROM THE ORIGINAL NEGATIVE AND CAPTIONED IN 1978 BY THE CIA

Photo lab
Erkennugsdienst

THE AUSCHWITZ PHOTOGRAPHER

Anna Dobrowolska

Historical consultants:
Grzegorz Berendt, Ph.D., The Institute of National Remembrance
Aleksandra Namysło, Ph.D., The Institute of National Remembrance
Mirosław Obstarczyk, Auschwitz-Birkenau State Museum

The book is based on the full interview with Wilhelm Brasse for "The Portraitist" – a documentary by Irek Dobrowolski.

Additional materials and stories included in the book are the result of the author's research into the experiences of other prisoners, collected and kept at the Archives of The Auschwitz-Birkenau State Museum (APMA-B) since 1954. Those stories are recorded in 165 volumes of "Testimonials" ("Zespół Oświadczenia") and 275 volumes of "Memoirs" ("Zespół Wspomnienia") which contain over 5,300 thousand official accounts by former prisoners, witnesses of events, forced laborers and depositions given by the Nazi crew members at their trial in Krakow, 1947 (Proces ZO). The book includes also prisoners' recollections from their own memoirs, referenced by the author.

If not otherwise stated, the illustrations come from The Archive of the Auschwitz-Birkenau Memorial and State Museum. (APMA-B)

Correction: Anna Morrison
Graphic Designer: Ryszard Kajzer
Typesetting: zerkaj studio
Color Expert: Oleh Diakon

No part of this book may be used or reproduced in any manner whatsoever without written permission except in the case of brief quotations embodied in articles and reviews.

"The Auschwitz Photographer" may be purchased for educational, business, or sales promotional use.

OVER THE YEARS WILHELM BRASSE MADE A FEW VISITS TO THE AUSCHWITZ-BIRKENAU STATE MUSEUM. HE WAS INTERVIEWED THERE BY HISTORIANS WHO RECORDED HIS FOUR TESTIMONIALS. THOSE WERE RARE INSTANCES SINCE THE PHOTOGRAPHER WAS RELUCTANT TO REVISIT HIS EXPERIENCES. THIS RELUCTANCE CHANGED IN 2006 WITH THE MAKING OF "THE PORTRAITIST" - A DOCUMENTARY BY IREK DOBROWOLSKI. AFTER THAT BRASSE CONSIDERED IT HIS MISSION TO SHARE HIS STORY, ESPECIALLY WITH GERMAN YOUTHS VISITING AUSCHWITZ, WITH WHOM HE COMMUNICATED IN GERMAN.

Publisher: REKONTRPLAN Film Group

www.rekontrplan.pl
info@rekontrplan.pl

www.auschwitzphotographer.com
www.portrecista.com
www.rekontrplanshop.pl

The moral right of the author has been asserted.
All rights reserved.
Copyright © 2015 Anna Dobrowolska
Translation copyright © Anna Samborska and Clay Young

Originally published as "Fotograf z Auschwitz" by Rekontrplan, Warsaw, Poland 2013
Printed in Poland.
ISBN 978-83-937261-6-5